AF540201

Coalition Government and Politics

UPA-II to 2014 Lok Sabha Elections

C.P. Bhambhri

Rs. 995; US$ 49.75

ISBN: 978-81-7541-692-5

First Published in India in 2014

Coalition Government and Politics: UPA-II to 2014 Lok Sabha Elections

Published by:
SHIPRA PUBLICATIONS
H.O.: LG 18-19, Pankaj Central Market, Patparganj,
I.P. Ext., Delhi-110092, Tel: 91-11-2223 5152, 2223 6152
Br.Off.: 4617/18, Ansari Road, Darya Ganj,
New Delhi-110002, Tel: 9650028065, 9810522367
E-mail: info@shiprapublication.com
www.shiprapublication.com

Preface

The focus of this study is to narrate significant happenings during the United Progressive Alliance government at the Centre especially during its second phase of power. The politics of coalition government led by Manmohan Singh-Sonia Gandhi leadership in its second phase has been comprehensively and analytically discussed and explained. The Prime Minister oftenly referred to the "compulsions of coalition government" which operated during the actual decision making processes of his leadership of the Central government, and in-spite of such coalitional constraints over the office of Prime Minister, the track record of UPA government at the Centre is a "mixed" one. If the Coalition government of UPA enthusiastically followed the politics of capitalist development with pro-American approach, a few remarkable welfare programmes, like the Food Security Act were also put on the statute book. It is also credited with the enactment of a powerful Lokpal Bill. The Foreign Policy is an extension of the domestic politics and in the age of globalization, the Indian foreign economic policy of collaborations has become quite central in the day-to-day activities of decision making and in this study, due attention has been paid to the foreign policy making during UPA-II.

The replacement of Manmohan Singh by Narendra Modi has been discussed and post-May 16, 2014 political developments are analysed here. *The Pioneer*, *The Financial World*, *The Hindustan Times*, *The Economic Times* and *The Seminar* deserve due acknowledgement and thanks. D. Kumar of Shipra Publications has been an enthusiastic publisher and deserves thanks.

July 2014

Chander Prakash Bhambhri
Jawaharlal Nehru University,
New Delhi

Contents

Introduction

A concrete social reality can best be studied, interpreted, explained and analysed in a scientific manner if one follows Karl Marx's Class Theory based on Materialist Interpretation of History because this approach leads us to demystify contradictions of a class-divided society by looking at the real historical content which at a given time impacts the course of developments of a particular society at a particular moment in history. Methodologically, social reality cannot be meaningfully explained without making a distinction between "apparent" and the "real" and without identifying the factors which really lie beyond and behind the seemingly visible social facts, not only the distinction between trees and wood will get blurred, the analysis will end up without really identifying the focus shaping the processes which are at work at a particular historical stage of social development of a specific reality. Moreover, any valid interpretation of concrete reality is possible if proper interconnections are made among the seemingly contrary and contradictory social facts.

On the basis of above mentioned insights provided by Marx's Class Theory and materialistic interpretation of History, a few salient facts about Indian society may be mentioned with a view to contextualise the social dialectical processes which are at work in India. India has followed the capitalist path of development and the state and dominant ruling bloc of classes and fractions of property-owning rural and urban groups are all committed to capitalist path where social surplus is accumulated by private appropriators of the main owners of the means of production and social wealth is socially produced and privately appropriated. Hence, the capitalist society of India is completely divided among classes and fractions of private appropriators and this productive system has logically led to the creation of an unequal society and absolute disparities of incomes and wealth have emerged in a big way.

India has become a country inhabited by many countries and a common factor which unites these many countries is "inequality of wealth and income". Further, the Indian state and every fraction of the capitalist classes is fully "integrated" with world capitalist system and collaboration between Monopoly Big Business Industrial Houses of India and every transnational corporation and financial institutions of every advanced capitalist country around the globe, especially the Western countries, has been institutionalized and the capitalist state of India which acts as a mid-wife of big Industrial and Business Houses of India. It has become a bridge between the Indian and global capitalism.

The Indian state has ceased to be an "autonomous" centre of power responsible for the management of public affairs for the whole society because of complete convergence which exists between the interest of the dominant exploiting classes and goals pursued by the Indian state. It has been suggested that in the contemporary age of globalisation, it is inter-dependence and not autonomy of national centres of power which has become a reality. It has been argued that in the age of globalisation of Finance—Capital, the state boundaries and concept of territoriality have lost all meaning because financial transactions have become global and investors travel down the whole world for financial investments. This trans-nationalization of finance capital has created transnational market economy leading to the end of any notion of "national economy or national state". The best evidence of this new phenomenon of globalisation was provided by the banking crisis of the United State of America in 2008 when financial crisis created by American banks impacted every country around the world and every country was faced with financial crises which was exported by the recklessness of American Banks. What is the politics of this economics?

Marx and Engels while writing on Capitalism observed its essential role has been "constant revolutionizing of production, uninterrupted disturbance of all social conditions (and) everlasting uncertainty and agitation, in sum, capitalism leads to "creative disruption". Has capitalism played this "historic" role in India by revolutionizing national forces of production? Has it succeeded in disrupting the ancient feudal, religion-dominated social order? The answer is a Big No. It deserves to be clearly stated that India had inherited an extremely backward underdeveloped economy as a direct consequence of colonial plunder of India's resources. The long standing income poverty and income and wealth inequality and disparities were inherited as aptly noted by Adam Smith, the founder of Modern Political Economy in his classic 'The wealth of Nations' (1776) that India in general, particularly Bengal was one of the most prosperous region on the globe and when national productive forces are allowed to remain backward, even primitive social productive relations continue to remain archaic and a backward economic structure and primitive social life and institutions remain stagnant.

Indian capitalism has succeeded up to a great extent in bringing qualitative changes in the material forces of production and politics has played an "activist" role in bringing many important break-throughs in national productive system of the country. History of societies has provided a lot of evidence to prove that development of new capitalist material forces may not keep pace with social changes at a particular stage of historical change in society.

Indian society has not kept pace with the changes brought by the new material forces which are at work in productive system and many new ways of social living co-exist with the "old" inherited past. Politics has to grapple with this "New" and its inter-play with the "past" and the best example is that every political party, whether all-India like Congress or BJP or other regional-state based parties, are compelled to make all kind of compromises with inherited social and cultural categories like that of "Identity" or "religion" or "language" et al. Further, competitive politics of Representative Electoral Democracy has provided enough evidence that all parties, groups and leaders make all kind of compromises and adjustments with categories like caste system or localism or religions as they are practiced by common man who are still under the shadow of priestly class and rituals sanctioned in the name of religion by visiting Temples, or Mosques or Churches or Gurdwaras. Political leaders who are laying down the foundations of modern science and technology based economy also visit temples, mosques, churches and gurdwaras especially at the time of elections. The best evidence is provided by the fact that all political parties, whether all-India like congress and BJP and every regional party and group are working on the basis of complete consensus on New Economic Policy framework of privatisation, deregulation, and every Prime Minister and Chief Minster, irrespective of party nomenclature, is standing in a queue to welcome with open hands foreign investors and transnational monopoly corporations from advanced capitalist countries of the West. Every political party is responsible for implementing policies of free market capitalism and every party is responsible for the deepening of disparities of income and wealth in society, a logical product of these policies followed by the Indian capitalist state. Every party represents the interests of dominant and exploiting classes and their fractions and this commonality of class-base of parties is an explanation for the march of capitalism and its integration with global capitalism and every party is willing to barter away the state sovereignty and even "relative anatonomy" at the altar of exploiting dominant ruling classes of India.

Every class-party has followed a path which has led to rising unemployment especially among the Dalits and Tribal communities and as Marx told that this reserve army of the unemployed leads to the depressing of wages of the under classes and it helps the property-owning classes to maximise their profits by paying extremely low wages. The ruling exploiting classes of India have to undertake some 'social welfare steps' to maintain their power over the exploited strata of society and this is the reason that the United Progressive Alliance government at the Centre led by Manmohan Singh and Sonia Gandhi got Mahatma Gandhi National Rural Employment Guarantee

Scheme, the Food Security Act, along with Right to Education Act et al. It is an imperative need for the exploiting classes specially in a country like India where voters after regular and competitive elections can punish political parties and leaders who are perceived to be anti-poor and anti-people because of lack of performance.

The Manmohan Singh-Sonia led UPA Coalition was inflicted a humiliating punishment by angry voters and on May 16, 2014 when election results of the Sixteenth Lok Sabha were declared, the Congress party obtained only 44 seats and with 19 per cent of votes polled by this party. The UPA and Congress were replaced and displaced by BJP which obtained an absolute majority of its own by winning 282 Lok Sabha seats and 31 per cent of votes were polled by the party. The new political dispensation led by Narendra Modi is committed to rigorously pursue politics of global integration of Indian capitalist classes and Modi has neither offered any alternative model to that pursued by Congress nor it has shown any new commitment to eradicate the sufferings of either people living under poverty line as defined by the government of India nor it has any recipe for tackling the accentuation of social cleavages because of growing poverty and persistence of income and wealth disparities in society. The BJP like its predecessors does not have any agenda for tackling the virus of acute social inequalities which have emerged because of the logic of the Laws of Motion of Capitalism.

The Narendra Modi-BJP-led government at the Centre like all other BJP State governments of Rajasthan, Madhya Pradesh, Chhattisgarh, and Gujarat has a distinct agenda of solidifying the foundations of *Hindu Rashtravad* where Hindus are first-class-citizens and minority religious communities like Muslims and Christians are expected to live like second-class-citizens. The Rashtriya Swayam Sevak Sangh led, guided and controlled every organization of Hindu joint family including the BJP, a political outfit or face of Hindu Sangh Parivar, is expected to aggressively implement the Hinduisation of society with the help of state apparatus and functionaries of the government, whether at the centre or the states. The power of Indian state in the hands of Hindu Joint Family including BJP will be ruthlessly exercised by the Narendra Modi government to consolidate the forces of Hindutva in society. If on the one hand the BJP-led governments are committed to pursue economic policies for the capitalist development of an unequal India, on the other, the Sangh Parivar and the BJP will consolidate Hindutva on the basis of its control over the levers of government powers. The "two faces" of BJP and Sangh Parivar-in-government will be clearly visible during the Narendra Modi-BJP-led Central Government. The Sangh Parivar's ideology of Hindu, Hindi and Hindustan, or one country, one Nation and one culture is at work in the BJP-controlled states of India and the same story will be replicated by Modi at the helm of affairs in the country.

Chapter 1
Coalition Politics

Unmitigated Disaster Called 'Third Front'

CPI(M) general secretary Prakash Karat is busy organising an anti-Congress and anti-BJP Third Front Alternative with the support of other marginal communist groups like the CPI, the Forward Bloc and the Revolutionary Socialist Party. He has also succeeded in motivating committed anti-Congress regional parties like Chandra Babu Naidu's TDP, Om Prakash Chauthala's Lok Dal and a few other not very significant region-based political fractions.

The rationale behind this exercise of Karat is that pro-capitalist Congress and Hindu majoritarian BJP are unable to form any Government at the Centre. Under such circumstances there is a political space for non-Congress and non-BJP political formations to come together and provide the choice of a third political alternative to voters. The Indian voters have been feeling burdened with the only choice between the Congress and the BJP. They have even shown their disinclination to exercise their electoral verdict in favour of either of these two political claimants, which provides sufficient space for a United Third Front.

A little reference to the post-independence history of democratic electoral politics of India may be helpful in understanding the genesis of the idea of the Third Front Alternative. First, the Congress has always secured the majority of Lok Saba seats on the basis of less than 50 per cent of votes. The Opposition parties always lost in the electoral game because they competed not only against the Congress but also against one another. Thus the Congress's winning the Lok Sabha elections because Opposition parties' remaining disunited and their voters split gave birth to a spurious idea that a United Opposition could defeat the Congress. It needs to be clearly stated that calculations based on anti-Congress vote falling in the lap of the United opposition deserves to be rejected with contempt.

Second, post-Nehru-Indira and Rajiv Gandhi phases of politics, the Congress was reduced to the status of just one political player among many emerging powerful regional political players along with the gradual growth of the Jan Sangh or the BJP in Indian politics. Third, beginning with the 1990s if India was witnessing the emergence of two poles of politics ie the Congress and the BJP, it was also becoming very clear that the voters were not prepared to provide a clear majority support to either of these two claimants. In this context, if the Government had to be formed at the Centre by either of these two parties, they would have to seek support from multiple, disparate regional and sub-regional parties.

The Communists, on the other hand, were not comfortable if the Congress or the BJP as largest party in the Lok Sabha formed a coalition Government at the Centre with the help of regional players. The first concrete step taken by the Communists was in 1989 when VP Singh formed the Government at the Centre on the basis of an outside support of both the Communists and the BJP. This experiment of short-lived Governments of VP Singh, Chandrashekar, HD Dev Gowda, IK Gujral proved beyond any shadow of doubt that the Union Government could not be stable if any largest party either the BJP from 1998 to 2004 or the Congress from 2004 to 2011 was kept out of any arrangement of the Government formation at the Centre.

The Third Front Alternative champions realised that stability of the Governments had become an issue with the voters and VP Singh or Chandrashekhar or HD Dev Gowda or IK Gujral's experiment attracted adverse and negative response by the voters and even parties because frequent Lok Sabha elections were not welcomed by anyone. This is the reason that the Communist Front of more than sixty Lok Sabha MPs extended an outside support to the Congress-led coalition form 2004 to 2008 and on the issue of Nuclear deal with the United States, the Communists withdrew their support from the Manmohan Singh-led coalition Government.

Karat again jumped into the fray and from 2008 to 2009 he made every effort to revive and launch and alterative front in politics on the basis of his doctrine of equi-distance from the Congress and the BJP. The Lok Sabha elections of 2009 gave a farewell to the idea of the Third Front and Karat himself realised the futility of bringing disparate groups on common front in politics. Incidentally, on the eve of Lok Sabha elections of 2009, Mayawati, who is a member of Karat's Third Front, declared herself as a candidate for the Prime Ministership after the elections. This announcement by Mayawati even before the elections of 2009 buried the very idea of the Third Front in politics because many other leaders of the so-called Third Front were themselves very ambitious and the whole thing collapsed.

It is expected that political leadership will make a serious analysis of its strategies and tactics especially when the whole idea of the Third Front alterative has repeatedly ended up in a fiasco. *The Pioneer, 05-09-2011*

Coalition Politics—Challenging

Mamata Banerjee has shown that allies cannot be taken for granted by the Union Government while formulating foreign policy.

Mamata Banerjee's performance as Chief Minister of West Bengal is projected as a great success on the completion of one hundred days of her in power. But a preliminary assessment suggests that nothing has changed in the responses of the most unpredictable Chief Minister. This also impacts the UPA at the Centre, of which her Trinamool Congress is a member.

The UPA has been crticised by many because of the conduct of the likes of Banerjee. Coalition Governments at the centre led by either Atal Bihari Vajpayee or Manmohan Singh have been in trouble because of her. Vajpayee had to spend a lot of energy in keeping Banerjee, who was a Minister in his Cabinet, in good humour.

The UPA Government had to hand over the Railways portfolio to Banerjee who shifted her 'headquarters' to Kolkata. Instead of focussing on Indian Railways, she remained busy preparing for the Assembly election.

Of course, it was a legitimate right of the president of the Trinamool Congress to launch political campaigns against the Left Front. But it was wrong to hand over Indian Railways to her.

Further, it is a fact that industrialisation and other economic development activities cannot be undertaken without a farmer-oriented Land Acquisition Act. Every State Government was in difficulty because of the problems faced by them on the question of land acquisition for development because India still has to reckon with an archaic colonial law of the mid-19th century to deal with the problems of the 21st century. Here the Manmohan Singh Government could not move an inch in the direction of a much-needed new Land Acquisition Bill because she had put her foot down on any new law because of her electoral imperatives in the West Bengal Assembly election.

By driving a hard bargain with the Government at the Centre, she has become a role model for every other party to corner the Manmohan Singh regime for its complete failure to frame a new Land Acquisition law in place of the British colonial law. It would seem political calculations based on the politics of West Bengal have become an overriding factor for policy-making of the UPA Government.

Through her serious acts of omission and commission, Banerjee has proved that coalition Governments cannot be in the driver's seat and the so-called federalists and defenders of the rights and autonomy of the federal units should be extremely worried about the weakening of the legitimate areas of authority of the Union Government which is beholden to regional allies.

Recently, Banerjee has completely knocked down Singh's efforts to improve India's relations with Bangladesh. Every other neighbouring country of South Asia wants to maintain a distance form India while Nepal and Shri Lanka have alleged that India wants to dominate its small neighbours and plays the role of 'Big Brother'. Pakistan's hostility towards India is well-known. The Islamist parties of Bangladesh had provided refuge to every anti-

India terrorist and insurgent group so that the Indian state could be put on a leash.

Sheikh Hasina Wajed, the daughter of Sheikh Mujibur Rahman, was always attacked by Islamist movements for being pro-India and incapable of defending her country's interests against a domineering neighbour. Sheikh Hasina is much more confident at present and has extended a much-needed hand of friendship and cordiality towards India.

Hence Singh's recent visit to Bangladesh could have created a new phase of bilateral friendship had Banerjee not sabotaged the Prime Minister's visit by refusing to endorse the Teesta water-sharing treaty with Bangladesh. This action of Banerjee has compelled rethinking on the part of every thinking Indian about the erosion of capability of a coalition Government to pursue foreign policy for the protection and promotion of national interests.

Bangladesh as a lower riparian country can inform the World Bank not to release its $1.5 billion aid to the West Bengal Government for improving its irrigation system. Banerjee has stalled a foreign policy initiative of the alliance Government at the Centre of which the Trinamool Congress is a member and, in the process, she has shown that she remains as unpredictable as ever.

Pioneer, 19-09-2011

A New Indian Model of Socialism may Still Work

An enlightened and dedicated leadership of the CPI(M) clearly spelt out its ideological and political position during its six-day long party congress held in Kozhikode from April 4 to 10. The party boldly discarded the idea of forming a Third Front that would have brought together regional parties on a common platform to oppose the Congress and the BJP. Indeed, it has buried the strategy of Front politics that it followed for more than two decades. Instead, it has opted for strengthening the Left platform and pursuing its own agenda of building a 'socialist model rooted in Indian conditions.'

This is the first time that the CPI(M) has expressed an unambiguous preference for an Indian model of socialism which will be firmly routed in this country's social reality. It, of course, will be a challenging task because Marxism-Leninism as a philosophical and theoretical framework does not lend itself easily to a territory-specific social project. It will be interesting to observe the direction in which Left politics proceed post the 20th party congress of the CPI(M).

Ram Manohar Lohia had talked of the Asian Model of socialism which was 'equi-distant from communism and capitalism'. Political leaders like Samajwadi Party chief Mulayam Singh Yadav, Chief Minister of Bihar Nitish Kumar, RJD chief Lalu Prasad Yadav and JD(U) leader Sharad Yadav never tire of publicly appropriating Lohia's ideology.

It is unfortunate that Lohia's legacy has emerged as the champion of those who practice the worst kind of casteism in politics. A socialist, by definition, is a modernist and a modernist is always committed to the idea of equality.

However, casteist socialists are pursuing a different kind of politics where the larger agenda of socialist equality is absent. Instead of moving forward, they have pushed society back to medieval times by institutionalising casteism and caste-based divisions in society. Lohia's model of Indian socialism was flawed and simplistic because his definition of the ruling class was equated to the then small English-speaking population. Since then, Lohia's followers have caricatured the socialist ideology, including its Indian version, by targetting symbols of inequality only.

India has not only experienced the Lohia model of socialism but has also witnessed former Prime Minister Jawaharlal Nehru's version which was described as the Third Path, subscribing to neither capitalism nor communism. Instead, it was a mix of both based on the system of economic planning. While Lohia looked backward, Nehru moved forward.

The Third Path envisioned a modern capitalist industrial society where the benefits of economic growth would trickle down to the poor and hence, the impoverished would be pulled out of centuries of backwardness. Nehru's model succeeded in firmly laying down the foundations of a modern, industrial capitalist country, but it failed to achieve the goal of egalitarianism.

In effect, both Nehru and Lohia's models failed because they were not based on an understanding of the socio-economic forces at work. The understanding of both these leaders was flawed. The historical time in which they lived and worked was a time of great contest between the ideas of capitalism and socialism—if the former created inequality, the latter, by challenging the foundations of capitalism, brought about equality. The 20th century saw battle lines being drawn between the ideologies of inequality-based capitalism and equality-based socialism. The Indian model had to make a clear choice between these two Big Ideas.

Even though the Indian experience with these desi variants of socialism has been largely disappointing, the CPI(M)'s new model may still be seen as an important step forward in the journey of socialism in India. The largest communist party of India has set before it the very challenging task of identifying the major social forces which are obstructing the country's growth.

But, the majority of people are no longer attracted to the idea of fighting a long and sustained struggle against an unequal social structure. While this will be a problem for the Indian Left, its biggest challenge will emerge from the entrenched land owning castes that exercise tremendous power. The labouring classes and other marginalised social groups need to be liberated from the tyranny of the land-owning classes. The Indian model of socialism will have a positive future if it can remove the foundations of India's pre-industrial society. Only then will the social super-structure of caste and casteism collapse.

Any struggle for equality can succeed only if the socialists and other progressive forces expose the fact that exploitation is not because of one's caste status but because the downtrodden are victims of a flawed social system.

The Pioneer, 03-04-2012

Wanted: A Neutral Umpire (President)

The forthcoming elections for the highest constitutional office of the President of India has assumed great political significance because the new occupant of Rashtrapati Bhawan in 2012 is expected to play a crucial and active role in the process of government formation at the Centre in 2014. It does not require a political magician to predict that the next general election, like all others since 1989, will bring a fractured electoral verdict. All-India national parties and state-based regional political groups and leaders will have to make great political efforts to form a coalition government at the Centre.

Indian voters will have to make their 'choice' from among about 45 recognised parties which are contesting for elections from their regions or sub-regions, or those parties which are described as all-India national parties. Such a diverse political map of India, where about 45 contenders for electoral victory are in competition against one another, has created a situation where no single party or group can win a majority of seats on its own. Hence, the role of President becomes crucial in determining and deciding the formation of a viable 'coalition government' at the Centre.

The President becomes the arbiter and neutral umpire and referee when the task of formation of central government becomes quite complex, because different parties or their combinations come forward to put their claim for the formation of government on the basis of a 'manufactured' majority of supporting parties and groups. The President has to evaluate the claims made by different coalitions of parties and find out methods to determine that their claim of a 'majority support' is not phoney. The ball is in the court of the Rashtrapati because, like Caesar's wife, he should be completely above suspicion when inviting a leader chosen by the coalition groups for forming a government.

This is the reason that an opinion has been expressed by a political leader that the office of President should be occupied by an 'apolitical' person who can be trusted by every group for his 'non-partisan' role while dealing with the claims of different groups that they have majority support behind them. The only objective criteria which is followed by the President at the time of formation of government is that the claim of majority support by group of coalition parties should not be 'spurious' and a viable an stable government should be constituted on the basis of majority support only.

The formation of coalition government at the Centre consisting of 22 parties and groups or 16 parties and groups—which has been the case in the past—should not lead to controversies about the President's neutrality. Otherwise, as head of government and sole symbol of the whole nation, he will lose his moral authority before the political public. Mulayam Singh Yadav of the Samajwadi Party, and a major player in the 2014 politics of government formation at the Centre, has openly rejected the idea of an 'apolitical' candidate for the forthcoming contest for President's office, and has publicly opted for a 'political' person for Rashtrapati Bhawan.

The process of consultation among the political stakeholders has begun and on 30 April, Sushma Swaraj of the BJP opposed the proposed candidature of Hamid Ansari, the present Vice-President of India, because she thought Ansari did not have the 'stature' to occupy the highest office of the country. Sushma of the BJP was castigated for her remark against Ansari. The JD(U), Samajwadi Party and CPI(M) distanced themselves from her remarks. On 1 May, Sharad Yadav, NDA convener, observed, 'There has been no discussion with us yet on this issue. The NDA has not yet decided its candidate.'

The BJP has been completely silenced because it has been politically isolated from its NDA allies and other important political players in the game of identifying a candidate. It is the concern of every political group 'a trustworthy' impartial kind of person should be the President in 2014. There is a lurking suspicion along all major political groups that the Congress party may not push a controversial Congress party leader for the office of the President. The explanation for the ongoing process of parleys and kite-flying arises from expectations of 'fractured and completely fragmented' verdict.

The Election of the President this year has assumed great significance because the President, whosoever he may be, would be expected to exercise his 'judgement' about the formation of a post-election 2014 coalition government. There is another important explanation for the hotly contested office of the President in 2012. Many political groups are haunted by the proclamation of Emergency by Indira Gandhi in June 1975, where President Fakhruddin Ali Ahmed was woken at midnight and blindly signed the proclamation that suspended all freedoms and fundamental rights.

It is not only this: many duly elected Chief Ministers of state governments during the last 63 years have been dismissed by an obliging and partisan President on the advice of the ruling party at the Centre on the basis of a spurious and disingenuous report of the state Governor, a ruling party nominee, that the constitutional machinery in the state has broken down. This memory haunts political leaders in spite of the fact that the letter and spirit of the Indian Constitution and judicial decisions of the Supreme Court have authoritatively laid down that the President is a constitutional head of a parliamentary system and he has no 'discretionary' powers of his own. It is felt that the Constitution can be twisted and tilted by the President in spite of the fact that he is a 'nominal' head of state. The Janata Party, which came to power in 1977 after defeating the Indira Gandhi Emergency regime, moved on 30 April 1979 the 44th Constitutional Amendment Act, which substantially changed the situation and curbed the arbitrary powers of any President in the future. Even Article 356, which was abused while dealing with state governments, was amended to ensure that the proclamation should be approved by both the Houses and if suspension of the Assembly at the state level is extended beyond six months, again Parliament should discuss and approve it.

Sea changes have occurred in the political situation in 2012 and it is difficult, even impossible, to proclaim for the whole country or in a particular state because coalition governments at the Centre have their built-in 'checks and balances' because so many groups share power at the Centre. It should not make the country complacent because the BJP and the Sangh Parivar are ideologically committed to the system of highly centralised Presidentialism for the country. *The Financial World, 20-05-2012*

Caught in its own Web

A salient feature of the Manmohan Singh led-UPA in its second term is that it is deadlocked with its own allies who had voluntarily joined in 2009 to form a coalition Government. That apart, there is also the Opposition with whom the UPA is forever at loggerheads. Of course, it is the responsibility of the Opposition in Parliament to keep a check on the ruling party or parties, but still, it is only fair to expect that it too will be taken into confidence when matters relating to national policy are discussed.

This narrative is helpful in understanding the real dynamics of a multi-party democracy which has two pillars of Government: The ruling party and the Opposition. The relationship between the two is based equally on conflict and cooperation. The Manmohan Singh Government has made it a habit to accuse the Opposition for not cooperating with the UPA in Parliament, forgetting the fact that the task of building consensus is the responsibility of the ruling party or coalition.

Still, the real challenge faced by the UPA Government comes from its own allies and partners. There is no reason why all these multiple parties should have joined the coalition Government if they do not agree on even some basic policies. After all, it is this disagreement among the coalition partners of the UPA Government that is responsible, at least in part, for the complete paralysis in policy-making and governance. A few important illustrations may be mentioned to substantiate the argument that the UPA Government is a divided house.

First, India's foreign policy should be formulated and implemented by the Union Government. However, in the formulation of that policy it is expected that the Union Government will accommodate the genuine concerns of the State Governments while still ensuring that the pan-Indian priorities and interests are protected. But the UPA Government has completely failed to convince even its own allies regarding its foreign policy decisions.

For instance, in September 2011, Singh undertook a special journey to neighbouring Bangladesh to meet that country's Prime Minister Sheikh Hasina. The sole aim of the visit was to strengthen bilateral relations between the two countries. But the trip was marred by West Bengal Chief Minister Mamata Banerjee, even though her party, the Trinamool Congress, is a Congress ally. Banerjee refused to accompany Singh on his trip and in effect threw cold water on the TeestaRiver water sharing agreement that was to be finalised. It was a great disappointment for Bangladesh because that country attached a high priority to the resolution of this water dispute. The question then is: Why did Singh not care to discuss the matter with Banerjee beforehand?

This setback with Bangladesh was only made worse when the politically disgraced patriarch of the DMK, M Karunanidhi, bullied the Union Government into voting against Sri Lanka in the United Nations' Human Rights Commission. This action of the UPA has not served any national interest. On the contrary, New Delhi has alienated Colombo which was quite peeved that India did not vote in its favour. In effect, the UPA Government was not been able to pursue a definite foreign policy that would safeguard national interests because its two allies in the coalition put their parochial and provincial interests ahead of the state.

The story of the UPA's imprisonment by its own coalition partners does not end here. The Union Government has not been able to push through even domestic policies because it could not arrive at a consensus with its coalition partners.

Sharad Pawar of the Nationalist Congress Party compelled his own Cabinet colleagues to permit the export of sugar and cotton, so that rich peasants could earn profits in the international market. If Pawar has changed the course of UPA's agriculture policy, Banerjee has scuttled the Government's efforts in land reform. Her ultimate aim is, however, to have the Union Government to impose a three-year moratorium on West Bengal's debt. She has caught Congress president Sonia Gandhi by the neck by offering conditional support to the party's presidential nominee.

How this issue and others such as those related to the proposed NCTC, are going to be resolved, is yet to be seen. However, that still does not answer the key question: Why does the UPA still not have a mechanism in place to resolve differences with its own allies before these issues are made known to the people?

The Pioneer, 22-05-2012

The Ideal President

Mulayam Singh Yadav set the cat among the pigeons when he said that the office of the President should not be occupied either by a bureaucrat or a non-political person. An extremely undesirable way to nominate a candidate is on sectarian considerations. The latest example of such sectarianism is the candidature of P A Sangma because he claims to belong to the tribal community and the office of the President has never been occupied by a tribal.

The BJP is dead set against any candidate with impeccable secular credentials. It nominated RSS leader Bhairon Singh Shekhawat in 2007, hoping that if elected, he would bend the secular fabric of India and promote the ideology of Hindu Rashtravad. The forces of Hindutva prefer a non-political candidate because he can be manipulated by the well-organised machinery of the Sangh Parivar. On April 30, Sushma Swaraj opposed the rumoured candidature of Hamid Ansari, the vice-president of India. Sharad Yadav of the JD(U) and convener of NDA, snubbed the BJP for jumping the queue before any decision had been taken by the NDA.

Mulayams warning against a non-political candidate is based on his experience of public life while struggling against communal forces. The President is not only a symbol of the nation, he is also protector and promoter of secular parliamentary democracy, and so, the Presidency should be insulated from sectarianism and religious fundamentalism.

The forthcoming elections have assumed political significance because the new occupant of Rashtrapati Bhavan in 2012 is expected to play a crucial and active role in the process of government formation at the Centre in 2014. It does not require a political magician to predict that the next general election, like all others since 1989, will bring up a fractured electoral verdict. National and regional parties will have to make great efforts to form a coalition government at the Centre. Indian voters will choose from around 45 recognised parties. Such a diverse political map, with nearly four dozen contenders for votes, has created a situation where no single party or group can win a majority on its own. This gives the President a vital role in coalition formation.

The President becomes the referee when the formation of the central government becomes complex, because different parties come forward to press their claims. The President has to evaluate the claims made by different coalitions of parties and establish whose claim of a majority is genuine. The ball is in the court of the Rashtrapati since, like Caesars wife, (s)he should be wholly above suspicion when inviting a leader chosen by coalition groups for forming a government.

The only objective criteria followed by the President at the time of formation of government is that the claim of majority support by group of coalition parties should not be spurious, and a viable and stable government should be constituted on the basis of majority support. A former President, Shankar Dayal Sharma, invited Atal Bihari Vajpayee to form the government in 1998 because the BJP was the single largest-minority party in the Lok Sabha, without fully applying his mind. He did not ask the BJP to seek written support from other parties to establish a majority in Parliament. The BJP could not prove its majority in the Lok Sabha and the government fell in 13 days.

A Presidential candidate should be clearly committed to the letter and spirit of Articles 74 and 75 of the Constitution because highly motivated and extremely dangerous interpretations of these Articles have been floated to suit the political requirements of involved political parties.

An ambitious, power-obsessed person should not be considered for President because (s)he can twist the Constitution by bending the real significance of Articles 74 and 75.

These Articles do not visualise that the President can override the Prime Minister and his council of ministers who are accountable to Parliament. The President is expected to act on the advice of the PM and his ministers: he cannot refuse, but only hope to ask the Cabinet to reconsider such advice.

Zail Singh, a former President, was very ambitious politically, and India narrowly escaped a constitutional crisis, when he decided to dismiss Rajiv Gandhi, who was clearly a leader of the majority of MPs in the Lok Sabha.

Many are haunted by the proclamation of Emergency by Indira Gandhi in June 1975, where President Fakhruddin Ali Ahmed was woken up at midnight and he signed the proclamation that suspended freedom and fundamental rights. Many elected chief ministers of state governments have been dismissed by an obliging and partisan President on advise of the ruling party at the Centre on the basis of disingenuous reports of governors. These powers have been much abridged over the years.

The ideal President should be secular, politically experienced but with no overarching political ambitions. *The Economic Times, 26-05-2012*

Democracy in the Hands of Crorepatis

The Election Commission has been making sincere attempts to clean up the electoral process for a while now. It is been vigilant about candidates with criminals records or those sponsored by the mafia. It has made every effort to curb the flow of unaccounted money in election by asking candidates to submit an affidavit disclosing his/her financial assets before filing the nomination. However, all hope has been belied because every contesting candidate violates all statuary limitations of expenditure incurred during the elections. It is simplistic to believe that Representation of People's Act or extra-vigilance by the Election Commission has in any way curbed the flow of illegal funds in elections because the larger context of democratic elections has ceased to be social or public service and has instead become an activity for the accumulation of funds for personal prosperity and riches.

A few facts can substantiate the argument that politics has become an activity of mercenaries in public life who benefited personally from political activity. First, it has been a common feature among Indian politicians to manage and control political parties like a family private business. It is not just the Congress which has always been accused of practicing dynastic politics, important regional parties like the Akali Dal of Punjab, Indian National Lok Dal of Haryana, Samajwadi Party of Uttar Pradesh, Rashtriya Janata Dal of Bihar, Biju Janata Dal of Orissa and the DMK of Tamil Nadu are patronising and promoting the cult of nepotism. Family members are being promoted as the sole custodians of 'financial resources' accumulated by these party-personal. Leaders like Pradash Singh Badal, Om Prakash Chautala, Ajit Singh, Mulayam Singh Yadav, Lalu Prasad Yadav, Navin Patnaik, K Karunanidhi—all practitioners of dynastic party system exercise authoritarian control over their respective organisations because the party funds are 'controlled' by them.

Loyal party members are given some share in party funds as a quid-pro-quo for blind obedience to the leader. The story does not end here. If the party bosses use their political power to accumulate funds in the name of the party, MPS and MLAS individually make every effort to accumulate private funds for themselves. And the corporate sector is ready to pay the 'price' to politicians who can bend and break the rules in its favour.

Politicians do not have personal resources to remain in public life, they exercise their power to accumulate funds for their own benefits and this is possible only when they can 'oblige' the fund-givers. No surprise then Assembly or Lok Sabha elections become a matter of life and death for parties. Only from corridors of power, can they reciprocate their fund-givers with governmental contracts and assignments. Further, the coalition governments at the centre beginning from the 1990s have provided an opportunity to every small, or middle or single coalition partner to separately collect money for their own party. The Atal Bihari Vajpayee government from 1998 to 2004 was a coalition of 24 parties and every group in the coalition used its power to collect funds for itself. But the way NDA allies such as DMK and AIADMK went ahead and joined the winning coalition led by the Congress later, it became clear that coalition had become a matter of convenience without any principle or ideology. Indian politicians keep harping on the secularism-communalism ideological divide, but in 1998 all the so-called practitioners of secularism like George Fernandes, Nitish Kumar, Chandrababu Naidu willingly and enthusiastically participated in the Vajpayee government and some of them even joined the secular government of UPA I and II.

The above context is to be kept in mind while discussing the emergence of multi-millionaires leaders in a democracy of more than 500 million below the poverty line. A political system ceases to be a democracy where the filthy rich claim to be elected 'representatives' of the majority poor.

A recent survey of affidavits filed by contesting candidates in the Lok Sabha or State Assembly elections shows that a large majority of contestants and winning candidates are multi-millionaires. Badal, Mulayam and Karunanidhi and other such patriarchs of family-run party businesses were very ordinary citizens with ordinary economic status before entering the elections. Evidently, the so-called 'discretionary' powers given to political leaders by the law have been exercised only to oblige the fund-giver businessmen.

But the question is can these crorepati elected representatives feel the pain of 500 million deprived Indians? Indian democracy has become an 'oligarchy' only because the moneyed class can win an election. This is a threat to democracy. *The Financial World, 28-08-2012*

Holding Parliament to Ransom is Unfair

The BJP has demanded Prime Minister Manmohan Singh's resignation because he is solely accountable for all acts of omission and commission which have been committed while allocating coal mines to private entrepreneurs. The BJP has also served notice to the UPA's coalition allies that Singh's hands are dirty due to the huge losses suffered by the country because he, not just as Prime Minister but also as Coal Minister, decided to allocate, not auction, coal mines to the highest bidder.

The battle-line between the BJP and the Congress has been clearly drawn. If Singh resigns, the UPA Government will collapse. Also, the Sonia Gandhi-led Congress can never accept such a demand because it will not only be an admission of guilt but it will also be politically indefensible for the party. This is the reason that Gandhi on August 23 said: "We have done no wrong, there is no need to be defensive." She further urged her party's MPs that they should "aggressively" confront BJP leaders for the tactics adopted by the latter to obstruct the functioning of Parliament. Clearly, there is no meeting ground between the BJP and the Congress. Such a confrontation has immobilised the whole political system of India.

The resolution of differences of opinion should take place either inside Parliament or by the independent judiciary according to the rules of the parliamentary game. In the case of a complete breakdown, the only option is to launch political protest movement and mobilise public opinion. It is inherent in the logic of polarisation that the whole society gets divided. Will elections held in this milieu lead to political solutions? Is one electoral verdict enough to douse the fire of antagonism between the Congress and the BJP? What will be the cost of such deadlocked political machinery wherein established institutions are now considered irrelevant for the resolution of conflicts?

India is facing a serious economic crisis. But this not the central concern of political parties even though an economic crisis along with deepening social cleavages can lead to unrest and violence. This is not to say that galloping levels of corruption in public life have not to be exposed and those responsible for it should not be punished. Accountability for misuse and abuse of power by the political executive has to be enforced. At the same time, it deserves to be re-emphasised Parliament is the only forum provided by the Constitution to hold the Union Cabinet accountable. The Opposition can move a vote of no-confidence in Parliament against the Cabinet, for instance. These procedures of parliamentary forum of Government are quite adequate to punish the guilty.

Imagine a situation wherein the Government starts taking decisions without referring them to Parliament, as provided by the Constitution. It would be the end of democracy. Similarly, on the other side of the coin, if the Opposition derails Parliament and takes to street politics for the resolution of disputes with the Government, it will lead to a complete de-legitimisation of politics based on debate and dissent.

The current deadlock of Parliament and the breakdown of dialogue between the Government and the Opposition raise several short-term and long-term issues concerning the future of Indian democracy. It is substantiated by historical experience of many modern Western democracies that democracy based on debate and dissent is destroyed if rules of the games are not followed. Politicians must believe in the Constitution, in its letter and spirit. Those who do not accept the fundamentals of constitutional democracy are simply making efforts to destroy democracy through politics of the bullet which will then eventually replace politics of the ballot. *The Pioneer, 31-08-2012*

No Coalitions, Only Marriages of Inconvenience

The Indian experience with the coalition system of government at the central level beginning with VP Singh's prime ministership in 1989 deserves a close scrutiny because many infirmities had emerged during the highly centralised system of governance due to the one party dominance of Indian politics for forty years post-Independence.

The imposition of Emergency by Indira Gandhi from 1975 to 1977 had completely delegitimized the system of political control by a single party which was impervious to any system of democratic checks and balance of power.

It has been assumed that replacement and displacement of single majority party rule by a coalition system of sharing of power by many groups will be more democratic and federal than its opposite, represented by a fully dominant party. India's experience with coalition system of government at the centre for about more than two decades has not at all proved positive as expected by its vocal defenders.

A few facts may be mentioned to substantiate the argument that rigorous analysis of coalition governments completely belies the expectations of pro-coalition advocates. The successful functioning of coalition governments in Kerala is just an exception because Congress-led or Communist-led governments are mirror images of each other and the problems of governance faced by state governments are not as complex and complicated as the ones dealt with by the central governments.

Prime Ministers of coalition governments at the centre like VP Singh or Chandra Shekar or HD Deve Gowda or Inder Kumar Gujral or Atal Bihari Vajpayee's first short term in power clearly showed the fragility of coalitions. Not only this. All these five Prime Ministers were just 'caretakers' because their political support structure was weak, and incoherent.

VP Singh in 1989-90 claimed support from two antagonists like the BJP and Communist parties and in spite of his self-proclaimed quality of governance by 'managing contradictions', he could not survive for more than ten months in office because his own patchwork Janata Party kicked him out. This story was repeated in the case of all these purely temporary and transitory Prime Ministers and even PV Narasimha Rao could form a central government in 1991 to 1996 on the basis of all kinds of tricks to sustain himself in power. (Comment).

All post-single party majority central governments have been continuously engaged in a fight for survival in office. Survivability of these Prime Ministers remained central concern of all coalition governments at the centre which has directly impacted the whole system because long term policies for governance at the Centre could not be formulated by coalition governments which were politically inherently weak from the inside. Second, Indian innovation of 'political groups' without joining the coalition government have oftenly opted to 'support from outside' the coalition-in-power.

VP Singh was supported from outside by Hindu Communalists and secular communists, the Manmohan Singh government was supported from 'outside' by the communists from 2004 to 2008 and Mulayam Singh Yadav. The Samajwadi Party and the Bahujan Samaj Party have extended 'outside' support to the current coalition government led by the Congress. Can such a coalition system provide an effective governmental leadership to a complex country when its own survival depends on 'oxygen' provided by groups enjoying great influence over government-in-power without any commitment of any kind to the policies of the ruling coalition?

Illustration is not an argument, but facts speak for themselves because beginning with VP Singh's 'outside supporters' to ManMohan Singh's 'Mulayam-Maya' have not only kept the government under pressure and whenever it is politically convenient, outsiders abandon the shaky ship of government.

Third, a coalition government at the centre has to entice and persuade regional and sub-regional parties, groups and leaders for manufacturing a 'majority support' to face the Lok Sabha. The public record of these regionalists speaks for itself because their 'support' or 'denial of support' to a coalition system of government at the centre is not at all based on any 'ideological or 'principled' political considerations.

The BJP, a party of the anti-minority Hindu Communalists, or a weak secular democratic Congress party have succeeded in building a coalition under their leadership of diverse regional political groups, irrespective of so-called publicly stated beliefs. *The Economics Times, 29-12-2012*

Dynasty Politics—No Place in Modern India

An extremely undemocratic practice of dynasticism has been solidified by Messrs M Karunanidhi of the DMK, Shibu Soren of the Jharkhand Mukti Morcha and Parkash Singh Badal of the Akali Dal, in the New Year. All of these leaders have recently crowned their sons as their successors.

The ageing leaders have said that their children are politically equipped to succeed them because the latter were initiated into politics at an early age and some have even worked as apprentices within the party. A case in point is Congress general secretary Rahul Gandhi and his brigade of young leaders such as Union Minister of State for Corporate Affairs Sachin Pilot and Union Minister of State for Power Jyotiraditya Scindia et al.

Similarly, Punjab Chief Minister Parkash Singh Badal, JMM's Shibu Soren and DMK's M Karunanidhi have tested the competence of their children by having them work as Deputy Chief Ministers or Ministers.

These 'special' children have contested elections, held responsible political positions either in Government or in their party organisation. And it is on the basis of this 'rich' political experience, that they are ready to become the Chief Minister or even the Prime Minister.

Another common denominator for these new leaders is that they have all grown up in a party culture where inner democracy is not practised at all. Gandhi had once made tall claims about holding organisational elections, but has long since abandoned the project. The fact is that most regional parties have practised the culture of nominating successors.

The idea that these nominated dynasty leaders will bring any substantial change in this dynastic style of Indian politics needs to be rejected outright as they will surely continue the traditions of their party patriarchs. This is the real meaning of dynastic politics.

It is unfortunate that political parties and leaders are completely out of sync with the demands of a changing India. The popular movements of 2012 and early 2013 show that new groups are demanding different things from their elected Governments. The Anna Hazare-led anti-corruption movement of 2011 was supported by moneyed classes and publicised by television channels. It fizzled out because its wanted to eradicate corruption in governance without going into the causes of graft.

While Team Anna was successful in creating some *tamasha*, the brutal gang rape in Delhi on December 16 led to an outburst of genuine anger across the country. A new generation of educated, young Indians spontaneously took to the streets to express their anguish against inept governance and the degradation of society's moral fabric. The issues raised by the young demonstrators clearly reflected their desire to alter the social and political system so that it is in tune with the real life aspirations of 21st century India.

Have our politicians drawn any message from these protests? Has any Chief Minister, Deputy Chief Minister or a Prime Ministerial aspirant, nominated to the top post by virtue of family, shown, through actions or statements, an understanding of this new politics? The old style has proved to be incapable of dealing with the aspirations of a young and new India.

It is quite clear that much like the old beneficiaries of dynasty politics—Odisha Chief Minister Naveen Patnaik (son of Biju Patnaik), Uttar Pradesh Chief Minister Akhilesh Yadav (son of Mulayam Singh Yadav), and Union Civil Aviation Minister Ajit Singh (son of Charan Singh)—who have continued in the footsteps of their fathers, the 'new' nominees will also walk the same path.

The political system of new India is not safe in the hands of these dynasts because they are all old wine in new bottles. *The Pioneer, 18-01-2013*

Riding High on Local Politics

The Forthcoming 16th Lok Sabha elections of 2014 have made every party-be it all-India and multiple regionalists—to think about their political strategies as political stakes of every party and group are quite high. Neither any all-India nor a regionalist can hope to come to power on the basis of its own electoral successes during the elections. It has become a fashion to suggest that India has entered the stage of coalition governments at the Centre and every coalition government whether of VP Singh-Chandra Shekar 1989-91 or HD Dev Gowda-Inder Kumar Gujral 1996-1998 or Atal Bihari Vajpayee-led National Democratic Alliance 1998-8-2004 or the Congress-led United Progressive Alliance I and II 2004-2009 and 2009-2013 depended on the support of regional parties and groups. Supreme leaders of regional parties like Prakash Singh Badal of Akali Dal of Punjab or Devi Lal-Om Prakash Chauthala of Lok Dals of Haryana, or Mulayam Singh Yadav or Mayawati of Samajvadi Party or Bahujan Samajavadi Party or Sharad Yadav, Nitish Kumar, Lalu Prasad Yadav, Ram Vilas Paswan of Bihar, or Shibu Sbren of Jharkhand or Navin Patanik of Biju Janata Dal of Orissa, or Mamata Banerjee of Trinamool Congress of Bengal, or Shiv Senas of Maharashtra or Telugu Desam and the latest YSR party of Jagan Reddy of Andhra or M. Karunanidhi or Km. Jayalalitha, of Tamil Nadu *et al.* have been active players in the formation of every coalition government at the Centre especially beginning with VP Singh's National Front government of 1989.

The current situation is BJP Alliance at the Centre, i.e. NDA, is shaky and quite weak to face mighty regional forces across the country. The Congress, another all-India political formation, in this pre-Lok Sabha election year is also faced with the ongoing process of desertion by its regional coalitional partners. It has led Sharad Pawar, the leader of Nationalist Congress party, and an alliance partner of the UPA government I and II to ask Sonia Gandhi on April 12, 2013 to call a meeting and take stock of the new situation which has arisen with the walking out of coalition partners and with such a dwindling political support to the Congress-led UPA II, it would be advisable to prepone the Lok Sabha elections to October-November 2013. It deserves to be clearly stated that Sharad Pawar is not only a tall leader in his own right, the Maharashtra State government also depends on the smooth functioning of Congress and Pawar's NCP. The purpose of above narrative is to contextualise the pre-Lok Sabha election's political situation and on the basis of this brief description, a few facts need to be clearly emphasised.

First the electoral performance of either the Congress or the BJP is expected to be quite average, rather below average for the 453 Lok Sabha seats of 2014f The Congress party's strong performance in Lok Sabha elections in Andhra in 2009 is not at all expected to be repeated because its Andhra wing is split and completely fac-tionalised. It is the same story for the Congress in Uttar Pradesh where Mulayam Singh Yadav in State Assembly elections of 2012, and inspite of Rahul Gandhi's great efforts in the state, reduced Congress to the status of nonexistent'. If Congress in large states is confronted with serious challenges either by powerful regionalists or the BJP, its capacity to get elected after the 16th Lok Sabha elections is quite doubtful. The second key party, the BJP, has double 'disadvantage' because if its trusted ally like Janata Dal (United) is threatening to walk out of the NDA, the other regionalists will find it difficult to align with communal brand of politics of the BJP. It is a truism to state that a coalition of parties and groups can successfully function if it is linked with a strong political 'pole' like Congress or the BJP and the experience of all other coalitions has been a failure. Political parties—whether national or regional, big or small—have a right to dream and given the Indian situation, every supreme leader of every regional party is a megalomaniac and wants to occupy the highest position of Prime Ministership of India even if it is for 10 months like VP Singh or HD Dev Gowda or for six months like Chandra Shekar or Inder Kumar Gujral or even for only thirteen days as Atal Bihari Vajpayee.

It deserves to be clearly stated that on the basis of all available public facts, Indian experience has been quite problematic. European coalition governments in England, France or Germany, unlike Italy, have been stable because, coalitions consist of two or three parties and work on the basis of agreed minimum common programme. Parties join coalition bargain with one another but the goals of governance are well-defined before coalition government is formed. Indian experiment in coalition making process is quite unique because partners join a coalition, not on the basis of any fundamental agreements, but on the basis of 'price' which they can successfully extract from coalition partners. The allotment of ministries and portfolios to the coalition partners is not decided on any principled basis but on the demand of a regional 'supremo' and the prime minister is expected to sign on the dotted lines. The regional supporters of the coalition at the centre have a power to. 'dictate' and 'veto' any decision including that of 'appointments' by the prime minister of a coalition government. India has experienced two models of coalition governments at the centre where either coalition was led by one largest party like the BJP or the Congress or the regionalists themselves occupied the post of prime minister. The worst model of coalition government was where both the all India parties remained 'outsiders' and the 'insiders' like VP Singh or Chandra Shekhar or Dev Gowda or Gujral exercised power without any responsibility for the future of the country.

It is too much to expect 'sons-of-the-soil' regionalists to have an all-India perspective and have an understanding of complex global politics. Regionalists are specialists, while playing the role of native 'brokers' and 'fixers' because they know the 'local milieu' and balance of social power. If the localists are made to occupy the office of prime minister, not only they will disturb the all-India social equilibrium by pursuing benefits for their states alone, they will not inspire any confidence from the leadership of neighbouring regions like Kaveri River Water Dispute between Karnataka and Tamil Nadu. The upshot of above description is that India cannot be governed by a coalition led by 'regionalist party supremo' because 'local boss' of one state is a 'foreigner' in another state and it is better for regionalists to realise their limitations and forget about their ambitions which are far away from the realities of complex India. *The Financial World, 02-05-2013*

Opportunists or Secularists?

Prime Minister Manmohan Singh has unambiguously drawn country's attention that coalition politics is a game of opportunist alliances when he observed on June 18 that 'in politics there are no permanent friends or enemies. We take decisions as the situation evolves.' Manmohan himself provided evidence about completely shifting loyalties of coalition partners when on June 18 he described Bihar Chief Minister Nitish Kumar as 'secular' precisely on the occasion of separation between Janata Dal (United) a full fledged and full blooded communal BJP. It is essential to spell out the track record of Nitish Kumar of fully 17 years for understanding his dubious political games which he has played to remain in the centre stage of power without any concern or regard for minimum ideological and principled commitment to the ideology of secularism in Indian politics.

Nitish Kumar forgot about secularism when he got associated with Hindu nationalist. Atal Bihari Vajpayee's led coalition government at the centre from 1998 to 2004. It is precisely at that time when Vajpayee was prime minister and Nitish Kumar and his Janata Dal (United) was part of coalition government at the centre that post-Godhra anti-Muslim communal riots took place from March to April 2002 and Rashtriya Swyam Sevak Sangh mouthpiece prime minister did not act against Narendra Modi who as chief minister could have been held solely responsible for Gujarat communal carnage of 2002. Not only this. Nitish Kumar twice occupied the office of Bihar Chief Minister on the basis of a 'coalition' with Hindu communal party. Sharad Yadav and Nitish Kumar have never treated Sangh Parivar as 'political untouchable' on the basis of an ideological opposition between JD(U) and the BJP. The political gimmickry of JD(U) Sharad Yadav and Nitish Kumar came to public notice when they expressed their opposition only to Narendra Modi and they clearly stated that if LK Advani was the NDA candidate for leadership, JD(U) will be a part of the BJP.

It is essential to refer to the ideological and political track record of other regional bosses to substantiate the argument that politics of coalition governments in India is based on completely unprincipled search for power. Mayawati of Uttar Pradesh's Bahujan Samaj Party could become chief minister of Uttar Pradesh with the support of Hindu communal BJP forgetting that struggle for justice for the oppressed and downtrodden Dalits, her party's main social support base, can be fought only on the secular platform and not by making alliances with Brahmanical Hindu communal party. The Hindu priestly class—an active ideological support base of Hinduism-based BJP—has not discriminated against Dalits throughout history. These Hindu priests did not permit Dalit entry to Hindu temples and Dalit Movement in India emerged on the platform of Dalit rights which were denied to them by Hindu priestly class, the allies of the BJP. Mayawati who had taken support of communalists to become UP chief minister opted to join so called secular Left-Democratic Alliance for the Lok Sabha elections of 2009 to use secular card to fulfill her political ambitions to occupy a seat of power in the central government if so-called secular front was able to form a government at the centre. Not only this. The so-called secular front was able to form a government at the centre.

The so-called Left-Democratic front of a motley grouping of opportunist regionalists welcomed with an open hand all those who had enjoyed power on the support of the BJP. Naveen Patnaik of Janata Biju Dal also aligned with anti-Muslim and anti-Christian BJP to achieve his political ambition of chief ministership of Odisha while Christian churches and Missionaries were attacked in the state when he was in alliance with BJP. Naveen Patnaik, like Nitish Kumar, parted company with BJP when he realised that politically and electorally BJD would gain at the time of elections by dissociating himself from BJP. It was not that Hindu communal party had suddenly become a 'liability' for Naveen Patnaik and Nitish Kumar because of any 'ideological' differences, the alliance and break up was dictated purely on the basis of electoral calculation and voting arithmetic. The anti-Brahman Dra-vadian parties and their factions have formed coalitions with Brahmanical BJP for purely political considerations of power at the centre and without any ideological hang ups, the Dravadian political groups and leaders of Tamil Nadu had participated in BJP-led coalition governments at the centre from 1998 to 2004.

HD Dev Gowda of Janata Dal, on the basis of his so-called secular credentials, became prime minister from 1996 to 1997 and the same secularist formed a coalition government in Karnataka, his state of political activity, with BJP. The above illustrations of political alignments based on complete absence of ideology by regional political parties should be of great concern to those who believe that politics should be based on principles and values and in the Indian context secular versus communal ideology and politics should act as a real 'divider' between committed secularists who should form a United Front against Hindu communal parties. First, the struggle between secular versus communal parties and politics has become a matter of winning an electoral support of Muslim votes. It is a strange political situation where Muslim votes per se has become the object of parties which pretend to be 'secular' and the rabid and aggressive anti-Muslim politics of the BJP is not opposed by any so-called secular political leader and group. It is an open secret that Naveen Patnaik and Nitish Kumar, who were quite comfortable in the company of communalists, parted the communal party because of their greed for Muslim vote. Is it secularism?

How can secular leaders occupy the office of ministers or chief ministers in alliance with committed anti-secular practitioners of religion-based politics? Vajpayee of the Sangh Parivar could occupy the highest office pf prime minister of India only on the basis of support of those leaders who claim to be 'secularists'? The only explanation for non-ideological opportunist politics of self-appointed secular leaders is that the greed for holding office of power in the government, whether in the Centre or state, is the basis of forming coalitions with communalists like Vajpayee or others. Hence Nitish, like others who have co-habited with the BJP, cannot become 'secular' leader simply because he has parted company with BJP. The reality is that none of these so-called secular leaders have firm commitment against Hindu-religion-based politics of the BJP, which is socially 'divisive'. Not only this. The goal of getting Muslim votes by any party does not make it secular and tactical alliances for electoral gains and losses are not to be confused with ideological battles among parties and groups. *The Financial World, 24-06-2013*

The Centre has to Hold Together

West Bengal chief minister Mamata Banerjee has floated the idea of forming a federal front of states such as Odisha, West Bengal, Bihar and Jharkhand to organise a united struggle to compel the central government to allocate special funds for these backward states. Not only this. Mulayam Singh Yadav of the Samajwadi Party has extended 'outside political support' to the central government in return for providing extra funds for the development of the backward state of Uttar Pradesh.

These demands by some regional parties have once again brought to centre stage the crucial problem of uneven levels of growth faced by the 28 states and seven union territories of India. The Indian situation is special because tensions and conflicts among the relatively large, resource-rich and developed states like Tamil Nadu, Karnataka and Andhra Pradesh in the south, or Maharashtra and Gujarat in the west, or Punjab and Haryana in the north have to coexist with the concerns of the backward states.

It should be noted that the Constitution makers were not only conscious of the economic, political and cultural diversity of the country; they provided the institutional architecture to deal with the short-and long-term problems confronted by 'special category' states.

Article 280 of the Constitution provides for the establishment of a finance commission every five years for the division and allocation of fiscal resources between the Centre and state governments. This body also evolves the criteria for 'special grants' to backward states. The present 14th Finance Commission is grappling with this challenge.

Hence, the crux of the matter is political credibility and the acceptance of the central government's fairness, especially by regionalists such as Naveen Patnaik, Mamata Banerjee or Nitish Kumar. The Manmohan Singh government is responsible for creating an impression among non-coalition partners by giving positive signals to Mulayam Singh Yadav's demand for special grants. It is a fact that the regionalists are guided purely by 'local' economic and political considerations while taking anti-central government postures, and it also cannot be denied that coalition partners at the Centre are able to appropriate disproportionate benefits for their states.

This is not the first time that the party or parties in power at the Centre have been attacked by state governments ruled by the opposition parties or that a partisan central government has treated opposition party governments in an unfair manner while allocating special financial grants. The first communist government in Kerala in 1957 led by EMS Namboodiripad had a big clash with Prime Minister Jawaharlal Nehru for discriminating against the state.

The political distancing among parties ruling at the Centre and different parties in states has increased, even intensified, during the phase of coalition governments at the Centre. The Tamil Nadu government even suspected the neutrality of the Inter-State Water Dispute Tribunal with HD Deve Gowda occupying the office of prime minister.

Chandrababu Naidu, as chief minister of Andhra Pradesh, led a delegation to New Delhi and asked then PM Atal Bihari Vajpayee to set a tradition and consult chief ministers before selecting members of the finance commission because 'forward' states were supposedly getting discriminatory treatment in the allocation of funds.

The upshot of all this is that the demand for a federal front of economically-backward eastern Indian states will inspire confidence among federal units. However, a so-called non-BJP, non-Congress coalition of regionalists is not a solution to the problems of a diverse India.

At the end of the day, a politically and administratively effective central government will have to be in power to properly 'mediate' and find solutions for conflicts between the Centre and the states or among the states themselves.

Hindustan Times, 25-06-2013

The Politics of Targeting

The 9/11 attacks made President George W Bush announce his country's determination to pursue its anti-terrorism policy all over the world.

This 'globalisation' by the US impacted not only the strategic policies of various states engaged in the fight against terror, but the rise of terrorism has also given birth to a thinking process that associates Muslims with violence.

India is a major country engaged in a war against 'terrorism', which has become the central agenda of the 21st century. Hence the question arises, especially in the context of a complex multi-religious country like India: 'Who is a terrorist?'

While the central government or the states have always taken the correct position that the culprits will be caught after proper 'investigation', a large section of Indian society, and even a section of the print and audio visual media, do not show the same restraint. Pakistan's state policy of exporting terrorism has contributed to the large extent to this.

It cannot be denied that jihadist Islamic groups based in Pakistan often make anti-Indian statements, which provide a source of justification for a section of Indian society to pronounce judgements against Indian Muslims.

Further, there is no denying the fact that the rapid and ongoing process of communalisation of Indian society has contributed to the climate of mistrust. Religion-based politics in a multi-religious country like India has historically 'divided' society on a 'religious basis' and such a milieu—targeting religious communities for their real/fictitious acts of omission and commission—becomes a fact of political culture and discourse of 'religious majority versus religious minority'.

The spark behind 'religious terrorism' is in the ideology that makes people act against 'other religions', an ideology based on a one-sided and biased interpretation of the meaning of religion, conveyed to the youth by priests and politicians.

Second, if a chief minister says, "I am a Hindu nationalist because I am a born Hindu. I am patriotic ...", any discerning mind can understand that such patriotism divides nationalists around religions.

There is no denying the fact that Muslims in India have become a 'suspect' in every act of terrorism. A telling example of 'Muslim are terrorists' is provided by the National Investigation Agency, involved in finding who is behind the bomb blasts in Bodh Gaya.

When the investigation process was underway, an NIA official on July 18 said, "Going by the modus operandi, the nature of explosive and eye witness ... it is now almost certain that the Indian Mujahideen or a local outfit owing allegiance to it carried out the multiple blasts".

If this can be the position of the NIA, it is not unreasonable to expect a 'hurt and concerned' community to reject every police encounter—whether at Batla House in Delhi or the one involving Ishrat Jahan in Gujarat—as fake. All hell broke loose when the minister for minority affairs, K Rahman Khan, "asked the government to constitute a task force and review terror cases against Muslims youth languishing in jails across the country".

It is apt to compare the mistrust between the African-Americans and Whites in the US to Hindu and Muslims in India because they (the African-Americans and Muslims) are always an object of the 'politics of targeting'.

Barack Obama in his speech on the death of Trayvon Martin, an African-American, said, "That includes me and I don't want to exaggerate this, but these sets of experiences inform how the African-American community interprets what happened one night in Florida".

Indian Muslims must be super-human if they are not conditioned by their daily experience of facing discrimination and getting targeted as terrorists.

Hindustan Times, 31-07-2013

Chapter 2
Congress Coalition and Government

Politics Ruining Economy

The Budget session of the Lok Sabha is expected to be devoted to serious discussion on issues concerning the fundamentals of economic health. The annual Railway Budget and the Union Budget are not mere statements of income and expenditure, nor are they confined to matters of new taxation for the augmentation of fiscal resources for future investments for developmental and welfare schemes for the country. These budget discussions in Parliament from February to May reveal the real situation of the national economy and future challenges which lie ahead for the forward march of the country.

Finance Minister Pranab Mukherjee's speech conveyed a message that the Indian economy was on the growth track and in spite of the deteriorating financial and economic situation, especially the European Unioncrisis, India has managed its economy and fiscal situation quite well. He did not convey even a hint of anxiety on the health of the economy. On a different note, in the second week of May while winding up the budgetary annual exercise, he threw a bombshell by declaring that the rate of growth will slow down because of crisis in the international market and also because ofadverse impact of the falling value on exchange rate. Mukherjee observed that the country is faced with the prospect of low rate of growth, like 6 per cent of the GDP only, or deteriorating value of the Indian rupee in the international market, the food-related inflation was becoming uncontrollable and the rising inflationary pressure on the economy was becoming unbearable for the common man. Finally, Mukherjee warned that the country will have to face 'austerity' because of the rising budgetary deficit, which was quite alarming.

Democracy is based on a social contract between the government and the people and it is the duty of the government to take public opinion into confidence on such a serious situation facing the Indian economy, but the UPA government did not deem it fit to inform the public about the country's real problems except when Pranab Mukherjee threw a shocker in the middle of May 2012 while winding up the annual budgetary exercise in Parliament. If Mukerjee announced some immediate austerity steps to cut the deficit, the

Prime Minister's Office suddenly came out with proposals to streamline the fast implementation of economic projects of the government. The PMO in the middle of May 2012 enlightened the country, especially business and industrial classes, that the Licence Raj of pre-1990s India has been replaced by a very obstructive and negative system of the 'clearance Raj or regime' because at least 58 clearances were required by public or private sector to launch any developmental or infrastructure project, including power-related projects.

These 58 'clearances', which were to be obtained by public or private investors, required everyone to knock at the door of various ministers at the Centre at the level of state governments. Not to be left behind, some 'clearances' were to be given by Panchayati Raj institutions. The toughest task for an investor was to chase the environmental ministry for clearances and pursue doggedly various government agencies which dealt with issues concerning 'land acquisition' for setting up as project.

This analysis of the working of 'clearance Raj or regime' by the PMO clearly shows that in spite of the fact that international economic and fiscal crisis has adversely impacted India, at the same time, it is the domestic political and administrative decision-making process which is the real villain of the piece and is becoming a roadblock in the way of acceleration of the rate of growth of the GDP of the economy. A few facts may be mentioned to substantiate the argument that the prevailing economic crisis is a direct consequence of political directionless of leadership and over bureaucratisation of decision making in the area of economic life of the country.

It is the duty of the government to protect environmental degradation but it is another issue to make environmental clearness an uphill task for investors. Further, the UPA government has adopted a time-consuming strategy of making a Group of Ministers to process each and every proposal of economic ministries where a policy decision is required. A minister of coal or mines or industry or any other infrastructural development minister or department may evolve a 'proposal' for speedy implementation of projects which fall under the jurisdiction of a particular minister. But then either the PMO or the GoM sits over the proposals of individual ministers before clearances are given. This is a politico-administrative problem which directly concerns the actual functioning style of the government which Lakshmi Mittal, a big industrialist, publicly observed is 'a slow moving' government.

Another very important issue is of land acquisition, compensation and rehabilitation, because the anachronistic colonial law of 1894 for land acquisition is completely out of sync with new realities of the 21st century. Land is required for developmental projects but if a proper policy of land acquisition does not exist, serious disputes are bound to arise between the seller and buyer of land. Indian courts are flooded with cases where involved parties have complained that either the land was forcibly taken or inadequate compensation was paid or agricultural land was acquired for construction of industries.

The UPA government, which has completed three years of its term, has kept the land acquisition law hanging fire for three years. How can any government keep out of the issue of land acquisition, especially when the distinction between public sector and private economic players is getting completely blurred? During the economic regime of Public-Private Partnership, the government cannot keep itself away from land acquisition processes.

The above narrative based on important facts clearly shows that the economy is slowing down because of purely 'domestic' political situation where decision-making processes have become quite complicated because so many ministries, departments, bureaucracy are involved in clearing a project. There is no political push or a political will to push the decision for a project or a scheme which is considered important for growth. If the Supreme Court has laid down a policy of 'auctions' for national resources, it has abrogated the policy-making powers of the political executive, which is dithering and confused.

The crisis of economy is a challenge and an opportunity for the political executive to sit in the 'driver's seat' and resolve domestic deadlocks and delays in decision-making by the government departments. It is only purposeful politics which can meet the challenge of economic crisis.

The Financial World, 25-05-2012

CONGRESS PARTY POLITICS

Grand Mess All Around as UPA Fumbles

The Congress-led UPA Government is completely encircled by critics including some of its regional allies and, of course, by the Opposition which has a legitimate a role to expose every act of omission and commission of the Government. The story of attacks on the functioning and malfunctioning of the Union Government does not end here.

A very popular movement against the Government has been led by Anna Hazare and his team of publicity-hungry activists who have succeeded in cornering the Government on the issue of widespread corruption in politics and bureaucracy. Anna Hazare has built up public pressure on a reluctant and hesitant Government to approach Parliament for the enactment of the Jan Lok Pal Bill.

While campaigning in favour of their Lokpal Bill, Team Anna showed a lot of indecent haste by commanding Parliament to perform its basic role of law-making within a time-frame laid down by these self-appointed and non-elected individual campaigners.

A legitimate anti-Government movement completely devalued itself by its approach and attitude towards procedures of Parliamentary democracy and other well-established norms of law-making in democracy. Team Anna failed to make a distinction between the Manmohan Singh-led Union Government and the role and responsibilities of elected representatives of Parliament.

Anna and his team has set a dangerous precedent by downgrading the sanctity of elected representatives who are solely responsible for law-making according to their own thinking of the issue of corruption in public life. The atmospherics created by Anna Hazare-led agitation helped in the creation of an image of weak and vacillating Government and this opportunity was fully exploited by powerful captains of the industry who started castigating the Government by addressing open letters to Singh.

On October 11, fourteen 'eminent citizens' led by the likes of Azim Premji, Deepak Parekh *et al.* accused the Government for the "absence of decision-making". The open letter stated that "continuing impasse" has led to "delay in clearing projects". It concluded that the "policy uncertainties and delays in approvals are forcing many large corporate entities to seek out opportunities in other geographies".

If Team Anna has been accused of 'blackmailing' elected political representatives by putting them on 'notice' to legislate or face music, in this atmosphere the leading industrialists are also 'blackmailing' the Government. Premji repeated his warning on November 20, in an open letter, that policy paralysis along with the existence of a "strong nexus among certain corporations, bureaucrats and power-brokers is corroding the fabric of our nation" because in such a situation "large scale corruption in public life has become the order of the day."

Singh has many a time emphasised that India is suffering because of the growth of crony capitalism but he forgets to mention that powerful cronies can turn against its own political and bureaucratic benefactors and patrons. Singh's crony capitalists have prospered under the full patronage of decision-makers who are either sitting in the corridors of power or those who exercise extra-constitutional authority.

It is not only the unelected Anna Hazare who has succeeded in dictating Singh's Government. Even the unelected industry captains who have enough financial resources to directly influence the corridors of power have a hold on the Government. Americans are always engaged in a public discourse on whether to rein in the power of big corporations. American conservatives and their intellectual collaborators are always targetting the role of state because they view the state as the villain and have pleaded to minimise the role of state appointed market regulators.

Believers in the free market economy like Donald Regan or Margaret Thatcher believe in the ideology of a "lean and thin state and freedom for entrepreneurs". Their ideological and political opponents attack the status occupied by big corporations as the fountain source of all evils in society and opt for a regulated capitalist economy where the state should be in the driver's seat.

Indians have also been engaged in this basic debate about the relationship between the Government and business. The Nehru-Indira Gandhi model of state-led economic planning was based on the principle of commanding heights which should be occupied by public institutions including public sector enterprises.

The beginning of 1990's experienced a break with the past. It was suggested by then Prime Minister Narasimha Rao and his Finance Minister Manmohan Singh that the model of planned economy had become completely dysfunctional, and be replaced by a new model of 'retreat of the state'.

From a regulated economy to one that has since been deregulated, liberalised and globalised, India today is a competitive market economic system. The Union and State Governments in the 1990's and the first decade of the 21st century practiced very enthusiastically the New Economic Policy of free market-led capitalism.

This new euphoria for a deregulated economy brought cheers from politicians, bureaucrats, corporate and the media. But everyone forgot that politicians require financial resources and big businesses favours from the Government. It is surprising that Premji and others are alleging a nexus between politicians and power-brokers when industry captains themselves are often found in the corridors of power. *Pioneer, 14-11-2011*

Time to Call the Bluff on Economic Policies

The new economic policy of globalisation, privatisation, deregulation and the opening of Indian market to foreign private investors was uncritically implemented by the Congress in 1991 and then the BJP and other political parties. Two decades after it was first introduced, there is a public debate has over the role of foreign direct investment in various economic sectors of India.

The Manmohan Singh-led Government abruptly announced on November 24 that up to 51 per cent of FDI in multi-brand retail would be allowed in India. All hell broke loose, and soon the Congress was completely isolated on the issue. Not only the Opposition but even allies of the Congress-led UPA chose to dissociate themselves from their new policy. Indeed, the opposition to the UPA's unilateral decision was so strong and widespread that the Government was compelled to beat a hasty retreat.

Yet, the opening of the retail sector to foreign investors is a logical step that follows the opening up of the Indian economy that began in 1991. In fact, at the time it was launched, the so-called New Economic Policy was hailed as the solution to India's balance of payment crisis. Also, it was then rightly argued by the supporters of the new policy that India's rate of economic growth was low because it had a closed economic model of planning. Even the balance of payment crisis faced by the country was because of rigidities in economic management.

Ultimately, the proof of the pudding is in the eating, and there is no doubt that the policy of liberalisation, privatisation and globalisation spurred India's economic growth to such an extent that the country is now noticed globally as an 'emerging economy' along with China. In the past two decades, the success of the policy was considered sufficient to sell it to the masses.

Yet, when the Government announced its decision to allow FDI in multi-brand retail, every erstwhile enthusiastic supporter of Singh's economic regime abandoned ship. In fact, Union Minister for Finance Pranab Mukerjee, while addressing Congress MPs on December 6, even said that, if the Government had not withdrawn the policy, it would have been ousted from power. Moreover, with the spectre of Assembly elections in several States across the country looming, the Government was compelled to abandon its foolhardy decision.

Nonetheless, the fact remains that the issue of FDI in multi-brand retail tradehas sharply divided Indian politics while also bringing the whole package of economic reforms under political scrutiny and public discourse. The Government of India, after announcing its policy on the opening of retail trade to foreign investors, was to announce the policy of foreign investment in the aviation sector, and in insurance and banking too. The Government has been compelled to halt its whole project of liberalisation and the opening of markets because of stiff opposition by political parties. It often happens in politics that one controversial policy decision about just one aspect of a large public policy opens a Pandora's Box and the whole framework of that policy becomes a target of public scrutiny. This is precisely the situation created by the Government and all political parties.

Several important sections of society have thought it appropriate to critically examine the meanings and consequences of the economic policies followed by India during the last 20 years. It is an extremely positive development in Indian politics because a crucial area of public life like road to economic development was followed without any serious discussion and debate by major political parties because the so-called rate of growth success story had mesmerised every political party which started competing against one another on the basis of their economic performance and mega economic and industrial projects which they brought to their state.

A comic situation has developed during these two decades. Regional parties in power in the States have began competing against one another for attracting investors for the establishment of mega industrial projects without thinking about specific requirements of their own State. The State-based and State co-terminus parties like TMC or DMK or JD(U) *et al.* have not thought it fit to have a close look at the relevance or irrelevance of their economic choices and their political implications.

Captains of industry like Deepak Parekh, Ashok Ganguly and many others have all supported the Government policy on the opening of multi-brand retail business to foreign investors and multinationals. The small traders have opposed the entry of foreigners in multi-brand trade because kirana stores, operators in local mandis or small and medium traders and shopkeepers cannot 'compete' against foreign retailers. India's domestic trading market is worth $600 billion, and more than 50 million shopkeepers are engaged in the domestic 'trade' business.

The fact is that, FDI in multi-brand retail business directly affects small and medium householders, small farmers, small and medium shopkeepers and traders that sell commodities to the neighbouring shopkeepers.

Pioneer, 23-11-2011

Rein in the Politicians

Power corrupts and absolute power corrupts absolutely. This old hackneyed description of politics has been replaced by new saying if power goes into the head of a politician, he behaves like a mentally challenged person. Power has made law minister Salman Khurshid not only arrogant, he has also violated all norms of constitutional legalities by showing complete defiance of the pronouncements of the Election Commission, which is a constitutional body responsible for the conduct of free, fair and fearless elections in the country. It is Khurshid's arrogant defiance of the censure note, which has compelled Chief Election Commissioner SY Quraishi to seek President's intervention for disciplining the defiant minister in the Manmohan Singh government.

It was a mild disapproval of the conduct of the minister when during the elections, contrary to the spirit of the Electoral Code of Conduct, he announced that a vote for the Congress would ensure nine per cent of reservation of public services for Muslims as a subquota of 27 per cent for the other backward castes. It was expected that Khurshid would get the message and move further after the views expressed by the Election Commission but, as power travels to head, he repeated that 'even if they (Election Commission) hang me', he would continue to ensure reservation for backward Muslims and such an affront to the authority of the Election Commission made it seek the intervention of the President for improper and unlawful action of Khurshid which could 'vitiate free and fair polls in Uttar Pradesh'. The above episode involving the Election Commission, a minister, the prime minister and the president provides an opportunity to reflect on the larger issue of the role of elections and the Election

Commission in a participatory electoral democracy based on the principle of universal adult franchise.

First, the provisions of the Representation of People's Act and the defined powers and functions of the Election Commission for the conduct and management of the Lok Sabha and state assembly elections lay down the broad framework for the conduct of elections, which are held generally after every five years. This legal arrangement is a necessary but not sufficient condition to ensure a fair elections. Politicians want to win at any cost and by any means. Politicians and political parties never hesitate to violate or completely break the laws to win elections.

Second, if the Election Commission is weakened or delegitimised, it would not be able to deal with money or muscle power, which is employed to completely rig and vitiate the electoral process.

Third, politics is a lucrative and profitable business, even rich and criminals participate in elections with the goal of maximising their wealth and power. Only a strong, impartial and effective Election Commission can act as a vigilant watchdog of the sanctity of ballot that is threatened by moneyed people and criminals. The Election Commission has been compelled to engage income tax officials, chartered accountants and others to exercise check the flow of illegal money during the elections. Money power makes elections a contest among unequals. In a democracy, it acts as a game changer because those who spend huge money make every attempt to earn it back after they are elected. When democracy becomes a playground of money power, it ceases to be people's democracy and becomes an oligarchy or plutocracy.

Fourth, elections in Uttar Pradesh or Bihar have their own specificity and the phenomenon of criminals involved in booth capturing or fraud voting has prevailed on a big scale. It is the vigilant Election Commission that has worked overtime to protect the sanctity of the ballot from the influence of money and muscle power. An innovation has been made in Uttar Pradesh of election coverage by webcasting (through internet) from polling booths. This webcasting from various polling stations ensures that the process takes place as per the rules. This webcast network has linked the Chief Election Commissioner, the Chief Election Commission of Uttar Pradesh and the district electoral officers, and this new technology is expected to ensure that the whole election activity is monitored properly.

Fifth, every Chief Election Commissioner has performed their duties quite effectively, TN Seshan, a maverick Chief Election Commissioner, brought the ills and maladies of elections into the public domain and he projected himself as one-man army for the cleansing of the electoral process of its ills like booth capturing, money power and the role of criminals. TN Seshan became a hero as citizens considered him a messiah of clean democracy. The moral of the Seshan phenomenon is that Indians want clean elections. They were fed up of the malpractices and illegalities committed by politicians and parties during the elections. That's why Khurshid does not have public support for his offensive attitude against the Election Commission. Narendra Modi, RSS pracharak and Chief Minister of Guajrat, attacked the interventions by the Chief Election Commissioner JM Lyndogh by calling him a Christian, in spite of media management by the Sangh Parivar in defence of Modi's insolence, Atal Bihari Vajapyee, the then Prime Minister, had to make a public statement that two constitutional authorities should not get involved in public abuse.

if the ruling party does not defend the autonomy of the pillars of constitution like the Election Commission or the judiciary or the Comptroller and Auditor General, democracy would end up in anarchy and chaos. Indians need to be reminded that it was only because of the independence of the Election Commission that electoral results against Indira Gandhi, the most powerful prime minster of India, were declared in March 1977 and electoral defeat saw the end of the Emergency regime of Indira Gandhi. India witnessed a big debate when a one-member Election Commission was converted into multi-member commission. The attempt to have three-member commission was considered an effort on the part of the political executive to plant its own favourites into the Election Commission. The taste of pudding is in the eating; the three-member Election Commission experiment has worked successfully.

The prime minister should restrain his ministers who are crossing the limits of legality and constitutionality by flouting the Election Commission, which is struggling hard to uphold the Election Code of Conduct. Do Indians want sham and fraudulent elections? Make up your mind. Political parties should take note of the Khurshid episode and add more teeth to the powers of the Election Commission to strengthen its capability to discipline the errant politicians. An amendment of the Constitution for providing more punitive powers to the Election Commission may be more opportune.

Financial World, 15-02-2012

All Hell Keeps Breaking Loose

It has been often pointed out that the Congress-party led UPA government at the Centre is in the 'intensive care unit' and the country is faced with the crisis of governance, clearly reflected in 'policy paralysis' the country is experiencing today. Nothing seems to be moving forward. If the UPA led central government has shown its complete incompetence to take any new policy initiative on the economic front, the BJP, the other claimant for the role of a national party playing the spoilt sport and is determined to play negative and obstructive role as an opposition party in Parliament and every economic policy initiative taken by the government has been nullified by the BJP which has mastered the art of disturbing the every policy move initiated by the government in the Parliament.

The consequence of completely weakened leadership of the Congress-government and the role of a negative role of the BJP as the key Opposition has only worked as a cog in the wheel for the country's economy. The wheels of government have refused to move forward and every important economic move by the government for the country has been vetoed by the BJP. Are these national parties pursuing any national interest whether in government or in Opposition?

A few facts may be mentioned to substantiate the argument that the prevailing 'deadlock' at the level of governance at the centre can be solely attributed to the present political situation. The regional fragments have to brought "on board" by the government so that they feel a part of the political formation. This will reduce the feeling of alienation and help the government push through its all important bills that are of prime interest to the common man.

The regional parties are not expected to provide 'national perspective' on public policy issues, they have to be led and persuaded by the national parties in power at the Centre. First, it is a lame excuse on the part of Prime Minister Manmohan Singh to publicly suggest that his government is functioning under the constraints of a coalition system of policy making. Has the Manmohan Singh–Sonia Gandhi Congress conveyed to their allies that compromises will not be made by the major partner on issues like Food Security Bill or the Land Acquisition and Rehabilitation Act. Has Congress leadership shown any strength while dealing with 'allies' about its own 'non-negotiable' agenda for governance? After all, Congress has its 207 Lok Sabha MPs. It can well flex its muscles.

In the Atal Bihari Vajpayee-led coalition government (1998-2004), the BJP did not have requisite numbers of its own neither did it have the same number of seats that Congress-led UPA has. Despite the lack of numbers, it had the coalition in control.

The agenda of Hindutva, the core ideology of the Sangh Parivar, was vigorously pursued by the BJP-led coalition from 1998 to 2004. The BJP-led government's coalition allies could not force Vajpayee to give marching orders to Narendra Modi of Gujarat after post-Godhra brutal riots of March 2002 in Ahmedabad and other parts of the state. Coalition compulsion was not an issue while BJP dealt with Narendra Modi.

The UPA II has not shown any firm commitment on any public issue of national and international importance and has always defended its 'inaction' either by talking about 'compulsions of coalition' or 'blaming the negativism of the BJP-led opposition. Why has the ruling UPA not succeeded in 'isolating' the BJP opposition in the Lok Sabha and aggressively hammering the issue of 'destructive role' of the BJP in the Rajya Sabha?

Second, Pranab Mukerjee, the Finance Minister, while addressing the Bengal Chamber of Commerce and Industry on April 1, 2012, made a brave statement that there was 'no policy paralysis' and mentioned that an initiative had been taken by the government while announcing the New Manufacturing Policy. Mukerjee swallowed his pride and observed 'My mandate is to carry people with me' and 'short-cuts cannot be taken' because 'divergent political views' have to be accommodated. Mukerjee should also have observed that 'diverse groups' have also to accommodate the policy agenda of the largest single party in the Lok Sabha while also has a mandate of the people to govern. Mukerjee admitted that even after third year of power of the government important laws remain in limbo and his statement of deadlocked Bills includes (a) Goods and Service Tax; b) Direct Tax Code; c) The Insurance Amendment Act; d) the Pension Fund Regulatory Act; and e) Amendments to be Banking Act. Mukerjee on April 1, 2012 was telling the Bengal Chamber of Commerce and Industry that there was 'no policy paralysis' and the UPA government announced on April 3 that fiscal reform agenda in the field of insurance, pension and banking cannot be pursued further because of political compulsions.

Third, it happened only in 2012, and never, before, that Dinesh Trivedi, the railway minister, presented UPA governments Budget in the Lok Sabha and all hell broke out because Mamata Banerjee, the Trinamool Congress chief, not only rejected all proposals announced by the railway minister, she demanded that Dinesh Trivedi of the TMC be replaced by her other party protégé Mukul Roy as railway minister. The Minister who had prepared and presented the budget in the Lok Sabha was not permitted to pilot his budgetary proposals in parliament.

The UPA government became a laughing stock because of political tsunami created by this drama in Parliament and the country. The 'reformist' railway minister, who got public support from all major railway trade unions, ended up as a political orphan and paid price for his efforts to improve sinking health of the Railway's fiscal situation.

The larger question is that a country is formally governed by a coalition government but in reality every political group, whether a self-appointed national party like the BJP, or small local state-regional parties in the Lok Sabha have empowered themselves to 'veto' every act of governance by the Congress-led central government. It is interesting to note that 'veto' power is exercised not only by the opposition parties or groups, even supporters of the coalition government apply brakes whenever it suits them.

The reality behind the above narrated story of the malfunctioning of the Congress-led UPA coalition is not because of its opponents. But the Congress itself has completely failed to show any firm commitment to any programme or policy which it is ready to own and pursue with firmness.

The Financial World, 11-04-2012

Rahul Gandhi: The Miracle that Failed

It has become a ritual for Congress leaders to propose at regular intervals that Rahul Gandhi should play an important role in Government. The latest to join the bandwagon is Union Minister for External Affairs SM Krishna who suggested on June 27 that Gandhi's entry into Government was necessary to solve the problems faced by the country. Earlier party general secretary Digvijay Singh had talked about Gandhi's leadership skills and how his active participation would save the sinking Government of Prime Minister Manmohan Singh.

But ever since the days of Mrs Indira Gandhi, the Congress has always depended on a leader from the 'family' because none of the other leaders could garner the kind of broad-based acceptability that a member of the Nehru-Gandhi family had.

The question that naturally arises now is if the Congress is called upon to form a coalition Government in 2014, will Gandhi pick her son to head the new regime? Gandhi's status in the Congress is quite different from the other dynasty successors in Punjab, Uttar Pradesh or even Tamil Nadu.

For instance, Akhilesh Yadav has been crowned Chief Minister of Uttar Pradesh with the full support of the Samajwadi Party that was created by his father, Mulayam Singh Yadav. But political inheritance is a tricky affair. Without the unquestioned loyalty and support of the party organisation, the successor can just be a one time wonder.

Gandhi's father himself could only win only one election in 1984 because that was the only time he could leverage public sympathy in his favour in the aftermath of his mother and then Prime Minister Indira Gandhi's assassination. Rajiv Gandhi was defeated in 1989 because VP Singh portrayed him as the middle man in the Bofor's scandal. Indeed, the Congress's defeat in 1989 was because Rajiv Gandhi had been was de-legitimised.

Between 2004 and 2012, Rajiv Gandhi's son was given the opportunity to prove his political capabilities. The young Gandhi assigned to himself the job of strengthening the party by the democratisation of the party organization and especially the Youth Congress. So, did he succeed in resurrecting the the grand old party? Not really, Gandhi made some half-hearted efforts to recharge the organisational structure of the party but left his task mid-way.

Additionally, Gandhi's leadership qualities have also failed to make a mark in Parliament. He did not make any contribution on the floor of the Lok Sabha between 2004 and 2012 that is worthy mention. His record of intervention in Parliament on crucial issues is abysmal. Even when the UPA Government was struggling to save its proposed Lok Pal legislation, Gandhi's absence was conspicuous.

Finally, a political party like the Congress only bows before a leader who can win elections but this has not been the case with Gandhi. He jumped into the electoral battle for the Bihar Legislative Assembly but could not make an impact.

It was then advertised that Gandhi would show his magic in Uttar Pradesh during the Assembly election. But he disappeared from the political scene after the results were announced. The votes were split between the Samajwadi Party and the Bahujan Samaj Party. The Congress had been completely marginalised.

When Mrs Indira Gandhi was asked to explain the secret of her 'unquestioned authority' among Congressmen, she had replied, "I win elections for them". The upshot of the above discussion is that Gandhi has proved a 'bad coin' for the Congress. His leadership is most uninspiring and he has not shown any capacity of new thinking. Gandhi is a non-starter.

Pioneer, 06-07-2012

Collective Irresponsibility?

The exit of Pranab Mukerjee as finance minister was welcomed by Big Business, which felt that the former finance minister was a real roadblock in the way of profit maximisation of crony business groups. Decisions of the finance ministry greatly impact the day-today and long-term business strategies followed by market players. Powerful multinational corporations and foreign funding agencies also have come to realise that India is a great emerging market for foreign investments and they along with their Indian business collaborators are also celebrating.

This is not the first time that a Prime Minister has filled a vacuum in this important ministry—even Jawaharlal Nehru had to do so. The atmospherics and the response of the media, which reflects the sentiments and feelings of Big Business, is that Manmohan Singh will amend, modify, even reverse some important economic and financial policies. A lot of noise had been made by foreign investors who had alleged that under Mukherjee, economic and fiscal policies, especially taxation policies, had not only become unpredictable but also sent out a negative signal.

The hostilities against Mukerjee started when on 16 March, during his annual Budget speech, he announced a proposal for 'retroactive tax penalty' of ` 11,000 crore to be imposed on Vodafone. All hell broke loose in foreign capital markets because 'the tax returns' of many foreign investors were expected to be 'reopened' by the income tax officials for finding liabilities of such investors with 'retrospective' effect. The Prime Minister, just a day after Mukherjee relinquished office, asked the finance ministry and the Prime Ministers' Office to review problems on the tax front which need to be addressed and especially make clarifications on the General Anti-Avoidance Rules (GAAR) which had become the bone of contention because Vodafone might get repeated in the case of 'tax liabilities' of other private investors, epically foreign.

The finance ministry also observed on 28 June that the GAAR is at a 'drafting' stage and 'meetings with the stakeholders will be held' before draft rules are finalised by the government. Vodafone executives were pleading for a 'level playing field', Mukherjee stood firm on his 16 March proposal on GAAR. Manmohan Singh is not only open to renew this scheme, he is stated to have told finance ministry officials on 27 June, 'reverse the climate of permission ...review the animal spirits in the country's economy.' The Prime Minister positively responded to the sentiments of HDFC Chairperson Deepak Parekh, who observed on 27 June that 'harassment by tax officials and corruption loom large. Things need to be in black and white and not in grey as they are today'.

An analytical question which needs to be addressed is the nature of collective responsibility of the cabinet led by Prime Minister Manmohan Singh, who is head of the Council of Ministers. A prime minister in parliamentary democracy is not just one among equals in the cabinet, he presides over every cabinet meeting where policy-making decisions are taken and his opinions carry greater weight than those of any individual cabinet minister.

Further, the Budget is a policy document of the government and after the ministry of finance sifts through all the proposals and suggestions of all the ministers, the finance minister and his officials prepare a fiscal document of income and expenditure estimate of the year.

The speech while presenting the Budget proposals is an announcement of proposals and polices of the government. Has the Indian parliamentary system evolved to a stage where the prime minister, head of the government, is kept in the dark about major policy proposals of the government? Is the finance minister king of his empire? Why was Mukherjee not told to refrain from following policies which were slowing economic growth because foreign investors were losing 'trust' over the UPA government?

The Truth seems to be that the Prime Minister of the UPA coalition government at the Centre does not exercise any authority over either the cabinet ministers of his own Congress party or ministers belonging to the coalition partners. Dinesh Trivedi, the railway minister, presented a Railway Budget which was highly appreciated by the Prime Minister but he was replaced by coalition partner All India Trinamool Congress. The cabinet at the Centre seems to be a like a pack of jokers who can be reshuffled or kicked out not by the Prime Minister but by regional party chiefs. In such a situation, every minister is a 'law into himself' and the Prime Minister has obvious not adhered to the principle of collective responsibility of the cabinet.

Thus every principle and practice of parliamentary democracy lies in the dust because Indian coalition system of government is a collective of disparate and disunited individuals who represent their own regional party and whose loyalty lies not with the Prime Minister but with their own regional leader who can make or unmake them as ministers. What's worse, Manmohan's writ does not run even over his party colleagues in the cabinet, because all of them, like representatives of individual coalition partners, owe their power to Sonia Gandhi, the real centre of power in the Congress. The source of authority of every minister is not the Prime Minister but party bosses, whether regional or national.

The National Democratic Alliance government of 1998 to 2004 led by Atal Bihari Vajpayee was not at all different from the UPA of 2004-12. The RSS made crucial decisions about the BJP's, role in the coalition government at the Centre and LK Advani, who was clamouring to become deputy prime minister, owed his elevation to the RSS. RSS interfered even in the allocation of portfolios to BJP ministers in the Vajpayee government.

Clearly, the cabinet system has completely deviated from the model of British or Australian or Canadian systems because from 1989 to 2012, except for a brief period of 1991-96, the central government's prime ministerial candidates had to work under extra-constitutional centres of power like the RSS or Sonia Gandhi. This is the real meaning of the exit of Pranab Mukherjee and the arrival of Manmohan Singh in the finance ministry.

The Financial World, 10-07-2012

Time for Self-introspection

The Grand Old Party of India is faced with a serious internal crisis. It is feared to pale into insignificance as a political force in the democracy if it fails to find immediate and appropriate political solutions to the challenges it faces. The Congress leadership cannot pretend that it did not receive timely warnings from its well wishers.

Time magazine in its 8 July issue quite unfairly described Prime Minister Manmohan Singh, 'an under-achiever' who is 'unwilling to stick his neck out' on economic reforms. The magazine noted that the 'Investors are beginning to get cold feet' and 'India does not need a Prime Minister who is a man in shadow'.

Visiting Singapore Prime Minister Lee Hsien Loong, last week while discussing the Indian business environment observed that "India has been working on improving the environment, but it is something that big companies pay careful attention to because they come here for the long-term. If you are not from the country, you will look at the prospects and the possibilities".

Not just foreign investors, India Inc too has been complaining of the Manmohan Singh government suffering from a 'policy paralysis' for long. It is quite simplistic to blame Prime Minister Singh's lack of leadership for the delays and deadlocks in decision-making. In a functioning parliamentary democracy, the effectiveness of the political executive also depends heavily on the support provided to it by the party and in this case, it is the Congress. The crisis faced by the UPA-2 government cannot just be attributed to Manmohan Singh and his Council of Ministers. The prime minister and his cabinet ministers are strong or weak, effective or ineffective if the party-in-government is committed to its own programme and is able to politically mobilise different sections of the society in support of its own government. In a Congress party-led government, if the system is suffering from a 'policy paralysis', it means that either party leadership is applying 'brakes' on the policy initiatives of its own government or party organisation is not in a position to mobilise people's support for its policies.

Last week, Congress leader Salman Khurshid lamented that his party was 'short on direction best provided by party number two', Rahul Gandhi. Though Khurshid later detracted from his statement, his most significant observation was that though the Congress party has no ideology and Rahul has to play an active role not only in articulating its ideological positions, he has also to energise the party organisation to spread the message of such an ideology to the people.

When a committed Gandhi-family loyalist like Khurshid is forced to express his concerns about the internal health of the party in the national media, it is quite plausible that he is expressing the frustrations of his party colleagues also worried about the Congress' downslide especially keeping in mind the 2014 Lok Sabha election. For party members, it is natural to be concerned about the forthcoming Lok Sabha elections and it is no surprise that they are looking for 'saviours' in Sonia Gandhi and her heir apparent, Rahul Gandhi.

The message from Khurshid and others in the Congress to Sonia and Rahul is to provide an effective, ideological and organisational leadership before it is too late.

Ironically, Rahul Gandhi's leadership did not bear any fruit in the recent Bihar and Uttar Pradesh Assembly elections. And it is not even a question of winning or losing an election in one or two states, on ground, the junior Gandhi completely failed to inspire his party. Unlike his grandmother Indira Gandhi, and Sonia Gandhi, he could not show the Congress in any new light. A close scrutiny of his election speeches during the Assembly elections clearly reveals his ideological bankruptcy, and if the Congress is expecting any miracle from him in the 2014 Lok Sabha elections, one can only pity their expectations. Mother's love for her son is one thing, but Rahul Gandhi has proved a 'non-starter'.

In such a scenario, Sonia Gandhi appears to be the last hope for the Congress and she has proved her leadership capabilities beyond any shadow of doubt. Congress was a sinking ship because of the disastrous leadership of

Narasimha Rao, Sitaram Kesari until Sonia revived it. Sonia's 'thinking' was clearly reflected in UPA 1 from 2004 to 2009 when she balanced the high rate of economic growth with progressive legislations like the Right to Information Act, Mahatma Gandhi Rural Employment Guarantee Scheme, Right to Education, Rural Health Programme et al. The Congress-in-government with full backing of Sonia Gandhi, was active and achievement-oriented between 2004 and 2009. Sonia provided leadership from the 'front' and it bore fruit when Congress party obtained 206 seats out of 543 in the 2009 Lok Sabha election.

But in its second term, Sonia's Congress lost all sense of purpose and directions and started searching for alibis and lame excuses by blaming the opposition parties or its own recalcitrant coalition allies for the government's non-performance. Just like the drowning man clutches a straw, an exhausted Sonia Gandhi is looking at Rahul to lead the party to electoral victories. Sonia as a leader is a better bet for the Congress, against a non-performing and uninspiring Rahul.

It is bad politics to blame everything on the leader of a coalition government or to expect a single leader to change the destiny of a big party like the Congress. The' well wishers of the Congress should stop shadow-boxing Manmohan Singh and should actively participate in the party's revival under Sonia Gandhi, the real leader of the party.

The Financial World, 17-07-2012

Sonia Gandhi: Crisis of Dualism

The UPA government has been blamed for paralysis in decision-making on public policy matters of great significance. Prime Minister Manmohan Singh, in his Independence Day address, observed that the government was unable to spur economic growth because of the lack of political consensus on many issues.

Absence of political support is only part of the explanation for policy immobilism. The other significant factor is Sonia Gandhis role as president of the Congress party and her chairmanship of a parallel centre of authority, the National Advisory Council.

A national newspaper on August 13 reported data provided in response to RTI queries about the formal relationship between the National Advisory Council (NAC) and the government from 2010. Gandhi, as chairman of the NAC, has intervened on policy issues by writing 25 letters to the Prime Minister and 17 letters to various Cabinet ministers during the last two years. Gandhi occupies a super status in the UPA government and the Prime Minister and Cabinet ministers have to make public policies as decided and directed by Gandhi.

The theory and practice of parliamentary-Cabinet system of democracy in every western country, without any exception, show that political executive headed by the prime minister and his council of ministers is solely accountable for the making and implementation of the governments policies, and the elected Parliament holds the PM accountable for all acts of omission and commission of the government.

Walter Bagehot observed that prime minister is the hyphen that joins and the buckle that binds the cabinet, and the system revolves around prime minister who is the kingpin of the government. The real first Labour party government was formed under Lord Attlee as Prime Minister of England. Prof Harold JLaski, who was chairman of the Labour party, asserted his authority vis-à-vis the Prime Minister because it was expected, as a Labour party government, to function according to the polices conveyed by the party chairman. The government was in office because of Labour, whose chairman carried authority of the whole party.

Lord Attlee conveyed to Prof Laski that the head of the Labour party government was accountable only to Parliament and the party chairman should confine himself to the problems of party only.

Jawaharlal Nehru, as Indias first Prime Minister, had to remind Acharya J B Kriplani that the prime minister is constitutionally recognised as the head of government and party president could not exercise any special authority, political or moral, over the prime minister. Another test for Nehru in the early days of post-Independence India came when Purushottam Das Tandon was elected Congress party president. Nehru wrote that he could not work with Tandon because of serious ideological differences with him, and the result was that Tandon had to resign as party president because the Prime Minister could not work with a socially-conservative person.

Indira Gandhi faced party president S Nijalingappa and some members of the Congress Working Committee who ignored the Prime Ministers choice of candidate for the president of India. She openly opposed the official candidate, Neelam Sanjiva Reddy, and asked MPs and MLAs for their conscience vote for V.V. Giri, who got elected. Nijalingappa served showcase notice to Indira Gandhi for indiscipline. Indira split the Congress in 1969.

The upshot of above narrative is clear that government-party relationship has to be based on the logic and conventions of Parliament-Cabinet system where the prime minister is the real centre of power and a parallel centre of authority of the party president is unacceptable and unworkable according to the principle of accountability of the prime minister to Parliament.

It is factually correct that Sonia Gandhi is the sole architect of the Congress-led UPA government at the Centre and that she, by her own efforts, revived and revitalised the sinking ship of the Congress. If she had continued to focus on the crisis-ridden Congress party organisation and allowed her coalition government to work on its own, asking only for implementation of her partys election manifesto, the present crisis faced by the Manmohan Singh would not have happened.

The situation is complicated by coalition politics, where every coalition member has its own agenda and is not constrained to accept Sonia Gandhi's leadership.

Sonia's NAC produces a social agenda for the government and expects the Prime Minister to implement it. The NAC has particular ideas on food security but these are not shared by Sharad Pawar, the agriculture minister belonging to the NCP. Dualism of the system of governance has crippled the UPA government and its functioning from 2004 to 2012. Sonia should follow parliamentary system and its practices and stop dictating policies to the Prime Minister. *The Economic Times, 24-08-2012*

Rahul Gandhi does not Have what it Takes

The Congress is setting its organisational structure in order for the forthcoming Lok Sabha election. The party's public rally in Delhi and the brainstorming session at Suraj Kund on November 9, the recent coronation of Gandhi-scion Rahul Gandhi as head of the election campaign committee, indicate the Congress's agenda for the 2014 electoral battle ahead.

Gandhi's new assignment is not just a formalisation of a well-known fact that he was his mother, Congress supremo Sonia Gandhi's choice, but also a clear message to everyone in the party that the face of leader in the 2014 poll will be the son and the mother will take a backseat.

Gandhi is seen as the architect of Congress's destiny—a party which was revived under her leadership to form a coalition Government in 2004. She repeated her electoral victories in 2009 and earned her pre-eminent leadership status solely on the basis of her own efforts. Also, like her late mother-in-lawIndira Gandhi she's transferred her party's 'ownership' to her son.

With an eye on the Lok Sabha election she has not only nominated Gandhi to 'lead the party's electoral campaign', but has also set up a six-member coordination panel to formulate and implement the electoral strategy.

It is probable that the present Lok Sabha may not complete its full five-year term. And in such an uncertain political situation, the Congress does not want to be caught unawares—the reason for the party's frenetic election preparations. It cannot be denied that Gandhi is the real leader-in-waiting. The only obstacle in his way is the uncertainty of Congress's electoral performance.

Electoral performance of all parties across the political spectrum has become completely unpredictable. The phenomenon of coalition-based politics in India is a direct reflection of the fractured electoral verdict of an electorate fragmented by socio-religious, cultural and linguistic issues.

Hence, Gandhi's ability to mobilise a disparate and diverse electorate in support of his party will be sorely tested. He failed miserably to win any election at a micro-state level, as in Bihar, Uttar Pradesh or Punjab Assembly elections.

He came across as an uninspiring campaigner during these elections and failed to establish a rapport with the voters. His focus that Congress stands for the welfare of aam aadmi sounds hollow and facile, because the aam aadmi wants solutions for his day-to-day problem that is compounded by inflation, price hike and corruption.

The issue, is not about Gandhi's presentation during the election campaigns, the issue is that he has failed to speak his mind on these crucial issues to inspire the voter.

His father, Rajiv Gandhi won the election on a 'sympathy wave' in 1984, but during his prime ministership, he conveyed many fresh ideas on technology, modernisation and a progressive foreign policy.

Gandhi, unlike his father, has been unable to project himself as a leader in spite of his second term in the Lok Sabha. It is ironical that he is projected by the Congress propaganda machine as a 'young leader', a young person who has completely failed to offer anything new and fresh in terms of goals for the second decade of 21st century.

The best forum for making a meaningful impact on country's thinking is the Lok Sabha. But even here, he has behaved as a 'non-existant MP'. How can a person, expected to lead India's 'grand old party' be a complete washout in the Lok Sabha and leave no impact during election campaigns?

The upshot of this discussion is that Gandhi has nothing to offer to the Indian voter because he is an ordinary person pushed into the highest position by a doting mother. And his record of losing elections, do not exhibit any special leadership trait or talent. *The Pioneer, 23-11-2012*

Beyond the Tears, It's Time for Action

At the Jaipur Chintan Shivir, the Congress Working Committee announced Rahul Gandhi as its vice-president. Following this, the Gandhi family scion occupies the number two position in Congress party hierarchy.

So far Rahul has served two terms as a Lok Sabha member and has also worked as the Youth Congress and NSUI president in 2008. He has also been on the party's Election Coordination Committee since November 14, 2012. The party leadership believes Rahul has attracted and infused more young blood into the party and therefore he is the most suitable candidate for Congress leadership if young voters are its focus.

In her opening speech at Jaipur on January 18, Congress chief Sonia Gandhi noted that the party has to face 'the new changing India' where youth with aspirations and impatience are asking for a fresh approach to politics and to the problems faced by the country.

In such a scenario, Rahul's new assignments does not end with shouldering the limited responsibility of making party organisation as a capable machine for political and electoral mobilisation. As Congress number two, he will have to play an active role in the formulation of Congress-governments' public policies and also lead the party from the front in the elections, apart from taking responsibility of party organisational.

Till now Rahul was sheltered from the rough and tumble of everyday politics and political dirt was never directed at him. However, things are likely to change dramatically after January 19. Even if he is a 'reluctant politician', Rahul is now the real face of the Congress. Whether it is strengthening the party organisation or leading it in elections, he will now be directly subjected to the brickbats of his political opponents.

Given his actions so far, Rahul appears to have a very limited understanding of party politics because he does not recognise that a strengthened and reformed party organisation though necessary, is not a sufficient condition to face the elections and confront political opponents in any competitive democracy including India. Has Rahul's Congress a programme for meeting the aspirations of his social constituencies in the whole of India?

Sonia Gandhi on January 18 had set the public policy agenda of the Congress when she supported the UPA government's economic policies of liberalisation and globalisation. She clearly said that a 'pragmatic' approach for foreign investments is essential to help job creation for ten million people with a special focus on youth and socially inclusive growth. But with inflationary pressures on the economy threatening the electoral prospects of the ruling party and its alliances, government policies have to be directed at benefiting the poor as well as the new rising middle class. It is to this end that Rahul has to now start working under the policy framework laid down at the Jaipur Party Declaration while also trying to get the electorate to accept his leadership.

So far Rahul has only confined himself to the task of strengthening the party organization. He has not yet spelt out any larger vision for India. It is one thing to give an emotional speech and describe politics as 'poison', and quite another to confront political dirt. With the party finalising its much-awaited reshuffle, his first test will be to present a team to strategise the 2014 general elections.

Congress leaders like Digvijaya Singh are already talking about team with a balance of experience and youth and more young faces with various party bodies including the Congress Working Committee. Though noone expects any sweeping changes, yet expectations are definitely high from the new leadership. Would Rahul be able to bring any significant change in the party's style of functioning, now that he is the face of the party? Will he be able to rough it out in Congress grind? These remain open questions.

The Financial World, 30-01-2013

Naive Rahul does not Know his Own Party

Congress vice-president Rahul Gandhi's statement to media on March 5 that he did not wish to be Prime Minister deserves close scrutiny. The two-time member of the Lok Sabha has rarely said anything noteworthy and has not been known to share with the public his ideas on any issue of national importance. Of course, none of this prevented other Congress leaders from making clear that 'Rahul is our leader' especially after media reported on Gandhi's lack of prime ministerial ambitions in 2014.

Still, the fact remains that for now Gandhi has given priority to his party. He has said that he wants to energise middle level leaders to strengthen the party organisation, empower the 720 odd MPs and the 5,000 legislators in various States. This is as it should be because if a party believes in inner democracy, every member of the party should actively participate in decision-making processes.

The question is: Will Gandhi succeed in changing the 'high-command' culture of the Congress? For now, Gandhi's tall claims of democratisation sound hollow given how the Punjab Pradesh Congress Committee president (himself a high command choice) was replaced on March 7 by yet another nominee of 10 Janpath without even being supposedly consulted in the process. And that is not all. The so-called young Congress leaders in the present Lok Sabha that Gandhi wishes to support are all political heirs themselves who have merely inherited the position occupied by their family members. Clearly, Gandhi's plan to empower MPs and MLAs so that they have a stake in the electoral success of the party is wishful thinking.

But even if Gandhi can be excused for his superficial understanding of Indian politics, he must learn from his mother, party president Sonia Gandhi's, struggle to reach the top of the Congress leadership. Gandhi took charge in 1998 and the party's electoral debacle under her watch led to great disenchantment. She was accepted as the undisputed leader only when she formed the first Congress-led coalition Government at the centre in 2004. But between 1998 and 2004, she was just a rallying point within the Congress.

But it seems like Gandhi is a slow learner or else he would have drawn important lessons from the Haryana Congress meeting where he witnessed conflict between Chief Minister Bhupinder Singh Hooda and MPs from the State. The point here is that the Congress is fighting against powerful political forces such as those represented by the BJP in Gujarat and regional parties in several large States. Yet, there is no ideological commitment which unites all Congressmen leading to factional fights within the party.

Gandhi introduced elections within the National Youth Congress but abandoned the exercise soon after as elections sharpened organisational cleavages. Also, before being anointed party vice-president, Gandhi had been party general secretary for a long time. Yet, he had not organised elections within the party and PCC presidents have been replaced at will by the central leadership.

Such centralisation of power in the hands of the 'Supreme Leader' has created a culture of sycophancy. This has adversely impacted the party. For instance, the Congress never announces the chief ministerial candidate before any State Assembly election because any candidate who is nominated faces electoral sabotage by his own party leaders. The inexperienced Gandhi had announced Amarinder Singh as the Congress's candidate for chief ministership in Punjab, and the result was for everyone to see. Gandhi is just shining in his mother's glory and all his goals will remain on paper only as he does not understand Congress-style politics. *Friday, 15-03-2013*

Rahul: The Style and Substance

Rahul Gandhi-in his first public encounter with business tycoons on April 4 at the Confederation of Indian Industry—spelt out his main ideas in a rambling informal style and took recourse to anecdotes to substantiate his main arguments. It deserves to be clearly mentioned that except during election campaigns of the Congress party, Rahul has never been heard in public and in a manner of speaking, he remained a mystery in politics.

It was always difficult to decipher his thinking and opinions on national issues, including many contentious challenges faced by his party during the last 10 years of his so-called active life in the Lok Sabha. Everything written about Rahul was at best speculative and at worst either laudatory or condemnatory because any serious analysis about any political leader can be made only on the basis of a leaders' public pronouncements and political actions. Rahul was dismissed because he completely failed to make any electoral impact especially during the state assembly elections of Bihar and Uttar Pradesh because of very high expectations from his sustained work for his party especially in Uttar Pradesh, and the election results showed that he was an empty shell. Rahul is solely responsible for negative comments in the media, audiovisual and print, because he generally remained aloof and uncommunicative. Hence, his major public exposure on April 4 before the scrutinising eyes of the big business of the CII deserves a very close attention and analysis. Let's focus on few important observations made by him at the event.

First, the most important statement and ideological commitment made by Rahul is about 'inclusive growth and how India's economic vision must be about compassion'. Rahul elaborated his thinking by observing "when you play the politics of alienating communities, you stop the movement of people and ideas. When that happens we all suffer. Businesses suffer and the seeds of disharmony are sown and the dreams of our people are severely disrupted." This was a clear philosophical and politico-ideological statement of Rahul, which is clearly the opposite of Sangh Parivar and Narendra Modi's 'exclusivist, anti-minority and culturally monolithic Hindutva blueprint of Hindu Rashtra or Bharat Mata (Mother India).

Rahul appropriately characterised India as a 'beehive', which to him means that "the biggest danger is excluding people, excluding the poor, the middle class, tribals, Dalits. Whenever we excluded women, the minutes, 200 million Muslims in India, we have always fallen back." Rahul's national vision is based on his commitment to secular, democratic, plural, culturally composite and federal India of diversities which are all united in a functioning democratic political system.

It must be a music to die hard and fanatic communal Hindu Rashtravadis who specialise in breaking mosques and churches and provoking violent situations against Muslims and Christians because Rahul's ideological and philosophical approach is not only just the opposite of completely divisive politics of the Sangh Parivar, it is for the first time in year 2013, a Congress leader, a real inheritor of Nehruvian philosophical and political commitments, has attempted to polarise India on the fundamental principles of cultural inclusiveness versus Hindutva's ideology of complete cultural 'exclusiveness'. Further, it is also a message to the fence sitter Congress leaders who have always taken refuge behind so-called 'soft Hindutva' and by following such a strategy and tactics, they have always failed to confront and contest against political Hindutva of the Sangh Parivar.

The Congress leadership silenced Sonia Gandhi when she very appropriately described Narendra Modi as 'Merchant of Death' because of an apprehension that it would 'alienate and create anger' among the Hindus of Gujarat who will solidly support Modi. Sonia Gandhi was also taught by the practitioner of soft Hindutva in the Congress that Shankar Singh Vagehela, a renegade RSS-BJP leader, should become Congress face in elections against Narendra Modi. The soft Hindu lobby in the Congress has shown an act of prudence by not restraining Rahul who has as a daredevil leader confronted the political Hindutva of divisive Sangh Parivar.

Another important agenda before Rahul was to win over the captains of big industry who had been giving certificates and testimonials to the pro-business style of governance of friendly Modi. Rahul argued for 'structural change in Indian political system' and offered a plea for decentralisation of decision-making to the local communities by 'giving people a voice'.

He argued in favour of a predicable economic policy and regulatory regime where business can operate efficiently because it is only when government is playing the role of a facilitator, business and industry can grow in such a stable environment.

Rahul frankly admitted that foreign investors get baffled and enraged on many 'complexities' of launching economic and industrial projects, however, if one can succeed in India, he can flourish 'even on the moon.'

Rahul was right when he warned the country that a prime minister alone cannot solve complex domestic and global problems, but, it cannot be denied this in a parliamentary democratic system, prime minister is expected to lead his team of ministers around well-defined goals, and this has been missing in UPA 2. If fiscal deficit and inflation are challenges to the government, the government has to find solutions and it cannot expect anyone else to bail out a government which parrot like keeps on repeating about growing deficit and rising inflation.

The upshot of above narration is that Rahul Gandhi, whether he becomes a future prime minister or not, as the most important leader in the Congress party hierarchy, has given some very positive signals on the meaning of Indian nationalism and at the same time, his escapist tendency has been quite visible on his April 4 performance. Rahul still remains a reluctant hero.

The Financial World, 12-04-2013

Stage set for Big Political Fight

The Congress-led United Progressive Alliance coalition government at the Centre completed its four years of power on May 22 during its second term in office beginning from 2009. It may be an opportune moment of stocktaking for the Congress leadership because the Opposition parties, which are making preparations for the forthcoming Lok Sabha elections of 2014 have to approach the voters with a catalogue of acts of omission and commission and failures of the UPA-in-government. With a view to replace and displace it from the Centre of power held by it for the last nine years, electoral competition for the forthcoming Lok Sabha elections is multipolar and the main contestants are the Congress, the BJP and many formidable regional parties and leaders who have become real decision makers for the formation of a coalition government at the Centre whether led by the Congress or the BJP or anti-Congress and anti-BJP third alternative of coalition of regionalists.

It deserves to be clearly and ambiguously stated that the regionalist parties have not shown any commitment to any ideology of any kind while deciding about post-electoral alliances and this is the reason that when Congress Party was out of power from 1996 to 2004, many of the regionalists had willingly and voluntarily joined the Hindu Rashtravadi Atal Bihari Vajpayee-led coalition government at the Centre from 1998 to 2004. The upshot of above narration is to state that irrespective of electoral verdict in the 2014 Lok Sabha elections, the real battle lines will be drawn between Congress versus the

BJP, the two main antagonistic contenders and competitors for power and this was evident on May 22 that even before the Congress-led UPA leadership could place its track-record of performance before the voter of India for completion of its four years in office during its second term, the BJP leadership jumped the queue and launched a pre-emptive attack on the lack of performance of the UPA government and especially targeted Manmohan Singh as unworthy person to hold the high office of Prime Minister of India.

Incidentally, Manmohan Singh has always been targeted by the BJP and LK Advani, BJP's Prime Minister-in-waiting, has described Manmohan as the 'weakest Prime Minister of India' and this line of attack was pursued by Sushma Swaray last week when she observed that the UPA prime minister was not a 'national leader' forgetting that unlike the Congress Party, the BJP is a pretender and all-India party because its political and electoral reach is quite limited and confined to a section of Hindu voters of North and North Western India. The BJP cannot buy any yardstick claim to be an all-India party because in the 2013 state assembly election of Gujarat, it did not nominated any Muslim candidate to contest on its platform. The Congress is an all-India social coalition in the real sense of the term and opposed to it is Hindu sectarian BJP and this can be seen from the list of its real tall leaders who are all RSS-supported Hindus.

Hence, the most important achievement of the UPA government during its first and, second term of office is that it has kept out of power the party of, by and for the Hindus-only and thus protected the secular and pluralist social fabric of Indian society. It will be very simplistic to suggest that highly diverse and multiple region-specific borders of India exercise their electoral choices for the Lok Sabha at and all-India level on the basis of only secular credentials of the Congress in preference to divisive Hindu Communal Ideology of the BJP. A common voter looks towards its elected government in a democracy for the redressal of his grievances and offer solutions to the needs of the voter. Has the party-in-government served the interests of especially those strata of Society who are needy and dependent for the welfare services? This is the only yardstick of performance by the government.

A party-in government in every competitive electoral democracy has to publicise and act as a salesman before the voters because reaching the voters is essential to persuade, even convince, him about the great useful work which their government has done while in office and May 22 had been an appropriate occasion for the UPA Government which has completed four years in office.

The Indian public has been greatly disappointed with the UPA Government because of its failure to contain the inflationary pressure on food prices which has hurt very adversely the household economy including family budgets. Inflation hits the middle and the lower middle classes but in India, it breaks the back of more than 500 million daily wage earners and self-employed labour classes. The voter shows his power of anger against the party and its candidates at the pollingbooths through the power of ballot. It is good classroom lecture by Manmohan Singh that global slowdown of economy has adversely impacted India rate of growth and the government is doing its best to meet the CDS challenges, however the voter judgment is based on his daily living experiences and not the so-called global economy slowdown. The discontented Indian voter targets and punishes its own political leaders who are perceived as no gooders and no doers. Sonia Gandhi, the real Centre of political power in the Congress, talked of government achievements like the Right to Information Act, the Mahatma Gandhi National Rural Employment Guaranty Scheme, the Right to Education, the protection of women dignity, et al. and squarely blamed the negativism of the BJP, the main Lok Sabha Opposition Party, which always disrupted the parliamentary proceedings and obstrcuted the government to get legislations approved which were pro-people and pro-poor and farmers like the Food Security Bill and the Land Acquisition Bill.

It is a legitimate right of the party in government to put the opposition party in the dock and on the defensive, and it is the duty of the opposition to castigate and confront the ruling coalition for its acts of omission and commission. Hence, the big political fight has officially begun. The battle lines have been drawn and Congress versus BJP *Dharam Yudh* is set to happen in 2014. Will the UPA, particularly the Congress, be able to clear the corruption charges on its ministers or will the voters be persuaded not to believe in this 'exaggerated propaganda' of corruption levelled against the government is yet to be seen. *The Financial World, 28-05-2013*

Rahul Gandhi and Hamlet's Dilemma

The All India Congress Committee session held in Delhi on January 17, 2014, was the final exercise for defining electoral strategies before the party plunges into the contest for the Lok Sabha elections of April-May this year. This pre-election meeting of the party leadership was meant to take a final and definitive decision on the role of Rahul Gandhi especially since Sonia Gandhi, the real moving force behind the revival of Congress, had decided to vacate the supreme leadership position and also manage, under her supervision, the smooth transition of the next generation of leadership. Was Rahul the obvious choice for Congress party's leadership? If Sonia Gandhi has decided to take the backseat, a frontline leader has to be found to fill in the vacuum created by her withdrawal.

The young Gandhi's formal journey began in the Jaipur session of the Congress in January 2013 when he was declared the vice-president of the party (the president being Sonia herself). It has taken just one year – from January 2013 to January 2014 – for Rahul to be formally made the chairman of the party's election campaign committee and perhaps informally, the party's prime ministerial candidate. Rahul has been gradually moving forward in the party organisation ever since he started as a leader of the Congress youth wing. He is now the chief of the party's election campaign for April-May 2014. The AICC session put a seal of approval on Rahul's new leading role and this fact was acknowledged by Rahul in his speech to the delegates when he observed that "as a sepoy of the party, every job is acceptable as decided by the party".

Rahul has always been seen as a "reluctant politician" and at the Jaipur session of the Congress in January 2013, his acceptance speech for the post of vice-president of the party had clearly shown his vacillations, ambiguities, and even doubts about his capacities to play an active role as new vice-president of the party. However, unlike the Jaipur session, Delhi's Rahul clearly showed his enthusiasm for taking over the responsibilities of "the leader" who was very much willing and happy to lead the party.

Has Rahul come out of the Hamlet's dilemma of "to be or not to be"? Has he overcome his tendency of leaving the stage mid-way without completing the tasks assigned to him?

Rahul, who had been perceived as a passive spectator in the Lok Sabha, made waves in September last year when he, in a press conference in Delhi, publicly asked for the rejection of an ordinance issued by his own party-led government which was meant to protect the "convicted lawmakers". He used strong language against the ordinance and demanded that it be thrown in the dustbin. Although Rahul's action drew a lot of flak, when seen in retrospect it appears that there was a calculated method behind this. With his action Rahul presented himself as the 'Clean' of politics.

Until then Rahul had nothing to offer to the Indian voter because of his explicit passivity. But people took note of him after this incident. He took another step in the same direction when he actively supported the passage of the Lokayukta Bill in Parliament and also castigated the Chief Minister of Maharashtra, a Congressman, in December 2013 for not-implementing the recommendations of inquiry committee into the Adarsh Housing Project scam.

Rahul Gandhi did not stop here. On January, while addressing the 4000 assembled AICC delegates, he observed, "We will go into this battle as warriors with our heads held high. We will not look back…go into the battle knowing who are and what we stand for". He clearly stated before the Congressmen that the forthcoming electoral battle has to be fought against divisive communal forces. He emphasized that the Congress stands for the defence of the "secular fabric" of diverse and plural society of India.

Rahul and Sonia laid down the Congress agenda of the forthcoming Lok Sabha elections by clearly emphasizing the fact that the values and philosophy of Indian constitution has to be defended because it is under attack by the so-called communal forces. Rahul summed up his commitment to India's secularism by observing: "...others, when weakened, incite riots while the Congress unites and believes in brotherhood, love and respect for each other". Finally, Rahul projected himself as a "youth leader" with Finance Minister P Chidambaram asking the gathering to nominate "young Congressmen" for the forthcoming elections.

It is clear that the Congress will promote and propagate the ideology of secularism versus communalism in 2014, and the new face of party will be of "Clean" who will lead the young brigade during the elections. Will Rahul be really able to defend the corruption-ridden UPA government simply on the basis of his 'Clean' image? It deserves to be mentioned that Rajiv Gandhi also began his political journey as prime minister with that same image which later got tarnished in the Bofors scam. Rajiv's own cabinet minister VP Singh cornered him personally on the issue of "bribery" in Bofors gun deal and on this single issue alone the Congress, led by Rajiv, was defeated in the Lok Sabha elections of 1989.

The truth is that 'Clean' is a very slippery plank to stand on and deal with complex political pressures which any party in government has to face. Rajiv was also the inventor of Congress party tradition of secularism but he fumbled and completely mishandled the politically sensitive issue of Babri Mosque demolition at Ayodhya. Rajiv, too, suffered from Hamlet's dilemma and committed political suicide with his 'to be or not to be' thoughts on secularism.

Another common thread between Rajiv and Rahul is that both were handed key political roles on a platter without them having any experience in leadership. Rahul's case is a little more complicated because as an MP for 10 years and party leader, in one capacity or the other, he has been "getting things done" by the Congress-led UPA government at the centre and he has enjoyed this special status without any responsibility. Every prime minister of India in the last 66 years has been involved in governance before occupying the apex post. Rahul has no experience in governance, not even as leader of opposition, and in spite of opportunities offered to him by Prime Minister Manmohan Singh, he has shirked from the responsibility of apprenticeship of a ministerial job.

It will be a miracle if a novice like Rahul tastes success in the top office of the country. But if past is any guide, Rahul cannot be a "different" personality than his father. *Newsyaps, 24-01-2014*

STATE POLITICS AND ELECTIONS

Regional Aspirations Prevail in Assembly Polls

Former Prime Minister, Mrs Indira Gandhi had delinked the Lok Sabha election from Assembly elections, which were held simultaneously throughout the country prior to 1971 and 1972. As a result of this decision, every State Assembly election now attracts national attention, and all-India parties along with State-specific regional parties engage in a tough electoral battle for survival.

This context is essential to understand the real significance of the forthcoming Assembly elections which will be held in Uttar Pradesh, Punjab, Uttarakhand, Manipur and Goa. The Assembly elections have once again brought the issue of unequal representation of States wherein large States like Uttar Pradesh carry more political weight than smaller ones like Manipur and Goa. Often, smaller States have even expressed their resentment against the larger States which dominate the country's political scene.

This federal imbalance should be rectified because it has already alienated some States. It is not only the politicians but even the mass media that remains focussed mainly on the Uttar Pradesh political scene while the election in Manipur or Goa have been accorded little importance.

However since the Uttar Pradesh Assembly election has assumed critical significance, it is worthwhile to highlight some of its salient features. Importantly, the two all-India parties, the Congress and the BJP, are not only competing against each other, they are also competing against regional parties like the Samajwadi Party led by Mulayam Singh Yadav and the Bahujan Samaj Party led by Chief Minister Mayawati.

Politics is a reflection of society, and the fragmented social structure of Uttar Pradesh is represented by its fragmented party politics. In this State, every political player is identified with only a section of a caste or sub-caste or a community; even the all-India parties do not represent the broad society of Uttar Pradesh. In effect, the regional parties are only representatives of specific groups within the State, and this has led to a phenomenon of 'divided loyalties'.

Rashtriya Lok Dal chief Ajit Singh, for instance, has openly claimed that his party has the support of the Jats of Western Uttar Pradesh. Similarly, Mulayam Singh Yadav believes he is the unquestioned leader of the Yadav caste. Along with the Muslim community's support, his party is politically invincible on the basis of such an assured vote-bank. Mayawati too never tires of proclaiming that the oppressed Dalits of Uttar Pradesh have found refuge under the protective umbrella of the BSP. From the Congress, party general secretary and heir apparent Rahul Gandhi has been trying to revive his party's fortunes in Uttar Pradesh on the basis of a caste-community coalition as well.

The general point which has emerged from the political and social scene of Uttar Pradesh is that every political contestant is representing an assured support base built around a particular caste or community. Uttar Pradesh is currently engaged in a caste struggle and the State has caste leaders masquerading as political leaders.

Akhilesh Yadav, heir-apparent of Yadav's political shop, has very aptly summed up the situation in Uttar Pradesh: "It is politics. Everyone wants to side with the winner. Many join politics because they want tickets. Many swap sides before polls. They are like fruits that fall during storms. Pick the ones that aren't damaged, throw the others." In Uttar Pradesh, it is not considered immoral to shift political loyalties because politics here is neither ideological nor does it have any large social goal. The only aim of an Uttar Pradesh politician is to win an election on the basis of his or her assured sectional support base.

This peculiar situation has worried the Election Commission which has decided to hold election in that State in seven phases so that it can perform its role of 'policing' the poll better. The Election Commission has asked for more than 700 battalions of central paramilitary forces, State Provincial Armed Constabulary and regular police to oversee election centres in Uttar Pradesh. and ensure that the electoral code of conduct is not violated.

Given this caste-based approach of regional parties, the national parties should be concerned about the political culture of Uttar Pradesh. At the end of the day, they will have to do business with the regional leaders for they will need their support to form coalition Governments in New Delhi.

And this is why Assembly elections have assumed national importance. Because the national parties need the regionalists to support their Governments, the regionalists tend to promote sectarian interests at the cost of national goals.

The Pioneer, 06-01-2012

Fractionalized Centre of Power

A modern state is considered a 'fully formed social organization of the whole society' once it has succeeded in creating a viable and capable 'centre of power' whose writ runs over every segment of society under its territorial jurisdiction. Philosophers of modern European state systems like Machiavelli and Hobbes considered a state as formed only when undisputed authority was exercised by a 'Prince', 'Leviathan' or a 'Sovereign'. In contrast, liberal democratic theorists argued that state sovereignty should reside in a constitutional democratically elected Parliament and political executive because only these 'centres of power' enjoy a democratic legitimacy and popular support. While absolutists, monarchists or democrats vigorously differed about the appropriate form of modern states, all agreed that the fundamental salient feature of the state lies in its capacity to exercise control over the whole society through an identifiable and visible 'centre of power'.

India cannot be an exception to this general story of historical evolution of modern state systems. A key justification of the extremely powerful anticolonial liberation movements was that state power should be controlled by the 'natives' and colonial rulers should be dislodged and compelled to vacate their illegal occupation of 'power at the centre' in the colonies. This historical context is essential to appreciate the fact that the current vulnerabilities and weaknesses of the authority of the Indian state can be best understood by focusing attention on the existing fractionalized nature of the 'centre of power'. The existing social situation is creating a feeling of 'pessimism' because the authority and writ of the real 'centre of power' is questioned not only by those, like the Communist Party of India (Maoists), who are fundamentally challenging the very foundational principles of the existing state and want to 'capture the centre of state power' to create a alternative state system. The unfortunate fact is that the 'centre of power' is divided and weak even when, in its own judgment, it is working in the interests of the leading ruling exploiting classes and its multiple class fractions and the state is confident of its military capability to confront these 'enemies of the state.' Rather, it is the friends of the state who are a problem.

Marx clearly stated that, 'The social relations of production (*i.e.*) social organization in its broadest sense, and the material forces of production to whose level they correspond, cannot be divorced', and this is the reason that 'the economic structure of society is formed by the totality of these relations.' This Marxist theoretical approach makes it clear that, 'Economic development cannot be discussed except in terms of a particular historical epoch and particular social structure.' It deserves to be recognized that despite the hegemony of the capitalist mode of production, the state in India has to operate in the specific situation where a mixture and coexistence of different 'forms' of social relations of production are in contest and competition for extending their own control over the 'centre of power'.

India has not arrived at a stage where a fully formed and mature capitalist mode of production has been completely successful in either weakening or eliminating pre-capitalist and pre-industrial surviving modes of production, especially the 'old' landlord, feudal remnants of the 'agrarian peasant societies and classes.' Thus, even as the capitalist mode of production has penetrated the agrarian sectors of economy and society, the leading strata of the capitalist classes face resistance from the agrarian surplus-generating peasant classes who refuse to be 'subservient' to the demands and interests of the big industrial houses, medium capitalists and professional educated middle classes who are an active social segment of the capitalist economy especially in the 'service sector', real estate and other commodity production activities of the growing consumerist classes.

While a kind of 'urban-rural' divide persists at a level of social relations of production, the 'surplus producing peasantry' which is materially, even technologically, linked with the modern capitalist economy, continues to maintain its traditional domination over 'village society'. India is at a historical stage where the peasant question remains a critical part of the social and political 'agenda' and only on its satisfactory resolution will the Indian 'centre of power' emerge as a fully 'formed source of authority.' The peasant question is integrally linked with the problematic of peasant power because traditionally in pre-capitalist societies, aristocracy, nobility, feudal, landlords, et al. dominated over the whole 'people' within their area of control, and this 'consciousness of power' to dominate over 'village society' persists among 'the surplus producing' peasant classes of agrarian India.

The means and instrumentalities of coming to power have no doubt changed because of a democratic electoral system; nevertheless, the political project of dominating over subordinate and marginal social groups in rural India remains the driving force among the peasant classes. It is not without reason that peasant-based parties have emerged on the political scene and are exercising substantial control over the state governments. Further, these peasant-leader led parties have more or less obliterated the distinction between the 'party' and 'elected state government' because of insufficiently evolved mediatory mechanisms between the exercise of power by chief ministers, ministers or MLAs and the peasant classes who have formed their own parties to directly pursue their class interests. The Akali Dal of Punjab is thus virtually indistinguishable from Sikh Jat peasantry; the Samajwadi Party of Mulayam Singh Yadav or the different Janata Dals and Lok Dals are essentially an extension of the dominant strata of the peasant classes which exercises control over 'village society'. Similarly, the surplus-producing peasantry of developed regions like Maharashtra or Andhra Pradesh or Karnataka constitutes the real backbone of the Sharad Pawar-led Nationalist Congress Party or Chandrababu Naidu's Telugu Desam Party. The argument is that the peasantry, while accepting the logic of the ongoing process of capitalist development and desirous of sharing the fruits of capitalist growth, is still imbued with the memory of its historical role of domination over its defined areas of control in agrarian society and that the democratic process is merely an instrument to capture government power for class domination over village society.

It is simplistic to reduce the issue to federal tensions and the conflicts between state governments and the Centre. The question is not about centralization versus decentralization of power, or a redistribution of powers between the central and state governments; the larger question is that to meet the logic of centralization and globalization, the capitalist classes and capitalism need a state which has an effective 'centre of power' so as to facilitate accumulation of profit in both the national and global markets. The peasantry in India finds itself at a crossroads because it finds the urban capitalist classes fully entrenched in the corridors of power at the Centre and realizes that to achieve its own goal of controlling the levers of governmental power, which it can achieve only at the state-regional levels of governance, it will have to accept the leadership of the capitalist classes. The real explanation for the fractionalization of the centre of power of the Indian state is that the Indian peasantry is finding it difficult to share power with the leading classes of the capitalist state because in doing so, it may have to surrender its own area of dominance which is coextensive with the boundaries of states, regions or sub-regions.

Even if the peasantry is on the wrong side of history, it has nevertheless shown great tenacity to hold on to power in its limited, social universe. The future of Indian state's 'centre of power' depends on the ability to structure an appropriate balance among the different strata of the exploiting ruling classes, especially the bourgeoisie and the peasantry, while resolving the contradictions and conflicts in which the peasantry finds itself. The Indian state is engaged in inter-class and intra-class conflict and competition and this conflict situation prevailing among the fractions and strata of the ruling classes has directly impacted the actual functioning of a coherent and cohesive 'centre of power'. History provides enough evidence that in situations when the ruling classes and their fractions are not threatened by a revolutionary force, they remain trapped in pursuing limited agendas, even if in the long-run, the process is counterproductive.

Seminar, May 2012

There is more to Elections than Winning Votes

A democratic political system can only be sustained, nurtured and nourished by political parties which have a strong grassroots organisation and which contest elections to seek a popular mandate that is based on specific ideologies and clearly defined social issues. Further, a society which is experiencing rapid social changes, cannot be effectively represented by leaders who simply make tall electoral promises that they do not intend to fulfill after the elections.

Against this backdrop, it is worrisome that political parties engaged in the forthcoming State Assembly elections in Uttar Pradesh, Punjab, Uttarakhand, Goa and Manipur haven't raised any important issues in their electoral campaigns.

A few facts may be mentioned to substantiate the argument that political parties are participating in elections on the basis of old and out-of-date electoral strategies.

First, Punjab, Uttarakhand, Goa, and Manipur have evolved a 'two party' system of politics. Like previous elections in Punjab, the Shiromani Akali Dal, along with the BJP, will be fighting the Congress. In fact ever since1966 the Akali Dal, the Jan Sangh and the Congress have been the only political formations which have occupied any significant political space in Punjab. Yet, the State has witnessed great changes in its economy, while more social changes are waiting to be addressed.

The most important challenge before the leaders of Punjab should be the fact that children of farmers do not wish to engage in agriculture any more. Also, an army of ill-educated youth in Punjab has taken to drugs because their dreams have not been articulated by policy makers.

The border State has become a haven for drug smugglers who have found for themselves a ready market here. But the main contenders for power have not come out with any manifesto or document devoted to youth policy Instead, they are raising the same old issues of corruption or engaging in mobilising 'local fixers' who can get them votes by luring in voters. The Election Commission is now faced with the problem of unaccounted money and the role of a partisan bureaucracy in 'managing' elections for one or the other party.

The story is much the same in Uttar Pradesh where the issues raised by the Samajwadi Party, the Bahujan Samaj Party, the Congress and the BJP have no relation to the problems faced by the people of the State.

But the 'Muslim question' remains an important component of electoral campaigns in Uttar Pradesh. If the Congress has announced a 4.5 per cent reservation for Muslims within the OBC quota, SP chief Mulayam Singh and State Chief Minister Mayawati, who do not wish to be left behind, have intensified their demands for minorities as well.

Peripheral issues that are specific to the Muslim community such as the Batla House encounter or the warning issued against the author of The Satanic Verses Salman Rushdie have been highlighted with a view to project one of these political parties as the real champion of the Muslim cause.

Further, like all previous elections in the past three decades, caste-based calculations have emerged as the real issue in Uttar Pradesh. It has been argued that Uttar Pradesh has achieved seven per cent economic 'growth rate' and hence, it is wrong to label it as a 'backward' State. But given the social inequalities in that State and the highly politicised administrative structure, the argument holds no water.

The electoral campaign for the 2012 election in Uttar Pradesh is a repeat of the 2007 campaign which was a copy of its predecessor. The politicians of Uttar Pradesh are oblivious to the fact that the State is facing a grim challenge of economic development, based on absolute levels of social inequality.

The moral of story is that old warhorses are practicing their tried and tested techniques for winning elections. They are convinced that challenges faced by the masses cannot become relevant issues in an electoral contest.

The general belief among political leaders is that basic issues concerning the people cannot be converted into a successful electoral strategy that will get them votes. Instead, they prefer the policy of 'divide and rule' that was followed earlier.

Many historians of pre-Independence India had written that the more India changes the more it remains the same. It is an unchanging society where caste and religion-based loyalties can be manipulated by the ruling class as the British had done to their benefit. 21st century politics has to be defined by new goals and new aspirations.

Or else, a dissatisfied citizenry will emerge as a threat to the country's democratic framework. That cannot be allowed to happen.

Pioneer, 19-01-2012

India's Divided-Identity Voters

It continues to be a great puzzle to identify the factors or events that motivate a voter to exercise his right to vote in highly-competitive elections that are regularly held in every democratic political system on the basis of universal adult franchise and secret ballot.

Every democratic political system has created powerful organisations like the Election Commission of India 'for the conduct of free, fair and fearless elections. A very important thinker, S M Lipset, in his classic The Political Man', has characterised the political contest during democratic elections as silent, peaceful and participatory class struggle that is organised by political parties.

Scholars have described Indian elections as a great festival where voters participate enthusiastically. This statement is corroborated by the percentage of voters' participation in the 15th Lok Sabha and hundreds of state assembly elections across the country.

Many historians have maintained that the more India changes, it still remains the same, and in this 'unchanging India', the past continues to survive and thrive in the present. This social and cultural historical essence of India is visible during electoral battles. Manifestoes or developmental programmes and promises that are made during the elections are mere talking points, the reality seems to be that the Indian voter exercises his right on the basis of 'just one issue' and on considerations like caste, sub-caste, religion or other sectarian identities. It is only in India that voters vote not on the basis of their 'opinions and views' about the performance of the party that has been in power for five years either in the state or at the central government levels.

V.P. Singh and L.K. Advani, by playing a very low level of politics, institutionalised and solidified identity-based politics around caste-versus-caste and Hindus-versus-religious and cultural minorities of India. If V.P. Singh and his successors gave birth to the backward and Dalit caste 'category' of voters, the Sangh Parivar has worked hard to create a Hindu identity-based 'bloc' of voters on the basis of their consistent policies and strategies of dividing society between Hindus and 'others'.

In a state like Gujarat, this has worked. Narendra Modi projects himself as a 'developmentalist', but completely vulnerable Muslim voters are maintaining a great distance from his style of politics and the Muslim vote in Gujarat is cast for 'personal security'. Here, Hindutva has become a reality for a segment of society and this Hindu section votes blindly for a 'Hindu party', just as Yadavs exercise their franchise for their caste leaders.

An important feature of Indian democratic politics, which has directly impacted electoral practices, is the ongoing process of emergence of new parties, and such a proliferation of parties is linked with the phenomenon of growing identity politics in society. The Congress and the Communists are the only parties that transcend social boundaries of caste or religions or regions while all others are based on local, parochial, caste and community support structure system.

It is only when levels of social consciousness of citizens, individuals or groups are liberated from primordialism and parochial loyalty structures and reference points, will voters, with a democratic level of consciousness, exercise their fundamental right to vote on the basis of a free choice as a citizen of India.

The experience of India during the last 60 years of electoral politics has been that battle lines are drawn during the elections and the rhetoric of leaders has no relationship with reality because the voter is conditioned by either an 'emotive' national or local event, or elections are held on the basis of mobilisation of assured identity-based constituencies where the individual voter just falls into place as a link.

This narrative can be substantiated by focusing attention on electoral politics of UP. Earlier, the Congress dominated the scene on the basis of a caste and community coalition of high castes, Dalits and Muslims. The Congress' caste-community coalition came to an end and its replacements were also parties and groups based on caste-versus-caste, sub-caste versus-sub-caste, religion versus-religion. It is a story of continuity with change around the same fragments of social structure.

The caste and community based social structure is continuing to dominate the level of social consciousness and franchise is exercised not on the basis of socio-economic needs of voters but on the basis of their loyalty towards their caste group or Hindutva politics. Issue-oriented electoral politics, in the real sense of the term, where citizens exercise choice by examining the merits and demerits of available political options, is at present kept hostage by the domination of group identities. *The Economics Times, 28-01-2012*

The Nature of Psephocracy

The ongoing assembly elections are the semifinals of the 2014 Lok Saba poll, said BJP President Nitin Gadkari recently. He was right. These elections have assumed national importance as parties involved in the race are fighting to keep their individual identities intact. In the current era of coalition governments, every national party—be it the Congress, the BJP or the communists has to negotiate and bargain with regional and sub-regional parties to form a coalition government at the centre. The era of coalition governments at the centre has brought a sea change in the meaning and significance of elections. Major political entities are not only eyeing state-level victories but they also to want their presence felt nationwide because a central government cannot be formed without the involvement of the regional parties. This context should be kept in mind while analysing the state elections.

Elections have become a secular festival in India. Under the umbrella of ideologies, manifestos and programmes, every political party plays every trick of the trade to grab power. Why and how do politicians do it? First, it is not only political organisations that participate in the elections. Individuals with money power at their disposal also enter electoral battles. Political parties do not nominate candidates for electoral contest on the basis of their loyalty or commitment to their party ideology but on the basis of their capacity to win an election. It is only in India that criminals lodged in jail like Mukhtar Aansari or gangster Brijesh Singh or Munna Bajrangi contest the elections and win.

Before these elections, Mayawati was compelled to sack more than two dozens ministers on charges of corruption as levelled by the UP Lokayukta. All of them were welcomed to contest on the party platform of Mulayam Singh Yadav's Samajwadi Party or the BJP. Principle and ideology are not therefore the criterion for nomination of a candidate. The only consideration is whether on caste or sub-caste basis, a candidate, corrupt or criminal, can win an election. The BJP, for example, welcomed Babu Singh Kushwaha, a former BSP minister, to win other backward caste voters' constituency. All hell broke out within the party and ultimately the party kept Kushwaha out of public attention. The votaries of Hindutva have always proclaimed from the rooftops that they are a party with a difference. But when it comes to winning elections, they get caught in dirty caste politics. The BJP has imported backward caste leader Uma Bharati from Madhya Pradesh to wow the OBC vote bank in the UP elections. A party which believes in the concept of one Hindu country and one Hindu nationhood plays caste versus caste games. Elections in India are either contested on the basis of caste-based vote banks or by criminals who flex their muscle power to win the polls by terrorising the voters.

Another dark side of the Indian elections has been identified by the Chief Election Commissioner SY Quraishi, who observed that elections are the main source of corruption in public life in India. Elections are contested on the basis of money power because party candidates have to spend between Rs. 5 crore and Rs. 10 crore to influence the voters and win over influential leaders and middlemen of caste or community groups in an electoral constituency. A vigilant election commission's expenditure monitoring cell seized over Rs. 42 crore of unaccounted cash in Uttar Pradesh, Uttarakhand, Punjab and Manipur until mid-January. History is repeating itself. More and more money bags are changing hands.

The Electoral Code of Conduct, enforced by the Election Commission, is being violated during the night of election campaigns when candidates and their middlemen approach the caste or sub-caste leaders with lucrative offers in exchange for votes of their caste or community followers. Free, fair and fearless elections based on universal adult franchise are being held under the shadow of illegalities practiced by the contesting candidates and parties. It is sad to state that every party, all-India or regional and every party boss, without exception, is in the game of bribing the voters.

Almost every politician tries to buy the voters by showing his influence of money, muscle power, caste or religion. The elections have become a market place activity where transactions are conducted on the basis of auction of votes in exchange for benefits and advantages, which a winning candidate can share with his supporters and voters. It is not without reason that the Election Commission has alerted the Income Tax Department and has taken the services of chartered accountants to keep vigil over the financial transactions undertaken by the parties and their contesting candidates during the elections. The bigger issue is that political parties have become a private shop of leaders who, as custodians of party funds, distribute money to party candidates during the elections.

Every Party collects money for politics and elections, except for a few big business leaders, who openly mention the amount donated to a party. The real collection of funds takes place secretly and not in the open and legal manner. Third, the management of the conduct of elections by the Election Commission has become a challenging job. Not only do security forces have to be deployed in large numbers to ensure that the polling stations are protected against criminal attacks but also because the number of contestants in each and every constituency remains unreasonably high.

A phenomenon of mushrooming of parties, groups and individuals is witnessed just after the schedule of elections is announced. Suddenly new parties are born overnight. The government remains shut during the elections because every leader of a party, from prime minster level to the level of assembly or minister is engaged in canvassing for their parties and candidates.

If five state assembly elections take about three months of campaigning from Punjab to Manipur, the decision-making machinery of the government will remain virtually paralysed for such a long time. Elections are staggered and they cannot be held on one or two days because without proper deployment of fully armed police forces and magistracy in every sub-region of a sate, free, fair and fearless elections are not possible. Democratic elections need to be protected by armed functionaries of the state from the assaults of ballot snatchers. Politics has to be reformed in a manner that a voter could neither be bribed nor feel threatened by powerful caste or community leaders or musclemen. India's parallel economy and black money within the country show ugly face during the elections and serious efforts should be made to check their money power during elections. If parties and individuals would spend huge money during the elections, they would like to recover it. This is a vicious circle and its harmful consequences are felt everywhere.

Tehelka, 02-02-2012

Establishing Durable Peace in the North-East

India cannot move an inch forward in pursuit of its 'Look East' policy without resolving the multi-dimensional violent conflict s which exist in the seven sister States in the North-East. Only if Assam, Manipur, Meghalaya, Mizoram, Nagaland, Arunchachal Pradesh and Tripura are at peace with one another and also within their own existing boundaries will New Delhi's foreign strategy work.

If the armed Naga insurgents' 65-year old struggle is not resolved, it can create a lot of difficulties that will stunt the development of India's relationship with Burma—the first step towards the realisation of the new policy. In this context, the recent Assembly election in Manipur deserves to be closely analysed so as to understand the co-relation between the politics of the ballot and the bullet in the North East.

The electoral battle in Manipur has brought into sharp focus all the features of electoral contests found in every State of India. Indeed, if democratic politics in Manipur is studied superficially and if electoral events are taken at face value, there will not be any visible difference between Manipur and the major States. Like the rest of India, Manipur has a multi-ethnic, multi-cultural population consisting of Meiteis, Muslims, Nagas and Kukis.

Manipur graduated from a Union Territory to a full-fledged State in 1956, and its journey is on the same lines as that of Mizoram, Meghalaya and Nagaland. The Manipur state Assembly has a strength of 60 members and 279 candidates are fighting for these seats. If in the 2007 Assembly election, 19 parties and 308 candidates were involved, in 2012, 17 parties and 279 candidates are in contest.

National parties like the Congress, the BJP, the CPI and CPI(M) are in the electoral battle while regional political formations like the Nationalist Congress party, the Trinamool Congress and the Naga People's Front sponsored by NSCN-IM is also contesting from Naga inhabited areas of Manipur. Manipur like all other States witnessed a multi-party contest and the Election Commission announced that 80 per cent of the voters participated in the elections held on January 28.

It deserves to be stated that Manipur's voter turnout during the elections has been remarkably extremely high. Even during the 2007 Assembly election the voter turnout was 80 per cent and for the Lok Sabha election of 2009, it was 67 per cent. It can be concluded that democracy has taken deep roots in the soil of Manipur. It can also be surmised, on the basis of a superficial understanding of the above mentioned facts, that Manipur should be a peaceful democratic State where people want to settle their problems on the basis of competitive electoral democratic contests based on the sanctity of the ballot paper.

However, the reality is not so simple and straightforward. Electoral politics in Manipur co-exists with the politics of the bullet. Separatist and other insurgent groups engage in violence. the Army and other paramilitary forces are permanently engaged in anti-insurgency warfare and democratically elected Governments depend on the Armed Forces to maintain law and order in the State.

Manipur is a 'disturbed' State and that is the reason that the Armed Forces (Special Powers) Act of 1958 is in full operation there. Activist Irom Sharmila has been on a hunger strike for the last 11 years, beginning in November 2000, to demand the scrapping of AFSPA.

The separatist movement in Manipur has been on since 1964, and now a new factor to destabilise the State has emerged. The Nagas have launched a movement for the hill areas of Manipur inhabited by Nagas to be merged with Nagaland. Also, the conflicts between the Kukis and the Meities and between Hill and the Valley remain unresolved, with at least one group having an economic blockade of the main areas of the Valley.

On the one hand, the January election to the Manipur Assembly does not seem to be any different than elections in any other State. But, on the other, a complete absence of normalcy prevails because an estimated 39 insurgent groups operate in this violence ridden and completely ethnically fragmented small State.

The politics of the ballot versus the bullet is the norm in the North-East where the authority of the democratically elected Governments are constantly challenged and threatened by insurgent groups in the region.

If democracy and a multi-party system has come to stay in all the seven States of the North-East, the other reality of organised violence has also become a permanent factor.

This is the complex and contradictory reality of the North-East.

The Pioneer, 03-02-2012

With Uttar Pradesh Polls Over, Hectic Times Lie Ahead

The essence of the seven-phase Assembly election being held in Uttar Pradesh from January through March can be really understood by focussing attention on the ongoing intensive struggle for political power involving not only the major regional parties but also the all-India parties. The latter cannot form any Union Government without forming alliances with the former. The present state of Indian politics has brought national and regional parties on a common political platform because both have come to depend on the other for political support.

It is in this context that the significance of the Uttar Pradesh Assembly election must be seen. The four major contestants in Uttar Pradesh—the Congress, the BJP, the Samajwadi Party and the BSP—are engaged in cut-throat political competition for the State Assembly. At the same time, all these four major contenders for power in Uttar Pradesh are also looking to occupy some place in the Government at the centre, whether in 2014 or later.

Much is at stake for certain politicians like Congress scion Rahul Gandhi, BJP leader Uma Bharati, SP chief Mulayam Singh Yadav and his son AkhileshYadav, BSP chief and State Chief Minister Mayawati and Rashtriya Lok Dal chief Ajit Singh and his son Jayant Chaudhary. This is especially the case when the State's politics is being seen as having a bearing on the shape the Union Government can take, now or later.

While Congress president Sonia Gandhi, her son Rahul Gandhi and daughter Priyanka Vadra have aggressively campaigned in Uttar Pradesh, with a view to revive their party, they are also quite clear that the electionwill have significant short-term and long-term consequences for the party. The Congress leadership indeed put much of its energy and resources into this electoral contest, not only for forming the State Government in Uttar Pradesh but also because it is related to national politics.

Like the Congress, the BJP understands that the after-effects of the State election will be felt beyond the territorial boundaries of Uttar Pradesh. Its own political prospects at the centre also depend on its performance in the Assembly election. The BJP occupies the position of the leading Opposition party because it has shown electoral strength in Himachal Pradesh, Punjab, Jharkhand, Uttaranchal, Chhattisgarh, Madhya Pradesh, Gujarat and Karnataka. It is because of its electoral successes in a large number of States that it has emerged as the largest Opposition party, both in 2004 and 2009.

The BJP is conscious of this political reality. It knows that it can emerge as the leader of a coalition Government at the centre only if, along with in other States, it can also perform well in Uttar Pradesh. This is the reason that the BJP has made former Prime Minister Atal Bihari Vajpayee as it most 'authentic face' during the election. It hopes that the voters will be attracted by the charisma of their leader. Further, the BJP has decided to contest the Assembly poll on its own without forming any alliance with the Janata Dal (United), which is its partner in Bihar's ruling coalition.

This is because what may be good for Bihar is not acceptable to the BJP in Uttar Pradesh. Instead, here Bharati has been projected as the chief mobiliser. The short-term and long-term goals of the BJP are inter-linked, because with good electoral performance in Uttar Pradesh this year it has bright prospects at the all-India level in 2014.

Mayawati and the father-son Yadav duo of the SP are no doubt sharply focussed because the poll is the key to their political existence. This is also the reason why Yadav has projected his young and educated son Akhilesh at the forefront of his party's leadership because he himself has been unable to come out of the shadow of his 'goonda raj' image.

Akhilesh Yadav may refer to Ram Manohar Lohia as the source of inspiration of the party but Lohiaism as practiced by his father has no takers in Uttar Pradesh. Instead, it is the alliance with the backward castes and the Muslims that has sustained the Yadavs in politics. Both Mulayam Singh Yadav and Mayawati are 'caste-based' political leaders.

Caste based politics is co-terminus with territorial boundaries of every State and this limitation is felt by all the regionalists. To overcome this, the regional parties have to look outside the boundaries of their State to wield power at the Centre.

This mutual need of the all-India and the regional parties has created a national political space for the likes of Mayawati and Mulayam Singh Yadav. How much can they exploit the opportunity, is to be seen.

The Pioneer, 02-03-2012

More to this UP Election than Anti-incumbency

A section of armchair analysts have taken the short cut to explaining the electoral defeat of the party-in-Government by offering the anti-incumbency sentiment as explanation. They have, in the process, unfortunately ignored the complexity of factors which determine an electoral verdict especially.

The anti-incumbency sentiment as explanation has repeatedly proved wrong not only during the recent Assembly elections for Punjab, Uttar Pradesh, Goa, Uttarakhand and Manipur but also earlier in the case of the incumbent Chief Ministers of Gujarat and Madhya Pradesh, Narendra Modi and Shivraj Singh Chauhan.

Coming back to the electoral results announced on March 6, the Akali Dal and BJP combine has been re-elected in Punjab. In the past, after every election in the State, a different party has formed the Government. The system has been described as the 'revolving door politics' of Punjab.

This time around, however, Punjab has broken that tradition. Clearly, the anti-incumbency factor stands rejected in this case. An in-depth analysis is required to identify the factors which have had an impact on the voters' choices during the elections.

For instance, Bahujan Samaj Party chief Mayawati's defeat in Uttar Pradesh also cannot be explained by the anti-incumbency factor. It is misleading to say that Mayawati's Government attracted strong mass opposition between 2007 and 2012, and hence it won only 80 Assembly seats out of the total of 403.

Instead, the Uttar Pradesh Assembly election deserves to be properly contextualised to understand the dynamics of the ongoing processes of social and political change within the matrix of a complex caste-community hyper conscious society. A few facts must be mentioned in this regard.

First, Uttar Pradesh has broken its inherited political apathy. In 1951-52, only 38 per cent of the voters participated in the elections while about 60 per cent of voters turned out this year. This is a significant development.

High level of voter participation shows shows that the electorate is becoming politically conscious. Democracy in Uttar Pradesh is clearly on the march and yet, at the same time, the State still carries the historical baggage of caste and community-based identity structures.

Uttar Pradesh is quite conscious about its political surroundings and is responsive to political issues as it views it in terms of benefits to its various caste, sub-castes and religious groups. This approach is further validated when voters' are segregated or classified on the basis of their caste and community credentials.

The electoral system of first-past-the-post has a built-in mechanism that gives a majority of seats to the 'winners' even if the winning party's electoral base when represented by the percentage of votes polled is much less than fifty per cent of the total votes.

In Uttar Pradesh, the winning Samajwadi Party got 224 Assembly seat while its main challenger, the BSP, has only 80 seats. However, inspite of such huge difference in the number of seats secured by these two parties, the difference in vote share between the winner and the loser is only about 2.5 per cent.

The SP got 29.15 per cent of votes and 224 seats, the BSP got 25.91 per cent of votes and 80 seats, the Congress and the RLD got 11.63 per cent of votes and have been limited to 31 seats and BJP has 15 per cent of the votes and 47 seats. Is it then really a landslide victory for the SP? Is it really a vote for stability? Is it a vote for good governance as distinguished from Mayawati's so-called 'bad governance.'

The answer is a big no because Mayawati's Dalit-Jatav social base and Mulayam Singh's Yadav caste-base vote bank, by and large, remain intact. Mayawati is correct when she says that the Muslim voters who have a sizable presence shifted their support to the SP since that was party was the perceived 'winner'.

Also, senior Congress leader and Union Minister for Law and Justice Salman Khurshid's foolish persistence with the Muslim quota within the OBC quota changed the political discourse during the elections. The Congress's star campaigners in the State came across as politically bankrupt, even immature, for not realising the implications of such a controversial policy on reservations in such a volatile and emotive society as the one in Uttar Pradesh.

The Pioneer, 16-03-2012

West Bengal Needs Governance, Not Rhetoric

There was hope that Trinamool Congress chief Mamata Banerjee would sober down her politics once she became Chief Minster of West Bengal following her thumping electoral victory in 2011. In the run-up to the State Assembly election, Banerjee had campaigned on the electoral plank of Poribortan (change).

It was expected that, as the leader of the ruling party, she would behave differently than the way she had when she was in Opposition. People had expected that she would evolve from being a street-fighter to a seasoned political leader.

The governance of a State like West Bengal, where the TMC has dislodged a deeply entrenched Left Front Government, requires special skills on the part of the Chief Minister. Banerjee has been expected to prove her administrative capabilities in a State where people have seen Chief Ministers like the legendary Jyoti Basu and Banerjee's predecessor, Buddhadeb Bhattacharjee.

After all, Jyoti Basu was the first communist leader to be offered the post of Prime Minister because of his reputation as an able administrator. Similarly, Prime Minister Jawaharlal Nehru also had great respect for the first Chief Minister of West Bengal, BC Roy.

But Banerjee is a practitioner of the politics of 'negativism'. She has not offered any positive programme for the development of her State. Also, her so-called copyright on the aam admi' has made her an opposition element within the UPA alliance of which she is a member. Take, for instance, the land acquisition policy for development projects. It has become a bone of contention between land owners and the buyers of land, whether they be private real estate developers or the Government. The public demands that the dated anachronistic Act of the colonial era should be scrapped and a new one formulated, keeping in mind today's requirements.

Besides, the State and the Union Governments have also misused their 'discretionary' powers for acquiring land on the pretext of 'public good' while 'displaced' landowners have been treated shabbily with respect to determining their compensation amount.

In fact, some times the policies of rehabilitation for the disposed families have been wholly ignored. There is hardly any need to prepare a catalogue of protests by 'dispossessed farmers' including those from Nandigram whose cause Banerjee championed, and which brought her into the national limelight. It was only to be expected that this 'heroine of Nandigram' would actively campaign for quick action on the Land Acquisition Act and possibly give it a more humane face.

However, Banerjee has vetoed the Bill prepared by the UPA Government. Disputes on land acquisition have not come to an end because the Union Government has completely failed to win over the approval of Banerjee. If the Congress-led UPA Government is known for its 'policy paralysis', Banerjee has now earned a reputation of vetoing every policy initiative.

This was particularly evident when she torpedoed the Railway Budget prepared by her party leader Dinesh Trivedi.

Consequently, the Union Government was criticised for allowing the Railway Budget to be so derailed, even though it had the approval of Union Minister for Finance Pranab Mukherjee. Banerjee had asked for a pound of flesh and she got it.

Trivedi made to resign and Banerjee's nominee, Mukul Roy, has taken charge as the new Minister for Railways. The future of Indian Railways is quite bleak if it is to be so whimsically governed.

On a different note, it must also be asked why Banerjee, a coalition ally of the UPA, join the so-called federal front formed by non-UPA Chief Ministers? It is, of course, understandable that State Governments managed by opposition parties may take a firm anti-Centre stand because of the latter's discriminatory attitude. It is quite legitimate for the Chief Ministers of Odisha, Gujarat, Madhya Pradesh and Chhattisgarh to oppose the Union Government's actions which erodes the federal spirit of the Constitution.

After all, the Chief Ministers of these States not ruled by the Congress or its allies had come together to oppose the setting up of the National Counter-Terrorism Centre because they saw in that an undue interference in their domain. But what was Banerjee doing in this group?

Either, Banerjee is ill-adjusted with the manner in which the UPA is functioning or she is simply using every opportunity she gets to bargain with the Centre for concessions and benefits for her State. Either way, she is proving to be a destablising factor for the UPA Government of which her party is an important player. It remains to be seen as to how long goes on.

The pioneer 30-03-2012

The Jostle for Political Space

The unilateral announcement by home minister P. Chidambaram of a National Counter Terrorism Centre (NCTC) showed that he failed to recognise that the political map of federal India has completely changed and the chief ministers of 2012 are not like their predecessors during the Nehru or Indira Gandhi phase of politics when they were treated as glorified municipalities. The phase of Congress party dominance over the central government and on absolute majority of state governments has come to an end.

This lapse by the Home Minister brought Manmohan Singh centre stage. He invited all the chief ministers to Delhi on 5 May to discuss issues related to the proposed NCTC setup. The chief ministers could not be won over by the central government and these deliberations proved futile. Sonia Gandhi, the leader of the Congress party, while addressing the Congress parliamentary party meeting, elaborated on this contentious issue and observed '….there are Centre-state issues of major national importance such as fighting terrorism or dealing with Left-Wing Extremism where the Centre cannot shirk its responsibility. Hence, in such case it has been our government's endeavour to work closely with the state governments so that ournational interest is protected. Trust and cooperation must be the anchor of Centre-state relations.'

The UPA government has completely failed to adjust and respond with the changing political map of India where 'regionalist' parties, groups and leaders have emerged as autonomous centres of power in their own areas of influence. It is quite simplistic and factually incorrect to maintain that Centre-state conflicts have arisen because of the prevailing 'trust deficit' between the government at the centre and the states. It is solely Congress party's failure to adapt itself to the new reality of political change when chief ministers have become real custodians of the interests of their states and are prepared to bargain, even confront, the central government on issues which are in the public domain.

Has the Congress party drawn any political lessons from the behaviour and conduct of opposition parties in Parliament beginning from May 2009 onwards? Is it only the issue of disruption of Parliamentary proceedings by the Opposition parties or is it a larger issue of basic political contest between the Congress and opposition parties, both within Parliament and at the level of states where these parties are in power and wish to displace the Congress from their zones of influence?

Political battles are fought both on the floor of the both Houses of Parliament and at the level of state governments because if regional parties succeed at the state level in competition against the all-India parties like the Congress or the BJP, only then these regionalists can be a part of coalition governments at the Centre. Every regionalist leader like Jayalalithaa of the AIADMK or M Karunanidhi of the DMK, or Chandrababu Naidu of the Telugu Desam party or Nitish Kumar of Bihar or Naveen Patnaik of Odisha or Akhilesh Yadav or Mayawati of Uttar Pradesh or Parkash Singh Badal of Punjab and Mamata Banerjee of Bengal are all potential claimants for power at the Centre while forming a new coalition government in 2014. How can such regionalists with political clout obey the dictat of the Centre on NCTC?

The BJP, along with its chief ministers in Gujarat, Karnataka, Madhya Pradesh, Jharkhand and Chhattisgarh and also with presence in the state governments of Bihar and Punjab is determined to displace the Congress-led UPA in the Lok Sabha elections of 2014. With this political goal, the BJP chief ministers cannot allow the Congress which is leading the central government to do things in its own way because the BJP and all its chief ministers are real opponents of the Congress. The Prime Minister and the home minister must keep this larger political scenario in their political calculations.

The essential argument of the above narrative is that the chief ministers have become major political players in Indian federation and every party or group is targeting the central government with a view to become an important part of the coalition government at the Centre. This new situation should make all-Indian parties think about new 'rules of the game' while forming a government at the Centre.

If regionalist parties and their leaders are engaged in finding political space at the level of central government, the central coalition has to evolve a consensus on every major public policy issue by winning over the support and concurrence of the chief ministers of states. There is no other alternative in a situation of changing political milieu of the country.

Financial World, 17-05-2012

Bodoland—Migrant Identities are Easy to Play On

Assam is just like a volcano. State Chief Minister Tarun Gogoi's observation about the unstoppable bleeding of inhabitants of Kokrajhar since 6 July said much about the state of affairs in his state. Peace has not been restored in Kokrajhar despite the deployment of Army as well as Central para-military forces. On the contrary, the fire of hatred has engulfed the whole country so much that now doctored images and viral threats are being spread across social networking siteslike Facebook, Twitter and YouTube to incite Muslims and create a scare among people of the Northeast living across India. The anonymous virtual threats have led to an exodus of migrant population and students of the Northeast from cities such as Mumbai, Pune, Chennai, Hyderabad, Bangalore and Lucknow impacting business and other activities.

State governments of Maharashtra, Andhra Pradesh, Karnataka, Tamil Nadu and Uttar Pradesh are clueless about this sudden phenomenon, only offering assurances in the name of security and safety to these migrants who are rushing back home to escape the wrath of non-Northeasterners. The Centre has ordered blocking of more than 250 websites in which morphed images and videos were uploaded to incite Muslims.

This situation in Assam compelled the Lok Sabha to discuss an adjournment motion on 7 August. But Opposition leader LK Advani chose the occasion to add fuel to the fire by raking up the old issue of illegal Bangadeshis in the Northeast and linking it with the present crisis. In one stroke, the BJP leader turned the argument into a Hindu versus Muslim conflict. But is that really the case?

Truth is that the so-called 'mainland' is completely ignorant that the Scheduled Tribe population of Northeast India belongs to the Austric, Tibeto-Chinese, Dravidian and Indi-European racial stock. The so-called 'mainland' Indians are completely unaware of the varied racial groups in the seven states—Assam, Manipur, Mizoram, Meghalaya, Tripura, Nagaland and Arunachal Pradesh, so it is impossible for the inhabitants of urban centres like Mumbai, Pune, Chennai, Hyderabad, Bengaluru, Lucknow to understand the finer distinctions between people from the Hill Area and Assam.

As for Advani's communal remark, the Kokrajhar crisis is more about problems of livelihood than communal biases. But that cannot be understood without going into the history of India's Northeast. For now, Advani would do good to know that a sizeable Bengali Hindu and Muslim population of Assam is completely indigenous to the region just like the Hindu and Muslim Assamese. Bengali Hindus and Muslims had settled in Assam long ago and worked along side the native Assamese in agriculture, trade and other professions. Hence, Bengali Muslim population along with Assamese Hindu, and tribals like Bodos, Santhals *et al.* are all 'local' as far as Assam is concerned. This history of composite culture of Assam cannot be wished away, but it is political manipulation of such historical facts by community leaders which is constantly fracturing the Assamese society. And now ignorant 'mainlanders' have jumped in to seek 'justice' for the Bengali Muslims who have become refugees in Bodoland—only to make things worse.

But the larger question here is that of the political manipulation of 'identities' of all kinds of migrants in a multi-linguistic and multicultural country. India consists of many diverse mini-Indias and this extremely diverse and heterogeneous country cannot be welded together into a harmonious universe of its own if 'separate identity' politics becomes the basis of electoral manipulations. Congress is the only secular social formation that is following in the footsteps of Nehru's 'national project', and the party should strengthen unity among diversities.

Opportunists destroyed the harmony in Bodoland and this fire of hatred is now consuming Indians at large. The lesson to be learnt here is that Northeast should be treated as a 'special' cultural mosaic and its peoples should feel that the whole of India belongs to all of them. The National Minorities Commission has clearly stated that the lakhs of people who have been accommodated in refugee camps are victims of hate campaign, arson, loot and murder indulged in by fanatics. Is anyone listening to this?

Tehelka, 21-08-2012

Great Power, Great Responsibility—Gujarat Elections

The upcoming assembly elections in Gujarat are extremely crucial for chief minister Narendra Modi not only for remaining in office but also positioning himself as a prime ministerial candidate.

His political ambitions cannot be achieved without establishing his pre-eminent position in Gujarat politics and also his supposed indispensability as regards the national goals of the Sangh parivar.

And this is the reason why he has chosen to attack Rahul Gandhi, widely expected to be the Congress's prime ministerial candidate in 2014 Lok Sabha elections.

How is he going about it? By silencing all voices of dissent, including that of former chief minister Keshubhai Patel, an undisputed leader of the powerful Patel community in Gujarat.

Though Modi has succeeded in establishing himself as the supreme leader of the Gujarat BJP, this alone cannot help him to succeed at the national level. He has to prove his worth as an acceptable and legitimate leader of the man on the streets of Gujarat. Modi's tall claims-that he has transformed the face of Gujarat by focussing attention on its unparalleled economic development; that he is the sole protector of the pride of 50 million Gujaratis; and his self-congratulatory statement that it is because of his administrative capability that the state has not witnessed a single communal riot and achieved social harmony-will be tested through a free and fair electoral process.

The greatest challenge Modi has to face is that the voters of Gujarat, especially the sizeable Muslim minority and other strata of society, have to accept his credentials as his track record remains tarnished by the 2002 Gujarat riots.

Modi has to do a lot of explaining for his government's acts of omission and commission in a situation where the Supreme Court had to order that the trials should be shifted outside the state because victims cannot expect justice in Gujarat and a special investigation team was appointed to ascertain the truth behind the riots.

Now Modi is making all efforts to project himself as a tolerant, liberal and democratically elected leader. He undertook the 'sadbhavna mission' and observed a fast in 2011. This year he organised a big show on Swami Vivekananda's birth anniversary. Here it needs to be pointed out that Swami Vivekananda's message to humanity was based on the principles of brotherhood, whereas Modi is a product of a tradition that has espoused social exclusion and discrimination against minorities.

While Modi was at his job, a verdict came in August from judge Jyotsna Yajnik, who awarded rigorous imprisonment to 32, including a former BJP minister, in the Naroda Patiya massacre case. She stated that the "riot victims were targeted on the basis of a conspiracy". Though the state government was criticised in her judgement, the Sangh parivar weekly, The Organiser, in its mid-September 2012 issue praised Modi for an "impartial, non-interfering approach" that ensured "every single riot case was investigated and arrest made".

Modi, like Caesar's wife, has to be above any kind of suspicion.

Further, his claim to being the "architect of modern developed Gujarat" will also be scrutinised because the ordinary voters know it very well that story of the developmental journey of the state precedes Modi.

Though political economists of great eminence have maintained that the human agency plays an important role in economic growth, they have also asserted that development can become self-accelerating and self-generating if the state or region concerned creates solid foundations for it. Modi is stating a half-truth when he takes full credit for bringing prosperity to Gujarat.

If a leader like Modi has built a personality cult around himself, he has to take full responsibility for his failures to ensure security, freedom and justice for Gujarat. Herein lies a contradiction and this is Modi's reality.

Hindustan Times, 26-09-2012

Will the Voter Take on the Modi Challenge?

Ending a 10-year boycott of Narendra Modi imposed after the 2002 riots, the UK government has decided to resume engagement with Gujarat on the eve of December 2012 elections in the state. While experts are debating if the EU and the US will follow the UK's embrace of Modi to boost trade with the most 'business-friendly' state in the country, there are voices questioning Modi's model of development and its 'excluvism' for the Hindus.

On 8 October, while campaigning for the upcoming assembly elections Modi asked the audience, "There was a time when before coming to Ahmedabad, you called up friends to inquire if there was a curfew or not. It has been 11 years. Has the curfew disappeared or not? Have the riots disappeared or not?" This is an astounding statement by a Chief Minister because maintenance of law and order' is the obligation of an elected political executive of a government. Why should Modi need to assure 60 million Gujaratis that their life and property is safe under his leadership?

To understand that here's a little recapitulation of the way Modi has emerged on the political scene of Gujarat and has completely overshadowed it. Modi became the Chief Minister in 2001 by displacing the then Chief Minister Keshubhai Patel, and in March-April 2002 the state witnessed the worst communal riots with the state apparatus aiding the killings of hapless

Muslims. But Modi's anti-Muslim propaganda still helped BJP win 127 seats of total 182 in the 2002 Assembly elections.

Since then Modi has earned notoriety for using state machinery to meet political ends. In 2005, three IPS officers were arrested for the killing of one Sohrabuddin in a fake encounter. Recently, the CBI named state minister Amit Shah for his involvement in the fake police encounter of Tulsiram Prajapati, who apparently knew something about the Sohrabuddin killing. Another special court in notorious Naroda Patiya riot case on 31 August 2012 pronounced 32 persons guilty including Bajrang Dal leader Babu Bajrangi, and former BJP minister and MLA Maya Kodnani sending them to life imprisonment with the message that 'this riot seems to be a case of conspiracy.' However, despite numerous such allegations, Modi won 117 state assembly seats out of 182 in 2007.

If Modi's comrades Kodnani and Shah are guilty of criminal offences, his minister Purushottam Solanki is facing corruption charges in fishing contracts. On 28 September, the Gujarat High Court upheld the Governor's sanction to 'prosecute the minister' despite the state cabinet twice rejecting the plea in this regard. The developmentalist Chief Minister is also obstructing the appointment of Lokayukta in the state to investigate corruption cases against his government. After the High Court upheld Governor's order for the appointment of the Lokayukta, the Modi government approached the Supreme Court. At a time when corruption in public institutions is such a major 'issue' in politics, why is it that the BJP government of Gujarat is fighting tooth and nail to prevent the appointment of a Lokayukta? Could it be the scare of more skeletons in his cupboard that Modi is not allowing an independent investigator in the state?

With the fight intensifying for the Assembly elections, Modi is trying hard to play up his 'inclusivist' model of development. Through events like the 'Sadbhavana Mission and the 'Vivekananda Vikas Yatra', he has been projecting himself as the sole protector of 60 million Gujaratis and how he has changed the fortunes of the state in his 11-year rule. During Swami Vivekananda's birthday celebrations, he even reminded the audience that the Ram Temple shilan-yas on 9 November 1989 was done by a Dalit from Bihar. He has even launched a TV channel, 'Vande Gujarat' to make emotive appeals for support. But Modi does not want to be reminded of Naroda Patia, Best Bakery and the fact that convictions of his supporters in these cases happened only because the Supreme Court was 'supervising' them. But more surprising was that Congress president too completely skirted the issue during her rally in Gujarat. When the political parties become hesitant to remind each other of their murky pasts, there has to be more to the story. Perhaps they are waiting for the voters' verdict to give it some clarity.

The Financial World, 17-10-2012

NCTC—Time to take Centre-stage

After the bomb blasts in Hyderabad last month, Union home minister Sushilkumar Shinde resurrected the idea of establishing a National Counter Terrorism Centre (NCTC) for undertaking investigations of terrorist attacks across India. He argued, as his predecessor P Chidambaram had done, that terrorism was a national threat and it was imperative that a national agency with necessary powers and resources should be in place.

This proposal of the central government has been stoutly opposed by chief ministers such as Naveen Patnaik and Nitish Kumar, and also by BJP leader Arun Jaitley. Their opposition is guided by apprehensions that this agency would lead to the erosion of the autonomy of state governments, which are constitutionally mandated to make arrangements for dealing with law and order situations.

There is considerable evidence that exposes the anti-federal postures of these self-appointed federalists. At the drop of a hat, chief ministers ask the central government to assist them in maintaining law and order. To cite a recent example, Akhilesh Yadav, chief minister of Uttar Pradesh, has asked for a Central Bureau of Investigation inquiry into the killing of a police official because the people of his state do not expect fair investigations by the local police. This is not the first time that such a thing has happened. Do the chief ministers then forget their constitutional mandate and autonomy? The National Investigation Agency (NIA) is routinely asked by state governments to take over the responsibility of handling anti-terrorist cases. The chief minister of Andhra Pradesh has asked for an NIA investigation into the Hyderabad blasts case.

Also, in the past 65 years, Parliament has enacted special laws like the Preventive Detention Act, Defence of India Act, Terrorist and Disruptive Activities (Prevention) Act, Prevention of Terrorism Act, or Unlawful Activities (Prevention) Act for the benefit of state governments. Have the states asked for the rescinding of these laws?

While the champions of state autonomy should be able to organise assembly elections with their own administrative and police organisations, free, fair and fearless elections are held under the supervision of central paramilitary forces. Narendra Modi, the man who provides 'model governance to his state', required 493 companies of central forces for the Gujarat elections, which took place in December.

Instead of fighting phoney battles of jurisdiction with the Centre, the state governments should strengthen their own administrative apparatus to deal with local challenges. If nine states are affected by well-armed left-wing extremism, they have to coordinate with the Centre to match the power of the extremists' gun. Terrorism, extremism or communal riots have transcended state boundaries and the central government has to be empowered to intervene, of course, with the support of the state governments. This point alone is sufficient defence for National Counter Terrorism Centre.

Hindustan Times, 22-03-2013

India's Democracy is Under Siege

The country's flawed model of economic development has produced an army of young, social rejects. But, instead of giving these youth opportunities to better themselves, political parties have deployed them to fight their dirty, electoral battles.

The tender plant of Indian democracy has to be nourished so that it can gather enough institutional capability and vitality to repel threats from anti-democratic forces which have scant respect for the principle of Rule of Law. The fundamental difference between a secular and pluralist system of political democracy and all other forms of authoritarian dictatorships is that citizens in a democracy are protected by the Rule of Law which is enforced by an accountable executive, an elected legislature and an independent judiciary.

The Constitution guarantees the citizens of this country the right to protest and express their grievances against the Government. However, these protests must be carried out within the legal framework of the country. When certain sections of society exercise their right to protest without caring for the letter and spirit of the law, they challenge the essence of Indian democracy. Take, for instance, the case of Kolkata student leader Sudipto Gupta who recently died in police custody.

Instead of following the law of the land that makes clear that a custodial death has to be investigated, West Bengal Chief Minister Mamata Banerjee jumped the gun and dismissed it as an ordinary accident. All hell broke loose in West Bengal and demonstrations were held even in New Delhi against the visiting Chief Minister. During the course of these protests, however, every norm and rule was broken.

First, supporters of the deceased from the Students Federation of India heckled Banerjee and her Finance Minister in New Delhi. Then, in retaliation, Trinamool Congress Chhatra Parishad cadre created havoc on the streets of Kolkata, while working under the protective umbrella of a passive Kolkata Police force.

But one wrong does not justify another. Especially in the case of West Bengal, it was the State Government's responsibility to maintain law and order, and prevent lumpen youth from vandalising the prestigious Presidency University. Such youths routinely take the law into their hands and often while wearing a political hat. For example, the Shiv Sainiks in Maharashtra have made it a habit to break the law to protest against real or imaginary grievances. But because the Shiv Sena is a political outfit, its goons remain above the law.

While it is completely undemocratic, even authoritarian, to suggest that college students should be kept out of the organisational structure of political parties, there should also be no doubt that if the youth wing of a political party violates the law of the land, the guilty should be punished. At the same time, this does not mean that all the youth of India must be kept out of politics.

Also, one must ask if any political party has, in the recent past, undertaken any serious investigation of the increasing frustration of the ill-educated, unemployed and unemployable young urban population. The answer is a resounding 'no'. This makes every political party equally accountable for the growing violence in society, much of which is driven by ill-educated youths who find themselves at the dead end of their hopes and aspirations.

After all, it is when the politics of development fail to provide the young the opportunities they deserve, that they join 'youth wing' of a party. Political ideology sometimes plays a part in this but mostly the youth who join politics end up providing the muscle power politicians need to win an election. And political parties are fully aware of this and know that they need these youths to do their dirty work.

Therefore, they patronise a large section of social rejects for exactly this purpose. While this helps achieve political gains in the short term, it does much damage in the long term by creating an army of young people who are paid to break the law. *The Pioneer, 26-04-2013*

They don't Caste their Vote

Political movements and the functioning of electoral democracy over the past 65 years have led to considerable social change in Karnataka, where old loyalties of caste and community are being substituted by the rising expectations which citizens have from their representatives. The fate of these representatives will be revealed today.

Let us look at a few examples. If proclaimed Lingayat leader BS Yeddyurappa had a strong caste backing, the BJP government in Karnataka should have collapsed with his resignation, but only 15 MLAs of his party resigned with him and in spite of the 'split', the government survived until May 2013.

Further, the Lingayats constitute only 17 per cent of the Karnataka population and the Vokkaligas constitute 15 per cent. While these dominant castes had chief ministers such as S Nijalingappa and Veerandra Patil of the Congress, Devaraj Urs, who came to power in 1972, did not belong to either of these two communities. Veerappa Moily, a former chief minister of the Congress in Karnataka, belonged to a backward caste. How could Indira Gandhi, a complete outsider, win a Lok Sabha election from Chikmagalur in 1978?

The ongoing process of inter-caste and intra-caste fragmentation has become unstoppable and many Vokkaligas or Lingayats from different political parties have competed against one another to win this election. Incidentally, HD Deve Gowda of the Janata Dal (S), a self-appointed representative of rural Karnataka, is a Vokkaliga but unfortunately for him, many Vokkaligas vote for the Congress. Hence no bloc of the dominant castes is a monolith, nor can caste-based leaders claim a monopoly of their kinsmen's support, especially in the 21st century.

Sonia Gandhi in her election campaign reminded BJP campaigners that corruption could not be an issue only for the central government and become irrelevant for Karnataka. Are the so-called caste-based voters unconcerned about corruption in Karnataka in the elections of 2013?

If just caste-based demographics determine electoral results, money power during the 2008 assembly elections should have failed in Bellary district, where the Reddy brothers secured eight out of nine seats for the BJP. But it didn't.

It should not be forgotten that Karnataka has 184 rural constituencies out of the 224 and Deve Gowda and HD Kumaraswamy, as self-appointed rural leaders of the JD (S), have always given a tough fight to the Congress. It is not only Deve Gowda who is campaigning for rural Karnataka's causes. Rahul Gandhi's representative in Karnataka, Madhusudan Mistry, is campaigning for the land rights of tribals and for a minimum support price for minor forest produce. Are these secular demands of different strata of society meaningless and irrelevant for the voters?

It is often forgotten that Karnataka has a history of limited representative government. In 1881, the Maharaja of Mysore had launched an experiment of socially inclusive politics, and Dalits, backward castes, Muslims and other minority groups were accommodated in governance.

In the end it is performance that counts. *Hindustan Times, 07-05-2013*

2013 State Assembly Elections: BJP *versus* Congress

The most important salient feature of the state assembly elections of November 2013 in the five states of India like Rajasthan, Madhya Pradesh, Chhattisgarh, Delhi, and Mizoram is that the Congress and the BJP, the two all-India political parties, are engaged in a great battle because the electoral verdict of these state assembly elections is expected to reveal the trend of electoral victories for the forthcoming Lok Sabha elections of April-May 2014. It is not only the media, or psephologists and observers of voting trends during the elections are actively engaged in the study of day-to-day developments of these elections; Congress and BJP, as two main contenders during these elections, are aggressively campaigning amongst the voters because stakes are very high for these two parties. The Congress has to defend its record of governance in

Delhi and Rajasthan where it has been in power from 2008 to 2013 and the BJP is making every effort to not only defeat the ruling Congress party in Rajasthan in Delhi, but also to win the state assembly elections of Madhya Pradesh and Chhattisgarh on the basis of its performance for the past 10 years of its rule in these two states.

Ashok Gehlot and Sheila Dikshit, the CMs of Rajasthan and Delhi, and Shivraj Singh Chouhan and Raman singh, CMs of Madhya Pradesh and Chhattisgarh, are individually leading their parties in the elections where the voters are expected to exercise their vote on the performance of these 'individual chief ministers'. If Congress and BJP have reposed confidence over the leadership qualities of its own state chief ministers, it is also important for the incumbents to show that they deserved this confidence of their own party and these chief ministers have to prove that they really performed well during five years of rule from 2008 to 2013.

Not only this, these are not ordinary state assembly elections for Congress and BJP, on the contrary, the verdict of the voters during these elections will determine, in an unambiguous manner, the voters' preference for the forthcoming sixteenth Lok Sabha elections of April-May 2014. If one of the salient features of these state assembly elections is that Congress and BJP are fighting elections directly against one another and this direct confrontation is likely to show the way wind blows in 2014, a few other salient features of these elections may be mentioned to highlight the fact that electoral politics in India is showing many worrisome trends and tendencies which deserve to be rectified with a view to make politics a healthy, competitive activity.

First, the Election Commission is concerned about the non-observance of the model code of conduct during the period of election campaign, both by the major all-India parties and their tall leaders like Rahul Gandhi and Narendra Modi. It is not only that the Election Commission reminded Rahul and Modi for breach of model code of conduct, the Election Commission expressed its anguish on November 21st2013 and asked for an amendment to have 'more teeth for the code of conduct.' Second, it is nothing new for the Indian democracy that 'money has become a deciding factor.' During the elections, and political parties, and individual candidates spend huge financial resources to win an election. Of late, the Election Commission has evolved many 'surveillance' methods to detect and check the flow of illegal money during the elections and on November 19th 2013, more than Rs 16 crores were caught by the surveillance teams consisting of income tax officers, service tax officers, customs and police. The salient feature of these assembly elections is that a bombshell exploded when an individual filed a PIL in high court on 'foreign funds' received by Aam Aadmi Party for elections of the Delhi state assembly and the Delhi High Court asked the Home Ministry of the Government of India to investigate the foreign sources of funding for elections for the AAP.

Incumbency and anti-incumbency factors do not hold weight if the performance of a CM and his party in government is found acceptable by the voter. This election will test the factor of incumbency both for the BJP and the Congress.

Arvind Kejriwal, the chief of AAP, asked for investigation into the foreign sources of election funding not only for his own party but also of the Congress and the BJP. It deserves to be clearly stated that the issue of funds for elections, both foreign and domestic has become quite hot and people are demanding answers from parties to declare in public the sources of their funds. Third, if the BJP is fighting the elections in MP and Chhattisgarh to prove that their performance is in open and the so called 'anti-incumbency' factor against the BJP state CMs will not work and Chouhan and Raman Singh will win for the third term in the elections of December 2013. Congress is also working hard to prove that the anti-incumbency factor in Rajasthan and Delhi will not work against their party because Gehlot and Sheila Dikshit have performed well as CMs.

The incumbency factor that a party in power for five years is generally re-elected by the voters is to test because it has been disapproved many a times. The psephologists had coined incumbency factor where the projected it as an explanatory factor for the failure of re-election of a party in power, however, incumbency and anti-incumbency factors do not hold weight if the performance of a CM and his party in government is found acceptable by the voter. This election will test the factor of incumbency both for the BJP and the Congress. It is unfortunate that election manifestos issued by political parties on the eve of elections are not taken seriously by the voters because it is believed that party make tall promises to win an election an after the elections, these manifestos and promises made by parties are simply forgotten.

A cynical attitude has developed about election manifestos and this election is not an exception to this general rule. However, Arvind Kejriwal's AAP, a new entrant to electoral politics, has made many promises to the voter and he has taken a high moral ground in politics, he is on trial during this election. Will AAP be like any other party and breach its electoral promises or it will be different than the others? This is a salient fact of this election. Fifth, if on the one hand, usual allegations and counter-allegations against one another are in the public domain, during the elections, Narendra Modi is on 'trial'. Because it is alleged that he has misused and abused his office of Gujarat Chief Minister to keep an eye on a daughter of his friend. This election is seeing a lot of mud-slinging and character assassinations, and emotive issues are dominating the real political issues. Finally, these elections are a great 'test' for Arvind Kejriwal, at a local level, and Narendra Modi.

Kejriwal has projected his party and politics in a manner that it is different than the others and Modi, BJP prime ministerial candidate, is on a 'probation' during these elections because his 'acceptability' as an all-India leader of the BJP will be tested. Modi is the only all-India leader who is campaigning every state on behalf of the BJP and if the party can show a hat-trick, credit will go to Modi's leadership. The BJP will think that it is safe in the hands of Modi who is a winning horse. If not, Modi will be challenged from within his own party. Rajnath Singh, the BJP president has pre-empted this possibility when he observed that electoral results during the state assembly elections of Nov.-Dec. 2013 are irrelevant because Modi is a PM candidate of the BJP for 2014 irrespective of election results of MP, Chhattisgarh, Delhi and Rajasthan.

The upshot of above narrative is quite clean that these state assembly elections are significant pointers not only for the forthcoming LokSabha elections, but these elections and campaigning for electoral democracy in Nov. 2013 is a warning for the future because the level of public discourse and debate has touched the lowest level of decency and if the flow of foreign funds during the elections is not stopped, electoral democracy of India will become the private property of foreign donors who will like panchayats, state assemblies and politicians to function as 'agents' of their foreign masters.

newsyaps.com, 05-12-2013

Electoral verdict of December 2013: An Analysis

The recently concluded assembly elections in five states of the country were hotly contested by both the Congress and the BJP. The December 8, 2013, electoral verdict of Rajasthan, Madhya Pradesh, Chhattisgarh and Delhi (the verdict of Mizoram came out a day later) has sent a clear signal to the two all-India competitors that the journey to the forthcoming Lok Sabha elections of March-April 2014 will not be a smooth ride for both.

The message of December 8, 2013, verdict is not only for the two national parties but also for every powerful regional leader and political formation in the 28 states and seven Union Territories of India. Although it is premature to write off the Congress party as a force in Indian politics, an obvious conclusion that can be drawn from the December 8 outcome is that a determined BJP, under the leadership of Narendra Modi, will fight like there is no tomorrow to win the 2014 Lok Sabha election.

There are a few salient facts emerging from the election results of the four states that deserve to be highlighted to substantiate the argument that there are lessons to be learnt by all parties and political observers.

First, the validity of holding the anti-incumbency factor responsible behind the defeat, or victory, of a party in elections has been established. The December 8 verdict has gone against the Congress governments which were in office in Rajasthan and Delhi, but BJP governments in MP and Chhattisgarh got voters' endorsement winning electoral victory for the third time in succession. Not only this, Sheila Dikshit, who led the Congress government as Delhi chief minister for 15 years, met with a humiliating defeat in the elections at the hands of Arvind Kejriwal of the Aam Aadmi Party – a political novice.

But it deserves to be clearly mentioned that electoral victories or defeats of leaders or parties cannot be explained by much simplistic arguments of anti-incumbency factors because a deeper analysis is required to understand electoral performance of parties. What is the explanation for a less than one-year-old party like AAP scoring 32 per cent of the votes polled in Delhi assembly elections with 28 seats out of 70?

Second, there is no denying the fact that the performance of the party in government for five years in office influences the choice of voters when they go to the polling booth. Generally, the perception of the voters about the performance of a ruling government is formed by the events that build up to the voting day. Situations such as the rising prices of onions, potatoes and other commodities of daily use during the last six months leave an impact on the minds of the voters who may ignore the good work, if any, done by the same government.

Unlike Modi's aggressive campaign for the BJP, Rahul's presence in Delhi campaigns was next to negligible. The campaigns of the BJP and Congress were a study in contrast in the four major states that went to polls.

Parties have to keep in mind the fact that it is the immediate content of elections which determines voters' choices. A few salient features about major contenders for power may be mentioned to understand the dynamics of electoral politics. Shivraj Singh Chauhan, Chief Minister of Madhya Pradesh; Raman Singh of Chhattisgarh; Vasundhara Raje of Rajasthan; and, Harsh Vardhan of Delhi were projected by the RSS and the BJP as the best performers from their respective states. The local BJP party units stood solidly behind their leaders in accordance to the strategy of the core BJP and RSS leadership. Not only this, the BJP's prime ministerial candidate Narendra Modi was accepted by every party worker as their national leader during the election and the local BJP organizations made every effort to make Modi's election meetings a grand success.

Nitin Gadkari, a former BJP president, was entrusted with the campaigning for the Delhi state assembly election while Modi addressed many public meetings in the national capital to influence the voters in favour of his party. The unified machine of the RSS-BJP organization was at work during the elections with lines of command clear to the state leaders, who were in full authority of their local-level election campaign with Modi acting as a national campaigner. Its exact opposite was the campaign of the Congress party where Sheila Dikshit was left alone to fend for herself. Unlike Modi's aggressive campaign for the BJP, Rahul's presence in Delhi campaigns was next to negligible. The campaigns of the BJP and Congress were a study in contrast in the four major states that went to polls. The Congress party campaign during the elections lacked the stamina and the energy of the BJP.

It is expected that the Congress will learn a lesson from the assembly elections because BJP is proving to be a tough challenger to the Congress leadership and its organizational capabilities. Question marks have arisen about Rahul Gandhi's leadership, and his capacity to attract and influence voters in favour of his party. Modi, the RSS and the BJP appear to be succeeding in making electoral politics in India look like a 'Modi vs Rahul' contest.

The electoral verdict of December 8 has also made everyone stand up and seriously analyze the phenomena of the AAP led by Arvind Kejriwal. The AAP has successfully decimated Congress in Delhi elections and has also succeeded in halting the march of the BJP to a thumping electoral victory. The AAP made tall claims during the hustings about maintaining equal distance from the old 'discredited' parties such as the Congress and the BJP. But the big question is: Will the AAP be able to hold on to its high moral ideals or will it eventually become like any other party in India?

Many questions and doubts have already been raised about the funding of this party especially those from foreign sources. A Public Interest Litigation (PIL) has been filed against the party over foreign money which it allegedly received during the elections. The election campaign organized by the AAP did not show that it was in any way short of financial resources.

It is very easy to oppose and criticize from the outside, but when a party is asked to participate in a legislative process, its negativism is bound to hurt it further. Every present leader of the AAP has come out of Anna Hazare's anti-corruption crusade and they have definitely left a mark in Delhi. But the party's expansion and extension into other states and metro cities over the long run is worth observing.

What is clear is that the Indian voter is actively participating in elections and major political parties will now have to fulfill the demands which a voter is placing before his elected representative. Where did Sheila Dikshit go wrong? Where did Ashok Gehlot go wrong? How did Shivraj Singh and Raman Singh get a renewed mandate for the third time? Is the AAP of crusaders a temporary political anomaly without any future or is it a wrecker of the established old parties? Is AAP also like other parties collecting funds for elections who, in return, oblige the donators as a quid pro quo? Will Modi carry the national mood during the Lok Sabha elections of 2014 or will Rahul succeed in meeting the tough challenge of RSS supported Modi and BJP? These and other questions are in the public domain and answers to them will determine the future direction of Indian politics of 2014.

newsyaps.com, 23-12-2013

CASTE POLITICS

Communists must Steer Clear of Caste Politics

An effective and viable socialist movement or political formation can play a significant role in correcting social imbalances of power which are found in every parliamentary democracy, be it in the West or in India. India-born English social critic RH Tawney in his classic, 'Acquisitive Society', had shown how the socialist movement introduces social equilibrium in a society of private property owners. If only the conservative centrist or extremist forces were allowed in the corridors of power, the social inequality created by these forces which own private property will definitely create a situation for social disorder.

India is not an exception to this general rule of democracies where a political force based on an ideological commitment to social equality plays a positive and substantial role in providing a human face to politics. The Communist Party of India was established in the 1920s but, in spite of its long history and splits, it has been confined to three States only: West Bengal, Kerala and Tripura. This has compelled the communists to critically examine their ideology and its application in the changing reality of a complex and contradictory society like that of India.

Such an exercise was undertaken by the CPI(M) at its central committee meeting held between January 17 and January 20 in Kolkata. The full text of the 65-page long resolution deserves to be critically scrutinised before it is placed for consideration at the party's 20th congress which will be held in April. The urgent need for a deep and detailed discussion on ideological and political issues has been strongly felt by the communists especially after they lost power in West Bengal, where it had been at helm of affairs for 34 years, and in Kerala where too they had a populist stronghold.

The critique of globalisation and the economic reforms introduced in 1991 on the principles of privatisation, deregulation and liberalisation, has highlighted the negative consequences of the present economic policies which have only served to intensify social inequality in India. This criticism must be a message to every political party that, if the growing social inequalities are not politically tackled, the mass of dissatisfied people will take to extremist political positions.

This fact, as it emerges from the CPI(M) resolution, is very well taken. India has indeed become a grossly unequal society—while a long list of billionaires are perched at the top, more than 500 million people continue to live in extreme poverty across the country. The conspicuous level of income inequality is most ironically visible when 'crorepatis' fighting State Assembly elections claim to represent the poor. The crux of the issue is that in such an unequal society the communists have to intervene and provide an effective alternative.

Of late, the communists also seem to have finally realised that the poor are exploited by the ruling parties based on their caste identities and loyalties. But they have not launched any mass struggle against such blatant casteism; instead, they have supported casteist parties and leaders. Unfortunately, caste-based politics has not only fragmented India's social fabric; it has strengthened caste consciousness among the masses so much so that the people look to their caste leaders as messiahs. The communists cannot eliminate caste-based discrimination unless they declare that they are opposed to all caste leaders and parties that promote caste.

If caste-based policies continue, then million of landless agricultural workers, marginal farmers, poor artisans and daily wage earners will never be able to get social justice. Caste in India is a divisive social phenomenon and it is impossible to organise the poor on any united platform if public goods are distributed on the basis of caste categories. For instance, the struggling female labour population deserve special welfare programmes designed to suit their needs but if all Government programmes are caste-based, then these working women are unfairly left out.

Ultimately, the alternative communist model of creating a society based on equal rights has to be fundamentally different from that envisioned by the likes of Samajwadi Party chief Mulayam Singh Yadav, Uttar Pradesh Chief Minister Mayawati or even Bihar Chief Minister Nitish Kumar.

If the communists have to provide an alternative to the Indian voters, it has to be built on secular strategies and not on the basis of regressive caste identities.

How else can India achieve its goals of equality without raising the masses' level of political consciousness? *The Pioneer, 17-02-2012*

Heart of Darkness in Country's Villages

Social philosophers such as the Victorian-era English art critic, John Ruskin, American author and poet Henry David Thoreau and Russian novelist Leo Tolstoy in the West and Mohandas Karamchand Gandhi in India not only rejected the emerging industrial society of their time, they also romanticised the seemingly simple social patterns of small rural communities. Indeed, Tolstoy and Gandhi not only found great bliss in the simplicity of human beings insulated from the evils of industrialisation that had grown roots in urban societies, they even set up farms (Tolstoy) and ashrams (Gandhi) where residents could live lives 'close to nature'.

Unfortunately, they were living in a utopian world. Unlike in the dreams of Tolstoy or Gandhi, the villages of India have been victims of social oppression and caste domination. They have also been exploited by a few powerful individuals or families. Indeed, social exclusion and deprivation are common to a majority of Indian villages.

A few concrete facts may be mentioned to substantiate the above argument. First, the prosperous farmers of Punjab inflict informally sanctioned punishments on farm labourers if the latter dare to raise their voice and make a demand, the legitimacy of which is determined only by the landowners.

In fact, according to news reports, earlier this month the Punjab Government had to hammer out a compromise in a village between upper caste landlords and Dalit labourers. The latter had endured a month-long social boycott and loss of work for demanding fair wages. This is a typical story representing the socio-economic reality of Indian villages.

Second, Bollywood actor Aamir Khan in the July 13 episode of his weekly TV programme, 'Satyamev Jayate', brought before the whole country the harrowing experiences of a poor Dalit girl whose struggle for education in Haryana should shock Indian society. This struggle is not confined only to Haryana. Across rural India, social segregation exists in schools and children grow up with bitter experiences of social discrimination.

Third, on July 10, a village panchayat in the Baghpat district of Uttar Pradesh ordered that women below the age of 40 cannot move outside the house unescorted. The diktat has effectively imprisoned the village's young women in their own homes. Similar orders regarding marriage and financial sanctions have also been issued by community leaders in the rural areas of Haryana and Rajasthan. India's legal and political system has unfortunately failed to deal with this tyrannical and coercive social order as much of the country's legislation is meant only to decorate the statute books.

The above illustrations are a guide to viewing the different realities of a diverse India where modern cities and towns co-exist with villages still stuck in the medieval ages. However, the social oppression prevalent in Indian villages cannot just be explained away by pinning the blame on the country's historical past. In recent times, history, particularly India's colonial history, has become a convenient whipping boy.

The fact is that the ugly social reality of rural India exists not only due to 5, 000 years of historical baggage but also because post-independence, political and social leaders by their many acts of omission and commission have perpetuated a system of oppression in rural India. Public policies like caste-based reservations in public and educational institutions have only served to institutionalise such a system.

Indeed, it is the political economy of post-independence India that is the main reason for the existence of a tyrannical authority structure in rural India. Today's politicians have failed to liberate the oppressed rural society because they have promoted social policies that simply cannot help bring the teeming millions of rural India out of their social darkness. *The Pioneer, 20-07-2012*

Riot Survivors: Victims Who Retain the Memory

An inter-religious violent conflict, commonly described as a communal riot, not only leads to killing of innocent men and women and destruction of property, it leads to flight of those targeted from their residence. They end up in so-called relief camps. It is not only that more than 45 Muslims were killed in the Muzaffarnagar and Shamli riots of September 8-10, 2013 in Uttar Pradesh, 70,000 residents of these riot affected areas are still living as "displaced" persons in "refugee camps" because they do not feel secure to return to their homes.

According to home minister Sushil Kumar Shinde, there have been 451 communal incidents this year already while the total count last year was 410. The "survivors" of communal riots are not only condemned to live with painful memories of the "dead" but also expected to struggle with their new status as displaced persons, something bound to "condition" their whole personality, attitude and ways of life.

Riot survivors are likely to develop negative attitudes towards society on the basis of their experiences. First, a section of "victim-survivors" are, on the basis of their own bitter experiences, likely to lose their confidence in the capacity of the Indian state to protect the life and property of religious minorities. The victims of riots spoke to PM Manmohan Singh and Sonia Gandhi, when they visited "refugee camps" on September 6 that "we pleaded for help but the police did not come. We had to flee ...."

Second, a section, at least, of aggrieved survivors can be persuaded to take the law into their own hands and act in a vengeful manner. These refugee camps can become a breeding ground for hostile sentiments among the victims. Third, a refuge camp may become a place for shared bitterness among the victims not only against the other religious community but also against the whole system of governance of a country. Rahul Gandhi was "admonished" by the Election Commission and leaders of many political parties when he stated at Muzzaffarnagar that Pakistan's ISI is in contact with angry Muslim victims of the riot. The fact is that the feelings of anger, hurt and humiliation among a section of survivors of communal riots can tempt some to fall prey to forces inimical to society.

Those killed are no more. Their memory survives. But can it be denied that the Students Islamic Movement of India or the Indian Mujahideen or other violent and religiously motivated groups have emerged on the Indian scene after the 1990s? The Ram-Janmabhumi movement, which led to the destruction of the Babri Mosque at Ayodhya on December 6, 1992 and the large-scale communal riots which took place in the country clearly divided Indian society. Can these contexts be ignored? Fourth, frequent inter-religious riots have led to the ghettoisation of targeted Muslim minorities, who seek security of life by living together. Why are the Muslims of Muzzaffarnagar not volunteering, inspite of financial compensation, to go back to their home and villages? The refugee camps are considered safe because the victimised religious community has developed a feeling of togetherness with their co-religionists.

The worst impact of frequent communal violence is that the victims passively accept that they are fated to live along with the Hindu majority as "second-class citizens". The survivors of such tragedies transmit their experiences of deprivation and dispossession to coming generations and the best evidence is provided by the post-Partition "refugee population" which still remains tied to the bitter memories of the post-1947 communal holocaust. The past continues to haunt and every repetition of the same experiences, if faced by a new generation, strengthens the feeling of difference and separateness among religious communities.

The anti-Sikh riots of 1984 in Delhi are still part of the memory of this community and Muslims of Gujarat continue to live under the impact of post-Godhra riots of 2002. Narendra Modi is identified by the Muslims with the riots of 2002. Why is Modi making extra efforts to mobilise Muslims for his election meetings? Because he wants to erase the bitter memories of the Muslims of Gujarat.

The upshot of the above narrative is clear: frequent occurrences of collective violence in a multi-religious society solidify feelings of otherness and separateness. This is the reason the short-and-long-term consequences of these bitter memories should not be ignored by the political leadership.

Economics Times, 06-12-2013

REGIONALISTS

Is Small Beautiful — Splitting Uttar Pradesh?

Mayawati, the most authentic leader of the Dalits of Uttar Pradesh, has thrown a political bombshell by asking for splitting the state. This announcement has set the cat among the pigeons and all her political opponents are confused, even politically paralysed, because they are not sure about the direction of public opinion on the issue of a four-fold division of Uttar Pradesh.

The real difficulty is faced by all-India parties like the Congress and the BJP because every specific demand for the creation of a new state like Telangana cannot be treated as an isolated demand since regionalists and sub-regionalist political formations in every state can also launch movements for such division of states to satisfy political ambitions of powerful local groups.

The Congress cannot open this Pandoras box because it will find it impossible to handle the conflicting demands of various segments demanding a state for themselves. But the point is that reorganisation of states is an integral part of the ongoing democratic process of India, even though regionalists and sub-regionalists are fighting for their little empires and only the Hindutva forces are ideologically committed to completely redrawing Indias map, with the RSS idea of Hindu, Hindi, Hindustan, and reduce cultural and language-based diverse states to the level of mere administrative units.

There is a need for close scrutiny of the functioning of new small states like Punjab, Haryana and Himachal Pradesh out of the reorganisation of united Punjab or states like Jharkhand, Chhattisgarh and Uttarakhand or the small states of Goa or Nagaland, Mizoram, Meghalaya, Manipur, Arunachal Pradesh and Tripura in north-east India. The new small states present a very mixed picture on the basis of their performance and actual governance. The six small states of northeast India are dependent on the central government for funding their developmental programmes due to their limited availability of resources. The central government has been continuously involved in resolving inter-state and intra-state disputes and social conflicts that have plagued these states.

The smaller size and minuscule political representation in the Lok Sabha makes these states develop a feeling of neglect and alienation from the mainstream. The idea of small states is, in practice, full of problems as revealed by these six states of the northeast. Further, within the state assemblies of these states, floor-crossing and defections are quite common. Thus, limited representation of small states in the Lok Sabha acts as a handicap for them at the centre of power, and within the state assembly, with a smaller number of MLAs, governments can be destabilised easily. The BJP, on its part, has to answer about the actual functioning of three new states created in 2008 because the mining mafia in Jharkhand has been patronised by leaders of new states like Shibu Soren or the Mundas. The small states have not at all been models of good governance and their performance is comparable to the mother states from which they were separated.

The new states have been created in regions where a strong cultural or linguistic bond did not exist among the majority of inhabitants of that state. Dravidian cultural ties are a uniting factor among Tamilians or Kannadigas; cultural affinity among the people of Karnataka or the Malayali cultural reference point for Kerala keeps them united and the demand for separation has not been raised by any powerful section in these three states. The Punjabi language and culture is a cementing factor in keeping Punjab united but Hindi has lost its cultural vigour and people of the Hindi states do not consider language-based culture a uniting factor. Hence, strong cultural and linguistic affinity acts as a brake against separatist demands. It is appropriate to conclude with a reference to the seminal work of Robert Dahl, Democracy and Size, in which he conclusively proves that development, democracy and good governance are size neutral, and big or small hardly make a difference. This important argument is valid for all societies. A functional system of governance in every country should reflect the specific social realities. Therefore, Indias requirements can be met only if a political system is able to harmonise and accommodate the needs and aspirations of multiple diverse cultural communities.

The unifying democratic, secular and federal central government is needed to keep such a diverse society united, and a balance or an equilibrium can be achieved by creating federal units not because small parties have demanded small states, but by evolving a political mechanism of arriving at a consensus on the need for a new small state. Leaders of small parties like Nitish Kumar or Ajit Singh have welcomed Mayawatis announcement, but such demands are reflective of the desire of small party leaders to hold on to power in their areas of influence. *The Economic Times 26-11-2011*

On Terrorism (NCTC) and Federalism

The central government has proposed a National Counter-Terrorism Centre (NCTC) for pan-India coordination of intelligence agencies with a view to effectively deal with externally exported or internally-organised terrorist activities. This announcement created a storm in many states, led by either the opposition parties or even alliance partners of the Manmohan Singh government, as they think the NCTC is violative of the Constitution and an infringement of their constitutional responsibility for maintenance of law and order. The Constitution, in Part XI dealing with Relations between the Union and the States, clearly defines the Distribution of Legislative Powers and Administrative Relations, and if these articles of the Constitution from 245 to 261 are read along with Article 355—which says that it is the duty of the Union to protect the states against external aggression and internal disturbance—then, in constitutional letter and spirit, it is quite clear that the maintenance of law and order is the shared responsibility of the Centre and state governments.

All-India and regional parties have always treated terrorism as a national challenge and that is why Parliament, with the support of all parties, has approved laws like the Prevention of Terrorist Act (POTA) and the Unlawful Activities (Prevention) Act. State governments have also enacted laws like the Maharashtra Control of Organised Crime Act (MCOCA) for dealing with issues concerning internal security and the Delhi government has also exercised powers of detention by applying MCOCA provisions to deal with criminals. Political parties have always supported, without taking refuge behind federal principles, the creation of special agencies like the NIA and NSG.

States have also often asked the central government to deploy CRPF or BSF or other armed forces while dealing with problems or insurgencies in their areas. State governments have actively supported the idea of the National Intelligence Grid (NATGrid).

If the CMs maintain that maintenance of law and order lies in their jurisdiction, and there should not be any infringement by the central government, they should support the demand of Omar Abdullah to withdraw the extraordinary AFSPA. The 'federalists' should be consistent and also oppose the Combat Battalion for Resolute Action (CoBRA), which was created by the Centre in 2008 for anti-Maoist operations.

The point is that every political formation, national or regional, right from August 15, 1947, has supported and approved the making of extraordinary laws for tackling gun-wielding social and political groups that have challenged the authority of the Indian state. Aren't even state assembly elections held with the assistance of central paramilitary forces? Why can't these champions of federal autonomy organise assembly elections with the support of their own police machinery?

Actually, the issue raised by CMs goes beyond constitutional and legal technicalities concerning the jurisdictional sphere of central or state governments.

It has been suggested by civil liberty groups and intellectuals that India is governed by implementing extraordinary draconian laws with the help of police and armed forces for dealing with domestic social problems that are the product of social injustice. On the face of it, India looks like a very strong nuclear and military state. But isn't it surprising that the world's fourthlargest military power, with additional million-strong paramilitary armed forces, is not able to tackle its alienated, deprived and marginalised groups who have taken to arms against their own state? Why is it that the champions of federalism actively support massive modernisation programme of security forces fighting Leftextremist-Maoist groups? The argument that the central government has violated the essentials of Indian federalism by encroaching on the jurisdiction of states by establishing a supra counter-terrorism centre seems spurious after looking at the record of political parties, central and state governments during the last 63 years. The central and state governments have always coordinated and cooperated for tackling extraordinary challenges to the security and integrity of the country—be it buttressing armed forces or bringing in a plethora of special laws and Acts.

Now, political points are being scored with a view to corner the United Progressive Alliance government so that the new Budget session of the Lok Sabha is made dysfunctional, as it has been happening from 2009.

This, simply put, is the BJP's game-plan, and there is absolutely no substance in the controversy around the NCTC if every political party accepts that 'terrorism' is a national security concern.

The Economics Times, 25-02-2012

Bipolar Politics Leads to Stable Regimes

The current political trend in India is that, while the Union Government has become a multi-polar body, politics in the States has become largely bipolar. Power rotates between two major political parties, such as the BJP and the Congress, or between two regional parties. An interesting consequence of this emerging trend of 'bipolarity' is that the Governments in these States have become relatively stable.

If the State Governments are stable because of bipolar politics, the Union Government has become weak due to the inherent competitiveness of coalition partners, who often come together to form a Government without any agreement on the fundamentals of public policy. The minor political allies in a coalition Government soon begin to feel threatened by the largest single party which leads the coalition.

It is interesting to observe how the phenomenon of bipolarity has played out in Uttar Pradesh. In the 2007 State Assembly election, the verdict was clearly in favour of the Bahujan Samaj Party, which secured 206 seats out of 403. That year, the BSP had defeated its main opponent, the Samajwadi Party, which had won the previous election in 2002. Eventually, the SP also regained its 2002 electoral position in 2012 when it captured 224 of the Assembly seats. It is interesting to note that, while in Uttar Pradesh there are several players such as the Congress, the BJP and many smaller parties, it is only the dynamics between the SP and the BSP that determine the State's power equation.

However, it must be mentioned that this is not an entirely new political phenomenon; on the contrary, it has been in the works since the 1980s when parties opposing the domination of the Congress had begun to seek their own political identity. The process has now culminated in the kind of bipolar politics that we see in certain States.

In Uttar Pradesh, for instance, the battle is between Mulayam Singh Yadav (and now his son and Chief Minister Akhilesh Yadav) of the SP and Mayawati of the BSP. While the latter is the unquestioned leader of the backward castes peasantry, the latter commands the Dalit vote-bank. As for the upper castes—the Brahmins, the Thakurs and the Rajputs—they must fall in line either with Mayawati's Dalit politics or Yadav's backward caste politics.

Ms Mayawati, especially, provides for an interesting study. On the instructions of her mentor Kanshi Ram, she has practiced a political strategy that has led to the gradual consolidation of her Dalit vote-bank without it being related in any way to the stability of her Government or alliance. This strategy has served her well. In the State Assembly election of 1993, the BSP secured 11.12 per cent of the total votes; the number increased to 19.64 per cent in 996 and 23.06 per cent in 2002. The crowning glory was in 2007 when her party secured 30.43 per cent share in 2007. The figure came down only marginally in 2012 when the BSP won 25.91 per cent of the votes.

It must be mentioned that Mayawati scripted this Dalit success story in an extremely casteist and hostile Uttar Pradesh, where not only did the upper castes not accept the Dalits, even non-Dalit backward caste peasantry was at odds with Dalit community. Initially, the Congress had created a political platform based on a coalition of upper caste Hindus, Muslim-minorities and Dalit voters and it had served the party well for many years during which it held sway over the State. Post-Emergency, however, the middle caste peasantry became stronger under the leadership of Charan Singh, who actively challenged upper caste domination. The Mayawati-Dalit phenomenon emerged later in 1993 when the BSP made its presence significantly felt for the very first time in the State.

The process of bipolarism has now taken concrete shape. The electoral defeat of such leaders does not signal the end of their political career, mostly because their social vote-bank is intact—and hence, the politics of caste-appeasement shall continue.

Little else explains why Akhilesh Yadav, soon after taking over as Chief Minister, has changed the names of Government schemes launched by the Mayawati Government in a manner that is designed to please his backward caste voters. Furthermore, he has also 'scrapped' Dalit quota system in Government contracts which Mayawati had initiated. On her part, Mayawati has expectedly lambasted the incumbent Government for its 'anti-Dalit' stance.

Clearly, a grand social experiment is underway in Uttar Pradesh. Mayawati had played her cards well in 2007 when she stitched together her rainbow coalition that won her the election then but failed to stand the test of time. Now, it is Akhilesh Yadav's turn to make a move. *Pioneer, 25-05-2012*

Nitish: Call for Public Debate on PM Candidate of the NDA

It is irrelevant to focus attention on Nitish Kumar's political calculations while diagnosing the real significance of his statement that the BJP, as the largest group of the NDA, should declare its PM candidate for the Lok Sabha elections of 2014. Kumar further observed that "the leader of the coalition should have secular credentials and a liberal frame of mind". Kumar set the cat among the pigeons of the RSS-led Sangh Parivar who, according to their well-practised strategy, tried to camouflage the issue, and no less a person than RSS chief Mohan Bhagwat jumped into this public debate saying Hinduism is an 'all-inclusive' Rashtravad and asked why a Hindutvavadi 'should not become PM'.

Nitish Kumar, an unconscious tool of history, has again brought into the public domain the issue of secularism versus religion-based politics of the communal-fascist Sangh Parivar. It needs to be emphasised that while Indian Constitution-makers provided for the basic structure of a democratic secular republic, the idea of secularism for a plural society has been strongly opposed by the practitioners of the idea of 'Hindu nationhood'. The latter preach and practice the ideology of an exclusivist idea of India as a home for only Hindus, and for the Sangh Parivar, politics is an instrument to capture power for the purpose of establishing Hindu Raj. The ideology of Hindu Rashtravadis, whose political platform is the BJP, or the erstwhile Jan Sangh, is inseparable.

What has been the record of secular formations in their approach to the politics of the BJP? The BJP share of the average national vote for the Lok Sabhas during the last 14 years has been only 22. 58 per cent. The party on its own obtained only 23. 75 per cent of votes in 1998 and 1999, and despite its low electoral performance, it formed a coalition government at the Centre from 1998 to 2004 with the support of 24 parties and small groups. Its electoral performance shows it can never form a government on its own at the Centre and the reason is quite clear: its mythical Hindu majority voter does not exist, and except natural allies like the Akali Dal and Shiv Sena, it can control power at the Centre only with the support of non-Congress, non-Communist regional/ sub-regional so-called secular groups. In fact, the BJP has been always a beneficiary of opportunistic and non-ideological politics of 'secular' political formations.

The Jan Sangh, with 85 Lok Sabha members, was the single-largest bloc in the Janata formation of 1977-79. L K Advani as I&B minister in the Morarji Desai government succeeded in placing RSS activists or sympathisers in the print media. The regional media, especially of the large Hindi-speaking states, was also successfully targeted by the Jan Sangh/RSS via L K Advani. Second, V P Singh became PM from 1989 to 1990 on the basis of 'outside' active support of the BJP and the communists. Jagmohan was appointed Governor of the disturbed state of J&K by V P Singh on the recommendation of L K Advani. Jagmohan's tenure as Governor of that state attracted adverse comments as he was perceived as a promoter of a Hindu agenda in that troubled state. Third, the post-Godhra massacres of about 2,000 innocent Muslims could take place in 2002 only because the anti-Muslim Narendra Modi of the BJP was the CM.

Murli Manohar Joshi as minister of education in the Vajpayee government, in a single-handed manner not only placed Hindu ideologues in positions of decision-making in educational institutions, but under his directions, textbooks were completely rewritten with a distorted Hindutva perspective of history. The Vajpayee government also appointed a so-called Constitution Review Commission to suggest its revision, obviously keeping in mind the philosophy of a Hindu state as defined by Golwalkar. The then-President K R Narayanan warned against this tinkering of the Constitution by the Sangh Parivar, and the whole machine of the RSS campaigned against Narayanan for being an 'activist' President.

It is time to call the bluff and tear the mask off Nitish's face because he is pretending to form a future coalition government with a 'secular and liberal' leader of the Sangh Parivar while conveniently forgetting that Pracharaks like Vajpayee, Advani, Murli Manohar Joshi, Rajnath Singh or Nitin Gadkari are all products of the training school of fundamentalist Hindutva. Secular pretenders who have closely worked with the governments of the Sangh Parivar leaders are suffering from the same confusion that Hitler exploited to come to power because German socialist and communist parties could not make up their mind about the reality of Nazism and Hitler.

Nitish Kumar's desire to see a 'liberal and secular' face of the BJP is the pipe dream of a confused leader. The choice before all political actors is clear and Nitish, unwittingly, has asked every political formation to choose between secular nationalism or the Parivar's sectarian and exclusivist Hindu Rashtravad.

The Economic Times, 23-06-2012

In 2012, Uttar Pradesh Still Stuck in Time Warp

In the medieval ages, conquering armies would routinely destroy temples, mosques and churches to celebrate their victory at war. That was a dark phase in the history of human civilisation and it was spread across the world from Europe to Arabia to Asia. Unfortunately, the atrocious acts of that dark age are now being repeated in modern day India. Last month, miscreants belonging to Other Backward Castes smashed the statue of Dalit leader Mayawati in the capital of Uttar Pradesh on July 26 and then also vandalised the statue of BR Ambedkar, another Dalit leader, in Azamgarh.

With such acts, the OBCs announced their return to the power seat of Uttar Pradesh following the victory of the Yadav-led Samajwadi Party in the State Assembly election held early this year. Like the feudal chiefs of the medieval ages, the OBC miscreants celebrated their 'victory' by publicly humiliating Dalit leaders.

A deeper analysis of the politics and society of Uttar Pradesh is needed to bring out the implication of the vandalism of the statues of Mayawati and Ambedkar. The most important observation in this regard is that the political leaders of Uttar Pradesh are blind to the fact that India is an integral part of the ongoing historical processes of the 21st century, and they cannot turn their back on the new agenda of growth and development that this new century demands.

Self-appointed political analysts may claim that Uttar Pradesh is changing fast because a society that is on the path of transition has a high level of electoral participation—as is the case in India's most populated State. The underlying argument here is that voters have become aware of their problems and hence, are looking to the ballot to make themselves heard and persuade their leaders to better respond to their concerns.

It has also been suggested by analysts that unlike in the States of Odisha, Chhattisgarh and Jharkhand, the Maoist movement has not grown roots in Uttar Pradesh. This, they argue, is because the people have successfully negotiated their problems with the Government through political parties and civil society groups. Unfortunately, almost all of this is wishful thinking based on a superficial study of electoral data.

To truly understand the complex socio-political scheme of Uttar Pradesh, one must ask some key questions: Have the political leaders of the State evolved a new model of politics that can pull out the society from centuries-old social, cultural and economic backwardness? Have they shown any inclination to learn lessons from other countries and or even from other States within India regarding new and effective strategies of economic growth? The answer to both these questions is a resounding no. In fact, there is no evidence whatsoever that the leaders of Uttar Pradesh have any ideas to pull the State out of the medieval morass in which it has been stuck for centuries.

Instead, political parties in Uttar Pradesh continue to engage in practices that are supposed to provide growth opportunities to those castes which were denied these in the past but in reality only perpetuate the evils of caste-based, vote-bank politics. This is ironical. If indeed the caste system as it exists today was the primary reason for Uttar Pradesh's backwardness, then that State's leaders should have worked to dismantle the caste structure and liberate society. Instead, they have strengthened and institutionalised the caste system. This acts as a road block in bringing changes in society.

Also, the political reality of Uttar Pradesh is that all of the State's major parties work within clearly defined boundaries of caste and community. In fact, the entire political narrative of Uttar Pradesh can be summed up in the phrase: Caste versus caste. Consequently, every leader of the State is engaged in building up his or her specific caste-based constituency. In other words, they have no time (or the need) to think of alternative political models that will make the State a better place for its people. *The Pioneer, 03-08-2012*

The Three Musketeers of Indian Politics— Mamata Banerjee, Mayawati and Mulayam Singh Yadav

Mamata Banerjee of the Trinamool Congress in West Bengal, Mayawati of the Bahujan Samaj Party in Uttar Pradesh and Mulayam Singh Yadav of the Samajwadi Party, also from Uttar Pradesh, have one thing in common: Their naked quest for power without any ideological constraints that would require them to take a principled stand on any public issue of significance to the people. But they also share other characteristics.

First, all three leaders have emerged as serious players only in the era of coalition Governments. Second, they all lead 'personality-based' political parties which operate as their personal fiefdoms. Here, party bosses do not permit any dissenting voice. Third, these three leaders have mobilised specific parts of society in their favour, and it is on the basis of support from these constituencies that they have emerged as strong leaders. Banerjee has built a rural support base in West Bengal, Mayawati is the undisputed leader of the Dalits in Uttar Pradesh and Yadav, the unchallenged representative of the Other Backward Castes of Uttar Pradesh.

Fourth, both Bengal and Uttar Pradesh have a sizable Muslim minority population—and all three leaders portray themselves as protectors of that community's interest. But their approach is guided by purely tactical electoral calculations. They all wear a shapeless secular hat but still never hesitate to join hands with blatantly communal outfits. Fifth, all three are willing to practise every trick of the trade to win an election. For example, they spend vast amounts of money during elections and then for the rest of their tenure work to earn back that spent amount. Finally, all three leaders aspire to play a critical role in the Union Government.

Since 1989, it has been a trend in Indian politics that prior to any Lok Sabha election there will be talk of a so-called non-Congress, non-BJP Third Front. This happened on the eve of the 2009 Lok Sabha election when Mayawati suddenly annou-nced her candidature for prime ministership of the Third Front. Similarly, during his party's national executive meet held in Kolkata in early September, Yadav observed that he had a "natural ambition" to be Prime Minister. Banerjee on the other hand is consumed with ambition, as one look at her electoral record will show.

She lost the election in 2001 but swept the State Assembly election in 2011. The Lok Sabha election of 2004 had returned only one MP for the TMC but in the 2009 election, the TMC won 19 Lok Sabha seats.

It is worthwhile to mention that Banerjee has always joined the Union Government with the threat of resignation in her pocket. Former Prime Minister PV Narasimha Rao made her the Sports Minister, but she led a demonstration in Kolkata in 1993 alleging that she had been ignored in decision making. Martyrdom is her public face. Similarly, Atal Bihari Vajpayee and George Fernandes had to visit Kolkata to persuade her to rejoin the NDA Government from which she had resigned on the pretext of the Tehelka expose. Manmohan Singh and Sonia Gandhi faced this again when Banerjee resigned for the 'cause' of aam aadmi on September 18 to protest against anti-people policies announced by the UPA2 Government.

The point here is that these three regional leaders are playing a game of chess on the basis of opportunism and self-promotion. Supporters of regionalism in Indian politics should learn lesson from this. Regionalists have an electoral mandate for their State alone.

But to make them national political players is to invite disaster for the country. Yadav's record as Union Defence Minister in a coalition Government

at the Centre and Banerjee's management of railways are good examples of why regional bosses should be kept miles away from the national centre.
The Pioneer, 28-09-2012

Whither Communists—CPI, CPI(M), CPI(ML)

It has been maintained that in modern history, a pro-people party plays a critical and crucial role in a society where millions live below the poverty line. Communist theoreticians and leaders understand that successful struggles can be launched in a society of serious structural inequalities. So, why are the Indian communists a marginal political force in India where all the prerequisites for social struggles against mass poverty and great inequality are to be found across the country Further, why are the communists fragmented despite the fact that parties like CPI, CPI (M), CPI(ML) and Maoists claim loyalty to the same ideology of establishing an equal society It is worthwhile to examine the causes for the marginalisation of communist movements in societies supposedly conducive for such movements.

History shows that parties can be forgotten because major social constituencies shift away from an ideology if their changing socially-felt needs are not responded to. This happened after the fall of the Berlin Wall in 1989 and the collapse of the socialist state system of the USSR in 1990, when European communist parties felt the impact of this ideological earthquake. Not only did communist parties in Europe break away from their past, they renamed themselves as socialist parties. And the best example of continuing relevance of new socialism is the French Socialist. Ideological adaptation to the changing political situation has helped French Socialists to continue to struggle for the cause of the working classes and the lower middle class, and it has even won electoral victories. In Asia, even the Communist Party of China gradually abandoned its rigidities. The rise of the Chinese economy thereafter is a well-known story.

Indian communists too face new social situations and challenges. And without broadening their social base by winning over new constituencies, they cannot face these challenges. One reason for the reduced space for Indian communists is the emergence of a new, mobile middle class for whom communist party programmes do not seem relevant. The fact is that communists always had an important base in the socially-progressive and enlightened sections of the middle classes, but the new middle class seems alienated, even hostile to communist ideology. Communists seem to have abandoned this new powerful social constituency because every felt technological, and new, need of this class is always opposed by the communists.

A pro-people movement can be rejuvenated by attracting factions of professional and middle classes if some of the demands of different strata are included in the agenda of party programmes. Also, the communist movement in India cannot become viable and relevant without closely scrutinising the popular base of the elected political executive. Governments and coalitions at the Centre and a large number of states are following an economic policy based on the model of growth and development legitimised by almost all other parties by claiming a link between the rate of growth and availability of huge public resources being spent on social welfare programmes.

This rapid proliferation of welfare programmes for the aam aadmi, especially the underclasses and deprived, has become a reality because the high rate of growth has made it possible to make huge investments in public spending for the poor. Every party in a highly competitive electoral system based on universal adult franchise has to win an election, and for obtaining the mandate of the voter, every party has to win over popular social constituencies, which means that social welfarism is an essential part of governance in democracy.

Then, the communists in India have not been able to form a united front or a coalition of the oppressed classes because every political party has created a solid social constituency by following a policy of reservations in public services and institutions. Thus, society has consolidated into castes and sub-castes and parties and governments take special care of caste interests to win elections. Communists have become irrelevant because fragmented castes have their own specific caste-based parties, groups and leaders, and communists cannot compete on the basis of caste-based appeals as India has authentic caste leaders like Mayawati, Mulayam Singh, Lalu Prasad and Ramvilas *et al.*

The communists have failed to create new progressive levels of social consciousness among the struggling masses who are assured of some public benefits on the basis of their caste identity by other parties. Can communists support the march of casteism and be seen in the company of caste and communal elements and still hope to be the party of the poor and deprived This is the crux of the issue. The rules have fragmented the poor completely and the communists have been party to it. *Economics Times, 05-10-2012*

Militants should not be Treated as Martyrs

The murderous attack on retired Lieutenant-General KS Brar on October 1 in London was undoubtedly in retaliation for his leading role in Operation Blue Star that was carried out on June 6, 1984 to flush out militants, holed up inside the Golden Temple in Amritsar. It proves once again that Khalistani militant groups are still active. Occasionally, they have even succeeded in eliminating their targets who they consider to be enemies of the Khalsa Panth.

Lt Gen Brar has rightly blamed the Akali Dal's religion-based politics, which has been responsible for the disturbed conditions in Punjab, including brutal militancy of the 1980s. The root cause of all problems faced by the

Sikh community in Punjab is the manipulative politics of the Akali Dal which builds on the 'danger to Khalsa Panth' slogan.

A few facts may be mentioned to substantiate the argument that the Akalis have divided Punjabi society on the basis of religion-based identity for political purposes. First, the likes of Gurcharan Singh Tohra, Jathedar Jagdev Singh Talwandi, Sant Longowal and Parkash Singh Badal have been known to manipulate gurdwara politics to gain political mileage.

Second, the theocratic character of Akali politics is revealed clearly when elections are held to the Shiromani Gurdwara Parbandhak Committee. An Akali leader becomes a powerful politician only if he can control the SGPC and the high priests of the Golden Temple. Every Akali politician has exercised power over the Sikh community by asking his nominees, the high priests, to issuehukamnamas to ex-communicate any dissident political leader from the Sangat.

Third, the Akali Dal-led Punjab Government not only asked the Union Government on March 30 to show 'mercy' to Balwant Singh, the killer of former Punjab Chief Minister Beant Singh, but also created an anti-Centre atmosphere among the Sikhs of Punjab on this issue. Beant Singh was also a Sikh but the Akali Dal, which is supposed to ameliorate the grievances of the Sikh community, has nothing to say about the former Chief Minister's assassination. Also, these self-appointed defenders of Sikh maryada never condemned the killing of DIG Avtar Singh Atwal who was killed in 1983 while leaving the Golden Temple.

Fourth, if Jarnail Singh Bhindranwale of Damdami Taksal is guilty of many of the ugly events linked to the militancy of the 1980s, the Akalis also have to take the blame for the killing of thousands of innocents at the hands of Khalistani militants. No Akali leader has ever stood up against those killers. The Akali Dal's religion-based politics is dangerous. By playing on the religious sentiments of innocent Sikhs, the Akalis have encouraged violence against Nirankari Sikhs and Deras in Punjab.

The Akalis cannot survive in politics without raising emotive issues concerning the Sikh community. Hence, it comes as no surprise that they have permitted the construction of a memorial within the Golden Temple in honour of the terrorists killed in Operation Blue Star. Does one need any other evidence to substantiate the argument that the Akali Dal has always played and will continue to play the religion card in politics?

Chief Minister Parkash Singh Badal has many questions to answer about this role during the 1980's militancy period, and it is ironical that, today as Punjab Chief Minister he himself is legitimising those terrorists as martyrs. The construction of a martyr's monument with the full support of the Badal Government should ring alarm bells. If Khalistani terrorists of yesterday are portrayed as martyrs today, they can become a rallying point for future separatist movements.

Also, this glorification of terrorists sends out a wrong message to security force personnel who risk their lives to protect the country. But why is there this conspiracy of silence in favour of the Khalistani militants by the political class? It appears that vote-banks alone matter. *The Pioneer, 12-10-2012*

A Telangana Territorial Administration?

The argument in defence of small states is that these sub-regions, which have remained underdeveloped as part of large states, can tackle developmental issues better. Hence the argument that size matters and small states can focus their attention on development because they are nearer to the people. So the agitation for Telangana. However, in spite of six options given by the Justice Srikrishna Commission, which was set up to look into the Telangana tangle, the Centre has not been able to arrive at any conclusive decision.

The Constitution-makers had made elaborate provisions for dealing with such sub-regional demands by laying down a provision for the establishment of territorial administration without partitioning a state, and this provision has been in operation in Bodoland, Gorkhaland et al. A Telangana Territorial Administration can be set up with 'special status' for 10 backward districts of the region.

A few things must be pointed out. First, small states with 80-100 MLAs have a history of political instability because the defection of a few MLAs can bring down the government. The relatively new small state of Haryana, created in 1966, had gained notoriety for practising the 'politics of Aya Ram-Gaya Ram' (here today, gone tomorrow).

The latest to join the ranks of unstable states is Jharkhand. The state has experienced President's rule three times and eight governments have been formed in the state during the 12 years of its existence and the President had to suspend the assembly on January 18.

Second, the assertion that small states can manage development challenges better than large ones has not been substantiated. In the age of globalisation, every chief minister is competing for investment, and in this atmosphere of competition, the size of a state does not have any special advantage. The best illustration of the fact that investments flow in only if investors are given special incentives and the size of the state is not relevant was proved on January 11 at the sixth bi-annual Vibrant Gujarat Summit. Hence, a separate state of Telangana is not at all on the agenda of investors and solutions to regional backwardness can be found only within the existing state boundaries.

Third, it is not far-fetched to state that the proposed bifurcation of Andhra Pradesh is a signal to many other local regional bosses to spearhead similar movements. Is India prepared for violent, parochial and subregional movements manipulated by local powerbrokers? Has Maoism ended with the creation of a Chhattisgarh or a Jharkhand?

It is also a tall, even fallacious, argument that democracy will be deepened by creating small states. None of the small states has practised any new model of democracy different from the all-India democratic political system.

The Congress, as an inheritor of Nehru's legacy, should tread very cautiously because the former prime minister's experience with the states' re-organisation, beginning in 1956, was not at all happy and he had witnessed emotive, competitive and even violent, regional and sub-regional struggles for the creation of new states. This history is likely to repeat itself. Further, the Congress should also know that its real ideological antagonist and adversary, the BJP, does not believe in linguistic-cultural diversity and plurality of India and the Sangh parivar wants 50 or more 'administrative units' to be established. MS Golwalkar, the guru of the RSS, had stated in 1948 that India should have a centralised, presidential system with 'administrative units' for maintaining and defending the unity and territorial integrity of the whole Hindu rashtra.

The choice before the country is between Nehru's pluralist, secular and federal democracy or Golwalkar and his disciples' idea of a Hindu India where regional and 'sub-regional' autonomies will be a thing of the past.

Hindustran Times, 04-02-2013

Akhilesh Yadav: UP's Night Watchman

Recently, Akhilesh Yadav, the Chief Minister of Uttar Pradesh, completed his first year in office. His record of governance is for everyone to see. In this past year, Uttar Pradesh has experienced a rise in lawlessness and criminal activity, just as it had done between 2002 and 2007 when his father Mulayam Singh Yadav was the Chief Minister. In fact, the senior Yadav was defeated in 2007 by rival Mayawati after she promised to end the '*goonda raj*' of his Samajwadi Party. One would have expected the younger Yadav to learn from his father's mistakes, and make he deliverance of good governance his top priority.

The senior Yadav has himself acknowledged the failure and asked his son to act tough. But he and others too must recognise the fact that the young Chief Minister has inherited a deeply entrenched culture of criminals in politics. It is also expected of him to continue with that culture and accommodate the criminal comrades of his father as MLAs and Ministers. In other words, the shadow of his father's past continues to haunt the Chief Minister.

Yadav must do the bidding of his father and uncles so as to keep the 'Samajwadis' together for the 2014 poll. He is the so-called 'night watchman' for his father. How else does one explain the induction of the likes of Raja Bhaiyya in the State Cabinet? Mulayam Singh Yadav has to keep each one of his well-known musclemen, including influential criminals, in good humour for the forthcoming Lok Sabha election in 2014, which is essentially his last chance to make a mark at the national level.

Take, for example, Azam Khan, who is the de facto leader of the Samajwadi Party's Muslim constituency. He exercises his own authority which is not in consultation with the Chief Minister, but with his party chief. Mulayam Singh Yadav is the real court of appeal when, for instance, Muslim leaders in his party engage in many factional battles.

Similarly, look at what happened when Union Minister Beni Prasad Verma annoyed Mulayam Singh Yadav by casting aspersions against him. The parliamentary board of the Samajwadi Party agreed that'Netaji' will decide on how best to tackle the situation created by Verma. 'Netaji' responded by serving a notice to Prime Minister Manmohan Singh and UPA chairperson Sonia Gandhi to either 'discipline' Verma or face the consequences. Clearly, the Samajwadi Party, like almost every other regional party in India, is run as the personal fiefdom of its party chief.

Given that Akhilesh Yadav is just a proxy for his father, it comes as no surprise then that following Mulayam Singh Yadav's advice, the Chief Minister has now sought to actively mobilise foreign capital for the development of Uttar Pradesh. Of course, it is too much to expect from phoney socialists like Mulayam Singh Yadav to project an alternative model for economic development which is different from that of the Prime Minister's model of privatisation, deregulation and globalisation which has led to a complete dependence on foreign investment.

Hence, Akhilesh Yadav is simply imitating Singh's economic model. On March 12, he met World Bank chief Jim Yong Kim and sought assistance of over US$ 3.5 billion for the next three to four years. This was followed by another meeting of the Chief Minister with the head honchos of 39 US companies on March 13.

Will this economic model help deal with the backwardness of India's largest State? Uttar Pradesh is primarily an agrarian society and lacks even basic infrastructure for both industrial and agricultural development. But do the politicians really care? *The Pioneer, 28-03-2013*

Mulayam Singh Yadav—Not Tall Enough for the Prime Minister's Chair

Mulayam Singh Yadav is no doubt a powerful leader with much popular support. But his decades-long political career, during the course of which he failed to develop his State, is proof of why he's not fit to lead the country.

For a seasoned leader like Mulayam Singh Yadav, it is perfectly legitimate to eye the highest office of the country. After all, why should a tall leader like the Samajwadi Party supremo only play king-maker when he can well be in the race to be king himself? Besides, if the likes of VP Singh, Chandra Shekhar,

HD Deve Gowda or even Inder Kumar Gujral—none of them grassroots leaders—could occupy the Prime Minister's position, Yadav with his mass support base can surely aspire for the top job. So, it comes as no surprise that he is now aiming to win a sizeable number of seats in the 2014 Lok Sabha election. (Yadav is working on the premise that he will be a force to be reckoned with, if his party gets 40 to 50 out of the 80 Lok Sabha seats in Uttar Pradesh.)

In fact, it is keeping exactly this aim in mind that the three-time-Chief Minister of Uttar Pradesh, has now handed over the reins of the State to his son after the Samajwadi Party won the 2012 State Assembly election. Also, Yadav has ensured that his family members are all accommodated in positions of power. Finally, given his dynastic control over the Samajwadi Party organisation, there is no question of him facing challenges from within his party. This provides him with the conducive environment he needs to prepare for the forthcoming Lok Sabha election—and Yadav is already taking several steps towards that end.

First, the Samajwadi Party has begun to somewhat distance itself from the UPA regime, after having consistently supported the Congress-led coalition Government at the Centre (even if from outside) for the past nine years. In fact, the party's support has been crucial for both terms of the Manmohan Singh-led UPA regime, which, for instance, would have definitely collapsed in 2008 when the Left withdrew its support from the Government. So, why did this faithful supporter refuse to show solidarity with the regime on its ninth anniversary last month? The answer is simple. Yadav is now placing himself as a challenger to the Congress and, therefore, neither does he want to associate himself with his competitor nor save the tottering Government that it leads.

Second, Yadav is now actively building a coalition with the Brahmins and other high caste communities. It is because of this that his Chief Minister son recently announced at a Brahminsammelan that, "It is the samaj (society) which will ultimately decide who forms the Government". The reference here is clearly to the 'Brahmin Samaj's' support to the Samajwadi Party which is essential for an electoral victory. Yadav is well aware that even though he defeated Mayawati of the Bahujan Samajwadi Party in 2012, she can always script a comeback by creating another rainbow coalition that will have her formidable Dalit vote-bank on one end and Brahmins on the other.

Third, Yadav continues to pander to the Muslim constituency, his favourite hunting ground for votes. He has, of course, already surrounded himself with Muslim leaders like Azam Khan and the Shahi Imam of Jama Masjid, and now wishes to win over Muslim voters by championing the cause of reservations for them in public institutions.

The larger issue, however, is that Yadav does not have any plan for the development of either his State or the country. Today, his son maybe negotiating with foreign investors but that alone cannot lead to development in Uttar Pradesh. The fact is that the State has missed the bus to modernisation and progress, and Yadav cannot say that he is not responsible for it. Ultimately, the fact remains that Yadav does not have what it takes to lead the country.

The Pioneer, *07-06-2013*

J. Jayalalithaa, Mayawati and Mamata Banerjee—The Three Musketeers of Indian Politics

J. Jayalalithaa, Mayawati and Mamata Banerjee are all self-made female politicians who have broken the glass ceiling in a male-dominated field. Their success as leaders and rise to power as heads of State are testimony to the health of Indian democracy.

On the basis of their own abilities, Mayawati, Mamata Banerjee and J Jayalalithaa have emerged as formidable regional leaders in a patriarchal society where political and leadership spaces have always been monopolised by men. This does not mean that there were no women politicians before them, but it is just that they rarely occupied top positions either within their party or the Government. But these three women have broken that glass ceiling—Mayawati heads the Bahujan Samaj Party and has served four terms as Chief Minister of Uttar Pradesh, Banerjee leads the Trinamool Congress and is currently Chief Minister of West Bengal, while Jayalalithaa is chief of the AIADMK and presently serving her third term as Chief Minister of Tamil Nadu.

All these three women share some traits. They head important regional parties and exercise unquestioned authority both within their political outfits and in Government. They are also all strong-willed individuals with an undisputed streak of authoritarianism. None of them tolerate any dissent. They also prefer to communicate directly with their party rank and file as well as with voters. This forthright approach has also helped create a sense of personal loyalty towards them. Finally, none of the three leaders are comfortable within a power-sharing equation.

Let us take Mayawati, for instance: While Kanshi Ram was her mentor, it was she who single-handedly converted his party into the formidable political force that it is today especially in Uttar Pradesh. Similarly, the chief ministership of Uttar Pradesh was also not handed to her on a platter. She occupied this high office solely on the basis of her own political acumen. For instance, she has successfully mobilised the Dalits in her favour and even till this date, they remain her staunch supporters. But Mayawati has also proven that she can look beyond her Dalit vote base, when necessary. She was able to rule Uttar Pradesh from 2007 to 2012 only because she brought the high caste voters into her fray as well. The BSP supremo has also earned the reputation of an efficient and effective leader who deals ruthlessly with criminals.

The story of Banerjee is also similar. She has earned every inch of political space in West Bengal on the basis of a sustained political struggle. And it is this which brought her to power both in the State and at the Centre. However, unlike Mayawati, Banerjee has failed to prove her credentials as an administrator, as petty politics seem to have kept her busy. During the 2011 State Assembly election, she campaigned on the agenda of poribortan (change), yet the only thing that seems to have changed in West Bengal under her is growing lawlessness in the State.

As for Jayalalithaa, she was initially patronised by MG Ramachandran, a popular leader of Tamil Nadu who also founded the AIADMK that she now heads. But today, the Tamil Nadu Chief Minister has well established her credentials as a mass leader and it is primarily on the basis of her own personal appeal that she holds the office of Chief Minister of Tamil Nadu. Equally importantly, Jayalalithaa has also raised the AIADMK to such strengths that it may directly confront M Karunanidhi's family-run party, the DMK.

The Chief Minister is not only known for her administrative capabilities but also has strong nationalist credentials as proven by the firm stand she took against the LTTE in Sri Lanka even as the militant group found support with dubious regionalist chauvinists such as Karunanidhi. On the basis of their own abilities, Mayawati, Mamata Banerjee and J Jayalalithaa have emerged as formidable regional leaders in a patriarchal society where political and leadership spaces have always been monopolised by men. This does not mean that there were no women politicians before them, but it is just that they rarely occupied top positions either within their party or the Government. But these three women have broken that glass ceiling—Mayawati heads the Bahujan Samaj Party and has served four terms as Chief Minister of Uttar Pradesh, Banerjee leads the Trinamool Congress and is currently Chief Minister of West Bengal, while Jayalalithaa is chief of the AIADMK and presently serving her third term as Chief Minister of Tamil Nadu.

All these three women share some traits. They head important regional parties and exercise unquestioned authority both within their political outfits and in Government. They are also all strong-willed individuals with an undisputed streak of authoritarianism. None of them tolerate any dissent. They also prefer to communicate directly with their party rank and file as well as with voters. This forthright approach has also helped create a sense of personal loyalty towards them. Finally, none of the three leaders are comfortable within a power-sharing equation.

Let us take Mayawati, for instance: While Kanshi Ram was her mentor, it was she who single-handedly converted his party into the formidable political force that it is today especially in Uttar Pradesh. Similarly, the chief ministership of Uttar Pradesh was also not handed to her on a platter. She occupied this high office solely on the basis of her own political acumen. For instance, she has successfully mobilised the Dalits in her favour and even till this date, they remain her staunch supporters. But Mayawati has also proven that she can look beyond her Dalit vote base, when necessary. She was able to rule Uttar Pradesh from 2007 to 2012 only because she brought the high caste voters into her fray as well. The BSP supremo has also earned the reputation of an efficient and effective leader who deals ruthlessly with criminals.

The story of Banerjee is also similar. She has earned every inch of political space in West Bengal on the basis of a sustained political struggle. And it is this which brought her to power both in the State and at the Centre. However, unlike Mayawati, Banerjee has failed to prove her credentials as an administrator, as petty politics seem to have kept her busy. During the 2011 State Assembly election, she campaigned on the agenda of poribortan (change), yet the only thing that seems to have changed in West Bengal under her is growing lawlessness in the State.

As for Jayalalithaa, she was initially patronised by MG Ramachandran, a popular leader of Tamil Nadu who also founded the AIADMK that she now heads. But today, the Tamil Nadu Chief Minister has well established her credentials as a mass leader and it is primarily on the basis of her own personal appeal that she holds the office of Chief Minister of Tamil Nadu. Equally importantly, Jayalalithaa has also raised the AIADMK to such strengths that it may directly confront M Karunanidhi's family-run party, the DMK.

The Chief Minister is not only known for her administrative capabilities but also has strong nationalist credentials as proven by the firm stand she took against the LTTE in Sri Lanka even as the militant group found support with dubious regionalist chauvinists such as Karunanidhi.

The Pioneer, 21-06-2013

Neither Modi Nor Nitish has Prescription for India's Ills

The claims and counter-claims made by the Chief Ministers of Gujarat and Bihar about the superiority of the model of development implemented in their respective States has once again brought into sharp focus the issue of pan-national development. Narendra Modi has suggested that the success of his Gujarat model of development is the result of his good governance system that he has provided during his decade as Chief Minister of Gujarat. He has often pointed to the fact that Gujarat has become the favoured destination for investors, both domestic and foreign. Modi believes that if the Gujarat model is replicated across India, both in letter and spirit, it will work wonders for the whole country. His assertions, however, must be viewed against the backdrop of his rise to the national stage as a senior BJP leader.

As for Nitish Kumar, he is not impressed with Modi's claims. On the contrary, he has said that his Bihar model of development that has pulled his State out of the shackles of backwardness is the way to go. In his defence,

Nitish Kumar has pointed out that while once the labouring classes of Bihar migrated in large numbers to far-off States such as Punjab, Haryana and Delhi, today, they stay in their home State because of the success of his model of development.

Nitish Kumar has also refuted Modi's claims by mentioning the obvious fact that when comparing the success of the Gujarat and Bihar models of development, one cannot ignore the level of development (or lack of it) at which the either State already was. In other words, one must take into consideration that when Modi became Chief Minister of Gujarat, his State was already more developed than Bihar.

The crux of the argument here is that there cannot be a single model of development for all States because each one has its own specific problems that require tailor-made responses. For instance, a model of development that may accelerate growth in the relatively 'developed' States such as Maharashtra, Gujarat, Andhra Pradesh, Tamil Nadu, Karnataka, Punjab or Haryana will probably nor work in the 'backward' States of the North-East. After all, the most important accelerator for economic development in any case is basic infrastructure like roads and communication facility. While these are already in place in the developed States, they still have to be put together in the less developed States.

Further, Indian diversity is reflected in vertical and horizontal levels of development. Therefore, 'special State's' like Odisha, Jharkhand and Chhattisgarh have to adopt their own model of development because of the specific challenges posed, for instance, by their large tribal populations. While most tribal communities are themselves deprived and impoverished, their land is most often rich in natural resources. Any model of development aimed at the tribals must take into account this dichotomy. Or else, it is bound to fail. The mismanagement of tribal affairs has fuelled the politics of the bullet by Maoists.

Given the diverse challenges at hand, it is clear, therefore, that there can be no one model of development for India. In fact, it is this understanding that led the country to steer away from the centralised model of economic planning as the Union Government will deliver goods constructed on the basis of 'uniformity' while the imperatives of the country demand 'multiplicity'.

This, however, does not mean that the Union Government should retreat from its role in planning development for the country as a whole. It is unrealistic to talk about Union Government versus the State Governments regarding their roles in planning process. The real issue is the Union Government and the States have to 'cooperate' and not 'confront' one another on development.

The Pioneer, 05-07-2013

Soren Clan Scripts Sordid Tale of a 'Small State'

More than a decade after it was carved out of Bihar to serve as the adivasis' home State, Jharkhand today is politically unstable, corrupt and backward with a slew of tribal Chief Ministers.

In 2000, Jharkhand was created especially for its tribal communities with great fanfare. It was said that after a long and sustained struggle the tribals now had their own home State. Political parties had proclaimed from the rooftops that the aspirations of the tribal population had been fulfilled and now they would prosper in their own identity-based State.

But the reality is that, between 2001 and 2013, Jharkhand has experienced political instability, widespread corruption and its leaders have come to occupy a special status of criminality among politicians. The dreams and expectations of the tribals lie shattered, as they have been betrayed by their own leaders in their State.

After President's Rule was revoked on July 13, the ninth Government of Jharkhand was formed with Hemant Soren as Chief Minister leading a rag-tag coalition. After the Jharkhand Mukti Morcha-BJP alliance collapsed, the President, on the recommendation of the UPA Government at the Centre, had suspended the State Assembly while proclaiming emergency rule in the State. This allowed for political manipulations that set the stage for fractured groups to come together and cobble another coalition Government. This process of coalition formation often leads to corruption of the worst kind. For example: All the six independent MLAs who have extended support to the new regime have asked for Cabinet ministership in return.

Chief Minister Soren has proclaimed that, "This Government will launch itself into development works of the State with enthusiasm". Does his statement carry any conviction, considering the power-greedy Soren clan's past record? One must ask why his father and Jharkhand Mukti Morcha chief Shibu Soren withdrew support to the previous Government? Shibu Soren had demanded the 'rotation' of Chief Ministership, so that his son, who was then Deputy Chief Minister, could be elevated to the post of Chief Minister. Is there now any doubt that coalition Governments, formed as a consequence of fractured and fragmented electoral verdicts, practice opportunistic and non-ideological politics?

Also, a deeper understanding of Jharkhand's tribal society will reveal that there are four important groups that contend for power in the State whose tribal population is not a monolith. The result is that while one former tribal Chief Minister, Madhu Koda, has been cooling his heels in jail, another tribal Chief Minister, Arjun Munda of the BJP, has just lost power while being replaced by a third tribal Chief Minister, Hemant Soren. Does a home State for the tribals means only tribal leaders as Chief Ministers?

Also, a larger point to be made here is that the creation of smaller States on the basis of supposed demands of one section of society, whether tribal or non-tribal, is not the answer to their specific problems, be it in Jharkhand, Chhattisgarh or Uttaranchal or earlier in Haryana and Himachal Pradesh. This also applies to the regions of Telangana, Vidarbha and Bundelkhand clamouring for separate Statehood.

Any identity-based State offers an open invitation to parochial politics. By creating more such States, policy makers are encouraging more such movements for separate States. They are institutionalising the fragmentation of Indian society. Today Assam is faced with the Bodo problem while West Bengal must contend with the dispute over Gorkhaland. When regionalist groups in these areas see the experience of others across the country, such as the tribals in Jharkhand, they are emboldened to make similar demands themselves.

An unsubstantiated message has been spread by those championing the cause of smaller States that it is easier to develop such States. But if this was true, then Tamil Nadu, Karnataka and Gujarat would not have been some of India's most developed States.

The Pioneer, *19-07-2013*

Chapter 3
Coalition and Governance Issues

The Eclipsing of Parliament

Elected representative legislatures have evolved on the basis of struggles against sovereign powers enjoyed by hereditary kings and monarchs. Indian anticolonial struggles, like others around the world, were also based on a demand for the establishment of a representative Parliament. Parliaments were then accorded a sovereign status, and as representatives of the people, they had legitimate powers to make laws, impose taxes and hold other constituents of government accountable. If the source of power of Parliaments or legislatures was based on their representativeness, this journey came to an end when, after World War-II, many erstwhile colonies, especially India and later South Africa, achieved the goal of establishing their own elected representative Parliament. The institutions of society have to keep pace with processes of social change, and gradually it was realised that elected representatives will not be able to cope with new tasks facing industrialised or industrialising societies in the 20th century. This led a British commentator, Ramsay Muir, to observe in his seminal 'How Britain is Governed' that because of the emerging complexities of society, the real centre of power had shifted away from Parliament to the political executive and that councils of ministers and cabinet ministers have willingly or unwillingly surrendered their powers to the class of professionals and permanent civil servants. The role of elected representatives in Parliaments has been marginalised and the social and economic requirements of an industrial and post-industrial age have created a compulsion for governments to involve and accord a high-profile role to a professional, technocratic elite in the domain of real policymaking processes. In India, this was highlighted with the introduction of the model of globalisation, deregulation and privatisation during Narasimha Rao-Manmohan Singhs phase of leadership in the early 1990s. The so-called unregulated market economy has also revealed its incapacity to stop the emergence of monopolistic firms that can hold society to ransom. Here, Parliament comes into the picture only for the making of an ordinance as an legislature law, while the real decision-makers for the establishment of powerful

Regulatory Commissions are professional technocrats with whose expert advice the political executive issues an Ordinance and places that before Parliament for ratification. Professionals and technocrats have substituted Parliament in its basic activity of lawmaking as seen in the case of the creation of SEBI, TRAI, CERC, *et al.*, by Presidential Ordinances, which Acts were then rubber-stamped by Parliament. The dialectical process of interaction between politics and economics can create situations where managers of economic markets can come to occupy the drivers seat and make politics an appendage. Every Regulatory Commission from its day of creation has elbowed out the role of elected political institutions. Parliament, the real centre of democratic power in society, has been presented with a fait accompli because the political executive supported by bureaucratic and professional groups has taken recourse to Presidential Ordinances for the creation of expert watchdogs of the economy. Parliament, or its so-called Standing Committees, puts a seal of formal approval on laws that have been introduced in a finished form before the elected representatives. A perfunctory reading of Acts passed by Parliament for the creation of expert Regulatory Commissions, especially from the early 1990s, will reveal that many vague and grey areas have been left and within that available space, the political executive has been able to manipulate and manoeuvre the Constitution and the functioning of these commissions. Since Parliament deals with the Bills prepared by experts and the professional elite, it is natural for these real initiators of Bills to ensure that these very experts are appointed by the Cabinet on the governing boards of these socalled specialised institutions. It is not incidental that every parliamentary Act dealing with a regulatory institution mentions that persons with administrative experience shall be appointed to manage these regulatory, specialised and autonomous agencies. A cursory look at the boards of management of these regulatory institutions shows that either retired or even serving civil servants have occupied the positions of power meant for the regulation of the economy. Members of Parliament have no one to blame except themselves because they are ill-equipped to deal with the problems of governance of a complex technological society. This explains their conduct in Parliament, because in spite of their marginalisation in public governance, they keep themselves in the limelight by disrupting parliamentary sessions and staging walkouts for the sake of publicity. MPs have been left to fight shadows because they have lost real powers. *Times of India, 24-09-2011*

Keeping the Spirit of Federalism Alive

The National Development Council meeting held in New Delhi on October 22, was for discussion and approval of the Draft of the 12th Five Year Plan. However, during this 56th meeting of the Council, Chief Tamil Nadu Chief Minister Jayalalithaa and Gujarat Chief Minister Narendra Modi expressed their resentment against the 'discriminatory' treatment by the Union Government to their states, more so because they were ruled by non-UPA parties. It deserves to be clearly stated that the Indian political landscape has completely changed, and that such a political diversity was reflected in the NDC meet. Such a political diverse forum of the Union and the State Governments is structurally constituted on the principle of political pluralism and even dissent. Prime Minister Manmohan Singh, during his inaugural speech on October 22, expressed this view by stating, "What this means is that parliamentary parties have to strike a difficult balance between maintaining adversarial political positions on many issues, while also cooperating to advance long term national agenda. This balance is not easy to strike." Such a diverse political situation depends on institutional arrangements for evolving a national consensus by accommodating diverse demands of specific regional and State Governments.

The NDC is one such institutional mechanism where the Union and the States' conflicts of goals can be resolved. Further, it is inherent in such a situation that States ruled by different parties not only pressure the Union Government, they also compete with one another to get their demands conceded the Union Government. Jayalalitha accused the UPA regime of showing "special" interest over the demands of its partner and Chief Minister of West Bengal Mamata Banerjee The Tamil Nadu Chief Minister is angry with the Union Government on its handling of the agitation at the Koodankulum nuclear plant, and she not only described such NDC meetings as a "ritualistic exercise" but went a step further and maintained that proposed laws like the Communal Violence Bill or the Goods and Service Tax Act were "blatant attempts" to totally "bypass" State Governments and concentrate all powers with the Union Government. She characterised the UPA-led Government as "partisan."

The existing about 147 centrally sponsored schemes were also criticised. Bihar Chief Minister Nitish Kumar referred to the Right to Education Act and observed that "legal obligations under the RTE have no relationship with availability of states finances." It is a fact that the constitutionally-supported Finance Commissions have regularly 'tried to work out an equalising formula' for financial resource transfer to the states. India still has serious 'regional imbalances' and resource deficit states have always asked for 'special assistance' for development and welfare schemes. The role of state Governors as 'watchdogs' and 'policemen' of the Union Government has always been a bone of contention and disputes between the Union Government and its opponents and competing parties ruling over the States.

Modi was quite agitated with the Congress—nominated Governor of his State for appointing a Lokpal without the consent and approval of the State Council of Ministers. At the NDC meeting, he also alleged the UPA-led

Governmental for 'tinkering with the federal structure of the country and suggested that the Union Government should 'observe federal dharma'. Modi also made a political point by asking Singh whether the National Development Council was in any way more important than Sonia Gandhi's National Advisory Council, which incidentally keeps on making public policy suggestions to the Congress-led UPA Government. Union Minister of Rural Development Jairam Ramesh admitted that the Land Acquisition Bill prepared by his Ministry was based on consultations with Rahul Gandhi, (the heir-apparent) by citing a comical consideration that Gandhi has great experience of land acquisition issues.

The above narration needs to be contextualised and analysed in a broader context of the functioning of a federal system in a country of great diversities, pluralities and regional and sub-regional special needs and people's aspirations. A federal, democratic system cannot survive, even exit, without an effective and politically strong Union Government which has to be in the 'drivers seat'.

Pioneer, 27-10-2011

The Ungovernables of India

India has been facing a grave crisis of governance and this has once again been brought out in the public domain by the honourable judges of the Supreme Court, who on February 2 censured the government of India for following a completely flawed policy in allocating 122 licences to domestic and global telecom companies. The authoritative judicial pronouncements on the so-called 2G spectrum scam has indicted the political executive, the higher echelons of the bureaucracy and the Telecom Regulatory Authority of India for their serious acts of omission and commission while taking decisions about pubic national resources of the country. The whole operation of allocating of licences was completely devoid of fairness and transparency. A few important salient features that have emerged from the judgment deserve to be highlighted to substantiate the argument that India is faced with the most serious challenge of governance.

First, a worrisome fact that has emerged is that the council of ministers, whose lynchpin is the prime minister, does not function as a collective decision-making body on matters of national importance.

The council of ministers does not operate collectively in India and individual ministers run their own departments or portfolios according to their will and whim. It was left to the judges to bring into public the sad situation that exists within the council by observing that A Raja, the then telecom minister, did not pay heed to the suggestion by the prime minister who wrote to the minister on November 2007 to give due consideration to issues raised regarding transparency in the spectrum allocation process. Do we have a council of ministers or we are functioning under individual monarchs, who treat their ministry as private fiefdom? The court observed that allocation by Raja was arbitrary and unconstitutional and the Department of Telecommunication headed and its eminent bureaucrats were cowed down by their minister and if they had not done so, they would have incurred the wrath of the minister. It is not without reason that the Secretary, Department of Telecommunication, is cooling his heels alongwith his minister in Tihar Jail. Can India progress in the young 21st century with a completely rotten bureaucratic apparatus? A complex market economy can end up in chaos and crisis in the absence of effective and autonomous regulatory agencies of the government.

The above narrative about the complete paralysis of the institutions of governance should make everyone clinically examine the causes for the growing directionless system of governance in the country. First, a multiparty coalition system of government at the centre or in the states takes into consideration the interest of its own parties and other political partners.

The inherent logic of coalition governments—whether led by the Congress or the BJP at the centre or the erstwhile Left Front of West Bengal—is that the prime minister or the chief minister is unable to micro manage the functioning of ministers belonging to political allies. The argument is that coalition governments are compelled to leave autonomous spaces to allies is a justification for the role played by Raja or the maverick Mamata Banerjee as former railway minister of the UPA government. Second, if ministers belonging to different coalition parties cannot remain united, it becomes difficult to expect the bureaucrats to work in the interest of the government as a whole because the higher echelons of the bureaucracy are happy to toe the line of their own minister.

The story of the past 63 years of the Indian democracy is based on the reality of complete adjustment of IAS bureaucrats with their political bosses for private and personal advantages. These officials never retire from service because obliged political leaders reward obliging civil servants with post-retirement jobs and assignments. How can institutions of governance remain effective and function on the basis of rule of law and procedures laid down by law if a quid pro quo exists between ministers and bureaucrats for bending and breaking the laws for personal benefit?

Third, it is not only the Indian judiciary that has ripped open the deep-rooted crisis in the institutions of governance, the Election Commission during every election, whether the Lok Sabha or the state assemblies, has repeatedly shown that free, fair and fearless elections cannot be held because of the nexus between politicians, bureaucrats, money and muscle power. Thus, during every election, the poll panel demands the transfer of IAS and IPS officials to hold free elections. The large scale cleansing of bureaucracy during the elections by the Election Commission shows that the Indian bureaucracy cannot be trusted to perform its legal duties fairly. If a section of officials cannot be trusted during the elections and or transferred, after the elections same tainted officers are brought back by the elected political leaders.

The writ of the Election Commission ends after the elections, but politically aligned bureaucrats continue in their jobs by following the same route of bending and breaking rules and procedures to curry favour for the political bosses.

The state-led system of planned economic development of the Jawaharlal Nehru and Indira Gandhi phase of governance has been replaced by the model of privatisation, liberalisation and deregulation of markets. In spite of the fundamental change in the model of economic management during the past two decades, the institutions of governance have not seen a change for the better. Not only this, politicians and bureaucrats have felt quite comfortable both with the model of regulated economic planning and liberalised and deregulated market economy because the old style of using government institutions for personal benefit has not come to an end.

The power of governance is seen as an opportunity to maximise personal wealth and influence. Come what may, politics continues to be a lucrative and profitable business for politicians and bureaucrats. The country needs to undertake a surgical operation of its public institutions of governance. It is not a simplistic issue of corruption – the larger issue is erosion of the capability of the institutions of governance for social justice and inclusive growth. An excessive public emphasis on corruption in public life has unwittingly created a situation where the larger issue of a completely dysfunctional machinery of government has been pushed under the carpet. *Tehelka, 11-02-2012*

From Legacy to Lame Duck

Some time back, leading industrialists wrote 'open letters' to the Prime Minister inviting his attention to the 'paralysis' in the government while dealing with serious problems and challenges faced by the Indian economy. They pointed out that the government is showing great incapacity to tackle economic problems. If the leading industrialists have been at their wit's end while dealing with a 'paralysed' governmental machinery at the centre, the Chief of Staff VK Singh has set the cat among the pigeons by alleging that the political executive and civil bureaucracy of the Ministry of Defence are completely blind and deaf while dealing with the problems of 'ill-equipped' armed forces of the country.

The Congress-led UPA government lost its credibility when the Supreme Court had to intervene to see that proper investigations are held for finding out the real truth behind 2G spectrum scam in which the minister and bureaucracy of the telecom ministry are suspect. As if misuse of powers by the government in telecommunication was not enough to paint the UPA government as 'corrupt', the coal ministry is in the waiting to be exposed by the Comptroller and Auditor General's Report for handing over coal mines to individuals at the whim and fancy of the coal ministry.

Indians are very sensitive if anything goes wrong with the army because it is considered as a protector. After fighting five wars with Pakistan and China, not only has the army proved it competence, it is considered a 'guarantor' of national security. Army is in the news for wrong reasons and its impact will be felt even after General VK Singh leaves the office of the Army chief. He has alleged that India lacks modern arms to fight a war and it is also short of ammunition which is required to face the opponent—because on March 19 the Stockholm International Peace Research Institute (SIPRI) in its annual report has stated that since the Kargil war of 1999, 'India has been steadily buying arms and ammunition.'

Not only this. India is the largest arms' importer. From 2007 to 2011, 10 per cent of the global arms were imported by India. Further, because of inadequate domestic defence production, 70 per cent of the total defence expenditure is directed for purchasing India's requirements for defence from imports. The SIPRI annual report mentions that 'India has long been a major purchaser of weapons. Now it is the biggest in the world.' It is not without reason that all major arms exporters have assembled at Def-Expo to show their defence equipment for exports. It has been estimated that India may spend more than 100 billion sterling pounds in the next 15 years for the purchase of arms. India perceives Pakistan and China as a 'security threat' and always keeps an eagle's eye on arms and equipment of armies of these two countries.

While Pakistan imports major requirements of its arms from 'friendly China' and receives military aid from the United States to equip its professional armed forces, China during its last two decades of consistent economic growth has increased its military budget. The budget announced on March 4 showed an increase of 11 per cent, about $100 billion. It is not without reason that the Chinese describe their military as a 'formidable regional force' and they have stated that 'the military spending increase was in line with Chinese economic development'. India has never hesitated to declare itself as a 'nuclear weapons state', but the reality is that country's own Army chief maintains that India neither has the latest military equipment nor does it buy the best arms because of rampant corruption.

The larger issue is that the republic is leaderless and headless. If anything goes wrong, the alibi is that the quality of governance is suffering because of the 'compulsions and constraints of the coalition partners' and DMK support was essential to keep the UPA government in office. Is there any 'compulsion of coalition' in dealing with the problems and allegations of defence forces? National security issues have to be directly dealt with by the Prime Minster and the defence minister, who belong to the Congress party. Can it be surmised that the Prime Minister has no authority to oversee the affairs of the defence ministry led by the Congress party defence minister? Are these ministers managing autonomous empires where the Prime Minister's writ does not run?

The story does not end here. Every political crisis faced by the Congress-led UPA government is responded by a counter-attack on the working of autonomous institutions of governance like the Comptroller and Auditor General (CAG) or the Election Commission. If CAG points out that huge financial loss has been incurred by the country the way A Raja, the communication minister, dealt with the spectrum issue, Kapil Sibal, a minister, challenges the CAG and maintains that 'zero loss' had occurred and CAG estimates were wrong.

If the Election Commission censures Salman Khurshid, a minister, for violating the model code of conduct during the Uttar Pradesh assembly elections, the minister responds that the Election Commission could 'hang him' but he would continue to campaign by violating the Election Code. If the Supreme Court suggest that 'all national resources' should be 'auctioned' by the government in a transparent manner, the confused government wishes to ask for a 'review' of this judgement. Thomas Hobbes, a philosopher, described a state of society where there was no 'single sovereign' where everyone was fighting a nasty, brutish, war against everyone else'. In India, every institution of governance like judiciary, parliament, Election Commission, CAG are all fighting their own battles because the political executive is not firmly in the drivers' seat at the centre and a country cannot be governed without central friendship and guidance. An explanation for the present leadership crisis is that the Prime Minister is not head of the government in the real political sense of the term. It is a strange situation where chief ministers of states are in command of their governments and Prime Minister of India has to look over his shoulder before he takes any important decision in public affairs.

The explanation for the prevailing 'paralysis' and 'crisis' seems to be that in a fractured and fragmented multiparty political system, the head of the political executive at the centre does not have any social constituency of his own which can come into the public to support the Prime Ministers' actions and decisions. *The Financial World, 05-04-2012*

Silent on its own Success

There is nothing unusual in an opposition party like the BJP alleging that the Manmohan Singh led UPA government is suffering from policy paralysis. But an insider saying something similar is a different matter. It was, thus, a harsh indictment of an immobilised central government when Kaushik Basu, chief economic adviser, recently observed that real economic reform momentum can take place only in 2014 because the present coalition democracy has created a situation where nothing seems to be moving forward. Basu set the cat among the pigeons, and Montek Singh Ahluwalia responded sharply, "There are always reforms that need to be done, but that does not mean that you cant get the economy back on a high-growth path, and that is what we should be focusing on at the moment."

The point, however, is that in a highly competitive multi-polar party system, the political leadership has to be in the drivers seat and it is the task of the political executive to defend its performance from the front and not hide behind either bureaucrats or acts of omission and commission of coalition partners.

Electoral endorsement is the only yardstick in a democracy to find out the level of democratic legitimacy of the contesting parties if the path of development had not resulted in positive results. If the Lok Sabha elections of 2004 brought in the Congress to lead a coalition while its own tally was only 144 seats, in 2008, it emerged as the single-largest party, winning 206 seats out of 543. How could the Congress succeed in the Lok Sabha elections of 2008 if the people of India did not support its polices in preference to the other contenders to power A few salient facts may be mentioned to substantiate the argument that the Congress path of economic development has brought substantial benefits to multiple strata of society and that the party is expected to defend its own achievements while in government. First, Indian big business has emerged as a global player and Tatas, Birlas, Ambanis, Mittals *et al.* are showing their presence in the US, EU, Asia and Africa markets. Big business of India has become an active player in the ongoing and unstoppable processes of globalisation of economy and finance. And the Manmohan Singh government has facilitated this process of emergence of India as a global player. Why not acknowledge it? Second, it must have been the deft handling by political managers of the UPA government that saved the situation from adverse effects of the financial and banking great crisis of 2008. A globalised India cannot always expect goodies, it has to share the adverse consequences of a crisis in the global economy. Since the global economic and financial crisis is continuing, why should Pranab Mukherjee not alert Indians that the global situation is challenging and we are making every effort to face it?

A failure to educate Indians can be attributed only to the government-in-power at the Centre. In addition, it is worth remembering that the economic transition beginning in the 1990s has led to the emergence of an upwardly mobile professional, entrepreneurial and technocratic middle class visible on the streets of not only big Indian cities but even at the district level. These millions of new social achievers have not emerged on the scene by accident, they are the product of the ongoing technological revolutionary process in the country. This success is not being highlighted.

The Manmohan Singh government has also forgotten its main achievement of ushering in a telecommunication revolution. Instead, a government that could have taken legitimate credit for this revolution is stuck with the 2G scam of A Raja and other family members of the DMK czar.

It is true that during the last two decades of the new economic project, already-existing inequalities have deepened. The Manmohan Singh government could have publicly defended its programme of poverty reduction while promising to tackle the issue of inequality. Instead, we had a situation where opposition members of Parliament were demanding the head of Montek Singh Ahluwalia by alleging that his organisation was fudging poverty figures ! How could the government allow the Opposition to get away with the argument that nothing has been done for the people at the bottom of the pyramid during UPA-I and three years of UPA-II ?

Finally, a globalised world requires that every country follows an activist foreign policy because the distinction between external and internal policy has been quite blurred. Clearly, the Manmohan Singh government has followed a very successful and positive foreign policy in the region, and beyond. And yet, this hardly finds mention.

Doctor, heal thyself is the adage. And the government must begin by effectively projecting its achievements. *The Economics Times*, *28-04-2012*

It's a Riddle in an Enigma

Every democratic competitive political system, at one time or the other, has been confronted with a complex situation of resolving the knotty problem of finding funds for elections. Not only this, Western democratic countries have enacted laws for the regulation of expenditure by political parties and contesting candidates during elections.

A cursory reading of laws passed by Western legislatures regarding electoral expenditure reflects national specificities. The common thread in all these laws, whether Australian or American or Canadian, is that a 'ceiling' on expenditure during the elections is fixed by the law of the land and an effort has been made to keep electoral competition 'clean' from the ugly power of moneyed people. The Western countries have tried to check financial malpractices during the elections by asking every party and candidate to declare not only the amount of money spent during the elections, but also publicly declare the sources of funds collected by parties for contesting elections. The corrupting influence of 'money power' has been legally curbed by asking the parties to get their accounts properly 'audited' by public agencies and completely disclose the name of fund givers to the parties for elections.

So every Western democratic country has faced the challenge of 'moneyed' people hijacking the democratic verdict by bribing voters. Laws have been put on the statute book to deal with the malaise of money power in democracy.

India has also grappled with the monster of the role of money during the elections and on the basis of concrete experience, remedial methods have been adopted to curb thepower of money and compel the parties to submit public statements of the sources of funds and the names of fund-gives. The Tata Group maintains a public record of funds donated to parties for elections.

The situation in India is quite dire because every serious candidate who is involved an competitive electoral process whether of the State Assembly or the Lok Sabha, even in the Panchayat and Zila Parisahd elections, spends huge money. Electoral democracy has been completely vitiated and corrupted because it has become a competition among those only who can spend maximum money during the elections. Of late, the Election Commission of India has evolved mechanisms of checking the misuse of money power during the elections but these efforts, while praiseworthy, have hardly succeeded in curbing the role of money power, including huge black money, during the elections.

Political parties defend their actions by arguing that parties do not have their own funds, and this compels them to raise funds from private sources. Thus this should be considered a 'necessary evil' and price for democracy. Many a time, it has been suggested by parties and reformists that 'public funding' of elections from government sources is the only method which can cleanse the electoral system from corrupting the role of 'moneyed people'. This plea that government should provide 'funds' to political parties for contesting elections and such 'public funds' will ensure that parties would not approach and collect funds from private big business houses is in circulation. This suggestion has not found favour with any government-in-power because there is no guarantee that parties after receiving 'public funds' will stop collecting 'funds' from private 'donors'.

While everyone is concerned about the polluting impact of involvement of 'money power' during the elections, the mechanism to curb the role of money has been always found inadequate because parties do not follow, in practice, the rule of democratic game because the winning of an elections, by any means, foul or fair, has become the sole motive of every contestant in elections. Politics has become a lucrative business and it is not surprising that elected representatives of poor voters are filthy rich crorepatis.

If declaration of personal sources of income and wealth by elected representatives are taken at face value, there is no doubt that Indian politics is controlled by 'crorepatis'. Only one illustration will substantiate the argument. The Association for Democratic Reforms and Uttar Pradesh Election Watch observes that 'the average individual assets of the 285 contesting mlas for the 2012 UP election increased from Rs 1.21 crore (2007) to Rs 3.56 crore (2012).' Democracy has to be safeguarded form the penetration of 'moneyed people' who finance a politicians in return for benefits and a quid pro quo emerges between elected public policy makers and private business empires and government-in-action becomes 'privatised' in the service of the private fund givers'.

Big business is also worried about the growing demands of politicians for funds for private purposes in return for favours by the government. Party/parties-in-power discriminate against 'non-obliging' businessmen and this makes everyone fall in line. In desperation, Adi Godrej, Chairperson of Godrej Group, observed on 22 April that '…industry is ready to pay democratic cess to facilitate state funding of elections as it is the main cause of corruption.' The President of the Confederation of Industry set the cat among the pigeon by publicly suggesting that 'Electoral reforms are very important. Personally, I favour state funding of elections. We are very open to imposing a democratic cess to fund elections.' Adi Godrej said that tax could be paid by cheque and create an 'electoral/political pool of funds.'

Electoral reform, including cleansing of elections from the evil of money power, has been on the agenda of every Chief Election Commissioner from 1952-53 to 2012 and many committees and commissions have also been appointed during the last six decades to suggest the reform of elections, unfortunately, nothing substantial has happened in this direction. The opposite of electoral reforms has emerged where politics has become a means to enrich oneself by misusing the public office occupied by elected representative. If Godrej is pleading for a cess for elections, Laxmi Niwas Mittal, the world's largest steel maker in the presence of Prime Minister Manmohan Singh observed on 28 April that 'Things are moving slowly. There is no doubt. Process approval is taking time.' Delaying the clearances required by industrialists is a tactic adopted by politicians and bureaucrats to collect 'speed money' for quickening the process of decision-making. How can the state funding of elections curb the role of money power in elections? Files move only if decision-makers are given huge funds. Adi Godrej and the Tatas should think of some other method of dealing with the evil of money power.

The Financial World, 02-05-2012

Beware of the 'Hidden Hands' in Disputes

Every industrialist and investor expects profit from his business venture. And every business venture requires workers for production of goods and services. But the relationship between the business class and the working class is often conflict-ridden. If the employer is concerned only about profits and the working classes feel ignored or underpaid, a clash of interests between capital and labour becomes inevitable. Resolution of conflicting interests of the employer and the employee needs a strong legal framework and deft negotiation. Therefore every modern industrial country, including India, has comprehensive laws to deal with clashes of interest between employers and employees.

In India's worst industrial strife post liberalisation, Maruti's Manesar plant in Gurgaon on 19 July witnessed ugly scenes of union members going berserk, damaging machinery and attacking about 90 managers. Onesenior manager died in the fire. This incident forced the management to declare a 'lockout' at the plant and seek strict action against the union leaders from the Haryana government. It has also raised some important issues for a public debate into labour disputes.

It is government's duty to hold an inquiry into the genesis of mishap to find out if something is seriously wrong between the Maruti management and its workers. It is not appropriate to pin down the sole responsibility for hooliganism on the union leadership, because long-term remedial action into the case is possible only after careful scrutiny. The government also cannot escape its responsibility of finding solutions to specific problems facing one Maruti plant or those concerning the whole industrial belt of Gurgaon-Haryana. Politically, short-term and long-term remedies have to be found if Haryana wishes to attract foreign investors.

Indians need to be reminded that the thriving textile industry of Mumbai was completely destroyed by reckless trade union leader Datta Samant, who emerged from nowhere on the labour scene in the mid-1960s, and through his unreasonable demands left thousands of textile workers unemployed and their families suffering in penury. Working class should know that their adventurism under manipulators like Samant harms its own interests. Will the story of Mumbai of the mid-1960s repeat itself in Haryana? If Mumbai is too old to remember, we can look at Singur and Nandigram in West Bengal and what the Socialist Unity Centre of India did to them in the recent past. The state is still reeling under the complete de-industrialisation and flight of capital that occurred in the aftermath of the climate of militant trade unionism that this adventurist group of Communists started in 2007.

But all this does not in any way suggest that employers can indulge in 'illegal' activities to exploit their employees. Industrialists are seen to violate laws governing the management-working class in collusion with politicians and bureaucracy. Hence, trade unions are an integral part of political parties. Party leaders representing trade unions can help counter political influences of powerful patrons of the industrial classes. Politics acts as a bridge with economics and for different reasons, industrialists and the trade unionists turn to politics in labour disputes.

Politicians must realise that galloping unemployment in the country provides an opportunity to employers to hire contractual labour at lower wages. Maruti isn't the only company employing a large number of temporary and low wage contractual workers. Such labour makes a major chunk of the work force in every industry. These workers are insecure about their job and are exploited by their employers as well as the trade union leaders, who use them to armtwist each other. That they have no long-term stake in their industry makes them even more vulnerable.

It would be too simplistic to conclude that this is a union leaders versus Maruti management conflict which turned violent. Hidden hands are always at work to complicate small problems. It is common political culture where purely economic conflicts between investor and labour take a political turn and get magnified because 'outside forces' get involved. But it is not just politicians who fish in such troubled waters, competitors disturb the status quo to get ahead. Even rival trade union leaders play politics with internal relations to settle scores with rival leaders trade unions. There are many lessons to be learnt from the ugly events at Maruti. The employers have a responsibility to nip the conflict in the bud by following legal procedures of dealing with the demands of workers. It is wishful thinking that politics and political parties will maintain a distance from business and economic activities and the only remedy against manipulative political intervention is to strengthen the machinery of resolving labour disputes. *Financial World, 28-07-2012*

India did not have to Copy this, of All Things

By establishing a national policy framework that promotes the distribution of special privileges to every segment of society on the basis of quotas, India has made a salient contribution to the theory of Western democracy. The 65-year-old Republic has shown to older democracies that if they base their governance strategies on fixing quotas for public service and in institutions, and in effect divide society into pieces, it is possible to maintain control over the whole social order. This is because there will be no meeting ground for the divided people and the situation here will be quite orderly.

The question here is: How did the political parties, irrespective of their ideological differences, arrive at such a unanimous agreement? When did they all decide that social pacification, with a view to maintaining social order, can be achieved by 'quota-based' policies and strategies? This wisdom came to the Indian political class from its colonial predecessors who successfully governed a continental sized colony by following similar policies based on reserved quotas for representatives of various groups in public institutions.

India's post-Independence leaders learnt their strategies of governance from the colonial rulers. Only one illustration is sufficient to substantiate this argument. During the three Round Table Conferences held in the 1930s in London to discuss the 'India Question', all that was achieved was the infamous Ramsay MacDonald Award and its corrective Irwin-Gandhi Accord.

Yet, the fact remains that a quota-based approach to social problems has been legitimised by 'nationalist leaders' of every persuasion. The strategy for social pacification has been implemented by all political parties to buy social peace during the last 65 years.

Such a policy has not only been legitimised by political leaders but also promoted by their academic collaborators. The latter have supported these policies by applying upon them western value loaded, sugar-coated tags of 'positive discrimination', 'affirmative action' and 'social inclusion'.

The main thrust of their argument is that special rights, privileges and opportunities should be provided by the Indian state to certain groups that have earlier been victims of a discriminatory social order. Such a historical wrong must then be rectified by a modern state by establishing strategies that give these discriminated groups special support and concessions, usually in the form of quotas and reservations. However, there is enough evidence to prove that the political leaders are rarely, if ever, interested in improving the situation of the poor.

For instance, thousands in India live below the poverty line and there are many more who live on the margins of society either as daily wage labourers or migrant workers. They, the real 'victims' of an discriminatory social and economic order, have only single identity. The only common aspect which brings them together is that they are live in misery and deprivation.

The moot point here is that India's 5, 000 year long civilisational history is not as responsible for the poor living status of the majority of the country's population, as the existing economic system of society.

Besides, it is a well-known fact that in all societies, historical interpretations have been politically manipulated to favour the socially and economically powerful ruling groups. Intellectuals have been employed in the service of the powers-that-be so that they project history in a manner that suits the ruling class.

Hence, it is important to ensure the central issue of the social inequality in India is not obfuscated by linking it with historical legacies of discriminations. Instead, there has to be close scrutiny of India's social, political and economic journey in the last 65 years. *The Pioneer*, *14-09-2012*

Not with You, Not for You

It is not surprising to read about the ill-treatment of rape victims at the hands of policemen. It does not require a social philosopher to make the observation that police in India lack the trust of the citizens or that the majority of citizens consider the force as a 'necessary evil'. This is chiefly because the police's mentality has not changed since 1947 and it also suits the class structure of our society.

So far, police reform commissions or judges of the Supreme Court have focused on the top of the police hierarchy, while the need of the hour is to restructure the basic organisational unit like the police station (PS) or thana. The police need the cooperation of citizens. This mutual dependence is a facilitating factor in the day-to-day interaction and interface between them and citizens. Unfortunately, this social contract is disintegrating. Academic studies of police stations reveal that the police are themselves to blame for their negative image.

First, a citizen is hesitant about visiting a police station to file a complaint against a law-breaker because the first information report, instead of being treated as a fundamental right of the complainant, is met with great hostility. It has been observed that in police stations, either the police discourage complainants or they file complaints against innocent people under the influence of local village or town influentials to teach a lesson to the complainant for crossing the limits of his low-caste status against high-caste individuals, who have the support of the police. Caste and class statuses determine police responses while dealing with law and order issues.

The atmosphere in thanas is highly 'inhospitable' for a law-abiding citizen whose dignity is violated by the abusive language used by policemen. The background of people managing thanas is cited as a reason for this. However, the more weighty reason is the sense of power or authority wielded by them. It is a hangover of the colonial police culture where the police were expected to inspire great awe and fear among the colonised people.

It is simplistic to mention that Indian Police Service officials are unaware of this. They cannot avoid their responsibility of making the police behave as protectors of the rule of law in a democracy.

If the story of harassed and humiliated citizens is one side of the picture, the other dimension is that the police leadership is always pleading for modernisation and reform to make it 'accountable' to the citizens. However, when put on the defensive, the police present a list of complaints that affect their morale. But it is a flimsy argument that creating more battalions will improve their efficiency. *Hindustan Times, 11-01-2013*

Let the Army Object; Amend Harsh AFSPA

The Armed Forces can be consulted, but they cannot impose an opinion on policy-making processes. In a democracy, any legal framework or law made in the interest of national security has to ensure that the rights of ordinary citizens are not violated

Democracy in India is firmly entrenched and the principle of civilian control over the Armed Forces is well established. But that does not mean that things can be taken for granted because even Indian military generals can make every effort to establish their very 'special' status in the governance of the country.

A warning signal has come from a recent statement by the Union Minister for Finance P Chidambaram: "The Army has taken a strong stand against any dilution of the AFSPA. We can't move forward because there is no consensus. The present and former Army chiefs have taken a strong position that the Act should not be amended. They also do not want the Government notification (of bringing areas under the Act) to be taken back. How does the Government move forward to make AFSPA a more humanitarian law?" The contentious Armed Forces (Special Powers) Act is in force in many 'disturbed' regions of the country.

Chidambaram's statement and the public role and assertions made by General (retd) VK Singh needs to be dissected to restore the balance between the controlling authority of the Government and the boundaries in which the Forces and retired generals are expected to conduct their affairs.

This is not the first time that the Army's inner functioning has been publicly debated. India's humiliating defeat in the border war with China in 1962 highlighted the 'demoralisation' of the Armed Forces wrought by Krishna Menon's frequent interventions in appointing 'favourite 'generals as commandants during that war. The 1962 crisis alerted the politicians that the loyalty of the men in uniform can be guaranteed if the Army is not subjected to petty politics of the politicians.

More recently, General VK Singh brought the highest office of the Army under public scrutiny. The issue of the Army's non-political character is back in the news. The issue is not that retired military chiefs have to maintain silence and refrain from speaking on public issues facing the country; the issue is that just after retirement, General Singh jumped into public controversies, lending credence to the growing impression about his hidden political ambitions while he was holding the highest office of commander-in-chief.

Discretion is the better part of valour, and retired generals serve the country better if they keep out of routine political activities in the country. Also, it must be remembered that laws, including those regarding the Armed Forces or paramilitary organisations, are enacted after much thought and discussion by a democratically-elected Government.

The Army can be consulted but it cannot impose an opinion on policy-making processes. India faces multiple security challenges, but in a democracy any legal framework or law in the interest of national security has to ensure that rights of ordinary citizens are not violated.

The AFSPA has been in force for a long time. Strong reservations against it have been expressed by Jammu & Kashmir Chief Minister Omar Abdullah and Irom Sharmila who has been on fast in Imphal since November 4, 2000, seeking the Act's revocation.

The deployment of the Armed Forces to fight insurgencies, whether in Jammu & Kashmir or in the North-East, may be necessary, but the deployment can succeed only if the local population supports the move.

If Krishna Menon was accused of excessive interference in the Army's internal affairs in 1962; if General VK Singh has violated 'conventions', then the UPA Government too has set a bad precedent by not amending and humanising the AFSPA, merely because 'consensus' does not exist in the Army to make changes in the Act. *The Pioneer, 05-02-2013*

Use Both Bullets and Bricks to Fight Maoist Violence

In 2009, the Union Government evolved a National Coordinated Offensive plan to fight Maoists. This plan has since been vigorously followed by the Union Government especially after the success of the Greyhound Operation in Andhra Pradesh. The States of Bihar, Jharkhand, Chhattisgarh and Odisha have also been selected up by the Union Government for special quasi-military operations against Maoists on the lines of the Greyhound Operation.

This year, the Union Ministry of Home Affairs has already decided to deploy 8,000 additional troops and 14 IAF choppers, apart from the 80,000 CRPF personnel across 70,000 sq km of territory. The Government's strategy is to use maximum firepower in a concentrated manner in select regions where Maoists are active. Yet, gun battles between the Maoists and the Government's well-armed para-military forces have often not succeeded in the liquidation of the insurgents.

The ideologically-motivated movement of the Maoists requires deep scrutiny, especially as the democratically elected Union and State Governments attempt to eradicate the problems faced in backward regions of the country. A brief description of the origins of the Naxal movement in West Bengal and Andhra Pradesh should help contextualise the movement.

After separating from the CPI(M), Kanu Sanyal and Charu Majumdar launched an armed struggle in 1967 from Naxalbari village in West Bengal's Darjeeling district. Their 'war' was similar to the efforts of the People's War Group in Andhra Pradesh. Siddhartha Shankar Ray, the then Chief Minister of West Bengal, launched a ruthless offensive against the Naxal leaders and it yielded the desired results. But now, after a gap of many years, the Naxal movement in West Bengal has re-emerged. This should lead us to examine the appeal of this ideology for the poor and tribal population in extremely backward regions of India.

The manner in which economic development has happened in post-Independence India has created serious regional imbalances and much social inequity. Maoism, therefore, has found fertile ground in the underdeveloped, backward States of Jharkhand, Bihar, Chhattisgarh and Odisha and even in Andhra Pradesh where certain regions remain undeveloped. In these areas, the insurgents have mobilised the discontented, dissatisfied and disempowered masses. But note that the Maoists have not been able to take violent movement outside the backward regions. Clearly, then it is the lack of development that breeds non-conformist, anti-democracy movements.

The only way to eliminate the Maoist challenge, once and for all, is to follow the policy of bullet for bullet in the short term but also to push for development of the backward States in the long term. The first strategy is a legitimate response from any democratically elected government towards an armed insurgency. However, it has its limitations. The deployment of security personnel cannot be a substitute for good governance.

The Government recognises this fact, yet its development initiatives have not yielded the desired results. For example, there are many special schemes and plans for the poor, but they are often badly implemented. As a result, India is paying heavy price for misgovernance because the bureaucracy is insensitive to the poor. Further, Maoist also oppose every developmental scheme introduced by the Government. The only option here is to activate local institutions such as the panchayats which can then be responsible for the implementations of the development schemes.

Even this approach has limitations. After all, it is hard to imagine that the South Korean owners of Posco will understand the plight of the Indian poor.

Friday, 12-04-2013

Is our Bureaucracy Neutral?

It is generally assumed that in a highly competitive multi-polar party democracy, civil and police functionaries perform their duties of maintenance of law and order in a neutral manner. It is not too much to expect that permanent civil and police functionaries perform their roles as impartial guardians of the rule of law while dealing with highly differentiated strata of the citizenry, both during normal and conflict situations.

But if these assumptions were found valid, the Congress-led UPA government would not have put its seal of approval on a highly diluted Communal Violence Bill.

Bill of a Problem

An important salient feature of this Bill, regarding collective violence committed against a religious or a linguistic community, is that the "toothless" National Human Rights Commission and State Human Rights Commissions are expected to "oversee" the performance of functionaries related to "maintaining of communal harmony".

It is for the first time that a Bill on communal violence has specifically fixed the responsibility of public servants in case of breach of command and failure to exercise control over subordinates "under their direct command".

The central government has recognised the harsh truth that civil and police functionaries of the government have not played a fair role while performing their duties during inter-community group violence. It can be argued that these functionaries have either been negligent during inter-community conflict situations or, worse, have shown a bias.

The Supreme Court had to intervene and transfer cases against the accused in the anti-Muslim post-Godhra riots of 2002 in Gujarat because the judges felt the victims could not expect justice from a partisan political and bureaucratic apparatus in the state. But it is not the first time that an independent and impartial judiciary has exposed biased and prejudiced interventions of local bureaucratic functionaries during inter-community conflicts.

Worming their Way In

Many judicial inquiry reports on "riots" have identified individual police officials who were actively involved in anti-minority riots—for example, Justice S Srikrishna was bold enough to single out police officials who did not protect Muslim victims during the Mumbai riots of 1993. Then, many examples exist where hidden biases of officials-inservice become public when, just after retirement, they choose to join a sectarian party. If senior officials themselves happen to be "Hindu Rashtravadis" of the Sangh Parivar, conflicts cannot be managed in a natural and impartial manner.

Also, it is a well-known fact that Sardar Patel, as home minister, in 1948, had openly "approved the reported action of the Bombay government banning the employment of Rashtriya Swayamsevak Sangh (RSS) men in government service... because it was not proper for government servants to identify with a communal organisation".

Much has happened since then, and Hindu communalism, and its para-army organisation of the RSS, has become a force to reckon with as its ideology has penetrated deep into the centres of power.

If the nationalists of post-Independence India could deal sternly with the RSS, Keshubhai Patel, former BJP CM of Gujarat with the full support of the RSS-controlled Sangh Parivar, in 2000 officially permitted the recruitment of individuals with an RSS background into the state civil services and A B Vajpayee, the then-PM, not only openly defended the Gujarat government order but "observed" that the RSS was a "cultural and social organisation".

So Not Secular

The RSS trains and indoctrinates its cadre in the belief system that Bharat Mata is the birthplace of Hindus only because other citizens like Muslims and Christians draw inspiration from outside Bharat Mata as their holy places of worship and religious reference points are located "outside" India. So, Hindus are "indigenous" and the "others" are "outsiders". Narendra Modi summed up this ideology when he observed, "I am a Hindu. I am a nationalist. Hence, I am a patriot."

It is not without reason that believers of this ideology are recruited by BJP-led state governments in state police forces, especially at the rank-and-file levels where recruitment is politically controlled by the BJP-in-government. It is not without reason that the BJP opposed the very idea of a law on the prevention of communal violence as interference in the domain of state governments. So, how can India be a secular democracy if its institutions of governance are managed by functionaries who believe that India is a Hindus-only nation?

The provision in the Communal Violence Bill for the overseeing of public personnel during situations of inter-religious communal violence needs to be strengthened and a special law is required to swiftly punish those who are found guilty of the dereliction of duty of protecting citizens' lives and property irrespective of religious identity. *The Economic Times, 30-12-2013*

Good Governance is not Always Good Economics

President Pranab Mukherjee, in his address to the nation on the eve of Republic Day, observed that "fractional mandates" had proved "catastrophic" and a situation had arisen when coalition governments at the Centre had become "hostage" to "whimsically" opportunistic aligned partners. Union minister Farooq Abdullah on February 2 said the government's "policies that should have been implemented three years back" could not be agreed upon because of the "veto" exercised by one partner or the other.

Even at the international level it has been maintained that the 'authoritarian Chinese political system' has an immense capacity to push forward a rate of economic growth that the democratic form of politics of India can't. The argument that stability is a prerequisite for achieving higher economic growth deserves clinical analysis because evidence from developing countries is not conclusive.

Based on the experiences of developing countries in Asia, Africa and Latin America political stability may be considered necessary but not at all sufficient for achieving the goals of social, economic and human resource development. State governments in India have been quite stable and some of them have not only completed five-year terms in office, a few of them have won elections continuously twice or thrice. Tamil Nadu may be ranked very high in delivering pro-poor and welfare services like the mid-day meal scheme. How could Tamil Nadu, Kerala and Andhra Pradesh achieve a consistently high rank in every sector of development? Why have Uttar Pradesh, Bihar, Madhya Pradesh and Rajasthan failed to come out of their inherited structures of backwardness?

On the basis of the data of the National Survey of the Central Statistics Office and the Planning Commission, of the 20 states for which the data are available, Bihar, UP, MP and Rajasthan rank 19th, 18th, 16th and 15th, respectively, on the basis of developmental indicators (2004, 2005). There is no evidence suggesting that the Centre had followed any discriminatory policies towards these states; on the contrary they enjoyed special political leverage.

Mukherjee, just after taking over as the President, warned that the high rates of economic growth could not automatically "trickle down". Political interventions are required in a determined manner if the needy are to get the benefits of growth. If some states are left behind the blame lies with the political leadership. The politics of communalism and caste leads to the allocation of resources for development in a differential and discriminatory manner. Politicians make choices while allocating resources for economic and social development and these choices are conditioned by their ideological preferences.

It is clear that a particular model of politics can lead to socially inclusive economic growth with social justice and a communal and casteist model of politics leads to social exclusivism practised by those who profess sectarian and communal ideologies. *Hindustan Times, 14–02-2014*

A Corrupt Middleman is not the Only Problem

It is not the first time that angry Members of Parliament, political parties, the media and self-appointed anti-corruption crusaders are discussing the role of corrupt middlemen in defence deals. It is also not the first time that a Cabinet Minister has innocently asked for the indigenisation of defence equipment to keep foreigners away. In fact, this is the story that plays out every time a corruption scandal in the defence sector becomes public. Then, there are demands for blacklisting corrupt foreign suppliers.

However, no one has cared to go to the root of the problem which is faced by the Indian Army, Navy and Air Force. The Armed Forces understandably want to modernise and upgrade themselves. The Government then has to go on a hunt for sellers from advanced industrial countries to purchase hardware for the Forces. If one country is dependent on other countries that produce and sell weapons, for its defence needs, then is only natural that middlemen will get involved.

Indians are shopping for weapons in a highly competitive and profitable global market. For example, the Swedes were not the only party involved in the sale of Bofors guns. In fact, when Indians were actively scouting the arms bazaar, every major gun-producing country was in the fray. The only difference was that eventually the lobbyists for Bofors succeeded, where others failed.

Similarly, Italy was not the only country competing to sell VVIP helicopters to India. But it was the Rs. 3,000 crore bribe that it offered which clinched the deal in its favour. Of course, this does not mean that the other competitors were not offering any money. The crux of the issue is that India is one of the biggest buyers of defence equipment because its own capacity to manufacture sophisticated hardware is limited.

Incidentally, India considers China as its economic and military competitor in the 21st century. However, China has strong domestic capabilities to meet not only its own galloping defence needs but also to take care of the needs of its strategic ally, Pakistan. The US also has been quite generous in providing arms to the Pakistani Army. The Indian journey in this regard has been quite interesting because of India's defence ties with the erstwhile Soviet Union which was a reliable and extremely helpful arms supplier. However, this journey came to an end when the Soviet Union collapsed, forcing India to enter the competitive global arms market. It is only during this new phase, that stories of kickbacks in defence deals surfaced.

Most recently, the UPA Government has been cornered by the Opposition in the Agusta Westland copter scam. This was followed by Defence Minister AK Antony announcing on February 20 that a new policy for the indigenisation of defence production will be actively pursued. But it should not be forgotten that former Defence Minister VK Krishna Menon had also talked about similar processes and how the public sector, the private sector and the defence production sector could eventually make India self-reliant economic and military power.

The fact remains that modern warfare compels every country to update its arsenal with state-of-the-art technology. If India wants the best in defence technologies, it has to allow foreign operators a free hand in joint venture enterprises. Already, Antony's statement of February 20 has activated the US India Business Council, which represents top multi-nationals. USIBC has asked the Indian Government to hike foreign direct investment in the defence sector from 26 to 74 per cent. But the larger issue is not that of unscrupulous middlemen but the role of Government in deciding the size of defence budget keeping in mind the strategic concerns of India. *The Pioneer, 01–03-2013*

It Takes Two to Tango

A premise of parliamentary democracy is that an elected and accountable political executive, with the assistance of an elaborate bureaucratic structure, will manage public affairs within the restrictions imposed by the Constitution and laws. It is further assumed that the supremacy, sanctity and majesty of the rule of law will be protected and promoted both by the elected and permanent executives in a professional and impartial manner.

However, the reality of politics in every democracy is complex and many deviations from 'legalities' take place. A few facts stand out in substantiating the argument that Indian democracy is in a great crisis because legal norms are being violated.

It deserves to be stated that the elected political executive cannot bend and break legally well-defined 'procedures of governance' without the full support of the professional public services. It is because of this collusion between politicians and bureaucrats that violations of law and procedures have occurred in governance. The judiciary, lokayuktas of the states, the Central

Bureau of Investigation and other inquiry commissions have indicted not only ministers but also civil servants because both have been in a cosy nexus. This became all the more clear when ministers and chief secretaries of the states and secretaries to the Government of India were found guilty of collaboration in abusing powers.

To cite another dimension of the problem, the Justice Srikrishna Commission's inquiry into the Mumbai riots of 1992-93 identified not only activists of Hindu communal organisations, it also clearly mentioned that many high officials of the Mumbai police were actively involved in the anti-Muslim riots. The Supreme Court has many a time intervened in Gujarat chief minister Narendra Modi's functioning and transferred the hearing of cases filed by riot victims to Maharashtra because of the suspicion that the prerequisites for a fair trial did not exist in Gujarat. It is well-known that some civil servants have developed an elaborate system of 'loyalties' towards politicians on the basis of caste and religion and in such a situation citizens find it difficult to get protection of life and property.

The story goes back many years. Indira Gandhi as PM asked for a 'committed bureaucracy' in the mid-70s. Though that ended in a fiasco, its other face is the current casteisation and communalisation, which the Election Commission of India has brought into focus by guiding and supervising the personnel involved in election duty during the Lok Sabha and assembly elections. The EC has often asked states to remove from election duty senior officials because of their suspected partisanship.

The real explanation for this is that many honest pubic functionaries are always at the receiving end and wilt under political pressure. Honesty and integrity have come to be regarded as deviations from the dominant culture of adjustment with the political masters for self-advancement and rewards. This situation makes it difficult for sincere public servants to survive.

Political democracy is a difficult form of government because powerful interest groups always try to enter the corridors of power and pubic decision-making. Hence, only a strong institutional system based on checks and balances and accountability can insulate to a great extent the political executive and its machinery of permanent functionaries from such elements.

The silver lining is that Indian democracy, like all western democracies, is engaged in a struggle to create a strong structure of rule of law. Many other countries have cleansed their governance systems and India is becoming conscious of the fact that things cannot go on like this.

Hindustan Times, 25-04-2014

Chapter 4

Corrution and Coalition

It's Oligarchy, not Democracy

A lot of attention has been focussed on corruption in the electoral process. The Election Commission of India has made many important interventions to cleanse the electoral process by maintaining vigilance over the role of criminals, mafia and musclemen who have been terrorising the voters to ensure that they exercise theirright to vote in favour of the candidates who are either themselves 'hardened criminals' or who are sponsored by local musclemen. If the practice of declaring assets was expected to curb the flow of unaccounted money during elections, this hope has been completely belied.

It is simplistic to believe that the Representation of People's Act or extra vigilance by the Election Commission will curb the flow of funds, mostly illegal, incurred for winning an election. Every attempt to cleanse the electoral process of malpractices is bound to achieve limited success because politics in India has become an activity for the accumulation of funds for personal prosperity and riches. Politics has ceased to be social or public service and large number of MPs, MLAs and other active participants in democratic politics are engaged in pursuing personal goals for their own advancement and welfare.

A few facts may be mentioned to substantiate the argument that politics has become an activity of mercenaries in public life who have personally benefited by joining political activity. First, it has been a common feature among Indian politicians to manage and control political parties like a private business. Not only the Congress—regional parties like the Akali Dal, or Indian National Lok Dal of Haryana or Samajwadi Party of Uttar Pradesh, or Rashtriya Janata Dal of Bihar or Biju Janata Dal of Odisha or DMK of Tamil Nadu are patronising, practising and promoting the cult of 'dynastic family politics'. It is not only that these leaders are promoting their close family members out of love and affection: These leaders are the sole custodians of 'financial resources' which cannot be trusted to other leaders. Party leaders like Pradash Singh Badal, Om Prakash Chautala, Ajit Singh, Mulayam Singh Yadav or Lalu Prasad, Navin Patnaik or M Karunanidhi exercise authoritarian control over the party because the party funds are 'controlled' by the family. Party MLAs and MPs are disciplined by their leaders because of the power of money which is in the hands of leaders only.

Party leaders and their families have to collect huge funds not only for themselves but also for these loyal party members who are given some share as a quid pro quo for blind obedience. If the party boss exercises political power to accumulate funds for family or party purposes, individual MPs, MLAs also individually make every effect to accumulateprivate funds for themselves. If power politics has come to be equated with 'money power in politics', the corporate sector and big business are very ready to pay the price to politicians for bending and breaking the rules and procedures in favour of fund-givers.

This is why an assembly or Lok Sabha election has become a matter of life and death for parties because only when they are in the corridors of governmental power, they are contacted and approached by other powerful shops who reciprocate if they get governmental contracts and other governmental assignments. Further, the coalition governments at the Centre beginning from the 1990s have provided an opportunity to every small or middle or single coalition partner to separately collect money for its own party.

The Atal Bihari Vajpayee coalition government at the Centre in 1998-2004 was a coalition of 24 parties or groups. Every party or group in the coalition used its power to collect funds for the self only. This is the reason that coalitions are formed without any principles or ideologies and erstwhile partners of Hindu Rashtravadis like Mamata Banerjee or DMK or AIADMK et al, had no hesitation in joining the winning coalition led by Congress party. Indian politicians talk about the secularism-communalism ideological divide but in 1998 when Hindu nationalists led by Atal Bihari Vajpayee formed coalition governments, all the so-called practitioners of secularism like George Fernandes, Nitish Kumar, Chandrababu Naidu *et al.* willingly and enthusiastically participated in the Vajpayee's government and some of them even joined the secular government of UPA 1 and 2 and these political climbers recognise the value of political power which has nothing to do with any ideology except the ideology of political power for self-advancement and self-promotion. The above context is to be kept in mind while discussing the emergence of the phenomenon of crorepatis or multi-millionaires in a democracy of more than 500 million below the poverty line or mere subsistence level population of the country.

Democracy is a government by elected representatives and it seems ironical that crorepatis or multi-millionaires, who are a microscopic minority of Indian population, claim to represent the wretched of the earth of India. It is a tip of the iceberg to point out Jagan Reddys or Rajas or Yedyurappas who have been caught red-handed for accumulating unlimited money while exercising political power. The recent survey of 'affidavits' filed by contesting candidates in the Lok Sabha or state assembly elections has shown that a large majority of contestants and winning candidates are crorepatis or multi-millionaires. The family patriarchs and their progeny of family-run party business like Badals or Mulayams or Karunanidhis or others are those who have astonishingly become crorepatis or multi-millionaires because of their active involvement in democratic politics of India. Many political leaders who are crorepatis or multimillionaires of 'today' were very ordinary citizens with ordinary economic status before entering politics. The so-called 'discretionary' powers given to the political leaders by the law of the country have been exercised only to oblige the fund-giver businessmen or mine owners.

A political system ceases to be a democracy where the filthy rich claim to be elected representatives of the people because democratically elected leaders should reflect the socio-economic reality of ordinary people. It is quite ironic that the struggling mass of the people of India are represented by multi-millionaires, especially those who got rich via the 'business of politics'. The question is: Who is the representative of the ordinary voter who stands in a queue during elections? Can crorepatis feel the pain of poverty of 500 million Indians? Indian democracy has become an 'oligarchy' because only the moneyed class can win an election. This is a threat to democracy.

Financial World, 23-6-2012

At the Service of their Political Masters

The biggest advantage of the democratic political process is that myths are broken at every stage. The political churn that is happening in the run upto the Assembly elections too is throwing up new faces and breaking a lot of myths along the way. Last week, senior Haryana IAS officer Ashok Khemka's questioning his transfer from Gurgaon within 45 days of his joining broke a big myth about civil servants having a cushyprofessional life which allows them to dictate terms to the lawmakers. Khemka's latest transfer came after he ordered a probe into the DLF-Robert Vadra land deal. The officer claims to have had 43 transfers during his 20-year service extending from 1992 to 2012.

Though it came as a shock to many, Khemka's 'transfer' record is hardly an exception in India where every party misuses its power either to reward cooperative bureaucrats or punish those unwilling to 'bend' rules. Our bureaucratic machinery is divided between the 'pliable' and the 'upright and procedure-oriented' bureaucrats, and while one is patronised and promoted by politicians, the other faces their hostility through 'transfer'. On 12 October, Khemka complained to the Haryana Chief Secretary against his 'abrupt transfer' only to be told by Chief Minister Bhupinder Singh Hooda that it was his government's prerogative to transfer civil servants. "I have asked the Chief Secretary to examine the assertions made by the IAS Officer and expect a report shortly," said Hooda adding, "And if Khemka has misquoted facts, action will be taken against him."

The cabinet secretary (at the centre) and chief secretary (in the state) are expected to protect the interests of civil servants within their jurisdiction as the heads of their establishment. But it is also an open secret that chief ministers appoint their 'favourites' as chief secretaries. Can these office bearers then be expected to honestly play 'guardians' to the civil service machinery? If former Telecom secretary Sidharth Behura was made a co-accused with former Minister A Raja for the 2G scam it wasn't without reason. Senior civil servants cannot violate law unless they are assured protection by their political masters on a quid pro quo basis. Explains why central cabinet ministers prefer to appoint personnel from their own state or home district in their favourite ministries. And this nexus between politicians and bureaucrats also includes senior police official. It is this prejudiced political executive that has divided public services along the lines of caste and religion and the sectarian divide is so deep now that it has started impacting the national ethos.

The Sri Krishna inquiry report on the 1993 Mumbai riots clearly identified 'high police officials' who were guilty of serious acts of bias against the minority community. The Narendra Modi government presided over the massacre of more than 2,000 innocent Muslims in 2002 with the willing involvement of the state police. With the officials at the beck and call of politicians, the recent Supreme Court directive to state governments to implement 'police reforms' seems like a bad joke on the governance. Sanjeev Bhatt, a Gujarat IPS official, was suspended by the Modi government because he dared to expose the latter's role in the post-Godhra riots. 'Politically obliging' civil servants, on the other hand, manage lucrative assignments even after retirement.

The Nehru-Indira model of economic planning which operated under rigid control of procedure-oriented bureaucracy is much criticised as the 'licence-permit' Raj and it was believed that the era of liberalisation will 'liberate' the economy from this obstructionist system. However, this myth too has been duly broken because all pliable retired civil servants now sit on regulatory commissions, the new 'centres of power' in the liberalised economy. Never was the Planning Commission as powerful as it is today under Montek Singh Ahluwalia. And the Telecom Regulatory Authority of India (TRAI) has only had retired IAS officers playing puppets to changing regimes.

The message is loud and clear that our public bureaucracy is actually a 'private' organisation at the service of the elected representatives. The 'yes men' are rewarded with appointments as governors, ambassadors and chairmen of commissions. The unrelenting like Ashok Khemka and Sanjeev Bhatt get the boot. Their integrity and efficiency is the least of the concerns of their political masters. Not even if it ensures better governance. Quite clearly, the 'inside story' of the Indian bureaucracy is in complete contrast with all the myths created around it. Largely, it is corrupt, prejudiced and dishonest. And this rot within is only impacting the miniscule good there is to it. Not a very encouraging scenario for India. *Financial World, 24-10-2012*

ANNA HAZARE'S MOVEMENT

Potential of Mass Movements

Anna Hazares agitation in defence of his version of the Lokpal Bill seems to have revived public memories of the 1974-75 Jayaprakash Narayan-led anti-corruption mass agitation, especially among the new generation of technology-driven middle class youth in metropolitan towns of India. But can Anna Hazares anti-corruption crusade become a benchmark comparable with the historical mass mobilisation movements launched by Gandhi from 1920 to 1947 or the one popularly known as the JP movement of 1974-75.

A mass movement has to be distinguished from political mobilisation undertaken by every political party in a competitive democracy because, unlike parties which mobilise their voters and supporters for winning an election, peoples movements are launched for cleansing the system of its fundamental ills. Gandhi prepared Indians to fight the struggle for Independence and for this mass struggle he created a united social bloc of castes, classes, religions, regions and women. The Gandhian movement was socially broad-based and inclusive of all major group identities of the country. The JP movement, unlike Gandhis struggles, had a limited reach, where he raised anti-corruption issues facing India. Further, JP, unlike Gandhi, had no mass base of his own, and he led the movement on the basis of cadre provided by Lohia socialists, the Rashtriya Swayamsevak Sangh (RSS) and the Jan Sangh. Essentially, JP launched a movement on the corruption issue primarily directed against Indira Gandhi as an individual and as a leader of a corrupt party and government. The lesson from the JP movement is that a large-scale mass movement has to be a product of preceding small-scale mobilisations as Gandhi did from the 1920s to 1947. Anna Hazares movement has some salient features that are a replication of the JP movement, but it has nothing in common with Gandhian movements. Hazares movement has spread in towns and cities, especially after his arrest by Delhi Police on August 16 and angry people have come out on the road in support of him. It is a repeat story, because the JP movement had assumed an all-India status only when the Allahabad High Court judgment of June 1975 set aside the election of Prime Minister Indira Gandhi. This support of the urban middle and lower middle class to Hazare is not only because of his anti-corruption crusade but because it is also an expression of their general frustration with the existing situation for which the easy whipping boy is the Manmohan Singh government. Further, Hazare himself and many of his supporters on the streets are targeting corrupt politicians, but in reality they are themselves apolitical, even anti-politics, in their daily life and ideological value system. Hazare has debunked the system of elections by publicly stating that elections are won by bribing the voter and his complete lack of faith in the democratic process of India can be summed up in his oft-repeated statement that the transfer of power after 1947 was from the white to the brown and black Indians and nothing has changed during the last 64 years of Indias Independence. Further, unlike Gandhi, Hazare who has no faith in democracy, has adopted fascistic methods to get a seal of approval by Parliament for his demand. This has nothing to do with Gandhian movements because Gandhi suspended his movements and never feared to negotiate with the colonial rulers. Anna, like JP, has been compelled to depend on the mobilisation machine of the Sangh Parivar and its communal-fascist cadre of the RSS. The BJP within Parliament and the whole joint family of the Sangh Parivar on the streets are providing the whole structure of support to keep the pot boiling to stigmatise the Congress, its main rival in politics. Gandhis movements had a long-term impact on Indian public life, Hazares movement, like the JP movement, has political consequences and its impact will be felt only in electoral politics. The age of large-scale united all-India mass movements has come to an end because a socially and regionally fragmented country will have, and has been, witnessing local/regional movements or caste-based movements. Our national identity, which was created by Gandhian struggles from Kohima to Peshawar, has been pushed to the background by movements launched by fragments on particularist demands of sections of society. Political competition among parties around local grievances has become the reality of democratic India. It is no ones case that politics will be missing from social movements; the only issue, as raised by the German philosopher Habermas, is that every social movement should be critically evaluated on the basis of its leadership, its social base, and the social cause pursued by the leaders. On the basis of the analytical yardstick suggested by Habermas, Hazares movement and the social support generated by it clearly reveals that the communal-fascist Sangh Parivar is the main driver of this movement.

Economic Times, 24-08-2011

State Response to Movement

The *Seminar* issue of September 2011 is devoted to the problematic of 'Combating Corruption' and contributors, a majority of them from civil society, have offered rich analysis focused on the Anna Hazare movement of August 2011. There is, however, need for broadening the discussion on the role of social movements in a democracy. Politics is the driving force in every society and it is no one's case that the activity of politics can be caged within the rules of the game as defined by the constitutional system of a democratic politics. The pillar of politics in democracy is the 'freedoms' that are available to citizens to exercise their right of dissent against the legally constituted institutions of the state. And dissenters and nonconformists define their own boundaries without caring for the limits imposed by the legal-institutional apparatuses of the state. The question is: How does the state respond to social movements launched by public spirited dissenters and diverse kinds of opposition groups?

The Indian state, during the sixty four years of its post-independence journey, has dealt with a large variety of movements which have emerged on the basis of felt-grievances of different segments and regions of society in a variety of ways. It used its organized and well-equipped armed forces in dealing with the Communist party-led Telangana movement from 1947 to 1950, despite the fact that it was an 'armed' struggle of the peasantry against feudal oppression and exploitation. The state did not address the genuine demands of an oppressed peasantry because it always uses its coercive forces against angry social groups, particularly if they launch an armed struggle against an unresponsive state which is protecting the interests of the exploiting classes.

The policy of bullet versus bullet has been consistently followed by the Indian state against armed groups which sought to opt out of India's territorially defined boundaries or against peasants and tribals who took to arms because the state was seen as protecting the oppressor landlords and mafias who have exploited the poor tribals and their natural resources.

It is not without reason that the managers of the Indian state have publicly observed that 'the Maoist insurgency is the greatest threat to the security of the state' and have sought to crush it. The above narrative clearly shows that our 'democratic' state has little concern for people's struggles if solutions are demanded by launching armed movements, either by suffering peasants or tribals or groups which claim to have the right to opt out of the Indian Union. A democratic state on the basis of its claim of moral superiority and democratic sanctions has legitimized its use of coercive power against anti-state armed struggles of groups who are fighting for their 'rights'.

While this is one facet of the relationship between state and movements, the other is that the functionaries of the state also negotiate with and accommodate the demands made by social movements which are described as 'normal activity of dissident groups in a competitive electoral democratic political system.' The Jayaprakash Narayan or Anna Hazare-led movements may rhetorically be described as extra-constitutional, but the functionaries of the state go out of their way to negotiate, bargain and accommodate the demands of these so-called social movements of civil society. Every such movement is concerned with the reform of the political system and while the state may resist some demands, it always keeps its doors open for settlement with the leadership of such intra-state reformist movements because they are spearheaded by leaders and social groups who are not 'outsiders' as far as the state system is concerned.

The JP movement was launched in 1974-75 to 'purify' a corrupted electoral system with a view to cleansing the democratic institutions by limiting the entry of MLAs and MPs accused of electoral malpractices. Jayaprakash Narayan launched his struggle against 'polluted' governmental institutions because those holding the reins had adopted 'foul' means to come to power. He wanted to restore the majesty and legitimacy of democratic institutions through his proposals for electoral reforms. Reforming democracy was the main agenda of the JP movement. Similarly, numerous other movements for the reorganization of state boundaries too have received a 'royal treatment' from negotiators and interlocutors of the government-in-power, by the opposition parties and media, both print and audiovisual. Anna's movement too was for a 'negotiated settlement' on the issue of an appropriate mechanism to check corruption in public life and public institutions. Anna led a popular struggle for a Jan Lokpal bill and like many other democratic struggles in post-independence India, this movement too achieved its goal on the basis of 'democratic accommodation' by the powers-that-be.

Clearly the state itself decides to adopt different yardsticks while dealing with different movements in a democracy. Depending upon the basic social issues raised by the movement and the methods chosen for achieving its goal, the state decides either to ruthlessly crush the movement or negotiate with its leaders. If on the one hand, the demands of a surplus generating peasantry or rural oligarchy, as articulated by the late Mahendra Singh Tikait's Bharatiya Kisan Union, are negotiated and conceded, struggles launched by landless agricultural labourers, share croppers, marginal farmers and tribals receive a cavalier response, often pushing them into taking up arms against the state.

The Anna Hazare movement too needs to be examined on the basis of its demands, and the support it garnered from the emerging middle classes who used modern means of communication to spread their message across the country. Is the emergence of the phenomenon of movements, actively supported by upwardly mobile technocratic, professional middle classes, any surprise? Instead of berating a social movement, which may have a broad social base among the rising Indian middle classes, the focus should be on analyzing the ideological driving force of this segment of our society, since middle class activism is here to stay.

By and large this 'moneyed class' is insecure and socially conservative, even status quoist. It is not sympathetically oriented towards movements for the rights of the 'real' poor, the basic classes, and usually supports every state action which, in its judgement, is needed to maintain and protect the existing social order. The mainstream of this 'new class', a product of fast-changing material forces of production, is status'-quoist', right-wing conservative and, in the specific Indian situation, a believer in and practitioner of ritualized religion.

Hence, the upshot is that the rapid, ongoing social change is creating a new strata of society and movements articulating demands which cannot be dismissed in a contemptuous manner. Social movements should be properly analysed. Further, historical evidence also testifies to the fact that even the essentially 'socially conservative middle class' can become an 'agency' for basic social transformations in society. The Indian middle class, old and new, has revealed its 'two faces' or two tendencies during the different struggles of the 20th century. At one level, every tall leader of the Indian national struggle against British colonial rule, despite different ideological persuasions, came from the middle classes and made every kind of personal sacrifice for the liberation of the country. The Indian middle class has been actively involved both in right of centre or left-of-centre or even full-fledged Communist party-led struggles. It is this complex and contradictory character of the emerging middle classes which influences both the goals and directions of the social movement, as also the response of the state.

Shades of Blue Seminar 626, October *2011*

Lokpal Movement: Whither Public Accountability?

Corruption crusader Anna Hazare's movement elicited public response because people have developed hatred against public functionaries. They perceive them as violators of laws of the land. Every democratic system has an elaborate system of checks and balances to ensure public accountability. India is not an exception. A complex system of institutions has been created to ensure that every public functionary is held accountable.

Legal institutions for governance are a necessary but not sufficient condition to ensure that an 'accountable' functionary of the state implements the rule of law. India has an elaborate structure for holding every public-decision maker accountable, but the reality is that a majority of 'insiders' are generally able to subvert the formally laiddown governance procedures.

A political executive in a democracy is expected to act as a defender of the rule of law and the Constitution. But the reality is that many of these custodians of the Constitution have been arrested and prosecuted for violations of law even while holding public office. Members of the union council of ministers have been hauled up by investigation agencies for violating laws and later prosecuted after a fair trial. Public servants—be they ministers or bureaucrats—are pillars of the democratic system to ensure that procedures are followed in government.

There is an internal chain of command among them. They are duty-bound to take decisions while dealing with the problems of citizens. However, this system, with a water-tight, built-in structure of control and supervision, has not yielded proper accountability of decision-makers in India.

Why has the formal system of accountability become so dysfunctional that its violators feel confident and subvert the whole system of checks and balances? The key reason is that the system is not foolproof. First, only internal mechanisms of public accountability have been defined.

However, the 'external' dimension of accountability was never integrally linked to the first. An open democracy and open government has never actually operated in India because every activity and decision of the government was 'open' only to a powerful strata of society. But it was 'secret' for a vast majority of citizens, who had to knock at the doors of decision-makers to resolve their problems.

Even today, most people in India do not have any access or information on the rationale or genesis of any public-decision taken by any public functionary that impinges on their day-to-day lives. The Right to Information Act, 2005 and the setting up of Central and State-level Information Commissions has opened the mysterious gates of the offices of decision-makers. This law has extended, to a great extent, the boundaries of accountability in public service.

Politicians or bureaucrats in the higher echelons of governance can 'close ranks' behind the Chinese wall of 'secrecy'. However, if the wall is broken, they will function with a sense of real accountability. Second, a democratic political system should guarantee that citizens will be served by functionaries of the state as a matter of 'right'.

The Grievance Redressal Bill along with a Citizens Charter, such as the RTI Act, will make public servants more accountable. As some social activists have observed, 'getting his bijli, sadak or paani' is far more important for the common man. The Grievance Bill, and not the Lokpal, will empower them to get these basic necessities.

The real innovation in enacting a Public Grievances Bill or Citizen's Charter is that a grievance redressal officer will 'be responsible for redressal of citizens' grievances within 30 days. Else, penal action will be taken against the errant officer.

India is a country that has several laws, including on very complex issues such as anti-corruption. Despite this, citizens often feel helpless while dealing with an 'allpowerful bureaucracy' and its consequence is that only powerful and influential persons can get their job done by a willing, compliant and obliging bureaucracy.

Ordinary citizens do not have any mechanism to hold non-performing bureaucrats accountable to any citizen-body that can oversee the actual functioning of public service.

India has continued with the British colonial structure of bureaucracy, where it is taken for granted that a well-knit chain of a command and hierarchical supervision system will keep the government machinery at work according to procedures laid down by the laws of the country. This system has not worked.

Hence, the process of decision-making by public authorities—be it the political executive or a permanent and professional civil servant—should be exposed to public scrutiny. Citizens must have a right to get their job done. The existing system of public accountability is dysfunctional.

It can be 'restored' only if offices of the government are 'open', not for powerful lobbyists or touts or middlemen, but for any citizen. The Official Secrecy Act should be replaced with a Citizens' Rights Act.

The Economic Times, 31-12-2011

More to Nation-building than Fighting Graft

Self-appointed and media projected messiahs of 'anti-corruption' campaigns in the country have now taken to painting the democratically elected representatives of the people as the villains that are solely responsible for India's present economic and social crises. According to them, the sources of corruption inpublic life today are the elected leaders. Hence, it is imperative to target these leaders to cleanse public life and rid India of the malaise of corruption.

These anti-corruption messiahs, of whom Team Anna is the most popular, believe that they have successfully identified the culprits and are hence building public opinion against the corrupt. They have also been quite successful—so much so that they have even been able to include the well-fed, professional middle class, which is otherwise indifferent, even contemptuous, of electoral politics. Yet, it does not require a magician to predict that the fragile structures of a young democracy may not necessarily be able to withstand such a challenge that has taken on the form of a highly organised 'hate campaign'.

Furthermore, a dangerous aspect of this anti-corruption campaign is that remedial action, according to this small group of anti-corruption activists, lies not in the strengthening of existing mechanisms of checks and balances that have been provided in the Constitution. Instead, remedies have to be found by assigning the responsibility of dealing with the corrupt to only nominated functionaries like retired members of the judiciary or the Comptroller and Auditor-General of India.

Many well-known Western theorists of elitism have often castigated democratically elected representatives by describing them as corrupt and incompetent. They have theorised that the virtuous and the knowledgeable experts can govern better, while mass-based politicians are essentially incapable of governing a society. Following in the footsteps of these Western critics of democracy, Anna Hazare and his team of musketeers have projected Parliament as an institution where criminals, rapists and the corrupt preside over the destiny of this country. Instead, Team Anna believes that the 'virtuous' and 'highly educated' professionals are the only saviours of this country. It is not without reason then, that former bureaucrats and judges who have made their fortunes at the Bar are in the driver's seat in this so-called mass campaign.

In other words, the anti-corruption campaigners are not champions of parliamentary democracy, because in essence their urban-based movement is directed against the very idea of universal adult suffrage. Their anti-corruption campaign is not only a threat to democracy in India, it has also created a climate where all other major challenges before the country have become irrelevant as public discourse has been hijacked by the single issue of corruption in politics.

It is time India seriously debate dand discussed the country's path of economic development on which it embarked in the beginning of the 1990s. After all, the economic policies that it has pursued for the last two decades have deepened social inequality. The idea of development of 'one India' has not been achieved; instead, many different Indias have emerged because of serious regional imbalances. Should this issue not be in the centre stage of political discourse?

Should Indians not be concerned about the widening of the rural-urban gap in terms of access to education and health facilities, for instance? Should Indians not be debating the issues emerging from demographic changes resulting in the addition of a millions of young people to the work-force? Is the large army of unemployed youth not a challenge worth finding solutions to? What kind of federal restructuring is necessary in a country that is composed of developed, developing and backward regions and States?

Many believe that India has entered the age of Chief Ministers. This could result in the weakening of the Centre's power and prove disastrous for the country. After all, it is only the Union Government which is solely responsible for the security and integrity of the whole country. Should the crisis faced by the all-India parties not be a focus of public discourse?

India cannot pursue any national policy at the global level if all-India parties which have a national and international perspective are weakened and hence dependent on regional parties for making foreign policy decisions. The UPA Government could not resolve the Teesta river water dispute with Bangladesh because a regional party vetoed a national foreign policy.

Post-independence, India has had a great tradition of discussions on 'alternatives' like the model of planned economic development versus free-market economy or foreign policy of non-alignment versus policy of joining a bloc in bipolar world etc.

Today, that discussion has been sidelined by the anti-corruption campaign.

The Pioneer, 08-06-2012

All is Fair in Business and Graft

It is a known fact that industrialists, manufacturers or other powerful players in the market compete against one another to control lion's share of market for maximisation of profits and in this cut-throat competitive game, the capitalists make every effort to win over and influence public policymakers for getting advantages for themselves at the cost of others. Every capitalist plays the same game and employs every trick of the trade to gain benefits at the cost of competitors, and for playing this game they employ hidden persuaders, the backroom boys and professional lobbyists who operate to get concessions for their masters. Further, rival capitalists do not act according to any rules of the game to achieve their own goal at the cost of competitors and the result is that professional and well-paid lobbyists are active in winning over pubic decision makers who are ready to bend and break rules, regulations and laws as a quid pro quo for personal favours receive from lobbyists. This made Prime Minister Manmohan Singh to castigate these 'crony capitalists' who are always engaged in creating conditions of unfair competition in the market by following unethical methods to influence public decision makers.

While championing the cause of 'fair' competition in public, crony capitalists create conditions for 'unfair' competition in their actual day-to-day dealings with public decision makers. It is not only Manmohan Singh who brought into public domain the ugly reality of dark side of capitalists in market, Veerapan Moily, Minister in the cabinet, also exposed this evil of lobbying by interested vested interests. Moily on June 14 stated that 'there are some lobbies which threaten every successive petroleum minister against taking decision to cut imports'. He elaborated 'I am telling you with all sense of responsibility that we are floating in oil and gas in this country. We are not exploring it, instead we are putting every obstruction to it. There are delays caused by bureaucrats in decision making and there are lobbies which don't want us to stop imports.' India imports around 80 per cent of oil and gas and it is a highly profitable business and this is the reason that every effort to cut imports and encourage domestic exploration is 'obstructed' by lobbyists.

The story that lobbyists 'exercise' pressure' on Civil Aviation Ministry was publicly expressed on July 3 by civil aviation minister Ajit Singh when bilateral air services agreement with Abu Dhabi was caught in the cross fire of 'corporate rivalry' and some politicians got involved in opposing this bilateral agreement. Yashwant Sinha of the BJP wanted a CBI investigation into the Jet-Etihad deal because 'it smacks of scam'. It has become a common practice by the lobbyists, opponents of any bilateral agreement, to spread the message that the agreement is the result of 'underhand deals' involving ministers and bureaucrats and thus the bilateral agreements get 'de-monised' to harm the interests of the successful bidder of an agreement. What are the social, economic and political implications of lobbying for rigging competitive transactions in any country including India? It deserves to be mentioned that every country either it is industrially developed or it is in the process of industrial development has been caught by the evil of lobbying for or against competitors in the market.

Hence, governments have created legal institutions to curb the phenomenon of unfair business practices indulged in by rival capitalists. The American Wal Mart Retail multinational corporation is facing an inquiry in the United States for indulging in malpractices through its lobbyists for influencing public decision makers for allowing Wal Mart to establish its retail business in countries around the globe. India has established statutory Competition Commission to launch investigations against industrialists and investors who are accused of rigging competition in the market. The existence of legal institutional mechanism for curbing the activities of lobbyists who indulge in tilting business deals in favour of their masters and against other competitors. It is not only Jet-Etihad India deal which has become the latest victim of 'corporate rivalry', the Air-Asia deal between Malaysia and India's Tata group has faced dirty tricks played by other existing Indian competitors in aviation. The Air-Asia group CEO Tony Fernandes stated in Delhi on July 3 that Naresh Goyal of Jet Airways has immense influence over decision making by public policy makers regarding Indian aviation sector.

This is the story of all sectors and it burst in open when Telecom Ministry, both its Political Executive and bureaucracy at the higher level were caught in which came to be known as 2 G spectrum deal involving 'all big players' and rules were bent and broken to favour some while distributing licences. The corporate sector has institutionalised the culture of corruption in public life because in its desire to break rules of the game of competition in market, it has let lose its 'lobbyists' to operate with no holds barred to secure concessions for a particular promoter and scuttle the chances of competitors to succeed. It is not only that pubic exchequer suffers huge losses in terms of public revenue from business like licensing costs of which it could earn from competitive pricing by distributing Telecom licenses on the basis of competition in a transparent manner, the consumers would also have benefited by paying low prices for services rendered by telecom service providers.

If the 'middlemen' have succeeded in 'rigging' the competition, the impact is clearly felt on the losses suffered by public exchequer and the high price paid by the consumers because the investors money spent in influencing the public decision making in the country has to be earned back by the investors who have succeeded in getting business concessions by indulging in illegal trade practices.

The Anna Hazare and Company launched public protest against corruption by politicians and political parties. However, these mass protests did not target the real culprits who have institutionalised the culture of corruption by bribing the public decision makers to get benefits for themselves at the cost of public good.

The big cats, the bribe givers, were not targeted either by Hazare and company or the corporate controlled media which went berserk in advertising Hazare's tirade against corruption in politics and the nexus which exists between politics and big business and industry was not mentioned by opinion makers. The upshot of above description is that crony capitalism and the institutionalised system of 'lobbying' for the promotion of malpractice's in public decision making process has brought immense losses to public exchequer and victimised the consumers who compensate the 'bribe givers' by paying high prices in the market. *The Financial World, 12-07-2013*

AAM AADMI PARTY

Well-meaning, but also Removed from Reality

Anna Hazare's erstwhile leading lights—Arvind Kejriwal, Shanti Bhushan, Prashant Bhushan and others—had made public statements against politicians and political parties. They have now abandoned non-party civil society crusades to launch a political outfit. An average Indian politician considers politics as a career for self-advancement and self-promotion. And in the quest for his individual prosperity, ideological commitments are considered expendable. How is Kejriwal any different from other non-ideological careerists in politics? The new entrants have a history of 'shifting' their goals and abandoning erstwhile allies in previous struggles such as for the Right to Information. They have also abandoned causes which brought them into public domain.

Arvind Kejriwal's recently launched Aam Aadmi Party is floating in the air. Its political agenda is nebulous and completely unrelated to the needs and aspirations of the common man. How is he any different from other non-ideological careerists in Indian politics?

Further, everyone in the Aam Aadmi Party has devoted time and energy on one public issue only—corruption. There is no evidence from that they can organise a political party which can confront the complexities of Indian politics. In fact, taking up causes like the hike in power tariff in Delhi further strengthens the argument that they are novices in the arena of competitive party politics. The political programme announced by Kejriwal shows that they have stitched some issues which had previously been raised by civil society. Kejriwal claims that his party is anti-Congress and anti-BJP, without realising that the Left has always practised politics of opposition to the Congress and the BJP. This kind of politics has only marginalised the communists. Today, Indian politics revolves around the Congress and the BJP. Almost every other party has found it necessary to join either one of them. Anti-BJP and anti-Congress political groups have occassionally floated a 'Third Front'. But such coalitions failed because of the political fragility of the alliance partners. Hence, the Aam Aadmi Party will remain a non-starter if it practises unrealistic anti-Congress and anti-BJP politics. If the party does not want to remain a drop in the ocean of Indian politics, it has to state its future plans in the context of coalition politics. A political party operates by establishing a network to connect with the people. By communicating its programme and policies, it is able to create its own constituency of supporters and voters. Kejriwal's AAP is floating in the air. Its political agenda is nebulous and completely unrelated to the needs and aspirations of the common man. And unlike other parties, the AAP lacks an organisational network and financial resources, vital to keep itself afloat. It is not without reason that Infosys founder NR Narayana Murthy who provided Kejriwal money for his struggle for Right to Information, has now refused to fund his party coffers. Of course, Shanti Bhushan has announced a donation of Rs1 crore to AAP but Kejriwal will need many more millions to keep in the business of electoral politics. The intent of Kejriwal and his party is to cleanse the political system of corruption. AAP is essentially a reformist platform, and understandably agonises about the dynamics of the country's politics. But all AAP luminaries have worked within the system and previously they have made no calls for a 'revolution' because they think that the political system can be reformed. Every party claims to stand for the welfare of the downtrodden. Every crorepati politician's heart bleeds for the poor and Kejriwal is sailing in the same boat. Hazare has been unable to make up his mind about 'politics' because on the one hand he has debunked politicians but on the other, has maintained that he will support good candidates. Both men are well-meaning but they do not either understand party-based politics or are pretenders in public life.*The Pioneer, 07-12-2012*

Aam Aadmi Party: Electoral Panacea or Unjustified Hype?

Indians seem to be enjoying the ongoing political drama of electoral political democracy and the best evidence of this addiction for politics is provided by the proliferation of parties throughout the country, whether for the Lok Sabha or state assembly or the panchayat elections.

The Election Commission of India is mandated to provide 'an election symbol' to contesting parties, groups and individuals, and often it has found it difficult to identify an 'election symbol' and ends up in providing the symbol of an appropriate mind. The best example of the ridiculous extent to which the election commission has to go in search for election symbol is the "broom or sweeping stick or jhadu" assigned to the AAP which is the latest entrant to the state assembly elections of Delhi in November 2013. How does one approach the issue of demystification of the essential reality of the AAP? A few facts may be mentioned to understand the essential reality of this new two-year-old party which has jumped into the electoral fray with great enthusiasm in the capital city of Delhi for November state assembly elections.

First, Arvind Kejriwal, the moving figure behind AAP, has been an activist and has received a prominent international award for his contribution to public causes, especially citizens' right to information which is essential for any helpless individual to get to know the decision-making reasons from 'secretive' and authoritarian Indian bureaucracy, from the highest levels to the lowest rung of the civil service hierarchy.

Second, the direct consequence of 'secrecy in decision-making' is that the harassed and humiliated citizens are compelled to take resort to illegal and unfair methods to get their work done for the public services. Corruption in public service and public life becomes the order of the day in an atmosphere of secrecy in decision-making. Arvind Kejriwal took the proverbial second step and mobilized a group of people including Anna Hazare, who had earned similar reputation as an anti-corruption crusader against powerful politicians of his home state of Maharashtra. During the 2011 Delhi experience, a large scale enthusiastic popular gathering of men, women young and old, was organised against corruption in politics, and Anna Hazare and Kejriwal's team during this big public event launched a struggle for the immediate enactment of Jan Lokpal Law for independent and autonomous investigation of public complaints against the highest functionaries of the government suspected of corruption.

This created a new kind of wave among the citizens of Delhi who wanted to move forward and create an organisation or a political platform to 'cleanse' the existing 'dirt' in public life created by established political parties, especially the Congress and the BJP in Delhi. A lot of controversy arose on the decision for the formation of a new party like AAP because anti-corruption platform launched under Anna Hazare and Kejriwal's group of 'non-party activists' has targeted 'party politics' and party and electoral politics were publically castigated and held responsible for the corruption in politics.

Parties and political leaders were accused of not only indulging in corruption, but were also held solely responsible for the complete pollution of public life in India. Hence, floating a political party by a group of activists who have organised an anti-politics movement seemed to be a somersault, an action of great opportunity and betrayal. The worst indictment of this idea of a new party came from Anna Hazare, who as the leading light of Delhi anti-corruption convention of 2011, completely distanced himself from Kejriwal and co.

Further, Kejriwal's Aam Aadmi, like all other parties, whether of the past or the present, is facing serious allegation of "collecting funds" for elections from dubious, especially foreign sources. Kejriwal's colleagues and friends already carry a stigma of setting foreign funds for their so-called NGOs, and AAP continues to be in a shadow of great doubt about money for party from foreign sources. All defences and alibis of Kejriwal or 'funds' have fallen flat because Indian public has become cynical about politicians and their sources of funds, public and secret; a climate of distrust against politicians created by Kejriwal and group, has now impacted AAP also. If every party or politician is a "suspect", Kejriwal, as a politician, cannot be a saint in politics. How can Kejriwal himself escape the inevitable predicaments surrounding Indian politics, politicians and parties?

What are the electoral appeals of AAP? Firstly, the most important asset of a new party is that it cannot be attached on the basis of its past acts of omission and commission. A party of two-years standing whose first test is in a local union territory election of a metropolitan capital city has a freshness and this is the reason that the "middle-class" colonies of the capital city are getting attracted to a "raw and fresh" face in politics. Further, a Delhi-based political formation with middle-class educated faces of leadership has an advantage over parties with vast rural or semi-urban constituencies. Delhi-based media and Delhi-based AAP are natural allies because both represent the middle classes.

Kejriwal is playing all tricks of the trade and his party is promising relief to the middle-class living in Delhi metropolis especially by appealing to their animal instincts of spending less money on public utilities like electricity, power and water to the residential areas. Kejriwal's tactics of individual-specific and special constituency-based "manifesto" which includes specific problems and difficulties faced by residence of a particular constituency may also have some impact on the voter's choice.

The essence of Kejriwal's party is that it is confined to "location" and its mental horizons are extremely "limited" and narrow-based that does not have any world view about the building of a new society. AAP is a "new", only two-years-old entrant in electoral politics and reality is that it has nothing new or fresh to offer to the Delhi-ites, and all its programmatic talks are around ordinary inconveniences faced by the residence. The AAP is neither an all-India party like the Congress or the BJP, nor it is a real grassroots-based regional party like the Dravidian parties of Tamil Nadu, BJD of Odisha, TMC of West Bengal, or Akali Dal of Punjab et al.

It is of little political shock, like a Lilliput facing the Gullivers of politics and its real status is on the "margins" of one capital city of India. Kejriwal and his group has exaggerated notions about itself leading to tall claims of it is setting the "agenda" of politics or the state assembly elections of Delhi in

November. The AAP leadership is suffering from self-delusion, forgetting that as a "minor", even a "marginal" player that will definitely be noted and noticed by a section of middle-class, Delhi-based voters who are always attracted towards the new fashions in clothes and shoes, and hence a new party with new faces.

AAP's talks are tall, its actions resemble those of ordinary, middle-class political activists, and its sources of funds are as suspect as of other parties. It is a different party than the others because it claims to be different. It is not the first time that a new face is seen in politics, the question is of its survivability because entry in politics is easy, but political endurance depends on acceptability and relevance. On the surface, this "baby" party does not seem to have any future prospects because, for the moment, it has offered nothing really "new" in politics. *newsyaps.com* 13-11-2013

Aam Aadmi Party: Fact or Fiction

A highly motivated small group of middle-class, educated professionals have taken the task of reforming the Indian public life to ensure that citizens are able to enjoy their rights in a democracy. It deserves to be clearly stated that only well-motivated individuals take up public causes and mobilize sections of society in support of their demands for a better life under a democracy.

It is not for the first time that agitations and struggles have been launched for the eradication of "corruption in public life" because the Jayaprakash Narayan movement of the early 1970s also had "cleansing" of Indian public life at its core with an objective that democracy in India truly becomes what it literally means. The second decade of the 21st century, like the JP movement, brought leaders like Anna Hazare, an anti-corruption crusader, on the scene. The city of Delhi witnessed a large-scale mobilization for the eradication of corruption in public life with a demand that a Jan Lokpal bill be passed by parliament to curb the cancer of corruption in public life.

Anna Hazare was supported by middle-class reformists like Arvind Kejriwal, Manish Sisodia and others who effectively articulated the demand for an effective law to curb corruption in public life. Some of these prominent anti-graft warriors launched a political party named AAP with the agenda of reforming Indian democracy by participating in the electoral process of the country. This is the life story of AAP.

In its very first attempt, this new entrant to electoral politics secured electoral victories in Delhi state assembly elections in 2013. The party leader Arvind Keriwal has now taken oath as Delhi's seventh chief minister. The special feature of this new party is that it prefers to reach the common man for his opinion on public issues like the decision of the AAP to form the government with the outside support of the Congress party. A kind of 'referendum' was held in Delhi and it was claimed by the AAP leadership that the majority of

Delhi residents supported the idea that this new party should form a government with the support of Congress party. Arvind Kejriwal, on the basis of this mandate, of the people on the basis of a referendum decided to stake his claim on December 23, 2013.

The upshot of the above narration is that the leadership of this new party is making every effort to project itself as a party with a difference, compared with other traditional parties like the Congress and the BJP, and this claim by the party is made because its methods of decision making are different than the older parties. The AAP leadership took 15 days from December 8 to 23 to arrive at a decision for accepting the office of CM of Delhi because they wanted the approval of citizens of Delhi for such a decision.

The AAP leadership is claiming that it will be guided only by the man on the street for all its important actions and activities. The AAP claims that it has followed a 'new grammar' of politics by involving ordinary citizens in decision-making in democracy. The days of decisions from "above" are over and decision will be taken only by involving ordinary citizens in governance. The secrecy of democracy as practiced by traditional parties has been replaced by "openness" of decision-making by the AAP. Hence Kejriwal and his team of activist-reformers have described their style and substance of politics as "new" because the "old" style of politics was based on the concept of high-command. The AAP decision making will be open, transparent, and also based on the seal of approval by ordinary citizens as the referendum organised by the party in Delhi.

The AAP is adept in playing the politics of shifting blames on others especially its political opponents. The AAP's first targets in case of its non-performance in government will be the Congress, its outside supporter in Delhi legislature, and the Central government.

What about "governance" by the party? Kejriwal, while addressing his supporters on December 22, observed that, "We will deliver whatever assurances we have made in our manifesto. It was prepared after wide consultation and a lot of thought went into it. Moreover, the people of Delhi are expecting much more from us and we will perform." Can Kejriwal's claim be taken on face value? It is a special feature of competitive electoral politics that parties make many promises to win an election and it has also been observed that a party, after winning an election, shows a lack of concern while implementing its promises made to the voters. A gap is observed between electoral promises made by parties during the elections and implementation of promises after winning the elections.

Can AAP be trusted to be any different from other parties in this respect? The euphoria of electoral victories comes to an end when voters start demanding performance from the government in office. Kejriwal's commitment that the Jan Lokpal bill will be his government's first priority on the agenda of governance may have smooth passage in the state assembly because every party has championed that the law to fight against corruption needs to be passed by the legislature. After all, the Indian parliament has shown the way by allowing the Lokpal bill in its last winter session and various state governments have placed Lokayukta on the stature books.

An ordinary voter of Delhi is expecting that the AAP government will provide "free supply of water" and drastically reduce the electricity bill for household consumption. It has been alleged by the critics of AAP that these two promises made to the citizens of Delhi will be extremely difficult for the government to implement. It has been alleged by the opponents of AAP that water and electricity cannot be realistically supplied on terms and conditions as announced by the new party during its election campaign.

The AAP will have two options while dealing with such promises made to the people. First, it can, on a priority basis, make public announcements that it sticks to its manifesto. Every citizen of Delhi will be provided guaranteed drinking water and asked to pay electricity bills for household consumptions at the rate of 50 per cent less than demanded by the suppliers of electricity in Delhi. This step by the AAP government will bring bouquets and great appreciation from ordinary households. Its second option is to claim that these two basic promises cannot be fulfilled unless the Congress-led UPA government at the Centre cooperates with the Delhi government's pro-citizen decision.

Possibly, the blame game will become the staple diet of politics in Delhi. The AAP government will broadcast its pro-people approach and shift the balance for the non-implementation of its pro-people policies to others, especially the Congress-led government at the Centre. Politics of shifting blames on opponents is always a handy gain for politicians. For "good public actions", the party in government tries to take credit and for non-implementation or failures, the opponent parties are held responsible.

The AAP is adept in playing the politics of shifting blames on others especially its political opponents. The AAP's first targets in case of its non-performance in government will be the Congress, its outside supporter in Delhi legislature, and the Central government. Congress will be held responsible for all of AAP's non-achievements and as practitioners of democracy from below, the AAP will go back to the voters in every street of Delhi to explain that the real villain is the Congress and not the Delhi government.

It will say that Congress is an obstructionist while AAP in government is a 'doer', 'a performer' et al. On the argument that if it were not a mandate given by the people of Delhi, the AAP would not have formed the government with Congress support, Kejriwal will claim innocence. The AAP leadership has maintained that every action taken by it is decided by the common man and if the government has been formed because of "referendum" in Delhi, its non-performance will be explained to the citizens of Delhi. It is the "fiction" of popular mandate which will be in currency of the AAP political rhetoric because like all other parties, the AAP has discovered that "fiction" is more relevant than "fact" in politics. *newsyaps.com,* 28-12-2013

Anti-corruption 'Champions': AAP, BJP and Rahul

The problem of corruption in the Indian public and political lives came to occupy a central space in India after the exposure of corruption deals involving the 2G spectrum auction or arbitrary allocation by the minister and ministry of telecommunications. But the story did not end with that because soon after the ministry of coal mines of the central government became allegedly involved in large-scale irregularities and acts of corruption while allocating coal mines to various private industrialists. The Supreme Court of India, disturbed by the growing disease of corruption in politics, decided to supervise and oversee the investigations into the activities of the ministry of telecommunications and coal mines.

Anna Hazare's movement against corruption in 2011 and his call for the enactment of a comprehensive anti-corruption law on the basis of Jan Lokpal attracted great popular public support. The Jan Lokpal Bill was presented by Anna Hazare's India Against Corruption movement as the panacea for curbing the monstrous evil of corruption in public life. This anti-corruption agenda of the non-political movement led to the birth of a political party by some of the comrade-in-arms of Anna. They floated a political party (the AAP) in 2013 with a view to contest the state assembly election in Delhi. When the results came, even the leaders of this new party must have been surprised when they won 28 out of 70 seats last year.

Kejriwal and a few other former associates of Hazare had kept the torch burning and they necessarily contested the state assembly elections on the basis of anti-corruption agenda demanding the enactment of Jan Lokpal law to investigate and punish the corrupt public functionaries. AAP is identified with the cause of fight against corruption in public life and the leaders of the party are perceived by the public and the media as crusaders against corruption. The leadership of AAP has dramatically captured public space by projecting the cause of struggle against corruption.

If AAP has taken upon itself the task of cleaning public life of the evil of corruption, the BJP, as the main opposition party in parliament, has quite often cornered the Congress-led UPA government on issues of corruption. The strategy adopted by the BJP to project itself as an anti-corruption champion was to disrupt the functioning of parliament to receive public attention. The BJP got great publicity for its disruptive activities in parliament because the mass media – always hungry for news – provided headline space to BJP for its boycott of parliament for exposing acts of corruption of the UPA government.

The BJP got actively engaged in the mobilisation of public opinion against Congress party on the allegations of corruption in government. Mohan Bhagwat, the RSS supremo, mentioned clearly that his organisation was actively, though informally, involved in the organisation and mobilisation of Anna's India Against Corruption campaign in Delhi in 2011. The BJP and the RSS are targeting the Congress for indulging in corrupt practices while in government at the centre, and have not let go of any opportunity of blaming the Congress for its failure to enact a Lokpal law in spite of BJP's full support to the government. But it deserves to be remembered that former BJP president Bangaru Laxman and the then chief minister of Karnataka, B S Yeddyurappa, were accused of corrupt practices.

Where does the Congress stand in public discourse on corruption in India? The Congress party and the Manmohan Singh-led UPA government has been on the receiving end because Anna Hazare and the BJP targeted the Congress not only for indulging in corruption in government but also dilly dallying on the issue of anti-corruption Lokpal law. The government and Congress party spokespersons always maintained that inquiries are on against allegations of corruption and because nothing has yet been proved, the Congress cannot be held guilty of wild and unproved allegations by the opposition. Many leaders within the Congress party have realised that anti-corruption campaign by its opponents has caught the imagination of the common man and it is high time that the Congress, like others, project itself as the anti-corruption champion.

Rahul Gandhi, the vice-president of the Congress, who is quite slow in his political responses on public issues, came on the scene in a dramatic manner when in a press conference he announced that the decision of his party-led government to issue an ordinance in protection of "accused MPs and MLAs" should be "torn into pieces and thrown in the waste paper basket". His action drew attention because he was seen as trying to disassociate himself from his own party-led coalition government and trying to project himself as an anti-corruption leader within his own party.

Rahul's well-known style is that he never pursues any public activity or action in a determined, consistent and continuous manner, and after this 'drama', he went into hibernation. Rahul again emerged in public view when he, and his party, projected him as a champion who actively participated in the enactment of the Lokpal Bill in parliament in December 2013. The Gandhi scion also wrote a letter to Anna Hazare on the passage of Lokpal Bill.

Since Rahul had woken up from his slumber, he also expressed his "disapproval" of Maharashtra Chief Minister Prithviraj Chauhan's decision to reject the Adarsh Commission report on the Colaba Housing Project in which many politicians and bureaucrats of the state had been indicted. The

Chief Minister, whose government had rejected the commission of inquiry report, had to eat a humble pie after Rahul's disapproval of his action, and the cabinet reversed its earlier decision on January 2, 2014, maintaining that the report is "accepted" and "action" would be taken against the bureaucrats indicted by the panel.

This was projected by Congress loyalists as Rahul's unambiguous commitment to 'clean public life'. Not only this, it has been also announced by the Congress that Rahul desires a brief Parliamentary session should be held in January 2014 to clear other anti-corruption bills like the Whistleblower Prevention Bill 2011, the Prevention of Corruption (Amendment) Bill 2013, the Prevention of Bribery of Foreign Public Officials and Public International Organisations Bill 2011, etc.

The above narrative clearly shows that three champions of anti-corruption have jumped into the fray in 2014 especially before the 15th Lok Sabha elections of April-May 2014. Which of the three will carry conviction with the public remains to be seen. The AAP, as a fresh face of Indian politics, seems to be in an advantageous position in this 'trilateral' competition because it was the first to unite the people against the cancer of corruption. Rahul is the last in the game. The issue of corruption has caught public imagination and Lok Sabha election of 2014 will witness a one of a kind contest on "corruption" among AAP, the BJP and Rahul Gandhi. Unfortunately for Rahul Gandhi, his party is not in a real good shape, to propagate effectively the idea that Congress is also anti-corruption force in public life.

newsyaps.com, 13-01-2014

Limitations of the AAP Political Model

Arvind Kejriwal writes in his "Swaraj" that "we need to tell our leaders we will work away our differences but we want power. You have misused the power we gave you on 26 January, 1950, and so we want it back." The AAP lays great stress on mohalla sabhas (ward meetings of residents) and public meetings where ordinary people will have a say in law-making.

The urgent need for good governance has not been only felt by different strata of Indian society, but also by the World Bank, transnational corporations and every foreign investor in the Indian market. Can the agenda of good governance be delinked from the larger ideological-political issues faced by a particular society? Is this agenda politically neutral?

Narendra Modi has projected himself as a "doer" and decision-maker who has led the state of Gujarat toeconomic development by providing good governance. Kejriwal said on December 26, 2013, in response to a question, "I really do not know how ideology driven the BJP is because both BJP and Congress have the same ideology—corruption".

In "Swaraj" he says, "our leaders, politicians, political parties and officers indulge in the politics of divide and rule". And he offers a solution: "The day gram sabhas begin in villages and mohalla sabhas in towns, the journey to eradicate segregation will have begun." Is it so?

AAP's invitation to everyone who wants to join the party is like the Gandhian model of making the Congress a mass movement with the participation of ordinary people for whom "membership" and "doors" of the Congress were open.

This "open membership" model of expansion of its catchment area is not the essence of Congress. The latter has been continuously engaged in political and ideological struggle both within itself and against opponents.

Congress has maintained its distinctiveness as a secular platform opposed to the ideology of communalism, and governs without discriminating against citizens on the basis of "religion, sect or creed". The BJP exercises its governmental powers on the basis of "open and subtle" policies of discrimination against religious minorities.

Does good governance mean the same thing for people in India when Congress is in power as when the BJP is in power? The answer is a big 'no'. The main, even the primary, analytical issue which emerges from the above narrative is that a party is formed on the basis of the support of various strata of society who identify themselves with its politics, ideology, world view worldview, policies and performances.

The AAP's support comes from groups, especially the middle and upwardly mobile urban class, who basically hate governmental regulations and are primarily interested in the redressal of their grievances while dealing with government agencies.

AAP is perceived primarily as a "grievance redressal" party by ordinary citizens, powerful middle classes and big industrial houses.

Unfortunately, governance cannot be reduced to 'grievance redressal' because, in reality, parties-in-government define the path of development and a manifesto for the idea of a good society.

The real confusion within AAP is that it is, on the one hand, attracting groups wanting efficient, accountable government, and, on the other, it has to compete against parties like the Congress and BJP which are in politics to create a new society in their own respective ideological mirror image.

The politics of a complex and conflict-ridden society like India cannot be properly led and managed by messiahs whose thinking is only limited to "one-issue politics" like that of India Against Corruption or the bijli-pani issues facing a limited segment of the population in Delhi.

The simplistic ad hocism of AAP was clearly revealed when it maintained that it is "cancelling" permission to foreign multi-brand retail multinationals, and at the same time, Kejriwal is on record saying "the AAP is not against FDI and every decision will be taken on a case-to-case basis".

Its inner contradictions will emerge when it takes a stand on the economic paradigm in force since 1991. AAP cannot become a "party" without defining its political world-view on basic issues facing this country in the second decade of the 21st century. *The Economics Times,* 30-01-2014

Don't Shy Away from Taking the Next Step

Anna Hazare and his associates of India Against Corruption must have been swept off their feet by the most unexpected popular response they received in 2011-12 for their demand for the enactment of a powerful Lokpal Bill to curb corruption.

It has been also argued that Hazare jumped into the fray when the public mood had already turned against corrupt politicians as the media highlighted the allegations against the high and mighty.

AAP, born of this movement, is busy in dramatising the anti-corruption political agenda by projecting itself as the sole practitioners of morality-based politics while all others are daily castigated as 'corrupt'.

This simplistic understanding of corruption makes them noticed in public but they will soon cease to be relevant because 'one-issue politics' is always quite short-lived. Hazare and Arvind Kejriwal's associates in AAP have done yeoman service by bringing the issue of corruption centre stage. Everyone in politics will have to respond because public pressure has been built by the media.

The major responsibility for cleaning up public life lies with every party, but more so with the Congress because it has been at the receiving end over this issue. What have been the responses of the party? It deserves to be clearly and unambiguously stated that the Congress could not rise to the occasion when the country was engaged in the discussions on corruption and it failed at the political level to snatch the initiative on the enactment of the Lokpal Bill.

The very fact that Parliament could get through the Lokpal Bill only at the end of 2013 speaks volumes for the Congress.

The Congress should have aggressively tackled the BJP's disruptions in Parliament and politically appropriated credit for the Bill the moment the situation became hot due to Hazare's antics at the Ramlila Ground.

It is unfortunate that very important anti-corruption Bills, such as the Prevention of Corruption (Amendment) Bill, the Citizen's Charter of Rights and Grievance Redress Bill, or the whistleblower's Bill could not see the light of day because a sagacious and wise President advised the government not to take the ordinance route at the end of the Lok Sabha term.

This failure of the Congress was not enough; it also failed to put the BJP on the mat because on corruption the saffron party has not fared any better.

Rahul Gandhi's style of functioning has not won him friends or admirers. In September 2013, at a press conference in Delhi, he said the ordinance to circumvent the Supreme Court ruling that convicted leaders immediately lost their seats should be torn up and thrown away.

The grand old party of India forgot that a public issue that had caught the imagination of every section of society had to be responded to. It is not only middle-class professionals or ordinary citizens who are eager to get a government that acts in a corruption-free atmosphere.

Corporate houses and entrepreneurs are also tired of corruption in the corridors of power.

NR Narayana Murthy of Infosys not only donated '65 lakh to Arvind Kejriwal for his public service, he welcomed the formation of AAP for 'clean governance'. Deepak Parekh, HDFC chairman, observed on the formation of AAP that it "is the beginning of a new era in Indian politics".

The Right to Information Act should have been immediately followed by anti-corruption laws and the Citizens' Charter of Rights and Demands and this package would have helped in cleansing public life and deepening Indian democracy.

It is not the ordinary voter but the political leadership that has to take the responsibility of correcting the situation by making India corruption-free. It is never too late in politics. *Hindustan Times*, *10-04-2014*

Chapter 5
Foreign Policy and UPA-II

America in South Asia

The US has reached the dead end of its decade-old anti-Taliban war in Afghanistan and is finding it difficult as to how to withdraw its bruised and humiliated forces without having achieved any goals even after spending an estimated one trillion dollars on the war.

America is a rich country and can squander its taxpayer's resources to promote its security and economic interests, but the consequences of its military misadventure have adversely impacted the security environment in south Asia. America could not have achieved its war goals in Afghanistan without the active cooperation and participation of its long-term ally Pakistan, but it was either ignored or forgotten that Pakistan also had its own security interests in Afghanistan.

The Pakistan military establishment has a legitimate apprehension that the growing influence and presence of India in Afghanistan is bound to checkmate, even obstruct, the solidification of Pakistani hold over Afghanistan. Pakistan is convinced that in a post-America situation in destabilised and conflict-ridden Afghanistan, Pakistan will be able to extend and expand its control over its neighbouring country.

But Pakistan's dream of consolidating its position in Afghanistan has suffered a setback as the Americans have realised their most trusted ally is playing a double game by supporting the Taliban and the Haqqani network.

But the recent barrage of anti-Pakistan statements by American policymakers does not mean that either of the two countries is on the verge of abandoning their 'tried-and-tested bilateral relationship'. It simply means that America wants a pound of flesh from Pakistan for playing a role in Afghanistan and, at the same time, Pakistan has created a relatively autonomous space for achieving its expansionist goals in Afghanistan.

Pakistan is asserting its autonomy not only because the US-led Nato forces are being compelled to withdraw within a time-frame, but also because America and Europe are in a state of serious economic crisis and do not have the capability to enforce their writ on erstwhile allies like Pakistan.

The once-upon-a-time global economic and military power like the US used to have a number of 'subservient' allies in all regions to protect and promote imperialist 'national interests' and Pakistan was its most 'reliable, subservient and dependent military collaborator' for the war in Afghanistan. Now, the Americans are being treated as paper tigers by Pakistan in an age of the decline of the US.

The whole apparatus of state-sponsored terrorism is intact and quite active inside Pakistan's territory. Pakistan feels encouraged to wage its 'proxy war' with neighbouring countries while the US is feeling helpless in controlling Pakistani adventurism.

India has invested more than two billion US dollars to build infrastructural facilities in Afghanistan, and the latter's army and police personnel are also getting training in India. Indian public and private sector companies are keen to undertake industrial and economic projects in Afghanistan, if its people and government are hospitable.

The failed policies of the US have created serious problems for India as a war-torn Afghanistan does not have any stable state system with which Indians can have a long-term strategic and business relationship. Also, the India-centred Pakistani army, which is the real centre of power in that country, cannot agree to conceding any space to India in Afghanistan.

It also deserves to be clearly mentioned that Pakistan itself is paying a heavy price for its military adventurism using terrorist networks. Pakistani society has suffered from religious extremists who are ready to take to guns against anyone, including the innocent people of the host country.

Terrorists located in Pakistan may be useful for the pursuit of short-sighted foreign policy goals of that country, but these elements have never hesitated to target Pakistan citizens and other Islamic groups whom they identify as opponents. How can India or Afghanistan escape Pakistani 'proxy interventions' when the army in Pakistan is not interested in domestic peace in its own country?

The Americans came to 'conquer' and will leave without a victory. The only contribution of America's war against the Taliban is that all the three countries, India, Pakistan and Afghanistan, are going to face more serious mutual conflict situations. This is the burden of American military intervention in Afghanistan.

The power vacuum in post-America Afghanistan will witness serious civil wars in that country and Pakistan will be directly involved in power struggles among Afghan warlords. That is only one part of the story. The intact terror machine in Pakistan will also continue to operate against both India and Afghanistan.

The Economic Times, 29-10-2011

Indian Foreign Policy: Foreign or Provincial?

The democratically elected political executive and Parliament are held solely responsible for the formulation and implementation of foreign and defence polices. On the basis of this logic, the Constitution makers had clearly defined and demarcated jurisdictional boundaries by assigning foreign and strategic policy makingroles only to the central government and limited the role of regional-state governments to deal with local law and order and developmental activities. So, in the more than six decades of post-Independence phase of democracy, foreign and defence policies have been pursued by the central government on the basis of its perceptions of national interests.

Jawaharlal Nehru, Indira Gandhi, Rajiv Gandhi as prime ministers followed the policy of non-alignment with two power blocs in the post-world war phase of the international structure of power. The collapse of the USSR meant this bipolarity in international relations was replaced by a unipolar global order and India adjusted and adapted its foreign and defence policies accordingly. But, unfortunately, we are now witnessing a new process where foreign policy-making is becoming subservient to short-sighted political interests of regional-state parties and leaders who are working contrary to the logic of our national foreign policy interests and objectives.

For example, Sheikh Hasina, as PM of Bangladesh, and leader of the secular and pro-India Awami League, extended a hand of friendship and PM Manmohan Singh, recognising the strategic importance of friendly neighbours like Bangladesh, decided to visit that country with a view to strengthen and cement the bonds of friendship. Mamata Banerjee, the maverick and temperamental chief minister of Bengal and a troublesome ally of the Congress-led UPA government, acted as a spoiler by not only vetoing the Teesta River watersharing talks but also by not joining the prime minister's delegation to Bangladesh. The national interest was subordinated to the minor river water issue of one state government and the UPA abdicated its national responsibility by keeping its alliance partner in good humour.

Then, M Karunanidhi, the electorally rejected leader of the DMK of Tamil Nadu, inflicted a long-term injury onforeign policy by raising the issue of the Sri Lankan Tamilian cause at a most inopportune time. The US-sponsored Resolution seems quite innocuous because it asks Sri Lanka to implement recommendations made by the Lessons Learnt and Reconciliation Commission to probe the killings in the 2009 war against the LTTE.

But the real goal is to investigate the 'war crimes' of a 'toxic war'. What happened between March14, when Pranab Mukherjee said that 'India does not vote on country-specific resolutions in the UNHRC', and March 19, when the PM told Parliament that 'We are inclined to vote'? It's just that a discredited DMK woke up from slumber to act as champion of the cause of Sri Lankan

Tamils with a view to curry favour with a section of the Tamil Nadu population. And Manmohan Singh bent foreign policy by mortgaging it to region-state leaders.

Was there a national consensus behind the government's foreign policy misadventure? Was any attempt made to involve all parties on such a serious issue? The vote in the UNHRC has not only isolated India from other Asian countries, it has conveyed a message that India is an interfering Big Brother as far as small neighbouring countries are concerned. The Sri Lankan government is not going to forget India's role on the US-led resolution and it will definitely exercise its options to provide more space and facilities to India's rivals like Pakistan and China.

India is likely to pay a very heavy price if it makes foreign policy a football game where 'regionalists' begin to dictate and decide the directions of policy. How would India react if Pakistan gets support in the UNHRC for gross violations of human rights by India in 'Indian-occupied Kashmir'? Would America allow a probe into its own war crimes in Iraq, Afghanistan and Pakistan? If India cannot agree to any probe on human rights violations in the 'disturbed' states of Jammu and Kashmir and the North East, it should, clearly, have remained neutral on Sri Lanka.

India is gradually losing the larger picture if its role in global affairs is to be determined by regional-state parties. It is a dangerous trend in foreign policy because 'local factors' cannot be allowed to dictate strategic and defence policies for the whole country.

It can be arguably said that localised political outfits and leaders do not have the capacity to comprehend forces which are at work and shape the power relations at the global, regional and bilateral levels among nation-states. The situation on this critical issue is becoming increasingly worrisome.

The Economic Times, 31-03-2012

Muscle-Flexing should become History

It has been suggested by foreign policymakers and defence security experts that robust economic and business interdependencies even among generally 'unfriendly' neighbouring countries like China, India and Pakistan can build bridges of friendly negotiations even on complex issues and disputes among the trading partners.

There is no denying the fact that India, China and Pakistan have 'bilateral disputes' and because of 'trust deficit', attempts to resolve political disputes like the Kashmir or 'border issues' between India and China have not achieved any meaningful 'breakthroughs'.

A great wall of suspicion exists among these neighbouring countries, who have in the past been at war with each other. Military skirmishes failed to alter the status quo. The three nations instead armed themselves with nuclear weapons making the region dangerous. Hence, steps taken by any of these three countries to achieve normalcy in South Asia and the whole of Asia should be welcomed as first step towards peace.

This is the context in which Pakistan President Asif Ali Zardari's one-day visit to India on 8 April evoked positive response. The government of India promptly accepted his suggestion that normal bilateral economic and trade relations should be strengthened and taken to new heights, like India-China trade ties.

Incidentally, India-China bilateral annual trade is around $75 billion. Pakistan Prime Minister Yousuf Raza Gillani enthusiastically endorsed his President's advocacy for normalisation of relations between the two neighbouring countries via expansion of economic and business engagements between them.

Events moved fast and on 12 April, Anand Sharma, minister of commerce, and his Pakistan counterpart Mukhdoom Mohammad Amin Fahim, opened the 'Lifestyle Pakistan Exhibition' in Delhi. The event has drawn about 650 business people here, which is the highest number to ever to come across the border.

Here Sharma observed, "We are writing a new history." A few more steps like the integrated check-post at Attari-Wagah border, liberalisation of visa for business, the opening of banks in two countries and Foreign Direct Investment from Pakistan to India have shown new light in the growth of 'bilateralisatism' among two territorially interlinked neighbours.

Home Minister P Chidambaram, while inaugurating the Attari-Wagah check-post on 13 April, observed, "The Wagah-Attari terminal is dedicated to traders in India and Pakistan." It is for the first time that a joint India-Pakistan Business Council has emerged as an 'institutionalised structure' for bilateral meetings between commerce and trade ministers of these two countries.

Where do these two countries go from here? It is relevant to state here that in spite of the frequent meetings between India-China political leadership at the annual India-China Business Council or Russia, India-China (RIC) meetings or Brazil, Russia, India, China (BRIC) countries or regular meetings of India China at ASEAN meetings, and inspite of sizeable and substantial trade and economic relations between these two countries, competition and unresolved conflicts exists.

Many a time, India and China have been found at the crossroads of history. India and China are emerging centres of economic power and they have clash of interests by dint of being serious competitors eager to capture space that would put Aisa on the world stage.

India and China keep flexing their muscles. The India-China dispute on South China Sea is the latest illustration to substantiate the argument that economic and business bilateral relations are not at all a 'substitute' for active political diplomacy for the resolution of knotty disputes generally inherited from history of the unresolved and leftover problems from the past: like partition of India and Pakistan, or China's so-called historical claims on territories including Arunachal Pradesh of India.

Vietnam along with Philippines has challenged China's claim on the whole of South China Sea and India has got involved in this conflict because India's Oil and Natural Gas Corporation or ONGC (Videsh) is jointly exploring oil fields in the Sea along with Vietnam.

China has sternly warned India not to get involved in oil exploration in 'disputed' South China.

China and India or India and Pakistan expected not to fight wars, but every diplomatic effort should be made to resolve pending bilateral disputes. Even 'Low Intensity Peace' is desirable and dialogue should be the means for conflict resolution. *The Financial World, 19-4-2012*

Making Sense of Pakistan's Peace Overture

In the second decade of the 21st century, a globalised India hardly has any option but to respond to every new foreign policy challenge. India and Pakistan have fought three wars—in 1947, 1965 and 1971—apart from the military confrontation in Kargil. These wars, along with the memories of partition, have made policy makers in both countries believe that the road to peace and friendship between India and Pakistan can never be built. Hence, both countries feel the need to be militarily strong and even possess nuclear weapons.

Unfortunately, democracy in Pakistan has often been disrupted by Army Generals who took power away from that country's civilian leaders and injected more poison into bilateral relations. A few abortive attempts were made to bring normalcy into the relations, however, the Mumbai terrorist attack of November 26, 2008 hardened public opinion against Pakistan in India. Indeed, all hope for a meaningful 'dialogue' that would ultimately lead to peace were dashed to the ground after the attack.

But 2012 has provided a 'new opportunity' to both countries to enter into a meaningful dialogue again. It is a well-known fact that trade relations between nations play a significant role in demolishing stereotyped images of the 'enemy'. Therefore, it won't be far-fetched to state that a new chapter in India-Pakistan relations has been initiated with the opening of the Attari-Wagah trade route and the expansion of the exports list.

In a joint statement on April 14, the Commerce Ministers of India and Pakistan made laudatory references to the opening of the Attari-Wagah integrated check post with both Ministers describing this as a 'historic' event. Union Minister for Home Affairs P Chidambaram while inaugurating the check post on April 13 even promised to ease the visa system for businessmen from Pakistan.

Further, for the first time, an institutional basis was laid down with the establishment of the India-Pakistan Joint Business Council. India has also Pakistan to open branches of its banks in India to facilitate trade transactions.

However, politics is always the driving force for finding solutions to issues ofnational interest. Trade and commerce may be necessary but that alone is not sufficient to dismantle the wall of suspicion and distrust that exists between India and Pakistan. The Pakistani President, Asif Ali Zardari, was in India on a private visit on April 8, but the fact that his visit received public approval in Pakistan is a sign of the changing times in that country.

Additionally, Nawaz Sharif who is the president of the Pakistan Muslim League (N) and a major contender for power, has also been publicly supporting the need for normalisation of relations with India.

This is significant because Sharif is from the Pakistan Province of Punjab—the hotbed of anti-India activity. Had he not had public support from the people of Punjab, Sharif would not stuck his neck out to support India.

Also, Ayaz Amir, a PML (N) MP observed on April 22 that "the threat of Taliban is not going to go away with the United States' withdrawal (from Afghanistan). It may get even worse. We have many more problems than India". Amir's comments came only days after Pakistani Army Chief Ashfaq Parvez Kayani surprised everyone on April 18 when he spoke about the need for 'peaceful co-existence with India', while visiting the accident site at Siachen. Gen Kayani suggested that, "the civilian and military leadership of the two countries... resolve the issue" of Siachen.

"We in the Army understand very well that there should be a balance between defence and development because ultimately security does not only mean a secure border but the welfare of the people. We would like to spend less on defence, any country should do the same way".

Gen Kayani has spoken well on behalf of his country. It is now clear that both Pakistan's military leaders and political bosses are ready to move forward on the peace process with India.

It will be a long and difficult process involving a lot of complex issues that have divided the countries for decades. Siachen and Sir Creek are just one of the many such issues that will have to be resolved to restore the much needed environment of peace and trust between the countries.

The crux of the matter now is whether India, as it stands today in 2012, is ready to accept this challenge for peace from Pakistan. The ball is in India's court and one can only hope that a Government suffering from chronic indecision will still be able to respond adequately and whole heartedly.

The Pioneer, 27-4-2012

A Window Opens on Look East Policy

The historic visit of Prime Minister Manmohan Singh to Myanmar in end-May has great significance not only for achieving India's foreign security and commercial goals, but in the opening ofnew opportunities for India's Northeastern states—because by linking the Northeast with Myanmar, India can accelerate the processes of economic development of these neighbouring states with Myanmar. Arunchal Pradesh, Nagaland, Mizoram and Manipur share a common border with Myammar and trade and commerce between these border states of Myanmar can get a big boost if India and Myanmar, both in their national interests, can create an appropriate physical infrastructure for the promotion of growth of interaction and exchanges among the business communities of these neighbours.

It is in India's enlightened self interest to understand that its friendly and openended relations with Myanmar shall provide great opportunities for the economic development of Northeastern states which, in spite of India's efforts to develop these underdeveloped regions, have not succeeded, leaving people alienated.

Many well-armed insurgent groups operate in 'disturbed' states of the Northeast region. Unfriendly, even hostile, governments of Bangladesh and Myanmar had provided sanctuaries to these insurgent groups to fight their battles within India. The government of Indiasucceeded in persuading Bhutan and Sheikh Hasina of Bangladesh to ban and kick out insurgent leaders who had taken refuge in these two countries. It is alleged that Chinese supply of arms to Indian insurgent groups keeps them active in waging war against India, but more important for anti-India insurgent groups is to seek sanctuary in neighbourng countries to launch their attacks against India in the Northeast. It is estimated that 50 rebel groups linked with National Socialist Council of Nagaland (Khapling action) and (I-M) faction are located in Myanmar who can successfully 'operate' in Nagaland or Manipur.

Perceived backwardness gives birth to feelings of neglect and this feeling of alienation is exploited by the insurgents. The only way to contain such well-armed groups is to block their escape routes to the neighbouring foreign countries where they make foreign soil a base to launch their violent movements. A big breakthrough has been achieved by Manmohan Singh's opening of a friendly dialogue with Myanmar. Countries like Bangladesh and Bhutan too can create situation which is quite inhospitable for Indian insurgent groups.

The government of Myanmar had promised Manmohan Singh that all insurgent camps will be closed on 10 June. This does not mean that the prime minister had gone there only to ensure this—a weighty foreign policy angle was uppermost in the mind of the Indian delegation. India's connectively and political understanding with Myanmar opens the gate for India to deepen its relations with Thailand and Malaysia but India also needs to collaborate with Myanmar for energy resources and commercial relations.

An unstated and underlying goal of Indian foreign policy in Myanmar is to have its presence in that country where China, India's main competitor in Asia, is already present in a big way. China's investments in Myanmar until 2010-11 were about $13. 6 billion and largely in the energy sector. India is a late-comer on the Myanmar scene because long military rule in Myanmar made Indians reluctant to enter into any large-scale economic transactions in spite of the fact that the Look East Policy of India was announced long back by Prime Minster PV Narasimha Rao in the beginning of the 1990s. Democratisation of Myanmar, opening of its political system and electoral victories of Aung San Suu Kyi provided an opportunity to India to rush to Myanmar.

At first, Chinese policymakers made negative comments on the visit. This provoked the prime minister to respond that 'India was not an expansionist' country. The Chinese changed their public position and on 28 May, Beijing observed that 'Both India and Myanmar are China's friendly neighbours. China is happy to see the development of relations between them.' The China 'factor' cannot be swept under the carpet.

So the Prime Minister's visit to Myanmar was not only for economic gains, the larger goal is to deepen its friendship with Myanmar for pursuing its Look East policy goals and also to curb domestic insurgency, which gets facilitated if Myanmar is friendly to India. The future contest in Asia is between two emerging and powerful countries: China and India. Both are competing in Asia for extending their areas of influence. Hence Myanmar is very important for both these countries. *The Financial World,* 07-06-2012

India and the US are Friends for Benefits

It is simplistic to state that America, the declining super economic power, and India, the new emerging economic power in Asia, need one another because there is no other way to survive in this globalised age. It is stating the obvious that the US and India have mutually reciprocal goals to pursue in the field of diplomacy, business, trade, defence and security and this is the explanation that these two countries have formalised and institutionalised their bilateral relations by setting up Joint India-US Business Council, India-US Strategic Dialogue, and such others.

But this does not mean that India or America have to evolve "joint strategies" while dealing with strategic issues which both of them have to separately resolve with a view to promoting their own national interests. This is the framework in which India-America relationships should be managed.

First, India has been attracting international policy-makers on the issue of anti-India state-sponsored terrorism originating from Pakistan. American strategic priorities in the 1990s were quite different and Pakistan was the best strategic ally of the US in war against Taliban in Afghanistan. American public policymakers did not take any interest in India's security concerns regarding the export of terrorism from Pakistan soil. This is the best illustration to substantiate the argument that there can be serious divergence of interests and policies between America and India. Only by following an independent foreign policy India can stand up on its own two feet.

This historical and significant fact should serve as a warning to the over-enthusiastic policy-makers of India who wish to see a partnership between these two countries. Partnership idea is out of question because in reality bilateral relationships between India and America, which have divergent security interests and goals, is just a matter of convenience and sometimes 'interests' converge.

Second, America is very apprehensive of the rising economic and military power of China. The US and China are in direct clash in the Asia-Pacific region. During and after the Cold War, America was a pre-eminent player in the Asia-Pacific region. But currently, China is staking its claim as a regional power. US Defence Secretary Leon Panetta, during his recent visit to India, observed that the US will raise its naval forces "so that 60 per cent of its battleships are placed in the Asia-Pacific by 2020".

How can China feel comfortable with this kind of military presence? Further, the US Defence Secretary declared in New Delhi that in this new shift in the US military strategy, "India is a lynchpin with one of the most capable militaries". The US, as an imperialist global military power, has always shown global interest to expand its military presence, but it should not expect India, to play its game.

India has its own strategic and economic priorities. So, decisions about national policies have to be taken solely by Indians themselves without any alignment with the super power. Union Minister for Defence AK Antony in his meeting with Panetta clearly stated that India wanted "unhindered freedom of navigation in international waters for all". India has its own policies about China and its assessment is that India and China are competitors but there is no need to operate on the basis of an anti-China phobia drummed up by other nations.

Still, there is no doubt that the post-2014 Afghanistan will definitely become a center of mini wars among warlords and the Taliban supported directly by Pakistan. In such a situation, Indian investment in the reconstruction of Afghanistan is akin to throwing water and oil in desert sands. Indian policy makers should clinically analyse the reasons and implications here.

It appears that the Americans want to fire from the shoulders of India in the Asia-Pacific region and in Afghanistan. This is not good for India. The US must be told that it cannot partner New Delhi in this dangerous game.

The Pioneer, 22-06-2012

India Faces an Afghan Riddle

Afghanistan has always paid a heavy price for its geographical location. Central Asia, on the one hand, and Iran, on the other, have been special targets of every big power for the past two centuries, and for controlling these coveted regions, every coloniser has tried to dominate and control the crucial and strategically located territory of Afghanistan. The country's 20th century tragedy began with Soviet Russia's invading it in 1979. To counter the Russian onslaught came the Americans, but the ensuing Russian-American conflict over Afghanistan only left the Afghan society bruised and scarred forever.

The Americans created and nourished religious fundamentalists and armed them to the hilt so they could resist atheistic communist Russia better. But peace failed to return to Afghanistan even after the humiliating retreat of Russian armed forces, because the American-created and well armed Talibans then set out to Islamise their own country. And now, despite the announced withdrawal of the American-led NATO armed forces from the region by 2014, Afghanistan's tragedy seems far from over. The United States, which has completely destroyed Afghanistan, has now decided to actively involve India in its efforts to strengthen the security, governing capability and the economic development in that country. On 13 June, India and the United States issued a joint statement in Delhi after their third strategic dialogue that intends to explore opportunities to work together to promote Afghanistan's development in areas such as agriculture, mining, energy, capacity building and infrastructure.

Already, India is actively engaged in the reconstruction of the war devastated country following the India-Afghanistan Strategic Agreement, which was signed in 2011. This June, India organised the South Asian Region Investment Summit to create investment opportunities in Afghanistan in the post NATO troops withdrawl scenario.

This was followed by the Tokyo International Meeting on Afghanistan on 8 July, for "creating capabilities to provide good governance and confront the al Qaeda and Taliban". The 70 nations attending the meeting expressed serious concern on the difficult security environment in Afghanistan, while emphasising that "the corporate sector was stepping into a relatively high risk market", and proposed special incentives, insurance covers and guarantees for investors in the region. The meeting also announced a financial aid of $16 billion for Afghanistan.

All this is part of the two-pronged cooperation programme planned by India, United States, Japan and others. The programme's first priority is to strengthen the military capabilities of the Hamid Karzai government in Afghanistan, while the second involves engaging multinational companies (MNCs) and corporate houses in the economic reconstruction of that country.

On 7 July, United States' Secretary of State Hillary Clinton announced that Afghanistan is the newest "major non-NATO ally", adding, "Our commitment to Afghanistan is long-term. A deeper look into the problems of Afghanistan's security and economic development on the basis of foreign investments indicates that normalcy may not be restored in that country for a very long time, because merely the retreat of the defeated American-led NATO forces after 2014 won't lead to restoration of peace in Afghanistan".

A lot of people might actually agree with Clinton for domestic reasons. First, Afghan President Hamid Karzai is on a very shaky ground. Though he represents a very important section of the divided tribal society, Karzai's support base does not extend to the whole country and even Kabul continues to witness violence by groups like al Qaeda, Taliban and other tribal chiefs. Second, Pakistan considers Afghanistan as its own 'zone of interest' and the Pakistani army can't seem to digest the expanding role of India there.

Logistically, Pakistan has every advantage over India for dealing directly with the Taliban and al Qaeda. Earlier this month, the United States had to eat a humble pie when the Obama administration was forced to apologise for deaths of Pakistani troops in airstrikes, only after which Pakistan reopened the NATO-supply lines into Afghanistan after seven long months. If America had to surrender before Pakistan for fighting its so-called anti-Taliban war in Afghanistan, India cannot expect to have a smooth sailing there.

Pakistan has already expressed its serious reservations to Karzai over Afghan army personnel being trained by Indians. Turbulence in Afghanistan is not going to end. On the contrary, it may get intensified even leading to a civil war, in the post-NATO withdrawal of 2014. Pakistan is actively engaged in the internal affairs of Afghanistan and it has the capability to checkmate India's efforts there. In time of trouble, the United States will develop a quid pro quo with Pakistan for mutual benefits in Afghanistan, with India ending up as a bad guy in the game. And it is not Pakistan alone, neighbouring Iran, too has its ambitions in regional politics, and Afghanistan will have to also deal with threats arising out of these.

But the finer point in all this is that it is not without reason that the world has suddenly opened its heart and pockets to Afghanistan, ignoring its disturbed security scenario. The United States, Japan, India and Pakistan among others are all eyeing the Asian country's abundant and untapped mineral and energy resources. The international community has sanctioned $16 billion for Afghanistan not as a charity, but for greater economic benefits.

If India is involved in Afghanistan at multi-dimensional levels, it is because it realises how influence over Afghanistan alone can help serve its legitimate national interests in central Asian republics. And the country's corporate sector is piggybacking on these government efforts to hunt for gold, copper and energy resources of Afghanistan.

So India can neither 'give up' nor can have a 'smooth sailing' in the Afghan country, while it deals with the problems there. Worse, it is in a 'trilateral' conflict with Pakistan and China, and their respective ambitions are bound to clash. India should play its diplomatic cards very cautiously while dealing with Afghanistan. *Financial World, 23-07-2012*

Some Lessons should Just be Forgotten

While there has recently been a clinical analysis of the factors which led to thearmed conflict between India and China, that analysis has been limited to investigating the domestic, military and political causes of conflict. The missing link is the international context of the 1960s which led to the deterioration of relationship between Nehru's non-aligned India and Mao's Communist China.

The early 1960s had witnessed a dangerous development in Cuba which brought Nikita Khrushchev of the Soviet Union and John F Kennedy of the US face to face. There was the possibility of a nuclear confrontation between the rival super powers in that bipolar era. Also, while the US and Russia were engaged in global brinkmanship, the Soviet Union and China—two Communist giants—were drifting away from one another as Khrushchev refused to give into Mao Tse Tung's demand for the transfer of nuclear technology to China.

Hence, there was a 'grand schism' in the global communist monolith. This prompted Italian Marxist Togliatti to announce that the movement had moved from the 'monolithic' to the 'polycentric' wherein Russia, China and other Communist nations would independently decide on their foreign policies.

Mao, following his dispute with Khrushchev, wanted to prove to the Communist world that the Soviet leader was a 'revisionist' and not a true Communist who cared more for non-aligned India than Communist China. To gain an upper-hand in his struggle against Khrushchev, Mao also wanted to prove that Soviet Russia was supporting the spurious non-aligned policy of Jawaharlal Nehru, who in reality was an American stooge. Indeed, the India-China conflict was so designed that it would compel a distressed Nehru to approach his natural allies—the US—and in the process, damage the India-Russia friendship.

This power game at the peak of the Cold War era was an important factor that made the Chinese to want to "teach Nehru a lesson". Indeed, when Nehru's Government approached Kennedy for help, China scored a point against Soviet Russia. However, Nehru's tilt in favour of America was short-lived. When he recovered from the shock of 1962, he asserted his commitment to a nonalignedforeign policy. Present day Indian analysts, obsessed with bilateralism, are oblivious of the linkages between the Cold War, the Sino-Soviet rift and the Sino-Indian conflict.

However, linking of the 1962 conflict with the larger global context of that time also shows that the global situation and the reality of India and China have qualitatively changed since 1962. Indeed, it will be blind ultra-nationalism, even jingoism, if New Delhi today incorporates lessons learnt from the India-China conflict of 1962 into its foreign policy vis-a-vis Beijing.

First, the economic and military prowess of neither China nor India in 2012 is comparable to what they were in the 1960s. Second, both countries are now emerging power centres who give stiff competition to the West. Third, the unipolar, America-led, global order has been a disaster for both the US and the European capitalist countries that supported the hegemon. Fourth, apart from India and China, other power centres are also emerging such as the Australia-Pacific Rim countries and Latin America. Consequently, the G-7 has now been expanded to G-20. Fifth, the lion's share of economic growth is spent on creating powerful military machines by modern nation-states, and India and China are no exception. Sixth, the West no longer has a monopoly over nuclear weapons—India, China, Pakistan, North Korea, are all nuclear weapon states.

Neither India nor China can afford to go to war against each other. There can be no repeat of 1962. Thus, a new perspective is required with which one can take a close look at the changing power equations, both economic and military, between the two nations. *The Pioneer, 26-10-2012*

Nation Must Pick

New Delhi's increasing proximity to Washington has not only alarmed Beijing but also left no space for a trust-based relationship to grow between the two Asian giants. As India shapes its foreign policy in the new world, it must keep in mind that it can choose its friends but not its neighbours.

The growing weakness of the Union Government has prevented any long-term planning regarding India's foreign policy which is often influenced by domestic politics. Domestic and foreign policy are two sides of the same coin and they are connected together by the overall political situation of the country. But, how can the country have a coherent foreign policy when its States and Union Territories are politically disconnected at the national level? India is governed by a coalition of parties at the Centre who have nothing in common with one another-their alliance is a marriage of convenience. As a result, India does not have a national policy framework for dealing with the emerging global challenges. Consequently, the country's foreign policy has been reduced to the level of 'bilateralism' or sometimes even 'regionalism'. A few facts may be mentioned to substantiate this argument. First, India celebrated the end of the Cold War by openly supporting American economic and military hegemony. India decisively broke from the Nehruvian model of self-reliance and independent existence that it had inherited, and enthusiastically accepted American leadership of the new world order. This new orientation in Indian foreign policy reduced this country's political leadership to passivity when, for instance, former US President George W Bush attacked Iraq to remove its leader Saddam Hussein on the false pretext that he possessed weapons of mass destruction. Hence, the activist legacy of the Nehruvian era was replaced by subservience to an aggressive American agenda. This in turn has made China suspicious of the India-US tie-up and removed any chances of a meaningful trust-based relationship between the two Asian giants. Also, the distrust has only been aggravated because America, with Indian support, is actively participating in almost every Asian forum. China is convinced that the India-US alliance is directed against it. To make matters worse, since 2011 India and the US are jointly cooperating with Japan with whom China has historically had a hostile relationship. China has reacted sharply to this trilateral relationship forged to ensure maritime security especially since Beijing is already in conflict with Tokyo in the East China Sea. It is no one's case that India not assert its rights in that region but problems arise when China finds America and India tied together. For example, America is already knocking at the doors of the recently formed Indian Ocean Rim Association for Regional Corporation for the status of a dialogue member. Clearly, America is trying to obtain institutional support in Asia so as to contain military and economic giant China.

America's global status is also diminishing but it cannot accept the emergence of a powerful rival like China. India and China can peacefully co-exist, cooperate and compete but India's growing proximity to the US is creating complications in the Asian balance of power. If India had a big picture view of its own interests, it would never have allowed itself to be viewed as an ally of America. But India is caught in the web of 'bilateralism'. Consequently, in the last two decades, it has not even cared to articulate its traditional foreign policy goal of achieving world peace. Finally, given the fact that neither Pakistan nor China is thinking of waging war against India, New Delhi should formulate a foreign policy that promotes friendship and cooperation within Asia. Old and out-of-date thinking regarding a hostile China and Pakistan should be buried. If India does not have any war-mongering enemy to confront, its present America-dependent foreign policy is irrelevant. India's imperatives of economic development should determine the foundation of peaceful foreign policy. *The Pioneer, 09-11-2012*

America has to Face the Dragon in Asia

The Sixth South East Asian summit followed by a meeting of heads of

Government and states of the Association for South East Asian countries on November 18 and 19 provided an opportunity to Indian, Chinese and American leaders to spell out their security and strategic concerns for the 21st century. India and China have multiple strategic concerns which often create conflicting situations. The US on the other hand, inspite of being a declining power, still has global interests. It also still has still the capacity to form powerful alliances with countries around the world and successfully pursue its national-global strategic and economic interests.

US President Barack Obama before proceeding to Bali in Indonesia, visited Australia. While there, on November 16, he referred to the Chinese role in the emerging new world order and said that, "It is important for them (China) to play by the rules of the road." He further observed, "I think the notion that we fear China is mistaken". He also asserted that, "Let there be no doubt in the Asian Pacific in the 21st century, the United States of America is all in."

Obama's policy message was conveyed in an unambiguous language to China and also to America's traditional allies in East Asia like Japan, the Philippines. He made clear to every country in Asia that "the US is a pacific power and we are here to stay".

It is but natural that China is wary of America's intentions especially about its 'activist' role in the region. The China versus US sentiment was clearly visible during both the high level meetings held on 17 and 18 November. During these meetings Chinese Premier Wen Jiabao told the Asian leaders that every issue should be settled "bilaterally" and "No outside power" should interfere in Asian affairs.

Naturally, the reference was to the US. And China's message was clear: Keep out of bilateral issues between Asian countries. Further, China asserted its right to play a central role in world affairs and especially in the Asian continent. China has emerged as an economic power house and has maintained an average economic growth rate of 7.5 per cent for the past two decades.

With such an economic base and a powerful military, the country is flexing its muscles. But before it challenges the existing hegemony of America and the European Union, it must consolidate its power base in Asia. Like all other powerful western countries, China too has made clear its desire to deal with its neighbours especially India, Vietnam, and the Philippines on its own terms.

If on the one hand China is competing against America for power in the region, on the other hand India's own strategic and commercial interests have also created several complex situations between China and itself. Prime Minister Manmohan Singh, while in Bali himself, clearly stated India's position on the South China Sea. He said that, "Issues of sovereignty should be resolved in consistence with international law and practice." Singh also made clear that India's oil and gas operations in the South China Sea were purely commercial activities.

Wen, on the other hand, made sugar-coated statements such as how the the "21st century belongs to Asia" and how there is enough space for every Asian country to 'cooperate.' Wen left many things vague and unsaid, especially China's own intentions and plans on the South China Sea which have created a worrisome situation for India, Vietnam, the Philippines and other countries that use the trading route that runs through the South China Sea.

It was understood by many countries that Wen's reference was against the US when he said that "outside forces should not, under any pretext, get involved". But thats not all. Even India was warned by the Chinese and put under the category of an 'outside power' interfering in the South China Sea. Without mincing any words, the Chinese specifically described as unacceptable ONGC Videsh's oil exploration activities in two Vietnamese blocks which have been claimed by China.

Beijing has identified the South China Sea under its sovereign rights and has told India that no foreign companies should 'engage in activities that will undermine China's sovereignty and rights and interests'. India and many other Asian countries have asserted that no one country has sovereign rights over the Sea, but China has dismissed such a view point and has asked for 'bilateral negotiations.'

The above narrative leads us to raise some questions about the emerging areas of cooperation and conflict among India, China and the US. China is challenging the existing arrangements of dealing with territorial claims based on its own definition of sovereign rights. Also, India and China are engaged in serious negotiations on boundary disputes but nothing significant has emerged. Chinese policies towards India are just to keep the pot boiling and keep the country on tenterhooks.

On the other hand, India's policy towards China has been that of a soft power which gets translated into a strategy of keeping the powder dry and not raising the conflict situation to a level of no-return. The India-China relationship is at a low-key level so that the situation does not escalate as it did in 1962. The best evidence of this soft-power approach was provided by Singh, who asked the Chinese to "respect international laws and practice."

A widespread impression exists among Chinese foreign and security policy makers that India is aligned with the US and that the two will stand together on issues concerning China. It must be clearly stated that the US is in search of allies in Asia to checkmate China's growing influence in the continent.

India has nothing to gain but a lot to lose by aligning with a declining US which is in no position to confront China because its own power cannot meet the challenge of rising Chinese influence. India cannot ignore its immediate neighbours like Pakistan and China and the real engagement of Indian foreign policy makers has to be with these two neighbouring countries in South Asia.

If India wants to play any effective role in international relations, it has to come out of the present limiting factors which have curbed its initiatives in strategies, especially its Look East policy. This picture has clearly emerged from the recent conferences held in Bali in Indonesia.

Asiance Magazine, 03-12-2012

Keep Dialogue Firmly in the Driver's Seat

Chief Justice Iftikhar Muhammad Chaudhry opened a new chapter in Pakistan's history on 5 November when in a direct message to the army leadership he observed that missiles and tanks are no longer symbols of national security.

"Gone are the days when the stability and security of a country was defined in terms of the number of missiles and tanks the state had as a manifestation of its hard power. Today, the concept of national security has been redefined as a polity wherein a state is bound to provide its citizens with overwhelming social security and welfare nets and to protect their natural and civil rights at all costs," said Chaudhry addressing a gathering at the National Management College in Lahore.

Post the ouster of military dictator Pervez Musharraf and the formation of a democratic government following popular protests in the country, this is probably the most vocal message from mainstream Pakistan to its military leadership _ that the society has opted for democracy based on competitive elections and it is willing to stand by its decision. That does not mean that army as one of the most important pillar of the Pakistani State has no role in its security and strategic policies. It simply means that the army prefers to work under a democratic civilian government.

However, the other side of the coin is that despite the emergence of democracy with the support of the masses, the Pakistani society is in turmoil and communal and fanaticism are posing a grave threat to not just the stability of the country but also to its newly established democratic regime.

To say the least, Pakistan is in an extremely fragile state. An essential that must constantly be borne in mind by India as it looks to normalise relations with its neighbour. Already there are too many sensitive thing's that the Indian establishment has to take care of while dealing with Pakistan. But following the resurgence of a very violent and radical Islam in that country, now the Indian foreign and security establishment, both political and bureaucratic, must be particularly attentive of Pakistan's vulnerable democratic government while deciding its strategies. That working in tandem with radical groups who are strongly against India, it may not have the mandate to offer any radical concessions to India on contentious issues such as Jammu and Kashmir must not be forgotten.

With a willing government in place, the timing only seems apt for the countries to engage in trade, travel and cultural contact by relaxing the rigidities on the Line of Control. The process has already been initiated. Pakistan has moved from a positive list of goods to be traded with India to a smaller negative list, India has allowed foreign direct investment from Pakistan, both countries have established a Joint Working Group to open more border points like the existing Attari-Wagah while initiating a liberalised visa pact that would allow greater freedom for travel for businessmen of both countries. "This process must be taken to its logical end by phasing out the negative list and eventually according MFN (most favoured nation) status to India," Commerce minister Anand Sharma said recently, adding that India will also consider the possibility of allowing its private banks to open branches in Pakistan.

Bilateralism is moving forward and its future potentialities will be observed at people to people level because these growing non-political, social and cultural contacts will demolish the 'stereotyped' enemy images which have persisted in the minds of the communities on both sides. And the gradualism will pay future dividends in normalising hostilities between the neighbours.

But this growing normalcy should not blind India and Pakistan to the fact that many hurdles still have to be crossed before mature friendly relations can be restored between them. Bilateral problems exist, and this is a compelling reason for both countries to actively negotiate to move forward. It is in India's national interests to actively promote normalisation and create an atmosphere of 'trust' with its most important neighbouring country, Pakistan. The pr-condition for Indian policy makers is that Pakistan's domestic violence-ridden social reality should always be kept in mind while dealing with its elected government.

Prime Minister Manmohan Singh may not have been able to visit Pakistan but political dialogue must go on. India should not give up on initiatives to break the inherited deadlocks of the past. *The Financial World, 07-12-2012*

New Friends Bring New Foes for India

India's 'Look East' foreign policy authorised by former Prime Minister PV Narasimha Rao and diligently pursued by his successors now seems to have matured. This was most evident on December 20, 2012, when the heads of state of 10 East-Asian countries assembled in New Delhi to strengthen their ties India at the India-Asean Commemorative Summit.

The evolution of the India-Asean relationship has been primarily determined by the principle of reciprocity and this has facilitated a slow but steady deepening of relationships, beginning with India being accorded the 'Dialogue' status at Asean meetings. Now, it enjoys a full-fledged 'strategic partnership' with Asean. India's Free Trade Agreement with Asean countries also matured on December 20, 2012, as the members agreed to include services in it, along with goods.

India-Asean relationship has also gone beyond the area of trade to include security cooperation. The Vision Statement released at the New Delhi Summit states: "We are committed to strengthening cooperation to ensure maritime security and freedom of navigation and safety of sea lanes of communication for unfettered movement of trade in accordance with international law". However, this new dimension can be problematic and must be carefully handled by India's foreign andsecurity policy makers. India must keep in mind its many old conflicts with neighbouring countries such as Pakistan, Bangladesh, Nepal and Sri Lanka in this respect.

It is one thing to issue a communiqué after a summit, demanding freedom of navigation and maritime rights under international law. But, it is quite another to deal with contentious issues regarding the rights of passage on the seas etc. These are problems that India will have to deal with, for instance, while enforcing a 'code of conduct' in the South China Sea where China is not prepared to concede even an inch to its other neighbours like Vietnam and the Philippines.

India itself has had to face Chinese anger when collaborating with Vietnam for gas exploration in the South China Sea. In fact, ONGC (Videsh) has had to withdraw from the area because China served a notice to India. In fact, Vietnamese Prime Minister Naugyen Tan Dung said at the New Delhi summit, "I hope India supports Asean in the full implementation of the declaration on the conduct of parties on the South China Sea". Now, can India refuse to take a stand on this contentious issue where it also has own interests to protect and promote?

India should look towards Asean only as a market for trade and commerce. However, this new security context also cannot be ignored and India has to deal with it while simultaneously also protecting its interests in the Indian Ocean. Indian policy-makers cannot delink this country's economic interests from its security and strategic interests—a fact that is perhaps become most evident in India's increasingly complex relations with Asean in which China has emerged as a major factor.

In fact, it is not only in the South China Sea that China is flexing its muscles, but also in the North China Sea and in its relations with Japan, a country with which India has maintained friendly relations.

The crux of the argument here is the India cannot cement its alliance with Asean or other East-Asian countries without making clear its position on China. India's 'Look East' policy has entered now a new phase where New Delhi will have to factor in the China angle if it wants to strengthen its relationship with Asean. After all, China has enough military and economic clout to impose its will on its smaller neighbours including Vietnam, the Philippines and Japan.

It is time India decides on how to respond to China's foreign and security goals in Asia. *The Pioneer, 14-01-2013*

US Wants to be Tutor, the World its Classroom

Barack Obama is speaking the language of imperialists. Indians do not need to be reminded that the British colonisers too had announced that they would gradually teach the art of democratic governance to their subjects in this country.

US President Barack Obama began his second four-year term by enunciating his policies and agenda at his inaugural address on January 21. His agenda merits a clinical analysis because, as the sole super military power, America's global policies determine the destinies of countries the world over.

Obama observed that "America will remain the anchor of strong alliances in every corner of the globe, and will renew those institutions that extend its capacity to manage crisis abroad", adding, "...because our interests and our conscience compel us to act on behalf of those who long for freedom".

The US President committed America to playing the role of global policeman and appropriated the role of 'guardianship' because it claims to be the 'most powerful nation'. Why did he adopt the tone of an arrogant imperialist, of a self-appointed global regulator? An American President is never a free agent, always constrained by powerful domestic groups which control the real levers of economic and military machine of the country. He cannot but pursue global interventionist policies to secure and safeguard interests of economic and military industrial czars of his country.

A few facts to substantiate the argument that Obama, like his predecessors, has little option of changing the course of history.

President Ronald Reagan had described the Communist Soviet regime as a "satanic civilisation" and pursued policies leading to the liquidation of the socialist state system in Russia and other East European countries.

President Bill Clinton, vigorously pursued interventionist military policies in Balkan countries especially while dealing with the dismemberment of Yugoslavia.

President George W Bush launched a full-fledged armed attack against Iraq's Saddam Hussein on the false pretext of destroying a dictator who possessed the 'most dangerous weapons of mass destruction'.

George Bush embarked on a mission against the Taliban regime in Afghanistan as part of the 'American war on terror' after the 9/11 World Trade Centre attacks in 2001.

Like his predecessors, Obama has not abandoned the path of interventionism in Syria and economic encirclement of Iran on the issue of nuclear weapons programme followed by the Iranians.

In his January 21 address, Obama clearly emphasised, "We will support democracy from Asia to Africa, from the Americas to the Middle East, because our interests and our conscience compel us to act on behalf of those who long for freedom". He remains committed to the idea of 'regime change' and 'export of democracy' with a view to create political systems in tune with the 'freedom' as determined by the US.

Anti-authoritarian struggles should be launched by the inhabitants of that country on their own and without any outside intervention. Obama is speaking the language of imperialists. Indians do not need to be reminded that the British colonisers too had announced that they would gradually teach the art of democratic governance to their subjects in India. Has the US succeeded in establishing democracy in Iraq? Has Obama been successful in making post-Taliban Afghanistan a real democracy?

Indian policy-makers must be cautious and never forget that for many decades now patronising, supporting and arming Pakistan's Army with the latest arsenal has topped the US agenda. And this has naturally affected relations between India and Pakistan. The latest is that the US is defining the Pakistani Army's role in the post-Nato withdrawal from Afghanistan in 2014, and is expecting Pakistan to act as its watchdog in post-2014 Afghanistan.

Pioneer, 01-02-2013

Their Politics Rule on Borders

The ruling coalition government and major opposition parties are engaged in politics of confrontation in 2013 and plausible explanation for such sharp political divisions among political parties on all major national and international policy issues seems to be the forthcoming Lok Sabha elections of 2014. A hell broke out in the media and not to be left behind, opposition parties, on the reported intrusion of Chinese troops on April 15 in Eastern Ladakh border area. It deserves to be clearly stated that such disputes between India and China are quite common because both these countries have yet to come to any firm agreement on the definition of borders between these two neighbouring countries. Because of this reason, the Manmohan Singh government plays down the issues of border intrusions.

Manmohan Singh's foreign policy towards China and Pakistan has been clearly based on 'moderation'. This is the reason why, inspite of jingoistic reactions of the media and opposition, the UPA government has not allowed itself to be swept off the feet on this contentious issues. The moderate response of Salman Khurshid, Minister of External Affairs, to the eastern Ladakh border issue of April 15 is fundamentally opposite to the extremely aggressive posture of Mulayam Singh Yadav of the Samajwadi Party, who is positioning himself as a future probable prime minister in case of fractured electoral verdict of 2014 for Lok Sabha. Mulayam Singh, one of the regionalist party leader of

Uttar Pradesh, made a highly provocative statement of April 26. "The Chinese army, without using force and weapons, easily captures strategic location. It is a big national crisis. There is no point talking to China. It is better to allow the army to deal with it" he said. Such statements by national chauvinists like Mualyam Singh Yadav provoke anti-China sentiment among gullible Indians and unfortunately, media also picks them up, adding fuel to the fire.

Finally, the prime minister threw cold water on the attitude of adventurists like Mulayam and others when on April 27, he clearly stated that the 'issue would be resolved and India does not want to accentuate the situation'. He emphasised, 'We do have a plan. We do believe that it is possible to resolve this problem. I think the talks are going on.' ManMohan clearly stated that it is a 'localised issue' Further, it deserves to be noted that India's minister of external affairs is visiting China and preparations are being made for the first visit of the new Chinese prime minister in May 2013. The exaggerated noises made of Mulayam Singh, the BJP and the media should be nipped in the bud. Te Sino-Indian border conflict of October-November 1962 had become ugly because of the anti-China hysteria created by the opposition parties, which tied the hands of the then prime minister Jawaharlal Nehru.

Hysterical nationalism cannot resolve border conflicts. It is only at the diplomatic levels that issues can be resolved. The larger issue is that China of 2013 is the single most Asian power, both militarily and economically, and as India's most important neighbour, both these countries have to keep the powder dry and remain engaged diplomatically with one another. Further, China, at present, is focused on disputes on seas, like South China Sea or its conflicts with Japan, and it is an elementary principle of diplomacy that immediate focal points of foreign policy of a neighoburing country should be always kept in mind for dealing with bilateral problems between India and China or India and Pakistan.

Separately, Narendra Modi, another prime ministerial aspirant for 2014, too jumped into the fray on assault on Sarabjit Singh, who succumbed to the injuries he got in a Lahore prison. The BJP leadership and Hindu communalists led by the joint family of the RSS are genetically anti-Muslim. Yes the assault of Sarabjit was unfortunate. But it should not give a licence to Sangh Parivar to either attack India's foreign policy towards Pakistan or indulge in spreading hatred against Muslims.

Indians should be cautious of leaders who are adept in manufacturing atmosphere of hatred against neighboring countries especially on issues which are purely bilateral in nature. India and China or India and Pakistan have enough maturity to resolve their mutual conflicts and safeguard their national strategic interests. A very negative wind is blowing in India which is adversely impacting the pursuit of Indian foreign policy and many a time, the central government has been paralysed in the pursuit of national interests because of aggressive attitudes of local chauvinist regionalists.

The DMK and the AIADMK, purely one-state based parties, have created difficulties for the central government on the issue of Tamilian population in Sri Lanka. Unfortunately, the government of India went to the international fora of the United National with its hands tied because Dravadian parties had created anti-Sri Lanka hysteria in Tamil Nadu. Local parties, which are co-terminus with the territorial boundaries of one state only for purely limited electoral purposes, have exercised veto over Manmohan Singh's foreign policy on Sri Lanka. It is forgotten by these local chauvinists that India needs friendly neighbours if it needs to grow. It has become a fashion to state that India has entered the stage of coalition governments at the centre and the leader of the coalition should follow 'coalition dharma' by accommodating interests and demands of alliance partners. But it is forgotten that it is only the central government, which has to formulate all-India foreign and security policies by keeping in mind the interaction and interplay of external with domestic needs of a country.

Should India take a stand at global fora as a sovereign country with its own national goals of should it have foreign policy of 27 state governments and seven union territories of the country? The US President, as leader of fifty states, decides about American foreign policy and as Head of the American centre of power, he decides what is good or bad for his country. American forces have been defeated and humiliated in war against Afghanistan, and Barack Obama in his second term in office, has decided to pull out its forces in 2014. An American President declared war against Afghanistan, and another President has decided to retreat from Afghanistan and such decisions are their prerogatives, irrespective of the fact that the US is a federation of 50 states. Hence, India cannot' be an exception to this rule. It is the central government which should set foreign policy keeping national interests in focus. The present state of affairs prevailing in India is not at all conducive to the formulation of a coherent all-India foreign policy. *The Financial World, 06-05-2013*

Pakistan's Bloody Road to Democracy

For the first time in its history, a civilian Government in Islamabad has completed its full-term and will hand over power to another elected regime. However, the military and the jihadists continue to threaten civilian rule in that country

Sarabjit Singh's tragic end in Pakistan understandably evoked strong reactions in India. It was the Pakistani Government's duty to protect the 49-year-old Indian convict who had spent more than two decades in a Lahore prison and it failed to do so. However, the death of Sarabjit Singh provides us with an opportunity to focus on the deep crisis that is faced by that country.

First, democracy was never allowed to strike strong roots in Pakistan, where men in uniform wielded all the power and suppressed public opinion. Consequently, the outside world does not know much about the aspirations of the Pakistani people. Moreover, military rule in Pakistan, as elsewhere in the world, has always been legitimised on the false pretext of a perennial threat to national security. The Pakistan Army rule has justified its rule by claiming that a well-equipped and powerful military alone stands between Pakistan and its enemy number one, India. The ordinary Pakistani, under military regime, has been raised on a staple anti-India diet.

Second, an authoritarian and brutal regime requires a certain kind of ideological support that is best rendered by religious fanatics. Hence, the Pakistani Army has patronised extremist mullahs and theirmadarssas which in turn, have produced an army of Pakistani youth who swear by an anti-Hindu-India ideology. These indoctrinated people today form the second line of defence for the Army against India—essentially by exporting terror and bloodshed to this country. Unfortunately for Pakistan, however, these terrorists are now actively perpetuating violence in their own country as well. Consequently, Pakistan has become a lawless mess where religious fanatics run wild. So grave is the threat from such extremists today that even the Pakistani Army chief, General Ashfaq Parvez Kayani, has publicly acknowledged that Islamists are the greatest threat to his country.

This is the first time a democratically elected Government has completed its full five year term—the PPP-led regime has been in office since 2008—and will be handing over power to another civilian administration. This has worried those with vested interests who now fear that public opinion will take a turn against jihadis elements. A direct result of this has been the shadow of death, perpetuated by gun-wielding terrorists, that now looms large on those contesting the general election scheduled for May 11.

The Pakistani Army has also been patronising jihadis so that it can use them as pawns in the power game to secure its interests in post-2014 Afghanistan. With the US-led Nato forces preparing to leave that war-torn country, the Pakistani Army's ambitions of controlling Afghanistan have only been emboldened. It has found an ally in the Taliban.

Ultimately, if Pakistan cannot control its own fanatical creations—which have now even turned against liberals and moderates in their own country—it is impossible for the Government to prevent from attacking India. Indeed, even as one pins the blame for Sarabjit Singh's death on the Pakistani Establishment, it is essential to understand the limitations of an elected democratic Government in that country.

The story of Pakistan is quite complex. This is perhaps best exemplified by the fact that even though the country's former dictatorial President Pervez

Musharraf is being tried for his various crimes on the eve of a historic general election, Pakistan cannot wholeheartedly celebrate the arrival of democracy as violence and bloodshed continues unabated. Pakistan is still a long road away from democracy as those opposed to such a system are still embedded within the system. One must take heart from the fact that at least elections are being held in Pakistan and some form of a multi-party political system is gaining ground.

The Pioneer, 10-05-2013

Meet the New Leaders in India's Neighbourhood

The lame duck, semi-paralysed regime led by Prime Minister Manmohan Singh has already had discussions with the new Premier of China and quite possibly will also be engaging the Government recently elected to power in Pakistan. The discussions take place against the backdrop of New Delhi's difficult bilateral relations with the two countries, which is sure to have a direct impact on the strategic concerns of India.

Let us start with Pakistan: It is a fact that in his previous tenures as Prime Minister, Nawaz Sharif, who will now once again be at the helm in Islamabad, had engaged the Indian leadership in positive dialogue. His Lahore summit of 1999 especially was a big step towards a meaningful resolution of bilateral conflicts, even though not much progress could be made because Sharif was overthrown by his Army chief.

However, it is also a fact that even this time around, Sharif has campaigned in favour of friendly relations with India. Now, his statements will be put to test. But the Prime Minister-elect may not have afree hand in the making of his foreign policy towards New Delhi because the Pakistani Army, the Taliban and other jihadi groups remain entrenched within the power structure of Pakistan—and they are avowedly anti-India.

Now, let's move to China: That country's new political leadership, led by President Xi Jinping and Prime Minister Li Keqiang, has already made clear that its relationship with New Delhi will not merely be bilateral in scope but also look at South and East Asia as a whole. Of course, the border dispute between these two countries will have to be discussed, negotiated and resolved. But there is a larger picture that both New Delhi and Beijing will have to consider.

The Chinese Premier's decision to make India the first stop on his maiden foreign trip, followed by Pakistan, is a clear indication that Beijing takes both countries seriously. Of course, much like Sharif who has talked of extending a hand of friendship towards India, the Chinese Premier has also made many positive statements about India-China ties.

However, these are all in the realm of diplomatic niceties which convey nothing as far as the hard issues of national interest are concerned. For instance, the Chinese Premier has said that Pakistan is still very much an ally.

But again, the larger picture should be kept in mind. In the existing multi-polar world order, China wants to be counted as one of the great powers. Already an economic and military powerhouse, it is determined not to play second fiddle, particularly to the US, the self-appointed policeman of the world. In fact, the US should be prepared to face more of Chinese 'veto-power' on the global arena—as it has had to grapple with in recent times. Traditionally, the Americans have always had the upper hand inWest Asia but on the matters of Iran and Syria, they now find themselves on tenterhooks as neither China nor Russia are prepared to follow in their footsteps.

This is a new and powerful China at work, for which India is both an important partner and a competitor particularly in Asia. Here, India is following its Look East policy in trying to strengthen ties with Japan, South Korea and Vietnam. In the process, it is coming in conflict with China which is also seeking to increase its footprint in the region.

Also, China is competing against the American dollar and pushing its own currency as an instrument of international trade and exchange—yet another reason why the Asia Pacific is set to enter a new stage of competition in international relations. *The Pioneer, 24-05-2013*

Sub-conventional Warfare Aimed Wrong

The brutal killing of two Indian soldiers by the Pakistani army along the Line of Control has once again escalated tension between India and Pakistan. The incident comes close on the heels of the beginning of Pakistan Army Chief Ashfaq Parvez Kayani's new 'Cold Start Doctrine'. Launching the doctrine early this month, Kayani is reported to have said that "Pakistan's armed forces were trained for conventional warfare but the current security situation necessitated a change. Because sub-conventional threat is a reality and is a part of threat matrix faced by our country." Last year, in his Independence Day speech, the army chief had announced that "no state can afford a parallel system or a militant force."

While initial guesses may link the 'Cold Start Doctrine' to the fight against Islamic terror groups likes the Taliban who are wreaking havoc in Pakistan, the cold-blooded murder and mutilation of two Indian jawans some how forces one to see in targeted towards India. There are several reasons why the new doctrine deserves serious attention by India. The Pakistan Army has always considered India as its enemy number one. If the Pakistan Army-is preparing itself for sun-conventional warfare with domestic enemies, the same may be tried against India at some point. Chances are, Pakistan has already started trying it with India, in the build-up to the exit of NATO forces from Afghanistan. Clearly, this is an attempt to derail the ongoing peace process between the two country and the bring to a nought the success that has been achieved so far through people-to-people exchanges. A flawed idea that the Pakistan Army seems to be working upon, when it should join India to counter the growing menace of terror in its own backyard.

The US has failed in its war against the Taliban in Afghanistan. Defeated and humiliated, it is negotiating a transfer of power to the Taliban. Now this extension of Taliban territorial authority from Pakistan to Afghanistan may temporarily serve Pakistan's strategic interests, but in the long run it will be upto Afghanistan, Pakistan and India to face the challenge of these Islamic fanatics. Any increase in the power of Taliban in Pakistan will automatically lead to the weakening of the authority of the state and its army and if Taliban strongholds like Peshawar become 'liberated states' within the state, the terror groups will have a free run from there not just against Pakistan, but also against India, especially in Jammu and Kashmir.

While talking about Afghanistan during his visit to New Delhi on January 2, Iranian National Security Advisor, Saeed Jalili is reported to have said, "A former Pakistani head of state said terrorism was planned by America, executed by Pakistan and funded by the Arabs." This threat to the security of India and destabilisation of Pakistan and Afghanistan by the Taliban is the legacy of American wars in the 21st century and this security threat cannot be faced by Afghanistan alone without the willing cooperation of its neighbours, Pakistan and India.

India has strategic and economic interests in Afghanistan and other countries of Central Asia. It has been looking for new transit routes to get better access to Afghanistan and Central Asia. Iran is a great source of energy for India but the Iran-Pakistan-India oil pipeline project could not move forward because of serious trust deficit between India and Pakistan.

Though itself seriously challenged by Islamic terrorists, Pakistan has made little effort to cooperate with India and evolve a joint strategy to deal with their common enemy. On the contrary, incidents such as the attack on Parliament, 26/11 Mumbai attack, and now the mutilation of the bodies of two jawans after their killing have further distanced the two Asian neighbours. External and domestic security challenges are inseparable because external threats to security have a direct impact on the domestic security situation.

India and Pakistan will have to sit around the table to evolve common strategy to deal with the challenge thrown by the Taliban or separately, these two countries will be facing a common enemy. The choice is clear. Post the exit of NATO forces from Afghanistion, India and Pakistan must seek a South Asian solution to the problem by together asking local groups in Afghanistan to arrive at agreement on their own. A peace settlement brokered by others will not be agreeable to them. *The Financial World, 12-08-2013*

Final Act of Foreign Policy

It is for the Central Government of India, irrespective of the fact that different political formations come to power at the Center, to formulate, implement and oversee foreign security and strategic policies for the promotion and protection of national interest.

The goals of foreign policy are defined and redefined by politically elected democratic governments at the Center while responding to the emerging global and regional challenges faced by the country. Manmohan Singh, as prime minister of Congress-led United Progressive Alliance (UPA) government from 2004 to 2013, has been at the helm of affairs and also actively engaged in the formulation of India's foreign policy. Going by the political wave in India, it is likely that his five-day visit to Russia and China from October 21 to 25, 2013, may mark as the culmination of his carrier as India's foreign policy maker.

It deserves to be clearly stated that foreign policy doesn't hang in the air by itself because the distinction between external and domestic politics is an illusory one. Domestic politics condition foreign policy making and events outside the territorial boundaries of a country exercise great impact on domestic politics in the broadest sense of the term.

If the US President Barack Obama quietly announces aid to Pakistan amounting to US Dollar 1.5 billion, Indians immediately begin calculating the meaning of this aid with respect to India's security concerns. This stems from the fact that India and Pakistan, as neighbouring countries, are not at the best of bilateral terms and any meaningful development in the region makes both the countries to sit down and reanalyze their individual policies.

Manmohan Singh's meeting with Russian President Vladimir Putin bore positive results and the joint statement by both these leaders as viewed on October 21, 2013, clearly shows that India and Russia have "very deep relations". Manmohan Singh himself observed that "relations with Russia are the higher strategic priority for us". India and erstwhile communist Russia were always the most dependable of friends and allies, and even after the collapse of the Soviet Union in 1989-90, bilateral relationships between the two countries have continued to grow. The most special, perhaps salient feature, of this visit was, as Indian foreign secretary observed on October 21, "a hefty paragraph on terrorism" because this time terrorism adversely impacted the whole climate of not only the South Asian region but also the world.

The same concern was mentioned clearly and unambiguously both by Manmohan Singh and President Putin who, in their joint statement said that the recurring terrorist attacks perpetrated under misleading slogans are "undermining the territorial integrity of our nation" and destabilizing "multi-ethnic and pluralist societies". Putin's declaration of war on terror is a message to Pakistan which Indians thinks is the epicenter of terrorist activities and attacks against India.

Manmohan Singh achieved an important breakthrough in dealing with the problem of terrorism exported from the neighbouring country when Russia, honouring it quite well that India's anti-terrorist struggle is against Pakistan based terrorist groups, came out openly and firmly against the challenges posed by terrorist groups sheltered and shielded by governments of some countries.

The joint statement must have been carefully read by the Pakistani ruling establishment because they cannot ignore the firm anti-terror stand of a country like Russia. It was also decided at a bilateral level in Moscow that "political interaction in the Russia-India-China triangular format" should be further intensified.

It deserves to be noted that this "trilateral" arrangement cannot proceed smoothly because India and Russia, and Russia and China are very close friends; however, India and China have many conflicts of interest at both bilateral and regional levels. India and Russia have very smooth dealings on defence equipments and defence productions.

This farewell visit of Manmohan Singh to Russia has further cemented the already strong bonds between these two countries and the new government formed after the Lok Sabha elections of 2014 would inherit a strong legacy of Manmohan Singh's foreign policy. Singh's very significant visit to China after completing the Russia trip focused on some bilateral issues like the balance of trade (which is abnormally in favour of China) and Brahmaputra river water management. Most important of all the issues was the problem at the borders between the armies of these two powerful neighboring countries. India and China are engaged in finding spaces in important countries of East Asia, South-East Asia and Asia Pacific and one common thread which runs in the foreign security policy of China is that it not only defines its own national interest but also flexes muscle power to protect those interests and achieve its goals.

China is suspicious of India's presence in East Asia, South East Asia and Asia Pacific, and the flash point came when India agreed to Vietnam's efforts to pursue energy resources in the South China Sea where Beijing doesn't want either Hanoi or Manila to make any claim. A fact that cannot be ignored is that China has emerged as an "economic power house", and this self-assured and self-confident country wants to deal with other countries on its own terms. It is in the interest of both China and India to ease their "visa regime" but the Communist leaders sitting in Beijing keep on irritating Indians when it hands "stapled visas" to visitors from Arunachal Pradesh to China.

The "visa agenda" was not on the menu of Manmohan Singh but the border issue definitely was. Singh's efforts were to arrive at more confidence building measures to keep peace between the two neighbours at the Line of Actual Control and this goal appears to have been achieved during his three-day Beijing visit. It has been decided between the leaders of the two countries not to take recourse to any unnecessary armed conflict at the border.

The Chinese had suggested in 2012 that India and China should have a Border Defence Cooperation Agreement and on October 24, an important step forward in this direction was taken. Manmohan Singh's visit appears to be a fruitful one in the direction of peace between India and its neighbor across the Himalayas. As Singh observed on October 22, 2013, that he has "attempted to put India-China relations on a stable growth path" further stating that "working together with the Chinese leadership, (my) attempt has been to create a forward looking agenda for our bilateral relations".

In spite of the prime minister' s hopeful declaration an impression that either China or Pakistan will arrive at a "normal" neighbourly relationship with India should not be created because there are many "core issues" that still remain unsolved and are divisive. Although Manmohan Singh has done his job, many unfinished contentious issues including "disputes" between China and India remain to be touched in the future.

Further, the main opposition party has been traditionally hostile to both Pakistan and China and the social constituency of the BJP, the Sangh Parivar, has a brand of 'hatred' for Pakistan and China. A section of Indian public opinion is also jingoist. It is expected that realism will be the guiding principal of the Government of India's dealing with extremely knotty conflicts because even though political visits are necessary, they are not sufficient condition to resolve all issues faced by India with both China and Pakistan.

newsyaps.com, 09-11-2013

Foreign and Defence Policy: Impact of Economy

It is a simple truism to state that the foreign defence policies of a country are not only reflected by domestic political factors, they are conditioned by the state of economic health of a country, too. The amount spent on the defence budget by a country is partly determined by the kind of security threat perceived by the country's government; it is also largely determined by the economic conditions. Foreign and defence policies are thus integrally linked with one another and this issue of inter-linkages deserves to be highlighted in the context of India's present slow economic growth.

The whole decade of the 1990s had witnessed a robust state of economic growth and India was perceived as an emerging regional power like that of China. Because of the bright situation of the economy, the budgetary allocations for defence were increased throughout the '90s. Of late, the Indian economic growth story has entered a stage of sluggishness; its impact on annual defence allocations has become either stationery or slightly gone down compared to the '90s. Unfortunately, this new situation in India has emerged at a time when the centres of power, whether global or regional, are "rebalancing" their foreign and defence policies.

Every country during such a phase of transition – when old balance of power is giving way to a new one – has to make appropriate adjustments and adaptations to the changing power relations among the nations. India can't be an exception to such a rule, especially in the present globalized interdependent world of the second decade of the 21st century. This is the reason that Prime Minister Manmohan Singh, while addressing a conference of Indian ambassadors in Delhi on November 4, 2013, explained the "principles" of foreign policy which act as guidelines for civil servants who are engaged in the task of implementation of these policies. Manmohan Singh observed:

A. Foreign policy does not serve only "our interests" but also promotes our "values".
B. He reminded the assembled ambassadors that our economic development is taking place within the framework of a "plural, secular and liberal democracy".
C. He also observed that India has shaped its foreign policy in a "global environment conducive to the well-being of our great country".
D. He also alerted that "great integration with the world economy benefits India". Hence, "stable, long-term and mutually beneficial relations with all "major powers" are beneficial.
E. Finally, India has "shared destiny with India subcontinent" on the basis of "regional co-operation and interconnectivity".

These five principles of foreign policy enunciated by Manmohan Singh on November 4 can be better understood by refering to his speech to top military commanders on November 22 in Delhi. Singh had observed that the powerful countries of the West are strategically shifting their attention to the East and that the decision of the United States to "rebalance" the US armed forces in Asia-Pacific is "fraught with uncertainty".

Asia is the centre of focus of America especially because it sees China as an economic and military global challenger. In such a scenario, India becomes a "pivot" or a "lynchpin" and this is why New Delhi automatically gets involved because as an important Asian country, it will be asked or expected to play its role in the changing power dynamics in the continent.

While Washington may be willing to deal with Beijing on its own terms, India is not prepared for any military confrontation against its northern neighbour because New Delhi's number one priority is economic growth on which it will not compromise. China already suspects India for developing very close relationship with Japan, with which Beijing has a long and bitter history. Not only this, a few important South East Asian countries like

Philippines, Malaysia, South Korea and Vietnam are either American allies or are very close to it. The same cannot be said about their relations with India or China. If China and India have mutual suspicion, India has serious conflict with its neighbouring countries such as Pakistan.

The brutal wars between India and Pakistan are intertwined with the history of the two countries since their birth 66 years ago. China as a factor in Pakistan's military cooperation has always irritated the Indians. The Maoist party of Nepal is suspected by Indians as pro-China and anti-India in approach. Sri Lanka is a strange story where Sri Lankan Tamil problem acts like a brake on the initiatives of Indian foreign policy makers. America is not going to support India against its South Asian neighbouring countries especially Pakistan. Americans do not have any influence over China's foreign and defence policy makers who autonomously decide their material goals.

It deserves to be clearly stated that India has on its own, without the support of any global power, whether of the West or the East, dealt with problems of security and defence created by Pakistan. But an extremely worrisome fact which emerged from Singh's address at the combined commanders' conference is the slow economic growth and its impact on defence budget. "We need to match our investment in military equipment and forces to our national resources," he urged adding that domestic defence industrial base needs to be strengthened. It requires to be mentioned here that India is world's top importer of military equipments and the lion's share of India's budget is spent on the import of defence products because domestic industrial base for production is quite weak. India is a developing country and it has serious fiscal limitations over defence expenditure especially because the country is an importer of defence equipment. What is the alternative?

There is no substitute to diplomacy and war is the last refuge of foreign policy of a country. India cannot live with the historical "ghosts" of the past, and nuclear India and Pakistan have to come to terms with one another. The status quo between South Asian neighbouring countries is harmful for the economic development of the whole region and it is a historically established fact that fiscal resources spent on defence, if spent for development, can pull out millions out of poverty in the region. Manmohan Singh has warned the country about the changing "shifts" in the balance of power from West (America) to East (China) and transition to Asia-Pacific as the real location of military concentration. Is it a new cold war in Asia as the centre?

newsyaps.com, 16-12-2013

Chapter 6
BJP in Opposition

Why BJP Opts for its Communal Icon

The National Executive meeting of the BJP held in Mumbai on 24-25 May brought into open the factionalism within the party. It deserves to be clearly stated that factional fights within the BJP have nothing to do with any ideological differences between factions or among the leaders: The battle for supremacy is purely confined to personal issues. The Sanjay Joshi vs Narendra Modi battle is not at all ideological issues as they were comrades-in-arms as pracharaks of the RSS. Modi felt highly offended when his enemy number one was given a special task by the BJP chief Nitin Gadkari during the UP election.

At Mumbai, Modi was unambiguously projected as the National Leader of the party not only for the assembly election of Gujarat in 2012-13 but also for the crucial Lok Sabha election of 2014. The cat was out of the bag when former disgraced Karnataka chief minister BS Yeddyurappa observed that 'Narendra Modi should be projected as Prime Minister-in-making.' He has also been calling the central leadership indecisive and weak. Keshubhai Patel, a former chief minister of Gujarat, said that Modi has successfully 'terrorised' the entire BJP high command.

A wizard is not required to explain a simple fact of Indian politics: Authority of the central leadership to discipline state leaders depends on control over the purse. If the present central leadership of LK Advani, Sushma Swaraj, Arun Jaitely, Yashwant Sinha, and Murli Manohar Joshi, including party President Nitin Gadkari depends on fund raisers like Modi, he becomes the real centre of power. The BJP is out of power in New Delhi and has to depend on its chief ministers, especially of rich Gujarat state, for funding party activities, 'including expenses incurred by the central leadership.

Modi has not only displaced the central leadership from its position of authority, he has also overshadowed all other BJP chief ministers of Himachal Pradesh, Madhya Pradesh, Chhattisgarh, Karnataka, Goa etc., because he proved his credentials as a practitioner of anti-minority ideology of the Sangh Parivar when more than about 2, 000 innocent Muslims became victims of post-Godhra riots in 2002 and Modi's government, including civil bureaucracy and men in khaki uniform, behaved as passive spectators of the ongoing genocide in that state. Advani vetoed Atal Bihari Vajpayee's idea of replacing Narender Modi after the riots, of which clear evidence has been provided by Jaswant Singh, who was asked by Vajpayee to seek Advani's opinion on dismissal of Modi after the riots. Jaswant Singh conveyed to Vajpayee that Advani was dead set against such an idea or action against Modi.

The Muslim minority in Gujarat after the riots of 2002 has been compelled to accept their status as 'second-class citizen' under Hindu Raj. Modi is the only Chief Minister who cannot visit the United States or UK because the governments of these two countries are not giving a visa to a violator of human rights. Such a leader is darling of the Sangh Parivar.

Modi has tried to shift public discourse away from his crimes of 2002 by projecting himself as the messiah of Gujarat development. But the state was on the developmental road even before Modi became CM. It is well known that Gujarati entrepreneurs like Dhirubhai Ambani relentlessly worked for the state's development, and the rate fo growth in terms of GDP of Gujarat even prior to Modi was always high, like other developed regions like Maharashtra or Tamil Nadu. Was Gujarat before Modi in the backward category of states like Bihar or Uttar Pradesh or Madhya Pradesh? Further, Modi is practising a 'socially exclusivist' model of development, where minorities who suffered during the riots have still not been paid compensation for the losses suffered by them. Is this development?

Advani had attained great eminence in the Sangh Parivar when he led a movement for the demolition of Babri Mosque at Ayodhya on 6 December 1992 by describing it as a 'monument of Muslim invasion'. Advani remained an unquestioned leader of the BJP from 1992 to 2008 because of his concrete achievement for the RSS goal of 'teaching a lesson to Muslims'. Advani has faded and Modi has replaced him because post-2002 riots, he has proved his credentials as a committed practitioner of RSS ideology of Hindu majority rule over minorities in India.

Modi has been crowned by the BJP and the Sangh Parivar because he contributes the lion's share of funds to the party and the RSS because he has proved his credentials as a good Swayamsevak. Will the country accept such a communal fascist as a leader? *Financial World, 01-06-2012*

The BJP Supports a Tribal?

It is in the fitness of things that the Congress has appealed to every political formation to extend their support to Pranab Mukerjee, but it is too much to expect that in the existing political situation any one consensus candidate for the highest office of the Indian state can be agreed upon by all the parties or political groups. Sushma Swaraj and Arun Jaitely, after the meeting of truncated

National Democratic Alliance of the BJP and the Akali Dal, made an announcement in support of PA Sangma, one of the 'tallest' leaders of the country and the 'tallest leader from the Northeast'. The BJP, the opposition party, observed on 21 June that during these elections, it cannot give any 'walkover' to the UPA.

The BJP was determined to oppose the Congress candidate, repeating the history of 2007, when Congress party candidate Pratibha Patil was opposed by RSS Pracharak Bhairon Singh Shekhawat. Sangma has offered himself as a representative candidate of the 'tribal population' of India by observing that none of the 12 previous Presidents, from Dr Rajendra Prasad to Pratibha Patil, belonged to this community. It is most surprising that the BJP and the Hindu Joint Family is supporting a candidate who is publicly claiming that he is representative of 'a particular section' of the Indian population. Sangma's self-definition about his tribal identity is fundamentally opposed to Sanga Parivar's concept of Hindu nationalism. Sangma is taking a public position that India is plural and a country of rich diverse cultures and traditions should have a 'representative' from diverse communities like Muslims or Dalit, or women or 'tribals'. This is Sangma's main claim and he is fighting these elections 'on the basis of his 'tribal identity', an idea of plural and diverse India rejected by the Sangh Parivar.

If the BJP, because of political expediency and opportunism, has decided to support Sangma, who is canvassing on the basis of his sectional 'tribal' identity, Sangma has also adopted a purely opportunistic political route by contesting these elections on the basis of support of antitribal and anti-Christian Hindu Rashtravadis. It should not be forgotten that the Sangh Parivar has a project of 'conversion' of tribals to Hindu religion and Sangma wants to be President by seeking support of such religious fanatics. Naveen Patnaik of the Biju Janata Dal has conveniently forgotten that he had kicked out BJP form his coalition government because under the protective umbrella of Hindu coalition partner, the activists of the Sangh Parivar were attacking Christians and churches in Odisha. Is public memory so short that Patnaik joins BJP for Sangma's contest against Pranab Mukherjee? This narrative clearly shows that principles and ideologies are expendable in elections and ideological opponents can sit on the same table to achieve small political gains.

If the election for the office of the President has clearly shown that 'secularists' are always willing to make compromises with their ideological opponents like the BJP, another very important fact which has shown the ugly face of Indian politics is that all alliances and coalitions in India are shortlived and extremely transitory. The four party alliance of the 'communists' remains intact in spite of the fact that the CPI(M) and Forward Bloc have decided to vote for Mukherjee and the CPI and RSP, other Left allies, have decided to 'abstain' from voting on this issue only.

The split in the NDA has taken an ideological turn because the Janata Dal (United), a partner of the NDA, has asked the BJP to announce the name of a Prime Ministerial candidate for the Lok Sabha election of 2014 because Nitish Kumar, the Chief Minister of Bihar, has shown his clear preference of a 'secular and liberal' candidate who should be worried about 'poor states'. The real reason for this so-called 'ideological' difference of opinion between the BJP and the JD(U) is not for the presidentship but for the prime ministerial candidate for 2014. The real focus of the JD(U) as an alliance partner of the BJP is the Lok Sabha election of 2014 and incidentally, the ideological debate between these two parties has taken place during the presidential election of 2012 which has not left any option for the JD(U) but to vote for Pranab Mukherjee, because the BJP is on the other side of the contest.

The debate between 'secularism versus communalism' between the JD(U) and the BJP has prematurely created a situation where these two partners, for the sake of consistency, are supporting candidates of two different camps. Sharad Yadav, the President of JD(U) has stopped the JD(U) leaders for expressing any differences with the BJP and on 24 June, Sharad Yadav clearly announced that the NDA remains united. The purpose of this above discussion is to highlight the fact that ideological divisions between 'secularists' and the 'communalists' are just a matter of convenience and such a controversy is raised at a particular moment when it is politically suitable.

It is not without reason that every non-Congress political formation has co-habited at one time or the other with the Hindu nationalists for the sake of political advantage. It is not unrealistic to affirm that if APJ Abdul Kalam had agreed to be a candidate for the July 2012 presidential election, the controversy about the communalism of the BJP would not have been raised and all pretenders to secularism would have been found in the great company of Hindu communalists. In sum, the Mukherjee-versus-Sangma contest has once against brought into sharp focus the complete de-ideologisation of politics of opportunism in India. Political parties have revealed their real face during the selections of July 2012 because for them ideology in politics is dead as a dodo and every alliance or coalition of parties can be sacrificed before the altar of rank opportunism. Sangma was for very long time with the Congress party yet he has absolutely no problem seeking support of the communal BJP in this contest. It has become difficult to identify any regional parties or leaders or groups as a firm and consistent believer of secularism because Naveen Patnaik kicked out BJP in Odisha because of communal politics of the party, and same Patnaik is supporting 'sectarian' Sangma who is dependent on the BJP for his electoral victory. Once again, politicians are seen as people of easy conscience and practitioners of unprincipled politics.

Financial World, 27-06-2012

The Politics of Development

Gujarat chief minister Narendra Modi is the most acceptable political leader for Indian and foreign big business. He is advertised as a developmentalist chief minister. HDFC chairman Deepak Parekh enthusiastically welcomed Modis electoral victory, terming it a vote for performance, development, growth and transparency. The results show that people want progress, be it in infrastructure or quality of life. CII chairman Adi Godrej, supported by Assocham president Raj Kumar Dhoot, observed, Gujarat has voted for development. The Gujarat government under Modi has been an epitome of good governance.

Modi's politics, which provides benefits, concessions and subsidies to big business, is clearly applauded. But ghettoisation of an insecure Muslim minority community should also be considered a part of the reality of the same state. Politics is multifaceted, and good politics for a particular social group may be bad politics for another social group and, thus, politics is in everyday motion and the direction and moral agenda of politics leads to either neglect of the needs of a vulnerable strata of society or operates for the welfare and benefits of other strata of society. This is the social dialectics of society.

If Modi has rolled out the red carpet for Tatas, Ambanis, Vodafone, Maruti Suzuki et al., he is a developmentalist CM, and if Gujarat has neglected tribals, fishermen and drought-hit sub-regions, they represent the neglected dark side of politics. Modi himself claimed victories in urban areas inhabited by the neo-middle class, however, his politics showed no interest in dealing with poor indictors of social development. How does one ignore the fact that his policies have brought prosperity and deprivation to different people in Gujarat? How is it that corporate India is in a welcoming mood towards the politics pursued by Modi, but there is an emptiness on the faces of underclasses and the mass of labouring classes who have been ignored on every indicator of social agenda by Modi's politics?

The larger issue is about the dominant ideology of politics that, while pursuing pro-industry, pro-business economic policies aimed at achieving the rate of economic growth, cannot ignore the logic of universal franchise and competitive electoral party politics. If pro-capital politics based on a growth-oriented economic agenda has clearly benefited 200-250 million of the population consisting of billionaires, multimillionaires and upwardly-mobile professional and entrepreneurial urban middle classes, the same model of politics has given birth to gross inequalities, and all kinds of sectoral and spatial imbalances, whether region-based or rural-versus-urban imbalances.

The agenda of society and economy is expected to be defined by politics in a democracy, however, in concrete reality, multiple social groups are actively involved in pushing their special and specific interests, and in such a situation, powerful social and economic groups are generally politically more successful than the unorganised labouring classes. Hence, politics is a game of competition among unequals and it is expected that political parties, groups and leaders are able to harmonise conflicting group interests in society. If a democratically-elected government feels the need for launching Mahatma Gandhi National Rozgar Yojana for the rural unemployed daily-wage earners, the same government actively responds to the complaint of 14 big business leaders who castigated the Manmohan Singh government in 2011 for 'public policy paralysis'. If a kind of American politics is hostile to any social insurance and security legislation for the poor, then some political groups demand that the Barack Obama government should 'pump taxpayer' money to salvage the subprime fiscal crisis of 2008.

Has the American state 'retreated' from market interventions and corrections as demanded by the extreme right-wing conservatives of the Republican party, champions of the 'rescue operation' for the banking system in 2008? Politics is omnipresent, and it is always in the driver's seat because modern industrial societies require active governmental interventions to manage the economy. The only issue is whether politics is pro-rich, pro-industrialist, pro-multinational or ideologically committed to perform welfare activities for the victims of an unequal society.

Politics is based on an ideology and because it is never ideologically 'neutral', this issue has to be continuously analysed and explained. The above narrative clearly shows that the essence of politics is to compete for control over public resources, and on the basis of this power alone, it distributes public resources to different social constituencies and groups in an unequal manner, depending on the ideology pursued by political leaders.

The Economic Times, 03-01-2013

Facts and Fiction about Modi

The National Executive and National Council meetings of the BJP from March 1 to 3, 2013 were formally held to endorse Rajnath Singh's presidency of the party, but in reality, the party wanted to test the popularity and acceptability of Narendra Modi especially within the large political stream represented essentially by the regional parties and leaders. It is a truism to state that whether the Congress or the BJP cannot form a central government in 2014 on their own strength and both these all-India parties have to hunt for allies and coalition partners for forming a government at the centre. It is the BJP which has to work hard for finding coalition partners because even the present truncated BJP-led National Democratic Alliance is under great strain because Nitish Kumar—the Janata Dal (United) Chief Minister of Bihar—has unambiguously opposed Modi's candidature for prime ministership of the NDA alliance at the centre in 2014.

Sharad Yadav, the other tall leader of the JD(U) has observed repeatedly that the future prime minister while belonging to the largest coalition partner has not at all expressed any positive opinion in favour of Modi. The Sangh Parivar's political shop, the BJP, has always been adept in obfuscation of true reality of political programme of its ideology of Hindustan and Hindu Rashtravad. This is the reason that Modi before 5,000 faithful of the BJP National Council presented himself as the champion of 'good governance' and the so-called 'Development Model' of Gujarat state governed by him. Every national leader of the BJP including LK Advani himself acknowledged that Modi including other BJP chief ministers like Shiv Raj Chauhan of Madhya Pradesh, Raman Singh of Chhat-tisgarh were 'great performers' and the electorate in these states have recognised this fact by re-electing Modi for the third time and Chauhan and Raman Singh twice as chief ministers.

Congress was painted as a failed performer and BJP, as opposed to its main national opponent, has shown performance by dynamic leaders both at the centre and at the state levels where it is in power. The media, both print and audio-visual, on the basis of public rhetoric of BJP leadership from March 1 to 3, faithfully not only informed the public about the proceedings of the BJP's National Executive and National Council, it enthusiastically played like a transistor' the rhetoric of 'Developmental' Chief Minister Modi.

It is one thing for the BJP and the Sangh Parivar to convince the faithful and committed Hinduvadis about BJP's tall claims, it is very difficult for the BJP to substantiate the claim of development on the basis of rigorous scrutiny of the real ideology of the Sangh Parivar. A few facts may be mentioned to substantiate the argument that Modi, the BJP and the Sangh Parivar are engaged in hiding facts and selling fiction to win an election to implement the agenda of Hindutva.

First, the BJP government in Karnataka from 2008 to 2013 has given a message that attackers on Christian churches or moral policing by its own workers for disciplining the Hindu women shall not be punished because under Hindu Ray, minorities have to be taught a lesson. Karnataka witnessed attack on Christian church on March 9 and the attackers are moving free. The minority community in Bihar strongly protested against the imposition of 'Surya Namaskar' a Hindu ritual, and Nitish Kumar who is chief minister with the support of BJP, had to intervene in this blatant anti-minority legitimisation of Hindu ritual.

Second, post-March 3, the dominant media, whether audio-visual or print, has indulged in vociferously counselling Modi that he would be acceptable if he follows in the footsteps of Atal Bihari Vajpayee who as prime minister from 1998 to 2004 was a 'liberal' face of Hindu BJP. The argument of media is that Modi will become acceptable to coalition partners if he acts as a new 'avatar' (incarnation) of Vajpayee, the liberal Sang Parivar mask.

Third, the Sangh Parivar and the BJP are engaged in the Hinduisation of India and the National Council of the BJP on March 3, where lullabies of 'good governance and development agenda' were sung, passed a resolution on Sethusamudram project for linking India and Sri Lanka for economic benefits.

The BJP and the Hindu priests do not consider Sethusamudram, an idea floated in 1963, as a 'project' designed to provide a shorter sailing route for trade and commerce because of their mythical and mythological belief of its association with Lord Rama. The resolution on March 3, 2013, stated its opposition to Sethusamundara by observing that 'Lord Rama epitomises the essence of India's cultural, spiritual and civilisational heritage. The identity of India is incomplete without him and the story of Rama is incomplete without Ram Sethu'. This opposition to a navigation project on the basis of this so-called sacredness, is a repeat of the arguments given by Sangh Parivar when they raised mosque-temple controversy and claimed it was a site of birth of Rama and on December 6, 1992, the Babri Mosque was destroyed by Kar Sevaks mobilised by the Sangh Parivar and led by Lal Krishna Advani.

It deserves to be highlighted that the media which is busy in telling Modi to project himself as Vajpayee has neither highlighted nor commented on the issue that was highlighted by the BJP and a resolution was passed on March 3. It is really surprising that a RSS Pracharak like Modi is being asked to project himself as a new face of 'liberal Hinduism' without realizing that liberal Hindutva of the Sangh Parivar is a contradiction in terms because the Sangh Parivar and all its affiliates and leaders are firm believers of an ideology where compromises are not made and never tolerated. LK Advani as a leader of Rama Janmabhoomi movement for 1990 to 1992 and Modi as a practitioner of anti-minority politics of Hindutva in 2002 were rewarded by the Sangh Parivar because they had proved their firm loyalty to its ideology.

Modi's two track strategy became crystal clear while on video-conferencing to NRI Hindus in Chicago on March 11 he asserted his commitment to the ideology of Hindutva by emphasising the idea of 'country first' and second he tried to win over upwardly mobile Hindu middle class by projecting himself as a 'developmentalist'. Do we need any other proof of Modi and BJP's consistency in sticking to their ideology of militant Hindutva? Incidentally, the idea of country first conceals the reality because the Sangh Parivar has always alleged that Muslims have extra-territorial loyalties as their places of pilgrimage are outside India. *The Financial World, 04-04-2013*

Bound by the Rules of the Greater Family

Narendra Modi's 1,000-word blog of December 27, just after the Ahmedabad judge dismissed a criminal case filed against him by Zakia Jafri, is just one in a series of attempts by him to hoodwink people by presenting the judgment as evidence that he, as chief minister of Gujarat, cannot be held guilty for the 2002 riots.

Modi, in his artificial, hyperbolic language, stated "yesterday's judgment culminated a process of unprecedented scrutiny … Gujarat's 12 years of trial by the fire have finally drawn to an end. I feel liberated and at peace". This self-congratulatory action is premature because Jafri has many legal rights and options before her to take up the cause of the massacred residents.

A few things may be mentioned to substantiate the argument that neither Modi nor his government and associates of the Sangh parivar can be absolved of their omission and commission during and after the anti-Muslim riots of 2002. A bandh call was given by associates of the Sangh parivar on February 28 and the messages, rumours and misinformation were spread throughout Gujarat that Muslims (unsubstantiated) had burnt Hindu kar sevaks who were coming back in a train from Ayodhya. Should the Modi government have allowed this bandh, whose only purpose was to create anti-Muslim feelings? The answer is: he could not stop it because he himself has been an RSS pracharak.

The RSS is committed to the ideology that Hindus are 'first-class' citizens of India and Muslims and Christians are 'second-class' and minorities can live only if they accept that they are citizens of the Hindu Rashtra as defined by the RSS. Modi is an ideologue of the RSS and his role during the riots of 2002 or as the PM candidate for 2014 can be understood by situating him in the Hindu joint family.

In an interview on July 12, 2013, he stated: "I'm nationalist. I'm patriotic. I'm Hindu nationalist …" Similarly, LK Advani, who as home minister in the NDA government had protected Modi, stated on July 17: "…our ideological family will always be the RSS. This is what binds us together…" This explains clearly why neither Modi nor his government can be exonerated. And this is the reason why the Supreme Court not only transferred cases filed by the riot victims outside Gujarat, the judges asked for the creation of a special investigation team.

The story does not end there. Modi did not show any concern for the 200,000 Muslim refugees. Former PM AB Vajpayee, in response to a letter from Sonia Gandhi, wrote back, saying: "I have directed the Gujarat government to set up a broad based committee, under the chairmanship of the governor of the state, to plan and implement rehabilitation measures on war-footing". The question that has emerged from the above narrative is whether the Sangh parivar can be trusted to perform its constitutional responsibilities of being the protectors of the rule of law and equality for every citizen in the country. The answer is: No. *Hindustan Times, 09-01-2014*

Narendra Modi's Indefensible Defence

Bharatiya Janata Party's prime ministerial candidate Narendra Modi has waited for a full 11 years to personally express his opinions on the great human tragedy which occurred in Gujarat under his chief ministership. It will not be an exaggeration to state that Modi is making every effort to project his clean image as an able administrator and competent chief minister who has left no stone unturned to develop his state.

More than a thousand Muslims were massacred, and 200,000 Muslims fled from their places of residence and sought refuge in relief camps during the anti-Muslim riots of 2002 in Gujarat. It is not only the human rights and civil rights groups, local, national and international, who have actively campaigned for the prosecution of guilty people who are responsible for the massacre, even the Supreme Court of India felt it necessary to transform the trials of criminals guilty of anti-Muslim riots to other states outside Gujarat. The highest court of the country constituted an SIT under its own supervision to undertake impartial investigations into the tragic happenings of 2002 Gujarat. Narendra Modi was himself questioned by the SC appointed special investigators about his actions during the riots especially because many victims had accused him of personal complicity.

The most famous case is of Zakia Jafri, the wife of Ehsan Jafri, a former Congress MP, who fought a legal battle against Modi accusing him of not taking any step in saving the lives of innocents who were trapped in Gulbarg society residential area. An Ahmedabad judge, in his verdict on December 26-27, 2013, gave a clean chit to Narendra Modi and dismissed all allegations against him levelled by Zakia Jafri of Gulbarg society. This one judgement from a local court of Ahmedabad prompted Narendra Modi on December 27, 2013 to breach his 11 years of silence on anti-Muslim massacres in Gujarat during 2002 riots and he wrote in a blog post of 1000 words that "I feel liberated and at peace" (because of court's judgement) and further "I was shaken to the core. Grief, sadness, misery, pain, anguish, agony – mere words could not capture the absolute emptiness one felt on witnessing such inhumanity".

Modi also believes that the story of tragedy with which his name is prominently associated has seen a closure when he observed "yesterday's judgement culminated a process of unprecedented scrutiny 'Gujarat's 12 years of trial by the fire have finally drawn to an end". Is it the end of the story? Is Modi really innocent? The answer to this question is a big no. Modi as a CM and the BJP and other affiliates of the Sangh Parivar like the RSS, VHP, *et al.* are on "trial" for their role in the riots.

Many of those who survived the riots are living a terrified existence. Has the Modi government done anything to restore confidence among the terrorised and terrified Muslim community in Gujarat?

The very first action of the Modi government set the stage for this large scale anti-Muslim massacre. Why did the Modi government allowed the burnt bodies of the railway compartment at Godhra on February 27 to be brought to Ahmedabad? Did the Gujarat police and intelligence agencies not inform the CM of serious backlash by Hindu organisations after the burnt bodies of the train passengers were put in public hospitals in Ahmedabad? Was it not an action of deliberate provocation by the Gujarat state government to play with the emotions of the people and members of the dead families? Was the state government and its police forces fully prepared to deal with the situation had it worsened after the "dead bodies" were brought from Godhra to Ahmedabad? There is no evidence that this action of the Modi government was an innocent response to a critical situation which arose in Godhra on February 27, 2002. Further, the direct involvement of the SC, the dissent shown by many senior police officials in Gujarat police force and other well-known facts clearly establish the point that a chief minister cannot be absolved of his responsibility of massacres of Muslims which took place in the riots.

While the finger of accusation needs to be directly pointed towards Narendra Modi, it should not be forgotten that his own Sangh Parivar was also actively involved. The BJP never leaves any opportunity of accusing the Congress of anti-Sikh riots of November 1984 in Delhi because the anti-Sikh mob was led by Congress party leaders like Jagdish Tytler, Sajjan Kumar and others. The same logic should be applied to the Gujarat riots of 2002 because the Ahmedabad court has already convicted a former lady MLA of the BJP and a prominent leader of the Bajrang Dal on charges of leading a mob to kill Muslims and burn their property.

If Congress cannot disown its own party leaders' involvement in the anti-Sikh riots of 1984, Modi, too, cannot dissociate the involvement of his own party members and convicted leaders in Gujarat riots of 2002. The targeting of Modi for anti-Muslim riots is only one part of the story; the other part is that Modi is an integral part of the Sangh Parivar whose involvement in the Gujarat riots has been legally established by the court. It is disingenuous to separate Modi from his larger family – the RSS, and its ideology, which is based on the Hindu versus Muslim way of thinking.

Many of those who survived the riots are living a terrified existence. Has the Modi government done anything to restore confidence among the terrorised and terrified Muslim community in Gujarat? The Modi government did not set up a panel to oversee "relief operations" meant for the displaced Muslims during the post-Godhra riots. The Gujarat state government with Modi as chief minister was made to set up a 13-member panel on orders from then prime minister Atal Bihari Vajpayee to "monitor operational running of relief camps". The wisdom of providing relief to the victims dawned upon Modi only after he got Vajpayee's letter written in response to Sonia Gandhi's missive to the prime minister.

Assuming for a moment that Narendra Modi had made earnest efforts to control the riots of 2002 under obligations as a chief minister, his complete neglect of relief arrangements for the victims deserves to be explained by him alone. Does it not reveal his anti-Muslim approach and ideology? Mulayam Singh Yadav and his son, the Uttar Pradesh Chief Minister Akhilesh Yadav, are facing brickbats for their complete failure to look after the welfare of more than 60,000 displaced victims of the Muzaffarnagar riots of September 2013. If Mulayam and Akhilesh are guilty of not performing their basic duty towards the riot affected people of Uttar Pradesh, Narendra Modi is equally guilty of pursuing his anti-Muslim policies during and after the Gujarat riots of 2002. Does Modi feel "grief, sadness, misery, pain, anguish, agony" for the victims and survivors of the riots? Modi's defence is completely indefensible because his acts of omission and commission as chief minister of Gujarat are many and unforgivable. *newsyaps.com, 09-01-2014*

Chapter 7
Elections 2014 and Modi in Government

Rahul vs Modi may Just Remain a Catchline

It still might be a year for the next general elections, but the mass media, both print and audio visual, has already started debating candidates for the office of India's next prime minister. Perhaps the media is simply reflecting the concerns of the political parties, the main being the Congress and the BJP.

Since his elevation as Congress vice-president, Rahul Gandhi has taken some significant steps for the resurgence and restructuring of the party organization with a view not only on the 2014 Lok Sabha elections but also on this year's assembly elections. Reportedly, he managed to pull huge crowds while campaigning in Tripura last week. While the party may not openly admit it, all indications are towards projecting him as the future leader of the party. The decision to elevate Rahul as vice-president, implicitly or explicitly, was taken to send a message to the voters that it would be Rahul, not Manmohan Singh who would lead the party in 2014.

But while the Congress seems to have settled the issue of Manmohan's successor, the BJP and the Sangh Parivar are having a tough time choosing the best of the many names with prime ministerial aspirations among their cadres. The exercise appears a little more complicated here than in the Congress or regional parties, which are mostly 'one man shows'. While NCP chief Sharad Pawar's prime ministerial aspirations seem to have waned with age, BSP chief Mayawati has made her ambitions loud and clear. This week she asked her party workers to ensure a "big victory" for her in the next Lok Sabha elections so that she can deliver the Independence Day speech from the Red Fort. Her bete noir, Samajwadi party chief Mulayam Singh Ya-dav too has told his party men that if they want their 'Netaji' as Prime Minister, they should send a maximum number of MPS from the Uttar Pradesh for the Lok Sabha of 2014. Janata Dal (United) leaders have for long been pitching for their party chief and Bihar Chief Minister Nitish Kumar as NDA'S prime ministerial candidate. JDU fases a tougher challenge pretending to be a 'secular' party while sailing with communal NDA.

But within the BJP, main component of the NDA, there's a battle simmering between the supporters of Sushma Swaraj, Arun Jaitley, Yashwant Sinha and Naren-dra Modi over who should be the party's face for 2014 elections. Newly elected BJP chief Rajnath Singh may have made it amply clear that no public discussion on the issue of prime minister should take place, but the buzz about Gujarat chief minister Narendra Modi being NDA'S PM candidate gets louder every passing day, specially in the wake of his third term as state chief minister. Modi too is deftly trying to get rid of his taint of the 2002 riots and project himself as a 'developmentalist' leader, supported by big business houses and a sound PR machinery.

Interestingly though, the only qualification for BJP prime ministerial candidate is that he must be an RSS pracharak. But even though Modi's a pracharak, the Gujarat Chief Minister's efforts to break Out of his communal image, have only distanced him from the RSS. No wonder then, Modi is trying to make it on his own performance.

In contrast, the Congress comes across as a lame duck, confused 'non-performer'. If the falling rate of economic growth and rising inflation weren't enough to turn public opinion against it, the flurry of scams that have broken out in the UPA rule are only likely to seal its fate.

With so many players in the fray, a fragmented verdict is all we can look forward to if elections are contested on 'routine' issues. And a fragmented verdict will only limit public choice. "Voters are forgotten when the verdict is ambiguous and politics of selecting a prime minister becomes a no holds barred game of manipulation among the multiple political groups. VP Singh, Chandrashekar, HD Dev Gowda; Inder Kumar Gujarat are examples that ultimately a dark horse may emerge victorious and Rahul versus Modi may end up just being a catchy slogan. *The Financial World, 21-02-2013*

Communists in Action for 2014 Elections

Political parties, whether national ones like the Congress and the BJP or state-based regional and sub-regional parties or groups, are evolving their electoral strategies for the upcoming Lok Sabha elections of April-May 2014.

It is clear that the electoral verdict of the Lok Sabha elections of 2014 will be completely fractured and fragmented which means that all victorious parties will have to work towards a pre-election or post-election alliance for the formation of a government at the Centre. Every coalition government is based on alliances among heterogeneous political groups who are united only on the basis of a marriage of opportunistic convenience.

Communist parties have a presence in West Bengal, Kerala and Tripura and as a united unit, communists can win 30 or 40 Lok Sabha seats; they are always active in the game of coalition making at the Centre.

The political journey of communists began with anti-Congressism and only recently have they shifted focus of their ideological politics to anti-communalism and anti-BJP. The communists mobilised some regional parties on October 30 when they organized a secular front meeting in Delhi. This meeting was interpreted as a gathering of anti-Congress and anti-BJP political alternative for secular politics where leaders from Samajwadi Party, Janta Dal (United), AIADMK, Biju Janata Dal, Janta Dal (Secular) and All Assam Student Union Representatives met under the so-called umbrella of secularism. The truth was that all of them were looking for "allies" in future coalition government at the centre. Although the slogan of the meeting of October 30 was on secularism, the absence of Bahujan Samaj Party, leaders like Lalu Prasad Yadav and Ram Vilas Paswan, and the Congress party clearly showed that the politics of factionalism between regional parties reigned supreme.

Sitaram Yechury, the CPI(M) leader, elaborated the strategy of an alternative on November 2013 by saying that the party was trying for a "combination" of secular parties "based on a common minimum programme". The CPI(M) is not only a committed anti-communalist and anti-BJP political formation, it is also fundamentally opposed to what is known as Manmohan Economics of globalisation, privatization, deregulation, open market economy for Indian and foreign investors, and it wants its allies of 2014 to "agree to an alternative economic policy trajectory". Sitaram, in his statement on November 9, 2013, made it clear that such a common minimum programme of this "combination" of the third alternative to Congress and BJP coalition "will take a concrete shape only post-election but it is working towards that".

Yechury observed, "A third front alliance should not be at a mercy of outside support. (Any) alternative policy trajectory is required to change the situation in the country and there is very little to choose between the Congress and the BJP. People want a government which will give them relief".

The above narrative deserves a clinical analysis because it is based on many premises about the shape of things of 2014 without any reference to the history of such shaky and extremely temporary experiments with so called Third Front government where neither the Congress nor the BJP were a part of the heterogeneous coalition government at the centre.

How have the coalitions from the decade of 1990s functioned without either the support of the Congress or the BJP? The first disastrous result of such an experiment was V.P. Singh-led government in 1989-90 supported from outside by the Congress, the BJP and the communists which made Singh boast that he was an expert in the "management of political contradictions".

His Janata Party revolted against him and he quit his post just after 10 months as prime minister. V.P. Singh is perhaps best remembered for announcing on August 9, 1990 the acceptance of Mandal Commission report on reservation in public services and publically funded institutes. Singh was kicked out; Mandal divided the country; Chadra Shekhar of Janta Party replaced Singh as PM with Congress support; the BJP walked out of the so called spurious alliance; and, L.K. Advani launched a highly emotive and socially divisive Ram Temple rath yatra in 1990.

Chandra Shekhar remained a prime minister for six months before the Lok Sabha election was again held in 1991, and the so called third alternative collapsed like a house of cards. The experiment was repeated and India again saw two shaky and unstable PMs from 1996-98 – H.D. Dewe Gowda and I.K. Gujral.

National politics gained some stability after Atal Bihari Vajpayee of the BJP led-coalition government completed its five-year term and Manmohan Singh-led UPA government successfully sailed through its two terms. It is clearly substantiated from past experience that either Congress or the BJP has performed the role of stabilizer at the Centre while disparate regionalists form part of a coalition.

The communists withdrew their 'outside support' from UPA in 2008 when India signed a nuclear energy treaty with the US. Post-2008, the story of communists has also changed because they were defeated in the state assembly elections of West Bengal by Mamata Banerjee's Trinamool Congress. This defeat shook the communists to the core because West Bengal had been a 'fortress' of left rule for more than three decades. Further, the defeat in Kerala state assembly elections added a sense of dependency and even gloom among the communist cadre.

Searching for an active role in politics, the announcement of Narendra Modi as BJP's PM candidate alerted communists because of fears that communal politics might take a vicious turn as it happened in Gujarat in 2002. There is no love lost between the Congress and the communists after their bitter separation in 2008 on the nuclear deal with US. Hence, the third alternative is the need of the communists and ambitious regionalists who have a dream of occupying the office of the PM irrespective of the lessons in failure history might provide.

Politics of power is based on 'dreams' and everyone has a right to have a 'dream', the real issue is that the coalition government at the Centre is already full of inner conflicts among the unprincipled allies, and a 'combination' or collection of disparate regionalists and parochial leaders will prove disastrous for the country. *Newsyaps, 28-11-2013*

Style vs Substance: Rahul-Modi Politics of Irrelevance

It is normal for every political party to launch a high-velocity campaign during the state assembly or Lok Sabha elections with a clear objective of winning the electoral battle on the basis of its public record of activities and services for the voter.

Political parties mobilize public supporters and voters with the goal of winning an election and during electoral mobilization, political parties compete against one another making such a competition a ruthless affair. Sometimes, during the heat of elections, parties or their leaders launch aggressive attacks against their political opponents and often in the process of electioneering parties or leaders stoop very low while attacking or suppressing the acts of omission and commission of their opponents. This "battle of democracy" has become quite aggressive with a no-holds-barred campaign launched by both the BJP and the Congress, the two major opponents at the national level.

Since this struggle for electoral victories is bound to continue till the forthcoming Lok Sabha elections of April-May 2014, it is essential to highlight the salient features of the election campaign launched by the BJP and the Congress against one another.

It can be no one's case that during election campaigning civility of behaviour of a kind of gentlemanly political "debate" will always be maintained and the limits of normal, decent public behaviour will be consciously observed by the contenders for power, but, it is expected that the "style" of campaigning adopted by the two major all-India parties will reflect less of "emotional" outbursts and more of reasoned arguments against the policies and performances of one's opponents.

Unfortunately, neither Narendra Modi, the BJP prime ministerial candidate, nor Rahul Gandhi, the vice president of the Congress party, restrained themselves during the electoral battle for five state assemblies. The Election Commission of India, a constitutional statutory body which is mandated to impose an election code of conduct, has already "expressed a mind of disapproval", even a mild reprimand to Rahul Gandhi on his unfounded statement on Muzaffarnagar riot victims. Rahul Gandhi has been clearly asked by the EC to maintain "restrain in his public speeches". Modi, not to be left behind, described the Congress election symbol of hand as "khooni panja" (bloody hand). The EC felt the need for asking Modi to maintain 'decency' during his election speeches.

It deserves to be clearly stated that the level and standard of political discourse during these elections has touched the lowest levels of public decency. Many tall political leaders, during these campaigns have shown a style of speech which at the best can be described as that of street level fighters and not of the level of national and important leaders of parties in India.

On the basis of quite a weighty public evidence it can be stated in an unambiguous manner that Narendra Modi's style of election campaigning is not at all worthy of a candidate who aspires to be the PM of India. The lowest level to which Modi reached was when he hit Sonia Gandhi below the belt by pointing out that "she was physically unwell" to undertake the responsibilities of Congress party leadership, and he arrogated to himself the right to advice Rahul to take over the command from her "ailing" mother.

Further, not to be left behind, Naresh Agarwal of Samajwadi Party asked on November 13 "how an ordinary worker at a street tea stall" (a reference to Narendra Modi) hope to become PM. Naresh forgot that in democracy, the most ordinary person can aspire to the highest office of any republican country.

It deserves to be clearly stated that the level and standard of political discourse during these elections has touched the lowest levels of public decency.

Modi, Agarwal and Rahul adopted the style of street fighters who in anger launch personal attacks on their rivals and level baseless charges. A few samples of Modi's 'words of jewel' spoken during the elections may be referred here to substantiate the argument that he alone is responsible for lowering the style of election campaigns.

Modi speaks:

a. "If you wish to save Chhattisgarh from the murderous hands, press the button alongside the lotus."
b. "I want to ask the Shehzada (prince – a reference to Rahul Gandhi), did the money come from his mama's (uncle) house?"
c. "Madam, you are ill. Let the Shehzada take over."

Modi was paid in his own coin by his political opponents. Salman Khurshid of Congress said, "What should I say about Modi. He is like a frog just out of well and at loss to find the right place for himself in the big wide world".

Naresh Agarwal, a socialist pretender, said: "Modi used to sell tea."

From Modi's 'khooni panja' remark, to frog in a well, to tea seller and madam you are ill; the level of election campaigning in 2013-14 has already hit a new low. It is no one's case that style of leaders during political election campaigning is to be considered be all and end all of democracy.

Unfortunately, in the dust of election campaign of a much low standard of public pronouncements, basic and "substantive" issues facing the people are not properly debated. Real public issues have been put under the carpet and petty personal issues have come to occupy the centre stage of elections.

The state of Chhattisgarh is infected by left extremism and the BJP and the Congress, should have educated the public during the election campaigning or the programme which will be followed by them to confront and resolve the problem of violence faced by common man as a result of Maoist challenge to democracy.

This is the central and basic issue of Chhattisgarh state and elections have been reduced to trivialities around the personality of Ajit Jogi, Congress party leader, or Modi's superficial statements on Congress party. Is it electoral democracy where voters exercise their franchise under the protective umbrella of well-armed Central Reserved Armed Forces of the country?

What kind of democracy exists in a country where "ballot" needs to be defended by "bullet" of the armed forces of the country? Sonia Gandhi on November 15 attacked Shivraj Singh Chouhan's leadership, MP CM, of BJP and alleged that the state government failed to deliver "welfare programmes" meant for the poorest of the poor of the state. This is the meaning of a "debate" during the elections when the performance of the ruling party is attached ruthlessly by the opponents because the role of elections in parliamentary democracy is to "elect a majority" for government formation and a minority in opposition to check the misuse and abuse of power by the government in power.

The upshot of above narrative is that the electoral process of India during the elections is getting hijacked by leaders who are raising "non-issues" and refusing to crossword or substantive issues. Style of politics has substituted the real substance of democratic public debate during the elections.

To say the least, it is "cheating" of the voter's right to know from competing parties about solutions to problems faced by citizens of the country. This mud-slinging during election campaign among political contenders is a clear warning that parties and leaders are shying away from their basic responsibilities of resolving ordinary citizens' daily problems faced in real life.

Indian democracy is faced with a serious challenge because those who are expected to manage democratic institutions of governance are not prefaced to discuss and debate their respective programmes and policies for public scrutiny. *newsyaps.com, 11-12-2013*

Deterioration of Political Debate

The politics of mobilisation has always been an essential and integral part of the Indian democracy. However, this time the only difference is that instead of talking about substantive issues facing the country, some leaders have debased the standard of political attacks. This deterioration of debate has intensified further after the nomination of Narendra Modi as the BJP's prime ministerial candidate.

It is not relevant whether it is Modi or the media that have projected the current political context just as one of rivalry between him and Congress vice-president Rahul Gandhi. Modi in his speeches, especially those delivered in October and November, has continuously referred to Gandhi as shahzada (prince). The allegation that the Congress is a 'dynastic' institution is not relevant to the understanding of the policies and programmes of the party. A party's politics has to be either supported or exposed. The substantive issues are centered around the politics pursued by the Congress and Gandhi. Modi, further, accused the Congress of dividing the country, starting from Partition (1947) to Telangana.

All these remarks along with some of Gandhi's forced the Election Commission of India (ECI) to observe on November 28 that "the gravity of the situation can be gauged from the fact that the ECI has seized petitions from two national parties seeking each other's derecognition for repeated violations of the model code."

Therefore, it becomes clear that Modi, for his highly personalised attacks and emotive public speeches, at the helm of public affairs is not a change for the better.

On November 28, Congress president Sonia Gandhi enumerated various social welfare programmes, including the Mahatma Gandhi National Rural Employment Guarantee Act, the Food Security Act, etc, that the UPA government has introduced.

She claimed that these schemes have benefited the whole of India. Now, the performance of the government has to be scrutinised, debated, contested and countered by political opponents. But instead of having a meaningful debate on issues of performance, the political class is busy indulging in the Modi vs Rahul debate.

Chhattisgarh chief minister Raman Singh claimed that the state's food law is better than the Centre's. A national political party like the BJP should not forget that the 28 states and seven Union Territories of India are categorised as highly developed, relatively developed, least developed and backward. And it is for the Centre to pull the least developed and backward states out of misery.

The Centre versus state argument raised by Singh reveals not only complete ignorance of the uneven growth of the regions and sub-regions of the country, it also shows that an all-India party has to have a capacity to think for the whole of India. *Hindustan Times*, *13-12-2013*

Politics: The Old and the New

The forthcoming Lok Sabha elections of April-May 2014 seem to be a little different, even unusual, than the preceding elections of the first decade of the 21st century because every established party and group at the all-India level, and important regionalists such as Mulayam Singh Yadav, Lalu Prasad, Mayawati, Nitish Kumar et al, are faced with a very new kind and style of politics from a one-year-old party – the AAP.

By playing politics on the basis of completely new rules of the game, which are a kind of 'break from the past' political culture of competitive electoral democracy of India, the AAP has set the cat among the pigeons. This fact that the AAP is a new kind of challenge for the old style of politics has been recognised by the Congress, the BJP, the Communists and other regional players of Indian politics.

Immediately after his party's humiliating defeat in the Delhi assembly elections, Congress vice-president Rahul Gandhi stated on December 8, 2013, that his party has "to learn from the AAP". He further observed that "we (Congress) will do better than the AAP in changing the style of electoral politics". Jairam Ramesh, an important leader of the Congress party, observed on January 8, 2014, that Congress "cannot ignore Aam Aadmi Party because they are agitating about corruption, austerity and simplicity in politics which are legitimate values. Today, Congress party is thinking about it."

It is ironic that those very parties, which had earlier dismissed AAP as insignificant, have woken up and taken note of the Arvind Kejriwal-led party. Other parties, too, have promised not only to learn from the new party but also practice a few things in public life as is done by the AAP.

The anti-corruption agenda became central to the political practice of all other parties especially since the birth of AAP in 2013 against the backdrop of Anna Hazare-led India Against Corruption movement in 2011. Rahul Gandhi and the Congress party have been shouting from the rooftops that the parliament passed the Lokpal Bill (now a law) because of Congress government's initiatives. The BJP has been a self-appointed champion of the war against corruption directed at the Congress party but could not carry conviction with the people because of chinks in its own armour (read Bangaru Laxman and BS Yeddyurappa). The party has also claimed credit for the Lokpal Law which will curb corruption in public life.

It is Anna Hazare and AAP leaders like Arvind Kejriwal, the erstwhile comrade-in-arms of Anna's movement, who have compelled established parties to accept the need for meeting the challenge of corruption in public life. Arvind Kejriwal and his team acted as catalysers for a new kind of politics and, feeling threatened, other parties are trying to change themselves so that they are able to meet the challenge posed by AAP.

It is Anna Hazare and AAP leaders like Arvind Kejriwal, the erstwhile comrade-in-arms of Anna's movement, who have compelled established parties to accept the need for meeting the challenge of corruption in public life.

The AAP has also made an extra effort to include public participation in Delhi's system of governance by creating *Mohalla Sabhas* (ward meetings of residents) to ensure that power flows from below to the top. Not only did Kejriwal took the oath of office before a mammoth crowd of Delhiites, the chief minister and his team of ministers also opened the gates and windows of the Delhi secretariat to the common man who can now get their grievances redressed by the officials. This new policy of AAP – "openness" of government offices and "approachability" of elected representatives including the chief minister – has made a great impact on ordinary citizens who, before now, were unable to establish a connection with their elected representatives.

Rahul Gandhi recently announced that ten "screening" committees of the Congress party have been set up to forward names of party candidates for the forthcoming Lok Sabha elections. He also observed on January 10, 2014, that the ordinary Congress workers will also be consulted about the suitability of a potential candidate from a constituency before their nomination.

This is the impact of AAP on the Congress because the former party nominated candidates on the basis of their "approval" by the voters of a constituency. Not only this, it is for the first time in the post-Independence history of India's Grand Old Party that a top Congress leader (Rahul Gandhi) is consulting and meeting different sections of society before finalising the Congress party's election manifesto for the Lok Sabha elections of 2014. The impact of AAP on the Congress can be clearly seen from the latter's changed style of functioning. Evidently, the 'sleeping elephant' has woken up to the new reality of politics which has been ushered in by the AAP.

The AAP has caught the imagination of the people of India as everyone is rushing to become members of this new party. An explanation for this new enthusiasm among the people could be the fact that AAP has shown that democratic politics can become meaningful if the distance between the "leaders" and the "led" is narrowed down and people's participation in not only the making of decisions of the government but also in the functioning of the party organisation is encouraged.

The rank and file of a party should not be reduced to a passive spectator waiting for the commands of the party "bosses" from above to be present whenever they are needed. The BJP, a political shop of the RSS, is integrally linked with RSS cadres who are actively involved in every activity of the BJP whether Ram Janmabhoomi Movement of 1991-92 or campaigning during elections. But the RSS cadre is always "ordered" from the above because the group is completely hierarchical, patterned like an army organisation where rank and file is expected only to follow and obey orders. The RSS and BJP leadership is quite worried about the AAP's challenge in politics and like the latter, the former and all the affiliates of the *Sangh Parivar* led by the RSS are actively moving around for mobilisation of voters for Narendra Modi, their prime ministerial candidate.

The RSS-led Sangh Parivar, including the BJP, has readymade committed cadre for mobilisation of every programme including elections whether Lok Sabha or state assembly. The difference which AAP has made is that even the *Sangh Parivar* has jumped quite early and launched campaigns for the Lok Sabha elections of April-May 2014. The AAP method of mobilisation has stirred the RSS leadership because the AAP is reaching the *mohallas* of ordinary families shattering the myth held by the RSS that only it could reach the voters because it has committed cadre.

The AAP has shown that enthusiastic public is a better alternative in politics than the rigid, hierarchical ideologies of the RSS. An element of "voluntariness" is clearly visible in AAP's workers and a voluntary army of workers can easily match the rigid ideology driven RSS workers. The AAP has been attracting public attention in towns and cities which were once considered pocket boroughs of the BJP and RSS. This is the reason that the RSS leadership is worried about the AAP.

If Congress is worried about the AAP it is because the latter's anti-corruption agenda has caught the imagination of the voters. This has forced the Congress on the defensive because the public sees Congress as the most corrupt party. The BJP is also worried about the rising AAP because the saffron party's city-based solid support structure is getting eroded with residents "shifting" their preference towards the AAP. This is the real development in Indian politics and its unfolding will have to be observed with great care and attention. *newsyaps.com, 20-01-2014*

Is Political Stability a Panacea?

President Pranab Mukherjee's address on the eve of the Republic Day has attracted a lot of attention because it appeared like a political indictment of the Aam Aadmi Party when he said that the government cannot be substituted by populist slogans and rhetoric. Mukherjee disapproved of "political anarchy", which seems to be directed against the action of the Delhi Chief Minister Arvind Kejriwal sitting on a *dharna* – a protest – against the Delhi Police.

The President further stated that the government is not a "charity shop" and "elections do not give any person the license to flirt with illusions". The observations of the President have been misinterpreted because his admonition of politicians is applicable to a large number of elected representatives who, under the influence of newly achieved power in politics, start behaving as supreme beings and tend to forget the problems faced by the people who have elected them. The President's observation only intended to convey a message to elected politicians that they should not forget their constitutional obligations while enjoying governmental powers.

The above interpretation of the spirit behind Mukherjee's observations is substantiated by a statement in his address according to which those in politics should understand that every election comes with a warning: perform or perish. The President has reminded politicians that voters have exercised their right to elect or reject a government. The President's cautionary address was not meant only for Kejriwal and his band of protestors. The real concern behind the President's address is about the possibility of fractured electoral verdict during the forthcoming Lok Sabha elections of April-May 2014.

How can any president ignore the political events such as the forthcoming General Elections? Mukherjee noted, "A fractured government, hostage to whimsical opportunists, is always an unhappy eventuality." He further buttressed this argument by saying, "It is the physician that heals itself, and 2014 must become a year of healing after the fractured and contentious politics of the last few years." The focus of attention and analysis should be on the President's anxiety about the electoral verdict of the forthcoming Lok Sabha elections because there is a general view among public policy makers that political stability is essential in achieving the goals of sustainable economic growth. A politically weak government cannot provide an effective and energetic leadership for economic growth.

The Indian experience is that if the party-in-government has clarity of goals and a model of economic development, it has already won half the battle because political stability without well-defined goals does not lead the country in any direction.

This quest for stability of government at the Centre is based on the bitter experience of the short-lived coalition governments of VP Singh and Chandra Shekhar (1989-91), and HD Deve Gowda and IK Gujral (1996-98) when Indian economy entered the stage of "crisis" because political leadership of these short-lived coalitions was engaged in efforts of survival and lacked the energy required to focus on economic challenges faced by the country. Not only this, it has also been maintained that even relatively speaking "stable governments" at the Centre led by Atal Bihari Vajpayee from 1998-2004 and Manmohan Singh from 2004-2014 faced serious infighting among coalition partners. Both the prime ministers have explained their incapacities to take firm decisions because they were expected to follow "coalition dharma" which in reality meant that on every crucial decisions, not only all the allies had to be consulted, even one ally could "veto" the consensus of the whole council of ministers.

A few facts may be mentioned to substantiate the argument that stability or instability of a government is not a precondition for good, purposeful and goal-oriented governance in a country. Political stability is hardly a panacea for the resolution of problems faced by the country. The only meaning of political and governmental stability is that a government-in-office should be able to complete its term of five years without any internal threat from its allies, in coalition or from outside, and opposition parties in the legislatures. A government should not have to worry about completing its term and should be able to focus on implementing its promised economic and social programmes.

But stability is not a guarantor of progress; India has serious regional imbalances. Tamil Nadu has witnessed political stability for many decades, and has also achieved high rates of growth and economic development. The argument of those who maintain that stability is a prerequisite for economic growth gets substantiated by Tamil Nadu's example. Compared to Tamil Nadu,

Bihar is a case in contrast. In spite of having long-ruling chief ministers, the state is yet to shed off its backward status tag. The same is the case with Uttar Pradesh. Neither Mayawati nor the father-son duo of Mulayam and Akhilesh Yadav has been able to pull out India's most populous state out of its backwardness.

The Indian experience is that if the party-in-government has clarity of goals and a model of economic development, it has already won half the battle because political stability without well-defined goals does not lead the country in any direction. If the leadership has clarity of goals, stability in politics becomes an asset for governance otherwise a stable government itself becomes the source of stagnation as proved by Uttar Pradesh's experience with Mayawati or the Yadavs.

President Mukherjee's concern for "stability" is well-taken, but only stability of government *per se* is insufficient for achieving the goal of purposeful governance. Ideology plays a critical and crucial role in determining the direction of economic development and a government without any ideology, even if it is stable, creates a situation of underdevelopment.

newsyaps.com, 31-01-2014

The Politics of Pre-election Alliances

Rats are the first to desert a sinking ship and just like them, political parties, groups and leaders are shifting and reshuffling their alliances, breaking away from the ruling Congress-led UPA government ahead of the 2014 General Election. The reason is obvious: Congress is not expected to show a good electoral performance in the forthcoming election.

The National Conference of Farooq and Omar Abdullah created a storm in January 2014 by indicating that the J&K-based party might withdraw from the Congress-led government and also terminate its relationship with the party, which is a part of coalition government in the state of J&K.

Before the Congress party could recover from this shock, Sharad Pawar – another coalition partner both at the Centre and in Maharashtra – said that his Nationalist Congress Party (NCP) had other "options" if the seat-sharing pact with the Congress was not resolved in five days.

Pawar thus set the cat among the insecure pigeons of Congress by floating a rumour that the NCP might strike a deal with the BJP. This somersault of parties – breaking away from the Congress-led coalition and joining the BJP-led coalition – is not something unexpected and unusual of opportunistic Indian politicians. While the Congress is facing problems in dealing with the tantrums of its existing coalition partners, BJP's traditional allies such as the Akali Dal and Shiv Sena are solidly behind it.

The story of the making and rotation of alliances for the forthcoming Lok Sabha elections is not complete without taking note of the effects made by "regional party bosses" to form so-called "alternative" coalition which is both anti-Congress and anti-BJP.

The communist parties have always tried to form such an anti-Congress and anti-BJP coalition, called the Third Front, of the so-called secular regionalists. Unfortunately for the communists, such a "secular Third Front" has a history of disintegration once the election results are out because regional political bosses jump onto the winning bandwagon irrespective of ideological differences.

Secular electoral alliances, or alternatives, in Indian politics have always been either still-born or short-lived because the regional political bosses do not believe that secularism is something for which they can opt out of a winning coalition.

The latest to float a secular front of allies is the Bihar Chief Minister and Janata Dal (United) leader Nitish Kumar who on January 3, 2014, stated that his party, along with Mulayam Singh Yadav's Samajwadi Party and HD Deve Gowda's Janata Dal (Secular), will work as a nucleus of other secular parties to come together on a common anti-Congress and anti-BJP stand. Nitish has given a call to all erstwhile comrade-in-arms of the JP Movement of 1974-75 to come on a common platform for the forthcoming Lok Sabha elections while forgetting his own track record in this respect. Nitish Kumar-Sharad Yadav, the so-called socialists and 'JPites' or 'Lohiaites', have been allies of the right-wing BJP for 17 long years before parting ways in 2013. Did they forget that the BJP was a full-fledged Hindu communal party?

The track record of such self-proclaimed secular ideologues clearly shows that they are fundamentally anti-Congress and they feel very comfortable in the company of the BJP irrespective of the fact that the latter has nothing to do with any kind of "secularism".

Further, to ensure that he remains a strong prime ministerial contender in 2014, Mulayam Singh Yadav has given a clarion call to his party – which heads the government in Uttar Pradesh – that every effort should be made and no stone be left unturned to win maximum Lok Sabha seats from the state.

The pre-election exercise to form alliances is purely opportunistic and unprincipled political efforts by the regional political bosses.

On the other hand Jayalalitha of the AIADMK and Mamata Banerjee of the Trinamool Congress have decided to contest the General Election with a view to secure maximum seats to ensure that they can become king-makers in 2014. Through her speeches to party cadres Mamata urged Trinamool to work harder in order to win maximum seats in the election so that their leader is able to play a decisive and crucial role in the formation of new coalition government at the centre.

Naveen Patnaik of the Biju Janata Dal of Odisha will also like to be taken seriously by the new leaders of post-2014 election. If Nitish Kumar can declare himself as a leader of a Third Front of secularists, Lalu Prasad Yadav and Ram Vilas Paswan, too, can claim to have all the credentials to be a part of any genuine secular coalition platform. If Mulayam can be invited by Nitish Kumar to join a secular electoral platform, Mayawati, an authentic Dalit leader of the Bahujan Samaj Party, also deserves to be a part of a Third Front.

The upshot of the above description is that all such ideas are pre-Lok Sabha election games played by every regional party boss to secure a place in the government in June 2014. It has become a habit with the regional party bosses who become active in the game of formation of alliances before every Lok Sabha election only to strengthen their positions vis-a-vis other regionalists and all-India parties during post-election phase of government formation at the centre. Every regional party boss wants a share in the pie of government formation at the centre. It is another thing that these regionalists walk in or walk out of a coalition government at the centre as and when they please.

This pre-election drama of electoral alliances does not have any significance because all these exercises are purely temporary in nature. It has been seen in the past that some regional allies part company even before the election process begins while others base their decisions on the post-election situation. The pre-election exercise to form alliances is purely opportunistic and unprincipled political efforts by regional political bosses. Coalition government at the Centre are marriages of inconvenience because such a government cannot be formed without the involvement of regionalists and regionalists can desert a ship at drop of the hat. *newsyaps.com, 10-02-2014*

Manmohan's Unfinished Agenda

Prime Minister Manmohan Singh can legitimately take credit for his achievements and his excellent performance in the field of foreign policy. Singh took over the leadership of India's foreign policy after former foreign minister K Natwar Singh was removed from his post in 2005. For eight years of UPA I and II rule, the Prime Minister himself took every initiative in the formulation and implementation of India's foreign policy.

Singh was very keen to establish strong bonds of friendship between India and the United States because he thought that India's national interests would be well served if a special strategic relationship could be established with the sole global military superpower. It must be stated here that former US president George W Bush and current President Barack Obama very enthusiastically reciprocated India's keenness to have "special relationship" with their country. The best evidence of that was when the US went out of its way to create conditions favourable to India for the signing of the Nuclear Energy Pact in 2008. Without that, Manmohan Singh's dream of getting India an entry in the global club of nuclear suppliers would have remained unfulfilled.

The PM single-handedly pushed the idea that India needed nuclear energy for economic development even though an important section within his own party was not very enthusiastic about the pact. The BJP and the communist parties were completely opposed to the idea of any nuclear energy pact with the US. In such circumstances, it was only Singh who successfully piloted this idea, leading to the signing of the pact in 2008.

Americans wanted a "special relationship" with India so as to have New Delhi play a counterweight to a rising Beijing in Asia. Foreign policy has necessary elements, and philanthropic considerations do not play any role in foreign policy calculations among the nations, whether at the global, regional or bilateral level. Manmohan succeeded with Americans in getting "special treatment" because the latter considers India a strategic partner in its goal to contain and counter China in Asia. One of Singh's foreign policy plans was to strengthen and solidify India's relationship with the US. His other foreign policy goal was to improve bilateral relationship with neighbouring countries especially China and Pakistan because without resolving India's longstanding problems with these two countries, New Delhi cannot achieve its goal of playing an important role in Asia, let alone at the international level.

The PM took all policy steps to resolve India-China and India-Pakistan disputes. However he must be a very disappointed man because he failed in his mission of strengthening ties with Islamabad. Singh spent a lot of time and energy on finding a common settlement with Pakistan on the Kashmir question, which still continues to remain a huge roadblock in the normalisation of bilateral ties between these two neighbours.

The PM can however breathe easy on China because Beijing may not go out of the way to show any special warmth toward India. The Chinese realise that India has enough strength to deal with any threat from China. India and China have achieved a level of relationship and mutual understanding on the basis of which they can have a good working relationship without any fear of aggression from one another.

But Pakistan is a different ball game. The country has its own domestic compulsions and militant anti-India groups in Pakistan cannot permit their country's leadership to make any special efforts to negotiate with India. Manmohan negotiated with Pervez Musharraf, Asif Ali Zardari and Nawaz Sharif, but no outcome was in accordance to the satisfaction and expectation of the Indian PM. It is not Pakistan alone where the Indian Prime Minister appears to have failed on the foreign policy front; a cooling off situation with the US too is visible.

In his second term, Barack Obama has not shown any special interest in India. Americans have not shown any inclination in involving India while dealing with Afghanistan, especially when NATO forces are all set to withdraw from the country. Singh must have been expecting that Americans would hold special negotiations with India about the future of Afghanistan especially because the entire South Asia would be affected with any destabilising political situation in Kabul. Americans are making extra efforts to stay on in Afghanistan even after the troop withdrawal but they seem to have forgotten that their "special strategic partner", India, also has its own national interests to protect there.

The PM was also not expecting that his sincere efforts in maintaining the 'special strategic partnership' with US will get a rude jolt with the Devyani Khobragade issue, which led to a rise in anti-American sentiments in the country.

It is a pity that Manmohan Singh, who perhaps wished to vacate the office of the Prime Minister with memories of foreign policy successes, is ending his term without leaving behind a legacy. He is completing his ten years in office without improving the India-Pakistan relationship. But the outgoing Prime Minister can take heart in the fact that he made the best efforts to resolve delicate issues of foreign policy. *newsyaps.com, 14-02-2014*

Why Capitalists Vote for Narendra Modi

It is a well-known and substantiated fact that Indian and foreign capitalists look towards Narendra Modi, currently the chief minister of Gujarat and the prime ministerial candidate of the BJP, as a "doer", who is committed to economic development and has always provided a red carpet treatment to investors and industrialists. The United States, too, has recognised the importance of Narendra Modi, whom it had denied visa to travel to that country; the US ambassador to India herself took the initiative to meet Modi on February 13, 2014 so that the existing barriers between the US and Modi are broken for future business relations between the two. The Americans have given a clear signal that like all other European and developed industrial countries of the West, they would not like to be left behind by ignoring Modi in Indian politics.

That Modi is a darling of the big industrial corporate houses became very clear when NR Narayan Murthy, the founder of Infosys, praised him in an interview saying that the Gujarat Chief Minister has demonstrated that "an individual can make a difference". Narendra Modi has his own public relations office and he makes it a point to invite every big industrialist to impress upon them that they are more than welcome to invest in Gujarat and set up their mega industrial projects. Ratan Tata certified that Modi's Gujarat is the most hospitable state for industry and investors after he succeeded in negotiating with the latter for the setting up of his Nano project, which could not take shape in West Bengal.

Modi gets free publicity because the big industrial houses and foreign business entrepreneurs show their business success story of Gujarat. Since the American capitalists, like all global capitalists, do not want to be left behind, the US government has decided to mend its relations with a somewhat estranged Modi on the issue of denial of visa to him. A critical question which needs to be addressed is that Modi, in spite of all his secular flaws, is able to carry conviction with capitalists, investors and industrialists. Are Indian and foreign capitalists interested only in maximising profits by making investments in Modi's Gujarat, where more than 1,500 Muslims were killed in the 2002 post-Godhra riots?

Not only this, the climate of hatred against Muslims in Modi's Gujarat after post-Godhra riots of 2002 had compelled more than 200,000 Muslims to run away from their homes to live in refugee camps. The Modi government failed to inspire confidence among Muslims who felt threatened by Hindu mobs roaming on the roads and targeting Muslims. Narayan Murthy claimed in his interview, "I don't think any of the coalitions can claim to be more secular than the other."

"The issue should not be 'who is more secular'...(but) 'who can lead the country to make it better," he stated. If Indian capitalists are not worried about the ideology of Hindutava practiced by Modi, it is too much to expect European and American governments and businessmen to treat Modi as an "outcast" simply because he believes in an ideology of treating Muslims as "second-class citizens" in their own country.

Modi and his party's 'One Vote, One Note' campaign is a political gimmick to hoodwink the Indian public because the firebrand leader is not short of funds. As a darling of the big businesses and industrialists, Modi is a natural candidate for support by the big donors.

This explains the urgency of a meeting between Modi and Nancy Powell, the American Ambassador to India. Business houses, and big, medium and small industrialists and manufacturers need political and governmental support to carry on their activities. Government help is required to acquire land for setting up industries. A government is expected to provide facilities for the smooth functioning of every business enterprise. The Congress-led UPA government at the Centre is under investigation for following faulty procedures in the allocation of coal mines to private industrialists. The Central Bureau of Investigation, under the direct supervision of Supreme Court of India, is engaged in the scrutiny of all government files dealing with allocation of coal mines with a view to find out if public decision-makers, both politicians and bureaucrats, have minted money by favouring particular allottees of the coal mines. The government of India has informed the Public Accounts Committee of Parliament, which is also investigating the coal mine deals, that lobbying was done, and many VIPs and chief ministers made recommendations for 'coal block allocations' for different industrialists.

Business and trade cannot be transacted without the support of ministers and bureaucrats, and such a support is never extended by any politician to any business concern without getting a price of government favour from the beneficiary. Business and industrial houses patronise politicians because the latter need funds for their multiple activities in the business of politics. It is a well-established fact that politicians need finances for contesting elections and these funds are provided by private business houses. It is obvious that the recipient of finances from private business owners is naturally expected to pay back after winning an election especially to the contributor who makes funds available to the politician. Politicians need money and moneyed people invest resources to get profit in return for their investment.

Modi and his party's 'One Vote, One Note' campaign is a political gimmick to hoodwink the Indian public because the firebrand leader is not short of funds. As a darling of the big businesses and industrialists, Modi is a natural candidate for support by the big donors. The Aam Aadmi Party is also fooling the Indian public by making a claim that the source of its funding is a common donor – the NRIs and the common people of India. Further, America's message to Modi, especially on the eve of Lok Sabha elections of 2014, is very significant because the global superpower has openly – and publicly – shown its preference for Modi as future prime ministerial candidate of the country.

Americans have to do business with India and the hand of friendship has been extended by the Americans to Modi, an expected future prime minister. America has put its great weight behind Modi by sending a clear signal that he is not persona non grata for the Americans. On the contrary, he is a friend and a buddy. The only goal of a businessman is to earn profit and they cannot succeed in this goal without the support of party-in-government, elected representatives in parliament and state legislatures. Hence, comradeship based on commonality of interests exists between profit earning businessmen who provide money and resources from these earned profits to politicians for their services to private industrialists.

This explains the importance of Modi for Indian and foreign investors because both need each other for performing their activities as businessmen and politicians. *newsyaps.com, 25-02-2014*

The Muslim Question

A very important test of any democratic political system is the treatment given to minority communities in a multi-religious and culturally pluralist country. Muslim religious community constitutes the single largest minority in India, with a population of about 180 million. The Indian Constitution guarantees fundamental rights in Chapter III in which it is mentioned very clearly that every citizen of the country will have equal rights irrespective of religious beliefs or cultural way of life.

It is one thing to mention rights in the constitution of the country; it is quite another to practice the same. It has been observed that minority communities in pluralistic societies are often discriminated against by a section of the religious majority, while dealing with the day-to-day interactions with public and government agencies. In this light, a few salient facts about Muslim community in India deserve to be highlighted to properly conceptualise and understand the specific problems faced by them due to their religious identity.

First, the partition of India was followed by communal holocaust, and besides widespread massacres, forced migration took place in both divided India and Pakistan. The Muslims, who on their own decided to remain in India in spite of the atmosphere of anti-Muslim hatred prevailing during post-partition years, felt assured about their safety because of their trust in a secular and democratic constitution, and political system of India. Jawaharlal Nehru, the first prime minister of independent India, through his speeches and actions had succeeded in creating a feeling of Indianness among Muslims. But the communal elements among the Hindus had a different plan.

Communal Hindus, led by the RSS-*Sangh Parivaar*, practised the politics of targeting of the Muslim community by falsely blaming them for not only the partition but also by alleging that Muslims in India were loyal to the Muslim-majority Pakistan. The *Sangh* has always demanded that Muslims should prove their patriotism. Even during cricket matches between two friendly teams from India and Pakistan, if some Muslims appreciated Pakistani cricket team's performance, the communalists advertised it as an anti-Indian act.

Muslims in India were always expected to prove their patriotism and belongingness to this country irrespective of the fact that Muslim soldiers, along with Hindus, fought in wars against Pakistan. If a religious minority is considered "suspect" by a communal section of the majority community, it is for the secular government to ensure that the minority do not become "second-class citizens" of this country.

Second, Muslims have always suffered more in violent attacks during riots. In every riot, whether the one following the Babri mosque demolition in Ayodhya or the post-Godhra riots or the latest Muzaffarnagar riots, victims have been largely from the minority community.

Third, the post-partition Muslim community in India has also faced some specific problems, like the lack of educational opportunities or employment opportunities. The Congress-led UPA government, while recognising that some special disadvantages were faced by the Muslims, appointed a commission under the chairmanship of Justice Rajendra Sachar; its recommendations are being gradually implemented by the Government of India's Ministry of Minority Affairs.

The Muslim minority is faced with some very significant social and political problems, and it is the task of political parties to pay attention to them. Unfortunately, the picture is quite complex. A few facts deserve to be highlighted to show that different parties have different kind of approaches and political agendas when dealing with the Muslim community.

First, the RSS-led *Sangh* openly speaks in public that Muslims and Christians living in this country have foreign links. As a support for their argument, they refer to the holiest places of worship of these religions which are located outside India. The fundamental belief of the *Sangh* – that Muslims are "outsiders" – conditions their politics towards Muslims.

Muslim voters keep away from the BJP because of their experiences with the communalist *Sangh Parivaar*. Narendra Modi has been making feeble attempts to attract Muslim community to vote for him in the upcoming general election but he knows that Muslims cannot forget the post-Godhra riots of 2002.

What is the track record of secular parties while dealing with Muslims? Look no further than Mulayam Singh Yadav of the Samajwadi Party, who has an ambition to become the Prime Minister of India in 2014. He cannot achieve this goal without polarising voters of Uttar Pradesh between Hindus and Muslims so that the Lok Sabha elections end up in a contest between the SP and the BJP. This politics of polarisation in UP has played havoc in Muslims of Muzaffarnagar and Shamli where anti-Muslim riots took place from September 7-9, 2013. How could the so-called secular Akhilesh Singh government allow such a horror to play in the state?

Muslims are targets. The BJP targets Muslims as "outsiders" who have to go through the test of loyalty and patriotism, and tactical and opportunistic secularists like Mulayam target Muslims by projecting his party as their only "saviour and protector" from Hindu communalists. For both Modi and Mulayam, the Muslim community is an expendable and disposable social group and for different reasons, both try to keep Muslims separate from other communities of the country. *newsyaps.com, 03-03-2014*

The Election-mode Politics

Political parties are getting actively involved in preparations for the forthcoming 16th Lok Sabha election of April-May 2014. The electoral contest for the Lok Sabha has become quite competitive because every single political unit of the country is trying to ensure its presence in the post-election composition of the Lok Sabha.

The Congress and the BJP are in direct competition against one another because of their ideological differences and their individual expectations to win this year's election. Political stakes for the Congress and the BJP are very high because whichever of these parties is able to secure sizeable number of seats in the Lok Sabha, will have a bigger chance of gathering the support of other elected political groups and independent MPs in making a coalition.

The coalition era of governments at the Centre began with the VP Singh government in 1989 but it lasted just two years. HD Deve Gowda repeated the same kind of government when he became prime minister in 1996 and like Singh, his government, too, lasted just two years. The reason behind the collapse of such coalitions was that neither government had the support of a reasonable number of coalition partners who could be kept together as a single unit.

The Atal Bihari Vajpayee-led NDA and Manmohan Singh-led UPA governments lasted their full terms because they provided a "stable government", the parties were in leading positions, the largest number of MPs were from the leading party and coalition partners needed a strong pillar to survive, which, naturally, was the bigger party. Hence, on the experiences of the past that a stable coalition government is possible at the Centre in 2014, if either Congress or BJP is able to get a sizeable strength on its own in the Lok Sabha, other small groups would tie themselves with the big fish.

A separate Third Front of non-Congress and non-BJP parties was floated on February 25, 2014 to contest the Lok Sabha elections and form a government at the Centre. The main players in this front are Mulayam Singh Yadav of Samajwadi Party, Nitish Kumar of Janata Dal (U), HD Deve Gowda of Janata Dal (S) and the four communist parties. But such an alliance is unstable because it is based on "negativism"; except for the communists, every leader in this coalition has political ambitions of their own.

If on the one hand a Third Front has come up to fight elections, some regional parties on the other hand are trying to cling to any big party by forming a tactical alliance with them – a case in point is Ram Vilas Paswan switching alliance from Congress to BJP. A salient feature of pre-election activities of parties is that ideological considerations become secondary in the calculations of different parties and political groups.

The forthcoming Lok Sabha elections have assumed special significance because of Narendra Modi, perhaps the most polarising prime ministerial candidate in the history of post-independent India. There is no ambiguity that Modi, as Chief Minister of Gujarat, is also responsible for the 2002 riots as much as those from his own party who were found guilty. It is expected that all political parties and groups which have spoken in public about their commitment to secularism and anti-communalism would come together on a common united electoral platform to defeat Modi.

It is clear that regional parties and leaders are prepared to form tactical and opportunistic pre-election alliances – secularism versus communalism are mere non-issues. Further, Modi is determined to sidetrack the issue of communalism and is, hence, projecting himself as someone who only works toward development. Modi is clearly shifting public attention from his anti-Muslim ideological politics and campaigning to the agenda of development.

The public relations machinery of the RSS-led *Sangh Parivar* is making extra special efforts to project Modi as the face of development. The BJP and RSS know it quite well that their prime ministerial candidate cannot easily wash his hands off the Gujarat riots which is why the BJP president Rajnath Singh remarked on February 25 that "whenever, wherever there has been any mistake and shortcoming on our (BJP) part, I assure you we'll apologise to you by bowing our heads". But Rajnath Singh knows it quite well that even this statement is not enough to salvage Modi's or the party's tarnished image.

A few facts about the election gymnastics of political parties deserve to be highlighted to keep in mind the unfolding of future events ahead of elections:

First, this is the season of alliances and coalitions, and all pre-election agreements among parties and groups are based on their calculations about their expected electoral performance for the 16th Lok Sabha.

Second, politics of opportunism is on display and so-called secularists like Paswan and Naidu have extended their hands of friendship towards communalists. Secularism is expendable and disposable commodity in the market of elections for 2014.

Third, media – audio-visual and print – has jumped into the game of electoral politics and in spite of the fact that opinion polls can be suspected, corporate-owned media is making every effort to remain relevant in making election forecasts. *newsyaps.com, 10-03-2014*

Caravan of Casteism Marches on

The ruling Congress party-led UPA government on March 3, 2014 – just a little before the model code of conduct for the 16th Lok Sabha election was to be declared – announced caste-based reservations for the Jats in nine states of North India. Different caste groups have always been demanding "reservations" in public services and educational institutions maintained by state or central government on the basis of a "quota", fixed for those castes and sub-castes whose demands and pressures for reservations are politically beneficial to parties in India. A brief perusal of the history of reservations in public services and educational institutions clearly shows that starting with post-independence journey of Indian democracy, the inclusion of castes and sub-castes in Reserved Lists has been determined on the basis of political factors of the time.

Reservations for Jat castes on the eve of Lok Sabha elections, like all earlier reservation policies, is determined solely on electoral considerations of the Congress party. The state of Rajasthan has a sizeable Jat population and traditionally Jats have been supporter of the Congress. The Congress party government of Ashok Gehlot suffered an electoral defeat and Vasundhara Raje-led BJP won the assembly election here in 2013. After this electoral defeat, the Congress party wanted to win over the Jat caste for the Lok Sabha elections of 2014 and it announced the inclusion of Jats of Rajasthan in the Central Government list of reservation in public services and educational institutions.

The party's low form in Punjab was a big reason for the state Congress leader Amrinder Singh to persuade the party to announce Jat reservations. There is a sizeable Jat population in Haryana and western Uttar Pradesh which can make or break the political equations of the region. This is the reason why Ajit Singh of the Rashtriya Lok Dal has been claiming to be an authentic leader of the Jat community of western Uttar Pradesh. Jats have been given reservation in nine out of 28 states and seven Union Territories based on their presence.

Political leaders argue that reservations are meant to redress the grievances of the downtrodden castes which have been traditionally discriminated against by the upper castes on the basis of hierarchical relationship of domination and sub-domination. It has been suggested that a section of the society, discriminated against on the basis of their low caste status by birth, deserve protection.

There is nothing wrong if the needy, poor and deprived are guaranteed some opportunities for upward mobility but it is perversion of the reservation policy if it is used for vote-bank purposes by the politicians.

The agenda of caste-based reservations has been defended by all political parties on the plea that the deprived castes suffering from social discrimination on the basis of status determined by birth require special advantages so that they can rise above their disabilities and disqualifications. On the face of it, public policy for reservation with a view to redress the discriminatory levels of social existence on the basis of "birth" seems plausible; however, in practice, political parties have used "reservations" as an instrument for bribing the voters to win over their support during elections.

There is nothing wrong if the needy, poor and deprived are guaranteed some opportunities for upward mobility but it is perversion of the reservation policy if it is used for vote-bank purposes by the politicians. It is the worst kind of perversion of reservation policy to include the Jat caste in the Central Government list of reservations and that, too, in those states where Jats form a sizeable vote-bank.

What is the social and economic background of the Jats in these parts of India? Jats are not traditional untouchables and cannot be equated with the Dalits. They have historically occupied a "middle status" in the caste hierarchy and have never been discriminated against on the basis of social or cultural status either as Hindus, Muslims or Sikhs. On the contrary, Jats are owners of lands, are dominant and often act as oppressors of landless agricultural workers.

Generally, Jats in rural society exercise great authority and power over the Dalit, landless agricultural workers. Broadly speaking, Jats are oppressors who wield enormous informal power over the village society because of their status as property owners. Because of their economic clout and social status in caste hierarchy, Jats are successful in capturing political power in the states where they have a dominant presence. Jats occupy special political status as MLAs, MPs and even chief ministers in some north Indian states.

Political parties "bribe" the powerful section of the society to win an election – an example is the Jat reservation. Reservations for Jats in the Central list can be justified only on the basis of pure political expediency of the Congress. Not only this, it also looks like a gamble by the Congress because the party does not seem to be a "winning horse" in north Indian states because there are many claimants for "backward caste" and they are bigger regional powers.

It is clear that caste-based reservation policy does not have social welfare at its core. The inclusion or exclusion of multiple caste and sub-caste groups in reservation lists, either of the state governments or of the central government, is decided by politicians-in-power on consideration of pure political expediency and opportunism. *newsyaps.com, 19-03-2014*

UPA-II: Time for an Honest Appraisal—State of the Congress

Something has gone seriously wrong within the political leadership of the Congress party which, despite winning 206 of the 543 Lok Sabha seats on its own in the 2009 elections, and unlike its own coalition government of 2004-09, seems to have nothing special to offer to the Indian voter. The Congress not only pulled off the India-US nuclear deal but the National Rural Employment Guarantee Scheme also brought enthusiastic support from the aam aadmi for the party which was re-elected in 2009. It cannot be denied that from 2004 to 2014, the Congress-led coalition government launched many social and economic welfare schemes and ensured citizens are empowered with certain important rights like Right to Education, Right to Information *et al*. But why has the same Sonia-Manmohan leadership seemingly failed to make any impact on the Indian voter. The political credibility of the Congress was eroded when in 2010 its ministers went to an airport to negotiate with the so-called Baba Ramdev who had threatened to launch a mass agitation against the Congress on the issue of black money. This approach of the party clearly showed its political bankruptcy because the message to the common man was that the Congress had something to hide and, hence, felt threatened by a small-town Baba. Congress ministers rushed to Ramlila Maidan in 2011 to negotiate with Anna Hazare who launched a mass movement for the enactment of the Jan Lokpal Bill to curb corruption in public life. The Congress was at the receiving end of Anna Hazare, whose anti-corruption movement, willynilly, came to be seen as directed against the Congress party. The Congress could not stand against the storm created by anti-corruption crusaders during 2011-

12 and an extremely defensive party could not politically seize the initiative and emerge as a champion of an anti-corruption Jan Lokpal Bill. So, the first explanation for the lacklustre performance of the Congressin-government from 2009 to 2014 is that it completely failed to understand the full implications of the anti-corruption sentiment at a popular mass level. How can it be a party of the aam aadmi if it cannot appreciate prevailing feelings among the masses That said, during the full term of the 15th Lok Sabha, it was the aggressive and disruptionist Opposition that determined the agenda of Parliament and succeeded in compelling the government to follow the dictates of the Opposition. It has been suggested by the Congress that it could not pursue its agenda because of hurdles placed in its way by the negativism of the Opposition. It is a strange argument by a government, with clear a majority of its own along with its coalition allies, that it was handicapped because of the tactics of the Opposition! How could a revolutionary welfare law like the National Food Security Act not be enacted in 2009 instead of 2013 The same story was repeated when the Right to Fair Compensation and Transparency in Land Acquisition, Rehabilitation and Compensation Act was enacted in 2013, while the difficulties in land acquisition for public and private projects had been brought to the notice of the government by its own ministers involved in developmental activities. The wheels of government were moving slowly and without any welldefined agenda from 2009 to 2014, and it is difficult to swallow that an obstructive Opposition or unreasonable coalition allies happen to be the villain of the piece. It also cannot be argued that the Prime Minister and Cabinet ministers were unable to take required political initiatives in the process of governance because of the existence of dual centres of power in their party because this so-called dual-authority system had worked quite successfully during UPA-I. There is no evidence to believe the Sonia-Manmohan Singh partnership came under strain from 2009 to 2014 while it worked smoothly from 2004 to 2009. The Congress partys political and governmental leadership is solely responsible for its patchy record of governance from 2009 to 2014 because it lacked courage of conviction in dealing with allegations, and a morally weakened leadership cannot lead from the front in politics. If the Bofors gun deal made Rajiv Gandhi morally weak in politics, history seems to be repeating itself, and Sonia and Rahul are facing an electoral defeat like Rajiv earlier on the issue of corruption in public life, whether proven or not. *The Economic Times, 03-04-2014*

BJP 2014 is All about RSS Ideology and Leadership

It has been suggested that the old order of BJP leaders—LK Advani, and some of his colleagues—is feeling quite unhappy and uncomfortable because they are being cut to size by the Mohan Bhagwat-led RSS' new strategy of projecting its *swayamsewak* Narendra Modi as the chief election campaigner and PM candidate for 2014. Is it just a power struggle between the old and the new or is it some new phenomena whose real meanings have yet to be understood? It is a common practice of politics in which leaders from the same party compete against one another to safeguard their interests with the whole battle fought around clash of personalities. BJP, like any other party, cannot be completely immune to the disease of greed for power of an entrenched leadership which fights back any new challengers from within.

Moreover, BJP is unlike any other party; it is a political shop—an extension of the RSS-controlled *Sangh Parivar*. Here the 'old' or the 'new' leaders are all, without any exception, mere instruments in the hands of the RSS and are expected to faithfully carry the flag of Hindu Nationalism. Hence, the present "conflicts" within the BJP should not be seen as 'ideological battles' between the old and the new or hardliners and moderates because the ideology is the same. Anyone even suspected as 'deviant' is simply purged from the party. BJP remains a party of Hindus and by Hindus, and everyone associated with the BJP is a certified practitioner and promoter of Hindutva ideology.

Because any party in democracy deserves a close scrutiny when something happens within that party, tremors within the BJP should not be ignored. Advani had expressed his public disapproval when Narendra Modi was appointed as the chief election campaigner of the BJP for the state assembly elections of 2013 and the Lok Sabha elections of 2014. Mohan Bhagwat, the RSS supremo, took another step and ensured that the BJP finally announce Narendra Modi the PM candidate. Modi, with the full backing of the RSS, in spite of some mild or open protests, is now the face of the RSS-led BJP for 2014. A few facts may be mentioned to grapple with the present state of affairs within the BJP.

First, instead of playing a decisive role beneath the surface, the RSS has decided to openly guide the 'change' in the organisation and leadership hierarchy of the party. Mohan Bhagwat personally started the "Operation Change BJP" when he single-handedly launched a sort of "remove Advani campaign" and make way for Nitin Gadkari as the BJP president. He succeeded. Now, Bhagwat has himself ensured that the current BJP President Rajnath Singh works in full cooperation with Modi for the Lok Sabha election of 2014. RSS leader Suresh Joshi said in *Panchajanya,* the organisation's mouthpiece, in March 2014, "There are manifold challenges before the nation and uncertainty about the future. Taking strong public sentiment into consideration, the Sangh has decided to play a special role." This is an authentic statement about the new activist role of the RSS in shaping of the BJP for 2014.

Bhagwat had observed in March 2014 that "vision needs to change with time….And this has been established". He continued that the RSS had worked hard on a difficult journey, "of sailing against the tide" which will "soon be completed successfully".

Second, RSS-led-and-directed changes will be implemented by its trusted *swayamsevak* Narendra Modi. Hence, everyone has to accept Modi's leadership. It is an illusion, even a propaganda, that BJP has been tolerant of any anti-Hindutva agendas of its opponents. Advani, who is the current target of the RSS-BJP, single-handedly launched the Ram Janmabhoomi campaign. He is one of the accused in the Babri Mosque demolition of December 6, 1992, which resulted in widespread riots across the country. If Advani is remembered for the demolition of the secular fabric of India in 1992, Modi repeated history with the 2002 Gujarat riots.

Muslims as targets is "core ideology" of RSS brand of Hindutva and everyone has to implement it, whether Advani or Modi. It is misinformation which is being spread across the country that "Modi is a polarizer who divides everything, including his party". Was Advani not a polarizer? It is propaganda that BJP is undergoing a big internal change, an old wine in an outwardly new bottle. The Hindutva ideology forms the core of BJP, and every leader of the party and in the government is committed to implement it aggressively. Hence, Narendra Modi and his team, if in government after May 2014, would be another chapter in the consolidation of Hindu Nationalism where religious, cultural and linguistic diversity will remain under threat from hegemonic Hindutva.

newsyaps.com, 05-04-2014

The Abandoned Prime Minister

It is always the bad workman who complains against his tools. The declining Congress party fits this description well especially after it launched a bitter tirade against a man most loyal to the party – Prime Minister Manmohan Singh.

Singh shouldered the heavy burden of prime ministership of the Congress-led UPA government at the Centre from 2004 to 2014 but, instead of feeling obliged for the leadership provided by Manmohan, the Congress leaders started accusing him for not successfully selling to the public the achievements of the Congress rule especially in the second term of the UPA government.

It appears that the Congress is quite nervous; its leaders worried sick about the party's electoral prospects for the 16th Lok Sabha. PC Chacko, a senior Congress leader, made an adverse statement against Singh on March 15, 2014, saying that the prime minister failed to highlight the government's achievements in his last press conference held after his foreign tours.

"He kept silent. At the same time the opposition took to the public the corruption charges against certain persons in the government," Chacko said.

"Losing patience over his silence and stifling negative publicity, we had repeatedly asked the Prime Minister to conduct weekly media briefings to present the government's achievements. The PM was unwilling to meet the media," he alleged.

Rahul Gandhi, in an interview to the PTI on March 16, 2014 also observed, "We have done transformative work. We could always be better in communication."

Sam Pitroda, the chairman of the National Innovation Council and advisor to the PM, observed on March 20, 2014 that the UPA's achievements have not been properly communicated to the public.

There is no denying the fact that media was a pillar of democracy especially during the early decades of the 21st century and it is also a fact that media has come to play a very crucial role in the shaping of public opinion in India. This reality has been recognised by all political parties across the country and this is why every party has established close ties with the media so that the party's views can be communicated to the people.

The Congress has a way with the media and some of its leaders are quite deft in utilising media to bolster the party's reputation. But targeting Manmohan Singh for his failure to effectively communicate the government's achievements is like barking up a wrong tree. The Congress party, starting January 2013, has indirectly sent out the message that Rahul Gandhi is the next PM-in-waiting. Now the vice-president of Congress, Rahul is treated as the "special leader" by everyone in the party. It is expected of Rahul to lead the Congress from the front and act as an authentic and authoritative communicator of the party.

> *Media publicity is a necessary condition for creating a favourable image of a "leader" or a "party", but it is not a sufficient condition to make any leader taller than the other if the reality is quite different.*

The issue is not that the PM has not risen to the occasion and provided effective leadership to the Congress, because he was not a pre-eminent leader of the Congress. The real centre of leadership has been Sonia Gandhi – the party president. Moreover, Manmohan Singh has publicly declared that he is not contending for the post of PM in this year's Lok Sabha election. Why should, therefore, the Congress expect a lame duck prime minister to actively and aggressively project his government's achievements to the public during the elections of April-May 2014?

Rahul, Narendra Modi and Arvind Kejriwal emerged as the three top leaders in 2013. Rahul was made vice-president of his party, Modi became the prime ministerial candidate of the BJP and its allies, and Aam Aadmi Party leader Kejriwal shook the political roots of the country with his chief ministerial debut in Delhi.

The Congress, the BJP and the AAP have been enjoying media attention because of their respective top leaders. With its coverage of every move of the three leaders from the three parties, the media has given the voters full opportunity to evaluate their capabilities and capacities in a comparative way.

It has been suggested that AAP is a metropolitan phenomenon and has no standing or influence in rural India. With a sterling performance in last year's Delhi assembly election, Arvind Kejriwal marginalised Congress in Delhi besides proving that Rahul Gandhi cannot salvage the plunging fortunes of the party.

Further, the actual battle-lines have been drawn between the Congress and the BJP via their respective candidates for the top job: Rahul and Modi. The RSS is making every effort to build a "personality cult" around Modi. The media is covering every single move made by Modi while the RSS is busy mobilising huge crowds for his meetings. Through his public meetings, the media shows that Modi has his own style of public speaking. The media is also making the public witness the election meetings addressed by Rahul and thus both Modi and Rahul have a fair opportunity to contradict each other's ideology and politics.

The media coverage of election campaign is quite exhaustive and informative. The impression the voters get of the leader can be manipulated by the media. But the people can form their own opinions, too. Media publicity is a necessary condition for creating a favourable image of a "leader" or a "party", but it is not a sufficient condition to make any leader taller than the other if the reality is quite different. Hence, it is not for Manmohan Singh to carry the burden of election campaign on his shoulders; it is for Rahul to confront and contest against Modi and prove himself the more effective leader of the two. *newsyaps.com, 12-04-2014*

Elections 2014: Dynasty *Versus* the Personality Cult

The prime ministerial candidate of the BJP, Narendra Modi, launched his very aggressive election campaign for Lok Sabha, by making it a kind of referendum between himself and Rahul Gandhi – an undeclared but probable prime ministerial candidate of the Congress party. The purpose of this style of election campaign was, like the American presidential campaign, to present before the voters a choice between 'two leaders', and if this plan of Modi had succeeded, the election campaign for 2014 would have centered around the personal qualities and capabilities of these two main contenders for power.

Modi began his campaign by directly targeting and focusing his attention on Congress party's 'shehzaada', Rahul. The sub-text of this campaign strategy was to corner Rahul by presenting him as a person without any experience of managing public and government affairs because he had never held any office in Congress-party led UPA government at the Centre from 2004 to 2014. Modi tried his best to draw Rahul into a debate on policies, programmes, and capacities to lead the country by juxtaposing his credentials as three-time elected Chief Minister of Gujarat and, while in office, he has to his credit a track record of administering a state government on the basis of his special Modi Model of Development of Gujarat.

Modi projected himself as a strong developmentalist leader and asked Rahul during election campaign to respond in public about his specific achievements to match Modi's record of governance. The media immediately jumped into fray and proclaimed that the 2014 Lok Sabha elections are a kind of direct presidential contest between "two leaders" of the two major contenders for electoral victory. The Congress party smelt a rat and immediately dismissed Modi's efforts to convert Parliamentary Electoral System into an American style of Presidential System where two leaders confront one another during the elections.

The main reason for Congress party's dissidence to pitch Rahul directly against Modi may be because Rahul's campaigning capacities are untested because unlike Modi, Rahul has remained confined to his own or to the constituency of his mother, Sonia Gandhi. Modi wanted to draw Rahul into the wrestling match of electoral politics knowing it quite well that there was enough material to corner Rahul especially by focusing attention on not only Rahul's meek personality but also on his complete lack of contribution to national public life. He also targeted Rahul for his dynastic links.

Rahul is benefitting from the hereditary qualifications bestowed upon him by his illustrious family. Modi, on the other hand, has climbed the ladder by his own efforts.

Rahul is benefitting from the hereditary qualifications bestowed upon him by his illustrious family. Modi, on the other hand, has climbed the ladder by his own efforts. This dynasty factor during elections has lost its value because every regional and sub-regional political party around the country has begun the practice of projecting and nominating their children for electoral offices. If the dynasty factor has lost its shine in politics because everyone is practicing it, Modi's image of a strong leader and an undisputed special campaigner of the BJP make sense. Modi has chalked out a programme of addressing 185 election rallies from Itanagar to Jammu. In fact such is the Modi cult that BJP candidates in the elections are asking the voters to vote for them to make Narendra Modi the Prime Minister. The election campaign of BJP is of, for and by Modi and even local BJP leaders are asking for votes in the name of Modi as the future prime minister. Modi has emerged as a larger-than-life figure in the BJP and, due to extensive media coverage, is seen as the leader of the BJP and prime-minister-in-waiting.

Modi raises the issues in elections and he himself is in the centre stage of political debate. Questions are asked and raised only about Modi, and all other leaders in the BJP have been reduced to secondary positions as compared to Modi who stands 'tall' in public life. Modi's qualities and weaknesses are the only subject matter of public debate during the elections, and decisions within the BJP are taken on the basis of Modi's preferences and choices. Outside BJP, other parties are also taking public positions either in support or opposition to Modi.

BJP and *Sangh Parivar*'s army of workers have also been relegated to the background and it is Modi who is in the driver's seat. This kind of development where a personality cult is built especially in a situation where democratic institutions of governance are yet to develop capabilities to check arbitrariness of the elected representatives is fraught with great danger to democracy. A functioning democracy depends on a complex constitutional network of checks and balances where ambitious, ruthless and capricious leaders like Modi are placed in chairs that govern the law of the country. Modi's reputation is that he is completely responsible for cutting every BJP leader to size and making all of them either completely subservient to his dictators compelling them to quit the BJP. In Gujarat BJP, there is no second who can be identified either as Modi's equal or a comrade-in-arm.

Modi does not tolerate 'equals' and his administrative ruthlessness has been witnessed when he did not allow any opposition to his choice of nominee for the office of Lokpal of Gujarat. Modi, like all other seminary of the *Rashtriya Swayamsevak Sangh*, has an anti-Muslim strain and a prime minister with personality of a fanatic is a great threat to democratic secular republic of India. Modi can govern only in a country which is without cultural, religious and lingual diversities. He is, therefore, a misfit to be Prime Minister of India because he does not accept that the essence of India lies in its rich diversity.

Modi, like all other *Swayamsevaks* and *Prachaaraks* of the RSS family, is a believer in the ideology of Hindutva where Hindus, as defined by the *Sangh Parivaar*, are privileged first-class citizens and all others are to be treated as second-class citizens. An individual with such rigidities can destroy the pluralist social fabric of rich India because having reduced Muslims in Gujarat to the status of second-class-citizenship in the eyes of his government, Modi cannot leave his ideology simply because he is Prime Minister. Personality cult built around Modi's persona is dangerous because he believes in dangerous ideology of Hindutva. This country is plural and Modi does not believe in pluralism because he sees only Hindus as special and privileged.

newsyaps.com, 21-4-2014

The Meaning of Lok Sabha Elections

The Indian muti-party political system has become quite competitive, robust, and even aggressive; however, some salient features of the ongoing battle for ballot for the Lok Sabha elections of 2014 deserve a clinical and analytical focus because a revived, rejuvenated and ideologically determined party is engaged in a very well-organized, large-scale political mobilization for achieving its goal of electoral victory in the 16thLok Sabha elections.

A few facts may be mentioned to properly contextualize and situate the exact features of this election which, unlike the previous ones, is witnessing the involvement of a highly-focused, ideologically committed and organized group such as the *Sangh Parivaar*, which is in a battle mood to win the majority of seats in the Lok Sabha of 543 members.

The *Sangh Parivaar* has recognized on the basis of its own actual experience from 1998 to 2004 that its goal of Hindu *Rastrawaad* can be achieved only if it is able to control levers of power of the central government. The Atal Bihari Vajpayee-led government from 1998 to 2004 succeeded in pushing forward the agenda of Saffronization of the Indian state apparatus and larger society. The *Sangh Parivaar*, not on the basis of any abstract theory but on the basis of its own achievement record became convinced that India could become the real Hindu Rashtra if it could occupy the seat of power at the centre.

The loss of power at the centre in 2004 election gave a feeling of great frustration to the forces of Hindutva and the electoral debacle of 2009 made the *Sangh Parivar* sit up and make the *Rashtriya Swayam Sevak Sangh* and its supremo Mohan Bhagwat the commanded of affairs of the BJP.

The RSS always played a supportive and guiding role for *Jan Sangh* of a weakened BJP in a discreet manner by keeping itself away from public scrutiny, came into the open for the first time in 2009 to mould the BJP and make it ready for the battle of 2014. Mohan Bhagwat supervised leadership changes and single-handedly performed a surgical operation marginalizing LK Advani and nominating Narendra Modi as the chief election campaigner and prime ministerial candidate.

From 2009 onwards every BJP leader made a public confession of firm loyalty to the RSS ending any ambiguity of relationship between the party and the group. Narendra Modi had publicly declared on July 12, 2013 that there is nothing wrong if he calls himself a nationalist, a patriotic, a born Hindu. On April 2, 2014 Modi was quoted declaring, "I got the inspiration to live for the nation from the RSS, I learnt to live for others, not for myself. I owe it all to RSS."

Even LK Advani, to re-establish his credentials, observed on July 17, 2013 that, the party's ideological family will always be with RSS. The veil of secrecy was ripped in public and electoral battle has become a collective responsibility of all members and affiliates of *Sangh Parivar* including the BJP. It is not unusual for *Sangh Parivar* and BJP political campaigners to employ Hindu mythological symbols during elections since they have a clear aim of establishing a deep and natural connect with its Hindu voters.

Narendra Modi, the prime ministerial candidate, is aggressively motivating Hindu voters by referring to their holy scriptures, and mythological significance of holy cities and places from where he launches his campaign. This fact has been dramatically highlighted by Modi's choice of Varanasi, a Hindu holy city, as his constituency.

Not only this, Modi specifically raised the issue of 'cow slaughter' on April 2 and 3 while reminding his Hindu audience that "while Congress-UPA give subsidies to slaughter houses, BJP government would not only ban, but severely punish those guilty of slaughtering of the holy mother, cow, of Hindus." It may appear to be an old story but repeated references to Hindu symbols of worship during elections by the BJP has a special message for the voters which is that Hindu religion needs special protection from government in power because its traditions include places of worship that need to be protected from its enemies who slaughter cows and indulge in religious conversions of Hindus into other 'external' religions such as Islam and Christianity. Hence, the anti-cow slaughter and anti-religious conversion issues raised by BJP are specifically meant to create a distance between the diverse religious communities.

It is generally forgotten that every appeal to Hindu sentiments through religious symbols leave a deep impact on the minds of voters. This reality is quite visible in public life when religious priests exchange their roles in temples with electoral campaigns acting as messengers of a Hindu party. Priests in politics not only bring votes for BJP, they also extend their own area of influence over the Hindu Samaj. This internal linkage between religion and politics, and priests and politicians fulfils both short term electoral goals and the long term goal of increasing the number of faithful believers in an attempt to consolidate the ritual base. The real agenda of *Sangh Parivar* is Hinduization of the society and each successive election since 2009, including the present one, is taking the Hinduization agenda forward with full energy. It is not without reason that Modi has decided to organize 185 public meetings to spread the message of Hindu Rashtra and it is also significant to note that he has described the election meetings as 'Bharat Vijay Rally'.

Big industrial and business houses have never actually got involved actively in the Indian political process and the leaders of industry had always maintained a respectable distance from parties, especially in public. It is no more the case. Big corporate houses have openly declared that Narendra Modi is a fit candidate for the prime minister's job and, as far as the ideology of Hindutava is concerned, its divisiveness does not matter to private big business houses.

The new media, whether print or audio-visual, national or regional, English or vernacular, has emerged as a new factor and force in the public life of Indians, and beginning with the economic liberalization change in the 1990s this media has become a vehicle and very powerful messenger of Hinduism.

Further, RSS supremo Mohan Bhagwat whether directly or indirectly addressing the big business stated on March 24, "The present scenario in the country is such that people are troubled as to where they will get stability. Where they find it, they are going that side. Those who are rooted in some ideology, only they can provide this stability."

This yearning for stable and predictive economic policy regime promised by the BJP has naturally attracted the support and approval of big business, and more than 300 to 350 million upwardly mobile and aspirational Hindu minded 'new middle class'. This is a solid constituency for a Hindu party and Modi has come to occupy a special place in this influential group.

The new media, whether print or audio-visual, national or regional, English or vernacular, has emerged as a new factor and force in the public life of Indians, and beginning with the economic liberalization change in the 1990s this media has become a vehicle and very powerful messenger of Hinduism. They directly link Hindu priestly classes with an audience comprising largely of the superstitious kind exposing them to daily religious sermons by *babas* and godmen. These media legitimized Hindu priests form a very important link between RSS politics of Hindu religion and the people. It has been argued that the corporate houses are directly playing an active role in politics on the basis of their ownership and control over media but no one has yet felt that this corporate-owned media is also strengthening the Hindu *Sangh Parivaar* by spreading to all corners of the country the Hindu belief system.

The media has played a crucial and critical role in spreading Hindu religious consciousness by its representation of Hindu temples and priests, and ritual based symbols. The BJP caught on this media promotion by projecting itself as the protectors, guardians and custodians of Hindus who are threatened by enemies. The Hindu vote bank has been created and solidified by RSS activists duly supported by this powerful media. This is the crux of the issue because politics does not hang in the air and ideological politics does not operate in a vacuum.

It is the spread of Hindu religious beliefs fully supported and propagated by corporate-owned media which provided a very hospitable, social and cultural soil for the *Sangh Parivar* to successfully construct a superstructure of Hindu Rashtras. Has this new challenge represented by Hindutva been comprehended and effectively responded to by defenders of basic secular structure of democratic republic of India? How can other religions, petty political operators and ambitious leaders, who are absolutely unconcerned and unaware of the fundamental ideological challenge posed by the *Sangh Parivaar* check mate a united Hindu front supported by big businesses, new media and the aggressively resurgent Hindu middle class?

If Narsimha Rao is legitimately accused of not defending Indian republic when a frenzied mob destroyed a historic mosque in Ayodhya on December 6, 1992, shouldn't someone question Atal Bihari Vajpayee for failing to prevent secular ideals of the constitution from getting hijacked by Modi in 2002? Even Vajpayee was acting as patron and chief of Hindu agenda when Keshubhai Patel, former chief minister of Gujarat, allowed banned RSS workers to be recruited for public services. HV Seshadri and other prominent leaders asked the central government to legalize entry of these *swayamsevaks* to public services. The then PM Atal Bihari Vajpayee not only defended Gujarat government order on recruitment, he also observed, like all other RSS propagandists, that "it was cultural and social organization" and, hence, legal.

Has Modi ever nominated a Muslim to contest an election for Gujarat state assembly? Did Modi and BJP show any hesitation while nominating three MLAs for the Lok Sabha elections accused of participation in anti-Muslim riots in September 2013 at Muzaffarnagar and Shamli?

The ongoing battle for ballot is been raged by fanatical right-wingers and in this ideological enterprise, beneficiaries of pro-capitalistic, free-market economy are enthusiastically supporting the RSS controlled BJP. Unfortunately, this crusade of a Hindu party cannot be stopped by a fragmented opposition, which is not even aware of the real threat if BJP is able to form a government at the centre in 2014. *newsyaps.com, 24-04-2014*

What the RSS Wants, and Plans for India

The fact that the 16th Lok Sabha election is special was highlighted by Sonia Gandhi in a televised message on April 14, when she said the electoral battle was against "divisive" forces who would lead to the "ruination of Bharatiyata and Hindustaniyat".

That this is an ideological contest was also underlined by Priyanka Gandhi, who on April 15, attacked Varun Gandhi for his association with the BJP. This ideological challenge by the oldest and largest social and political formation of India has been effectively responded to by its real and only opponent, the Rashtriya Swayamsevak Sangh (RSS).

The Mohan Bhagwat-led RSS has jumped into the election process with a determination, aggression and energy not seen in any election held from 1952 onwards. The RSS always preferred to be a backseat driver of the Jan Sangh/BJP during polls, while in public it wore the "mask" of a cultural organisation, but in 2014, the RSS has brought all its ideological and organisational resources to bear on mainstream electoral politics.

The Sangh Parivar recognised, on the basis of its experience from 1998 to 2014, that its basic goal of Hindu Rashtravad could be achieved only if it controlled the levels of power at the Centre. The Atal Bihari Vajpayee-led government did succeed in pushing forward the agenda of Hinduisation of the Indian state apparatus, but the loss of power in 2004 and failure of the BJP alerted the Sangh leadership.

So, Mohan Bhagwat purged all leaders of the Vajpayee era, and nominated Narendra Modi as the prime ministerial candidate. The RSS nominated Modi because he is expected to perform the same role for the cause of Hindutva as L K Advani did when he led a yatra for the Ram Temple at the site of the Babri Mosque.

Keshav B Hegdewar, the founder, and M S Golwalkar, the real consolidator of the RSS, built the organisation not only to create an army of Hindutva preachers but also invented, following in the footsteps of British colonisers, a Hindu Brahmanical monolith in place of a diverse and pluralist Hindu identity.

This narrative of the ideology, organisation and political parties of the RSS clearly shows that the "Idea of India", which is the real issue in the 2014 Lok Sabha elections, is defined in Hindu terms by the RSS.

What are the main social constituencies of the BJP, on whose support it comes to power either at the central or state level? A few important leaders of industry, business and trade are openly supporting the candidature of RSS-nominated Narendra Modi.

If profit-seeking billionaires are openly supporting the Sangh Parivar in these elections, irrespective of its ideology, the upwardly-mobile aspirational Hindu-at-heart middle and upper-middle classes have also enthusiastically come out in support of the BJP and Modi.

An added factor that has attracted Hindu professional and entrepreneurial classes towards the Hindu ideological party is that their sentiment of nationalism and patriotism is reflected in the Hindu party's programmes and policies. So, millions admire the militaristic approach of the BJP towards national security.

But where are the minority communities in this Hindu "Idea of India"? Do they really count? The BJP did not show any hesitation while applauding and nominating for the Lok Sabha polls three MLAs accused under the National Security Act for their role in anti-Muslim riots in Muzaffarnagar and Shamli. Is this action of the BJP not a clear signal to Muslims that they just do not matter in Hindu India?

The belief that Hindus of Bharat Mataare "first-class citizens" and other religious communities can at best be "second-class citizens" means the latter are often targeted. This anti-minority message is spread through its 44,982 shakhas across the country by the RSS, and with 50 RSSaffiliated organisations at work, to expect that Muslims will not be targeted would be fooling oneself.

In brief, on May 16, the hard choice between two antagonistic Ideas of India will become public. It can't be forgotten that any model of economic development represents a social philosophy of a particular kind, and the RSS-BJP is committed to the ideology of social exclusion of minorities. There is, simply, nothing like a "neutral development model".

The Economic Times, 28-04-2014

Two Manifestos: Congress vs BJP

A political party is always known on the basis of its policies and programmes. Every party competes against one another, especially during elections, on the basis of its policies for which voters are expected to support one or the other party. This is the reason that prior to every election, whether Lok Sabha or state assembly, parties make their election manifestos and on the basis of their public statements approach voters for their support during the elections.

Manifestos are 'promises' made by a party to the voters before an election with an assurance that the promises will be implemented if the party is elected. Many a times, election manifestos of parties are not taken seriously by the people because of a credible feeling that manifestos contain empty rhetoric and promises are forgotten after the elections are over. This does not mean that manifestos should be ignored or taken lightly because voters' choices and preferences are, to a large extent, guided by the manifesto of a party.

The Lok Sabha election of April-May 2014, like all the other previous elections, is witnessing a contest between Congress and BJP. The Congress is clearly and unambiguously distinguishing itself from its major opponent, the BJP, on the basis of its ideology of 'secularism'. The electoral battle lines between Congress and BJP have been drawn which means that the election manifestos of these two contenders for power deserve a scrutiny.

BJP's manifesto clearly states that the party "believes in India being one country, one people, one nation." The real essence of this assertion by the BJP in its manifesto lies in its public commitment to its idea of Hindu Rashtravaad because its real meaning of "one nation" is the Hindu majority nation, where all other diverse cultural and religious minorities should come to terms with the idea of Hindu Rashtra of the BJP government.

The BJP manifesto contains many sugar-coated statements about the "richness of Indian diversity". It is committed quite openly to the idea of Hindu India. It becomes quite clear when its manifesto, while explaining its policy of "India first", also talks of its favourite oft repeated quote of "appeasement of none". LK Advani coined a discouraging term for secularists by adding the word 'pseudo' to it meaning that their secularism was nothing but bowing before religious minorities. The BJP has sold its communal ideology of Hindu Rashtra by defining it in vague words such as "respect for all religions and appeasement of none".

The opposite of BJP's approach is contained in Congress party's manifesto which mentions not only its basic commitment to secularism and its determination to fight against Hindu communal BJP but also specifically mentions its priorities for the upliftment and welfare of the minority communities of India. The Congress manifesto not only mentions in detail programmes launched by its UPA government at the centre for 'minorities', it further assures the minorities that Congress will continue to protect and promote special interests of minorities.

BJP's idea of an aggressive and militarized Hindu Rashtravaad is unambiguously revealed by its manifesto in its assertion that if elected in 2014, it will "review India's nuclear policy of non-first-use". But Prime Minister Manmohan Singh called for a "global meeting for complete control over proliferation of nuclear weapons system". While both BJP and Congress are firmly committed to New Economic Policy of liberalisation, privatisation and globalisation, the BJP manifesto also assumes that both Indian and foreign multinationals, big industrial houses, and all leaders of industry are unhappy with Congress-led UPA government because of its lack of initiative in pushing forward the agenda of further reform of the economy.

It is not without reason that the captains of industry have quite often accused the UPA government of suffering from 'policy paralysis'. It is the big business which has launched a campaign stating that the rate of economic growth has slowed down and inflationary trends in economy have emerged because of lack of leadership and initiative by the UPA government at the centre. Business in India has completely shifted in support of the BJP and its prime ministerial candidate, Narendra Modi. In its manifesto addressing its election campaign, the BJP has effectively propagated its commitment to implement economic reforms and follow policies for accelerated growth of the economy.

Not only this, Modi has sold his so-called Gujarat Model of development to the country with the media blindly projecting stories, whether fact or fiction, of Modi's achievements in his home state. The BJP has cleverly used the media by launching a campaign against the misdeeds of the UPA government while in office and after gaining a lot of publicity in this campaign, it released its manifesto on April 7, 2014 when the election process had already begun. This timing of the BJP was a clever one because the Congress manifesto, which had been released much earlier in March 2014, had been completely forgotten by this time, and BJP's late release of manifesto gained great publicity because people could not compare it with the manifesto of the Congress.

The upshot of the above discussion about similarities and dissimilarities between Congress and BJP's manifestos clearly reveals that these two parties represent two fundamentally opposite poles in Indian politics. The voters are expected to make their choice either for one or the other because there is no meeting ground between BJP and Congress. This Lok Sabha election is crucial because the voters' choice will define the direction of the future of India.

newsyaps.com, 07-05-2014

Lok Sabha Elections 2014: Congress vs BJP is an unequal contest

The eighth phase of April-May 2014 16 thLok Sabha election has ended and one more phase will end on May 12. The results will be declared on May 16. The actual electoral battle is between the Congress and BJP – the two all India contestants and ideological opponents. The Congress has to defend its record of governance from 2009 to 2014 while the BJP wants to displace the Congress-led UPA coalition government at the centre and itself occupy the corridors of power. A very special issue which deserves to be addressed here is the quality of contest among these two competitors because the number of Lok Sabha seats won either by the Congress or the BJP will determine the direction of country's politics after May 16. Has the Congress really fought its electoral battle with determination against its major rival, the BJP?

A few facts may be mentioned to substantiate the argument that the Congress has not shown enough determination during its election campaign from March to May 2014. First, prominent Congress leaders, who were important cabinet ministers such as Defence Minister AK Antony, Finance Minister P Chidambaram and Information and Broadcasting Minister Manish Tewari, decided to opt out from the contest. Their decision not to face the electorate sent a negative message to voters because it helped in creating a widespread impression among the people that Congress leadership has accepted its electoral defeat even before the battle started. This mid-way desertion by these Congress ministers is a betrayal of the trust reposed by their own party on their loyalty. How can voters feel enthusiastic about a party whose leaders run away from the battle?

Second, it has been left only to Sonia Gandhi and Rahul Gandhi to lead the Congress in the election campaign, and an election campaign of an all-India party cannot be shouldered by two leaders alone. This vacuum of effective guidance to party cadres was seen during the phase of hectic Congress campaign. Not only this, although Sonia Gandhi is nationally accepted as the moving force of the party, Rahul's campaigning abilities and capacities have not made a strong impression on the voters and while Sonia succeeded, as always, in conveying her message of achievements of the ruling party, her son's style of canvassing during the elections could not carry much conviction.

> The Congress strategy should have been to target Modi aggressively and payback Modi in the same coin as he has been targeting the Congress.

Rahul made serious efforts to reach the voters but his efforts did not bear the fruits because unlike Sonia, he could not establish a natural link with his audience. A week of campaigning by Priyanka Gandhi at Rae Bareilly and Amethi constituencies was extremely effective and forceful; its impact was felt across the country. The BJP was so rattled by Priyanka that they stooped low and targeted her husband by leveling allegations of corruption besides character assassination. Priyanka's refutations and counter-attacks on the BJP attracted national attention. This quality of campaigning was missing in Rahul but, unfortunately, Priyanka has been brought on the scene when crucial phases of voting are over.

If on the one hand, Congress campaign seemed to be lacking in vigour and energy, then on the other the *Sangh Parivar*, led by an army-like organization of the *Rashtriya Swayamsevak Sangh* and Narendra Modi's 185 Vijay Bharat election rallies, showed aggression. Modi, fully supported by RSS workers and other organizations of the *Sangh Parivar,* plunged into the campaign with energy and determination of warrior fighting against an enemy with a view to win the battle.

Aggression has been the keyword in Modi-RSS campaign and every trick of the trade, including no holds barred sarcasm and personal attacks against the Congress, has been part of RSS strategy from the very first day of the election campaigns. Hitting below the belt has been the style and substance of Modi-led election campaign. Not only this, an ideologically anti-minority, anti-Muslim *Sangh Parivar*, BJP, and Narendra Modi have adopted the strategy of polarization of Hindu versus Muslim voters. Voters have been told that "those who vote against Modi should leave for Pakistan". Priests, preachers of Hindu Samaj in their religious garments are working as comrade-in-arms of the *Sangh Parivar* during these elections. Every Hindu symbol and every religious ritual is projected by the *Sangh Parivar* to influence the Hindu voters to convey the message that 2014 Lok Sabha elections are a decisive battle for the protection of Hindu Rashtra. A vote for Modi is a vote for Hindus, by the Hindus and the country will be in the hands of a Hindu prime minister. Congress has failed in the task of demolishing the myth around Modi.

The Congress strategy should have been to target Modi aggressively and payback Modi in the same coin as he has been targeting the Congress. The election campaign of 2014 has become Modi versus the others. Only Sonia Gandhi has the capacity to match the energy and aggression of her political enemy. Somewhere, the Congress has lost the plot and the initiative has slipped away from its hands. A successful election campaign is to build a case in one's favor and demolish the opponent and this mix of negative and positive elements makes an election campaign tilt the balance in favor of one or the other party.

The balance has been tilted in favor of Modi because Congress leadership failed to evolve a clear electoral strategy against him. Modi has campaigned against his enemy no.1: the Congress. It is expected that Congress will also treat him as their enemy no.1. Unfortunately, the Congress leadership failed to anticipate the real meaning of the challenge from Modi's army of RSS workers making the contest ending up somewhat benefiting the BJP. With a single round of voting left it can only be hoped that Congress will be able to minimize the loss resulting from missed opportunities in the previous phases of the ballot.

newsyaps.com, 08-05-2014

Organizing the Elections

It is a wonder of wonders that Indians have successfully managed to conduct regular, even frequent and highly competitive elections for the Lok Sabha in 28 states and 7 Union Territories of India. Elections in democracy have relevance only if voters believe that the rules of electoral game have not been violated and 'free, fair and fearless' voting has been exercised, organized, conducted and supervised by an election machinery under the overall guidance and direction of an independent and impartial Election Commission.

India's electoral process makes a very important study because management of elections, from Kashmir to Kanyakumari, South to North, North West and North-East, is a herculean task which is regularly undertaken by Election Commission. Not only this, a compelling reality of electoral process is that the contesting candidate, leaders, parties, and groups may not hesitate to adopt unfair, even high-handed, methods to win an election because losing an election means losing an opportunity to officially attain a position of prestige and power. An individual can rise in status in politics only if he wins an election. Because of this the constitution makers of India have provided many safeguards to the Election Commission of India so that it can autonomously, as a constitutional body, manage the complex and complicated task of holding regular elections.

Part XV of the constitution consisting of Articles 324 to 329 has clearly stated that "Superintendence, direction and control of elections to be vested in the Election Commission". It is essential to critically analyze the way election commission has actually functioned in tackling the problems that rose during the elections. The first challenge faced by the election commission from the early 1970s has been to curb and control the role of criminals and musclemen, who have tried to terrorize and coerce the voters into exercising their choice in favor of a candidate supported by bullies. If the voters did not obey the diktats of such criminals, entire polling booth is 'hijacked' and 'bogus' voting takes place. This challenge has been tackled with strong determination by the Election Commission by increasing its supervisory role over the personnel and government functionaries who were deployed to oversee the whole process of voting on a fixed day and time of elections of a constituency whether of the Lok Sabha or the State Assembly.

It would be a fair assessment of the role of Election Commission if we say that over the decades it has been able to tighten its control over the government functionaries, including the police and paramilitary forces, to ensure that voters are not intimidated by criminals and musclemen at the time of voting. Although the threat from 'criminals' has not been completely neutralized, it has been contained to a great extent and the phenomenon of criminalization of politics, which emerged in a big way in the early 1990s, appears to be a thing of the past.

The second challenge besides the rising influence of criminals over the voters' choice is the role of money power during the elections, where resource rich and resource surplus parties and candidates are able to spend huge funds to 'buy' the voter. It is quite difficult to completely check and contain the role of money power and flow of illegal money during elections because every electoral contest involves powerful candidates who want to win an election at any cost and, hence, money power is quite visible during the elections. The Election Commission, of late, has deployed a large number of Income Tax officials and functionaries of other enforcement agencies to supervise, probe and nab contestants who are spending huge sums of money to purchase voters.

The result of this vigilance exercise by the Election Commission, Income Tax and Enforcement Agencies is that everyday millions of rupees are seized from candidates or their nominees who are found carrying money in an illegal manner. Bribing the voter is a common disease during the elections and our vigilant election machinery is actively engaged in detecting the persons involved in the business of buying votes.

> It would be a fair assessment of the role of Election Commission if we say that over the decades it has been able to tighten its control over the government functionaries, including the police and paramilitary forces, to ensure that voters are not intimidated by criminals and musclemen at the time of voting.

Third, the Election Commission enforces a Model Code of Conduct during the period of elections and any complaint filed against the violator of this code of conduct is investigated, and punishment is imposed depending on the nature of complaint and act of violation of the code.

The 16th Lok Sabha election, like all previous elections, is also faced with the problem of 'intemperate' or 'threatening' language used by prominent party candidates to intimidate the voter. Leaders like Amit Shah of the BJP and Azam Khan of the Samajwadi Party have already been penalized by the Election Commission for "spreading hatred" against religious communities during the elections. Candidates are also often found using defamatory language against the competitor. In such cases either the candidate or the election commission on its own can file an FIR.

Fourth, a candidate, even after the election results are declared, can file a petition against a victorious opponent alleging serious electoral malpractice or corruption during the elections. The courts after scrutinizing the complaints contained in the election petition can either reject the petition or disqualify the defendant for six years, if found guilty. This system has also helped in cleansing the electoral process.

Fifth, convicted criminals sitting as elected MPs and MLAs has already agitated the general public who believe that Indian democracy cannot be handed over to proven criminals who keep on filing appeals against their 'conviction'. The Indian judicial process is notoriously time consuming, and even after conviction elected representatives used to enjoy all the power and privileges of elected office in democracy. The recent judgment of the Supreme Court says that if any MLA or MP has been convicted for two years by any court, such a person shall be disqualified even if an appeal against his conviction is pending before a higher court. The latest example is of Lalu Prasad Yadav who has been convicted and is on bail but has not been able to contest the 16th Lok Sabha elections under the new judgment because he stands disqualified. This judgment of the Supreme Court led to a unity among law breakers who succeeded in pressing the Congress-led UPA government to issue an 'ordinance' to get the judgment nullified. However the beleaguered UPA government did not succeed under counter-pressure from those who stood up against such a move.

Finally, more teeth should be added to the existing Representation of People Act because the Election Commission which has powers equivalent to a civil court – oversight, investigation, prosecution and sentencing – has limited impact on spending limits of parties and individuals during the elections. It is impossible to estimate the amount of money spent by the BJP on the projection of Narendra Modi in the 2014 Lok Sabha election. It is roughly estimated that "billions of rupees" have been spent by the party on election related advertisements for their party candidates especially, on their prime ministerial candidate Narendra Modi.

How does one curb the unlimited spending power of parties during the elections? The law has both limitations and serious loopholes on the issue of election spending by parties which collect huge money from big industrialists and other donors, both in India and abroad. The corrupting influence of money power is felt over all democratically elected institutions of government because the 'donors' expect a 'quid-pro-quo' from the beneficiary of such donations.

newsyaps.com, 12-05-2014

Electoral Verdict of 2014

The marathon race for the 16th Lok Sabha elections, which began on March 2014 when the Model Code of Conduct was enforced and set in motion on April 7 with the nine-phase voting, culminated on May 16, 2014 when the ballots were opened for the declaration of results of over 5000 candidates who contested in 543 Lok Sabha seats. It is not just the fact that about 10 candidates were in electoral contest per seat for the 543 seats that makes the Lok Sabha election mammoth; it is also the fact that an estimated 1600 political parties were also involved in competition to win over the loyalty of the voters.

Further, keeping in mind the rising cost of conducting elections in a large Lok Sabha constituency, the Election Commission raised the expenditure ceiling per candidate from an earlier 10 lakh rupees to 70 lakh. Political parties have ensured that there is no limit or ceiling on the expenditure incurred by them during the campaign period. This is the reason that parties not only spend the money at their own will, they also collect huge funds from all donors especially the big industrial houses. In return for these donations, parties oblige their benefactors by often breaking and bending rules and procedures in the latter's favor.

It has been alleged that huge sums of unaccounted money has been spent by major parties during the 2014 Lok Sabha election campaign. Further, huge funds were invested by the parties and the benefactors in all forms of media and in multiple languages in order to project their leaders, candidates and campaign agenda throughout the length and breadth of the country. While every major political party and leaders took full advantage of media projection, the Centre for Media Studies, based on prime time (from 8 pm to 10 pm) coverage by six leading news channels, informs that Narendra Modi occupied 2,500 minutes or 33.21 percent of the total air time from March 1 to April 30, 2014. Rahul Gandhi of the Congress party also was a frontrunner with 72 minutes to 108 minutes of television coverage during the same period.

The implication of this special feature of elections of 2014 is clear: money and media made Narendra Modi the only visible persona during the long period of election campaigning. Congress president Sonia Gandhi or vice-president Rahul Gandhi or any other leader of prominent parties appeared insignificant before the Modi portrayed by the media. Modi was omnipresent and it was only Priyanka Gandhi who managed to steal the show from him for a few days of campaigning at Amethi and Rae Bareilly constituency.

In this context, the results of the elections deserve to be studied in order to answer questions about the role played by money and media in influencing the electoral outcome. It is for the first time in the history of Indian electoral politics that media and moolah have emerged as a determining 'factor' of electoral results. In the 1952 Lok Sabha elections the BJP, then known as Jan Sangh, won three seats. Compared to that, the party's 2014 Lok Sabha performance is like a small fly metamorphosing into an elephant.

While BJP has achieved a level of success, which will be called a sterling achievement in the post-independence history of India, the 'almighty' Congress is lying in dust and its 2014 performance is its worst in its own long and chequered history. Even in its year of disgrace and humiliation in the post-emergency elections of 1977, the Congress had won 157 out of 543 seats. And, even after Narasimha Rao-Sitaram Kesri's destructive politics, the Congress had won a respectable number of seats in 1996 Lok Sabha elections.

The electoral defeat of Congress in 2014 is also its worst performance in its history because it has never been totally wiped out in the way it has been now with the BJP winning all seats in six states. States such as Gujarat and Rajasthan are but examples of the manner in which the BJP decimated its rival. BJP also humiliated Congress in states such as Maharashtra, Assam and Karnataka; the Congress and its allies got a double whammy in the form of regional powers such as Trinamool Congress in West Bengal, Biju Janata Dal in Odisha and AIADMK in Tamil Nadu. But the wonder of wonders for the BJP is Uttar Pradesh where two formidable caste-based powerful regionalists – Mulayam Singh of Samajwadi Party and Mayawati of Bahujan Samaj Party – have been completely marginalized. Amit Shah, a trusted lieutenant of Modi, has proved his mettle in turning the tide in Uttar Pradesh against regionalists. It is BJP all the way and therefore there is a note of warning.

Rashtriya Swayamsewak Sangh-led BJP and *Sangh Parivar* can prove disastrous for India because with such power in its hands at the central government levels, it can pursue and impose its sectarian agenda of Hindutva and majoritarian Hindu Rashtravaad on the whole country. Muslims are already feeling insecure. The opposition parties, in spite of fragmentation and weakness, will have to stand up united to curb the sectarian tendencies of Hindu BJP.

newsyaps.com, 19-05-2014

Modi and the Media

The most special, to some extent an exceptional feature of the Lok Sabha elections 2014, was that Narendra Modi loomed large over the entire country and was the only person around whom the electoral discussion was focused. Ever since the Election Commission of India brought into force the Model Code of Conduct on March 5, 2014, it was Modi who was seen from Itanagar to Srinagar and on television single-handedly setting the electoral agenda during his campaign rallies.

This fact was noticed in a prominent manner on May 8 when the entire city of Varanasi, a constituency from where Modi contested and won, was completely 'occupied' by his supporters. The BJP played every trick of the trade to occupy the centre-stage in an audio-visual display of the people rallying around their only 'hero' – Modi. The Varanasi returning officer dared to impose some restrictions on Modi's proposed public rally on that day because of the law and order problems which could have risen during Modi's public rally.

Modi and BJP converted this small administrative decision of the returning officer into a mammoth issue launching dharnas and protests in the whole city alleging that he has been deliberately stopped from addressing a large election rally by the partisan district magistrate of Varanasi. The television footages carried images of saffron clothed and capped crowd protesting against the discriminatory treatment by the returning officer. The media, both print and electronic, carried Modi's statement with full gusto that "Mother Ganges has called him to contest from the holy city of Kashi".

The media assisted Modi in conveying his campaign statements of May 8 where he played the Hindu card in a big way. Modi's complete identification with Hindu symbols, religious rituals and the act of touching feet of Hindu priests was displayed for the entire day to the country by the electronic media camped in Varanasi. Media and Modi became quite indistinguishable and, unfortunately, the media conveyed to the whole country Modi's allegation that the returning officer had restricted his desire to offer *aarti* (prayer by a Hindu devotee) to holy mother Ganges.

The media loudly and repeatedly broadcast every statement, mixed with fact and fiction, made by Modi. And, every campaign rally addressed by Modi from Kashmir to Kanyakumari during the 2014 election season was aired into every household because Modi's media reach has no limitations of time and space. The focus of media was not only on Modi addressing the election rally; it was also concentrated on the vast multitudes assembled at a Modi rally. The persona of Modi remained a constant factor and he was a permanent fixture during the long phase of election campaign.

Modi succeeded in reaching every nook and corner of the country thanks to the media, which performed a great service to the cause of promoting him. It deserves to be clearly mentioned that Modi had long made his intentions quite clear by converting electoral campaign of 2014 as a kind of American Presidential contest between him and Congress vice-president Rahul Gandhi. Modi's effort to make election campaign look like a presidential debate between two leaders of two parties was ridiculed by everyone and it was even suggested that Modi was unrealistic because in a competitive multi-polar political party system like that one in India, tall regional or state-level leaders and parties play a significant role during election campaign. Modi's desire of confrontational debate between two individuals is in fact a pipedream not possible in the Indian system. But, what was considered impractical became a reality and media helped Modi turn the election debate into a 'one man show' and everyone else, whether the Congress or regionalists, were left playing second fiddle to him.

Modi speaks, media spreads his message far and wide and other parties react and respond to Modi. Modi said the Congress is corrupt, the Congress replies back and attacks corruption activities of Modi and BJP leaders. Modi's allegations against Congress corruption are given prominent space by the media in the name of "news value" while others are only shown as reactions.

Campaigning in Amethi, the constituency of Rahul Gandhi, Modi was shown as a crowd-puller by the media which also claimed that such a rally against the Congress scion had never been held in the party's UP bastion. Modi, as shown by the media, is shown to have turned the tables against Rahul. Modi decides, media informs the whole country, and Rahul and others respond to Modi.

The whole of India should be highly concerned about such a development where one personality is projected taller than everyone. Not only this, the Lok Sabha elections of 2014 should be seen as an act around Modi alone; even his own BJP and other RSS-led Sangh were relegated into the background. The 16th Lok Sabha elections will be remembered, unlike all the previous elections, as a single man's show with the media at the beck-and-call of that one man. *newsyaps.com, 21-05-2014*

Foreign Policy Agenda 2014

The new government at the centre will be immediately confronted with a foreign policy agenda following NATO's withdrawal from Afghanistan coupled with Pakistan's determination to keep India out of reach from its own self-proclaimed natural strategic zone of influence. India's desire to keep itself fully engaged with the newly elected government of Afghanistan will demand urgent policy reforms from the BJP-led NDA government.

Not only this, Pakistan's Army Chief, General Raheel Sharif, had on May 1, 2014, described Kashmir as an internationally recognized dispute between India and Pakistan and rhetorically proclaimed that "matchless sacrifices offered by Kashmiris will not go in vain" and added, "Pakistan Army is in favor of peace but is always ready to respond to any aggression in a befitting manner."

Sharif's description of Kashmir as the "jugular vein" of Pakistan on May 1 assumes great significance because of its timing. Pakistan is preparing itself to deal with new government of India and Afghanistan and the army chief must have thought it appropriate to remind the to-be elected leaders of the two neighboring countries that Pakistan has clear security and strategic agenda for its own country and they should be ready to address Pakistan's core strategic agenda.

One must understand here that the army chief of Pakistan has the real authority to define, frame and execute the country's security policies. Prime Minister Nawaz Sharif knows this fact quite well because it was his former army chief, General Pervez Musharraf, who had on his own planned and executed Kargil attack in 1998 leading to an all out war with India.

It is Pakistan's army which is the real nerve centre of power and Islamabad has either passively, or tactically, accepted and supported the army's decisions for the prevailing fear that the men in uniform might pack up the elected leaders and send them into exile.

Hence, Raheel Sharif and not Prime Minister Nawaz Sharif who has publicly announced that the Pakistani army is prepared to protect its interests in Afghanistan and India should follow a hands-off policy there.

If on the one hand Pakistan has placed its cards on the table and clearly announced its priorities and agenda, on the other hand India has entered a stage of flux and uncertainties because there is every possibility of political rupture in policy-making process because the public discourse and manifesto of the BJP during the hustings did not reveal any significant idea regarding foreign policy challenges faced by India in 2014.

A few facts may be mentioned to substantiate the argument that Indian political leadership will take time to evolve a comprehensive foreign and strategic policy framework because 2013-2014 of the Congress-led UPA government's foreign policy record has been a washout and domestic issues overshadowed the thinking and action on the external policy front.

Former Prime Minister Manmohan Singh felt politically handicapped by domestic situations and the result was that his policy initiatives towards Pakistan remained just his unfinished wishes. Singh sincerely believed that normalcy could be restored between India and Pakistan, and the opening of trade routes and travel between these neighbors could be restarted in a big way. Unfortunately, nothing happened on the issue of bilateral relations and status quo remains, which will have to be broken by the new government.

Congress had a very balanced approach towards Pakistan but Manmohan Singh, a well-meaning prime minister, felt politically handicapped. But, Prime Minister Narendra Modi and the RSS-led Sangh is ideologically anti-Pakistan. This attitude of the BJP coupled with the fact that party's leadership have never showed any capacity to formulate foreign policy of India with a clear understanding of national interests poses serious questions. It is a propaganda that Atal Bihari Vajpayee, the prime minister from 1999 to 2004, has left behind a good record of his foreign policy towards Pakistan because there is no evidence to substantiate the statement that his so-called "foreign policy framework" can be a good guide for Narendra Modi in 2014. Further, Modi has serious intellectual deficiencies and the best evidence has been provided by his election campaign statements that he will ask Pakistan to hand over fugitive mafia criminal Dawood Ibrahim to India (as if India is in a position to dictate Pakistan on this or any other issue).

That Pakistan is the epicenter of anti-India terror-activities is a well-known fact and the challenge before Indian policy makers is to bring Pakistan to the negotiating table and not issue irresponsible statements. It is no denying the fact that the Kashmir dispute remains a bone of contention between India and Pakistan, and every effort has to be made to find a solution to ease the situation besides restore confidence between the two neighbours. India and Pakistan have vested interests in resolving this dispute at a bilateral level because any foreign involvement in the settlement of this dispute is bound to complicate matters. Not only this, armed conflicts between the two countries have failed to be decisive because military capabilities of both these countries are almost at an equal level.

Pakistan's low intensity war against India by export of Jihadi and mercenary terrorists has not succeeded in destabilizing India. On the contrary it is Pakistan which is under threat from its own creation. The genie is out of the bottle, and anti-India terrorists are threatening peace and stability of Pakistan itself. Hence, both India and Pakistan have to search for solutions to resolve bilateral disputes without any foreign intervention.

newsyaps.com, 24-05-2014

Election Verdict: 2014

A few salient, even exceptional, features of the 16th Lok Sabha electoral verdict of 2014 deserve to be highlighted for understanding the true meaning and significance of unprecedented voters 'turnout of 66.38 per cent. It has been always maintained by important theorists of electoral political Representative democracy that an exceptional voters' turnout happens only when elections are held and and voters feel that an extraordinary situation exists in society and because of much a special situation, the voters come out to exercise their right to vote. The first illustration to substantiate this theory of elections is that of the Lok Sabha elections of 1984 when large number of voters rushed towards the polling booths to exercise their right to vote because they all felt that country's security is threatened because even Indira Gandhi, Prime Minister of India, could not be saved from the bullets of the assassins. Post-Indira Gandhi elections took place under extraordinary conditions when people felt that India was under siege and the need of the hour was to elect a formidable government with a clear majority of seats in the Lok Sabha. Is 2014 a repeat story of the post-Indira Gandhi elections of 1984? If a common voter feels that he cannot sit at home, because his "vote" matters, otherwise the existing crisis will further deeper, if a government-in-power is politically weak and vulnerable to all kinds of competing and conflicting pressures. Did Indians feel that the Manmohan Singh at the Centre was not at all equal to face the challenges of 2014 India? Perhaps the voters in 2014 desired an alternative to the Congress-led UPA government because of their perception that is was only a capable and effective governmental and political leadership that could deliver the goods. The Manmohan Singh government for many reasons was perhaps perceived as incapable and weak to perform its responsibilities of proper governance of the country and hence its replacement and displacement have an absolute necessity for the present times. Hence, Narendra Modi-led Bharatiya Janata Party was given a clear mandate and for the first time the party received 282 seats in the Lok Sabha of 543 members.

May be, even BJP has been impressed by its robust electoral victory in its history of fighting ninteen Lok Sabha elections beginning from 1952 to 2014.

Table I: BJP's Performance

The Rise and Fall				
Year	*Contested*	*Won*	*Vote Share (in per cent)*	*Votes polled (in crore)*
1989	225	85	11.36	3.42
1991	468	120	20.11	5.53
1996	471	161	20.29	6.79
1998	388	182	25.59	9.43
1999	339	182	23.75	8.66
2004	364	138	22.16	8.64
2009	433	116	18.8	7.84

Source: Indian Express, Delhi, May 19, 2014-06-18

The Table I clearly shows that the Atal Bihari Vajpayee-led coalition government at the Centre could get only 182 Lok Sabha seats in 1996 and 1998 and on the basis of support of a large number of coalition partners, it was able to come to power at the centre in 1996 and 1998. This is BJP's past. Its present is quite different not only because it has majority of 282 seats of its own. L.K. Advani, while presiding over BJP's elected MPs on May 20, 2014, observed that this remarkable electoral victory of the party should be attributed to the single handed successful campaigning by Narender Modi and only Modi deserves full credit for winning 282 Lok Sabha seats in 2014. If the winning party itself has recognised the pre-eminent status of Modi, any other evidence is not required to state that the whole electoral battle for 2014 was fought around Modi as a leader.

Further, India has a competitive multi polar-party system, it is essential to mention the percentage of votes polled by other important contestants in 2014.

The Table II clearly shows that except the BJP and Congress which polled 31.0 per cent and 19.3 per cent of the total votes polled, all other state level based parties and groups received from 4 per cent to 0.3 per cent of votes polled because of their limited geographical reach and hence support of the voters. Only BJP and Congress are an all-India national parties and all others

Table II: Final Vote-Shares of Major Palyers—2014

Party	*Vote Share (in %)*
BJP	31
Congress	19.3
BSP	4.1
TMC	3.8
SP	3.4
AIADMK	3.3
CPM	3.2
Independents	3
TDP	2.5
YSRCP	2.5
AAP	2
Shiv Sena	1.9
DMK	1.7
BJD	1.7
NCP	1.6
RJD	1.3
TRS	1.2
JD(U)	1.1
CPI	0.8
JD(S)	0.7

Source: *Indian Express*, Delhi, May 19-2014

are limited to particular states of India. If BJP has obtained 282 seats, the congress (44), the ADMK (37), The Biju Janata Dal (20) and Trinamool Congress (34) and all others have limited number of seats in the 16th Lok Sabha. The picture of Lok Sabha elections cannot become clear without briefly referring to the status of once dominant majority party which ruled over India.

Table III: Congress-performance

Elections	*Winning Party*	*Seats Won*	*Total Seats*	*Vote Share*
1957	Congress	371	494	47.8
1962	Congress	361	494	44.7
1967	Congress	283	520	40.8
1971	Congress	352	518	43.7
1977	Janata Party	154	542	34.5
1980	Congress	353	529	42.7
1984-85	Congress	414	541	48.1
2014	Congress	44	543	19.3

Source: Indian Express, New Delhi, May 18, 2014

The once formidable Congress is lying in a shambles with 44 seats and a little more than 19 per cent of the retained votes.

The Table III gives a glimpse of the given situation in which Congress has fallen from high pedestal to an extremely miserable political status.

Indian Elections are very special because on the basis of 'Registered' and 'Non-registered' categories defined by the Election Commission of India, the present day India has 1,687 parties 'Registered' for the Lok Sabha elections. It does not mean that all Registered or Unregistered parties actually contest the elections, for example, in 2014, 53 parties actually contested and not to be left behind the contestant candidates, many frivolous and absentee, 5000 contested 2014 elections. If BJP has recorded slow and steadily growth, Congress has shown ups and downs during the last sixteen Lok Sabha Elections.

Table IV: Congress Decline in Varous States

Congress in power at state level	*States*	*Number of Seats (All India = 543 Seats)*
Congress has not been in power at state level in 25 years	West Bengal, Tamilnadu, Uttar Pradesh, Bihar, Sikkim, Tripura, Nagaland	205
Congress has not been in power at state level for more than 10 years	Gujarat, Odisha, Madhya Pradesh, Chhattisgarh,	87
Less likely that congress will be able to win power in state without an ally	Andhra Pradesh (Telangana and Seemandhara, (Delhi,. Jammu & Kashmir, Maharashtra, Jharkhand)	117
Congress still within striking distance of power at state level	Punjab, Himachal, Haryana, Kerala, Karnataka, Assam, Goa, Rajasthan, Northeastern States, Union Territories	134

Congress Performance in Key Elections Since 1977

Lok Sabha Election Year	*Seats Contested*	*Won*	*Number of Seats Fofeited Deposit*	*Vote Share (in %)*
1977	492	154	18	34.5
1989	510	197	5	39.5
1996	529	140	127	28.8
1999	453	114	88	28.3
2009	440	206	71	28.6
2014	464	44	178*	19.3

*Provisional

Source: Indian Express, Delhi. May 20, 2014.

The Table IV clearly shows that Congress has always shown a capacity to revive and reinvent itself. The future will show whether Congress is able to really face the new challenge before itself or remain a pale shadow of its former self.

To conclude the discussion about the meanings of verdict, Modi's contribution deserves to be highlighted. Modi addressed 440 rallies including185 Vijay Bharat elector rallies. Modi always appropriated Hindu popular symbols like launching his election campaign after offering prayers at Vaishno Devi Temple with Mata's blessings and addressed his own election rally at Varanasi with a slogan "Holy Ganga Ma has asked" him to come to Varanasi to contest the elections. Hindutva was always his shield and public face. This is an election victory of Modi only.

Modi Government and Opposition's Role: Focus must Shift to India's Inclusiveness and Diversity

The Narendra Modi model of governance can be analysed only if his personality traits and ideological worldview are scrutinised for an understanding of a leader of a party that has won 282 of the 543 Lok Sabha seats, and 31 per cent votes in a turnout of 66.4 per cent.

It is only after Jawaharlal Nehru, Indira Gandhi and Rajiv Gandhi that a party and its leader have a clear mandate to govern India from 2014 to 2019.

Who is Narendra Modi?

First, Modi is a product of the Hindu seminary of the RSS. The ideological foundation of the RSS is to work for the welfare of Hindu Bharat Mata that has supposedly been under siege from non-Hindu or Muslim invaders. Modi has said, "I am a Hindu, I am a nationalist and I am a patriot."

Second, as chief minister of Gujarat for over 10 years, he ran a government in which Muslims never found any representation. Not was there any Muslim candidate in the state polls of 2012.

Third, his style of governance was authoritarian, by empowering a bureaucracy loyal only to him. He did not appoint a Lokayukta for nine years, till he got a person who was loyal to him.

So, it is imperative to identify some important constitutional checks and balances that can keep the Modi administration within the constitutional "basic structure of India".

First, socially and spatially, the verdict of 2014 elections shows that in spite of 282 seats won by the BJP, its real support base is limited in terms of territorial dispersal among the 29 states and seven Union territories of India.

Even without Muslim votes, the BJP's geographical reach is concentrated in the eight states of Uttar Pradesh, Madhya Pradesh, Gujarat, Rajasthan, Bihar, Karnataka, Chhattisgarh and Maharashtra from where it has won 211 seats out of 282, and secured 11.7 crore, or two-thirds, of 17.2 crore voters.

But it does not represent the continental diversity of India and important "peripheries" like Assam, Meghalaya, Manipur, Mizoram, Nagaland, Tripura,

Arunachal Pradesh and Sikkim on the one hand, and Jammu and Kashmir on the other.

Arunachal Pradesh has a Congressled government, Tripura has a Leftled government, and even in 2014, Manipur has elected two Congress MPs and Mizoram's only one. In Assam, Tarun Gogoi's Congressled government watched as Modi's campaign split votes between Hindus and Muslims.

How will the Centre now help Assam maintain law and order in the volatile region? In its euphoria, the BJP should not forget that the aspirations of the northeast and J&K are complex, volatile and different from the Hindi mainland.

The RSS' idea of India is less nuanced with a more centralised government with a powerful, authoritarian figure at the helm. Centralising forces are diluted when we have checks and balances of a coalition government. But the BJP doesn't need the NDA any more. An alternative political alliance of opposition parties in the Lok Sabha seems to be a possibility.

Only a viable and effective opposition in the Lok Sabha can act as a real countervailing force to Modi's centralisation. The Congress party and its UPA allies with 66 members, Trinamool Congress with 34, AIADMK with 37 members, Biju Janata Dal with 20, SP with five and a few others can emerge as a compact opposition in the Lok Sabha.

In the first Lok Sabha, the Nehru-led Congress had a majority, but the combined opposition of communists and socialists acted as a vigilant watchdog of people's interests. Naveen Patnaik gave marching orders to the BJP after the anti-Christian Kandhamal riots.

Mamata Banerjee with J Jayalalithaa and Patnaik floated the idea of a federal opposition front before the Lok Sabha elections. The rationale for such an idea has assumed some significance in the changed political landscape.

The BJP is committed to the idea of a separate Gorkhaland from Bengal, which should bother Mamata. Modi had announced that he would take chief ministers on board while framing important national policies.

Will Mamata agree with Modi's formulation that Muslim Bangladeshis should be commanded to leave and Hindu Bangladeshis could continue to reside in the border areas of West Bengal and Assam? For the regional parties, anti-Congressism is dead and the focus must shift to maintaining India's inclusiveness and diversity.

The Economic Times, 10-06-2014

Index